CATHER STUDIES

VOLUME 7

Cather Studies

Willa Cather as Cultural Icon

EDITED BY GUY REYNOLDS

UNIVERSITY OF NEBRASKA PRESS

LINCOLN AND LONDON

Manufactured in the United States of America
∞
The series Cather Studies is sponsored by the University of Nebraska–Lincoln in cooperation with the Willa Cather Pioneer Memorial and Educational Foundation.
ISSN: 1045-9871
ISBN: 978-0-8032-6011-5

Frontispiece:
Willa Cather with Leon Bakst in his Paris studio (detail). Bakst painted Cather's portrait in 1923. At the bottom of the picture, Cather has inscribed to her sister: "For Elsie, a picture of Bakst and me in his beautiful studio. Willa Cather. Paris, October 1, 1923." Courtesy of the UNL Libraries Archives and Special Collections, the Philip L. and Helen Cather Southwick Collection.

CONTENTS

EDITORIAL POLICY

Cather Studies, a forum for Cather scholarship and criticism, is published biennially by the University of Nebraska Press. Submissions are invited on all aspects of Cather studies: biography, various critical approaches to the art of Cather, her literary relationships and reputation, the artistic, historical, intellectual, religious, economic, political, and social backgrounds to her work. Criteria for selection will be excellence and originality.

Manuscripts may vary in length from 4,000 to 12,000 words and should conform to the MLA Style Manual, 1998 edition. Please submit manuscripts in duplicate, accompanied by return postage; overseas contributors should enclose international reply coupons. Because *Cather Studies* adheres to a policy of anonymous submission, please include a title page providing author's name and address and delete identifying information from the manuscript. Manuscripts and editorial correspondence should be addressed to Guy Reynolds, Editor, *Cather Studies*, Department of English, University of Nebraska–Lincoln, Lincoln NE 68588-0333.

Introduction
Willa Cather as Icon

GUY REYNOLDS

That Willa Cather, in many ways the most elusive of early-twentieth-century American writers, might now be thought of as an "icon" is one of literary history's best jokes. Cather had a long career and moved through a variety of places and jobs and roles during her life. She was something of a moving target, able to transform herself from one literary identity to another. In the 1890s she was a wasp and a critical shrew, a precocious reviewer of books, plays, and music, armed with an acid pen. In the early years of the twentieth century she had become her mentor S. S. McClure's right-hand (wo)man, the managing editor of one of the age's leading magazines. Across her desk came works by many of the era's leading authors. She became an adept businesswoman. As she continually adjusted herself to the literary market, looking for cracks in the publishing industry, Cather took on odd projects that have to be fitted—somehow—into a map of her career. She helped to write, or "ghostwrite," McClure's autobiography, and she edited a muckraking exposé of the founder of Christian Science, Mary Baker Eddy, written by Georgine Milmine. Even before she became a novelist Cather had written across and within a number of literary discourses: reviewing, poetry, muckraking journalism, autobiography, short fiction.

One might put "novelist" in inverted commas, since Cather's inflection of this term was ongoing. Her novels sometimes seemed to their readers, in their plotlessness and episodic construction, to be barely novels at all. Cather herself would adopt the term *narrative*, in the 1920s, deploying this word in a flexible way to explain the experimentalism of her mature fiction. The range of her works, especially the geographical variety of their settings, would make Cather's identity problematic. Although Cather had achieved fame as a Nebraskan novelist and the author of those quintessential frontier or Old West texts, *My Ántonia* and *O Pioneers!*, her regionalist identity was in fact varied and even heterotopic. She wrote about Quebec, London, France, New York, Pittsburgh, New Mexico. There is probably *more* of North America's sheer geographical variety in her work than in fictions by her contemporaries. And at the end of her life she was working on a manuscript set in medieval Avignon.

These are the well-known facets of her career, but they need to be recapitulated because they bear on Cather's iconicity. An icon, one supposes, is singular. The religious and pictorial origins of the term suggest the meditative stillness of a medieval saint's image or, in the secular realm, the permanence of monarchical imagery (think of Elizabeth I as the Virgin Queen). A certain stasis is implicit in the original meaning of the term. But Cather's iconicity seems less fixed, less determined. In part, this is because Cather was in a continual and changing dialogue with the culture around her—and that culture was itself a highly mobile, commercialized, and transitional network of ideas, images, and narratives. In her relationship to iconicity and its associated themes (celebrity and publicity; literary canonicity and the place of the woman artist) one also senses Cather's ambivalent relationship to modern America. A good deal of evidence suggests that she disliked aspects of the contemporary culture of the icon. She became famous, was awarded honorary degrees, won the Pulitzer Prize for fiction. But she also stepped away from Hollywood, unlike Faulkner and Fitzgerald, and eventually prohibited the filming of her novels. She seems to have become uncomfortable with her own fame, and there are accounts of her resentment at being recognized in public. Cather was an icon discomfited by iconic status.

These biographical details underpin her work's ongoing interest in icons and in a related nexus of themes and scenarios. As many of the writers in this volume note, her stories touch on motifs that derive from a reading of icons and iconicity. A relatively humble figure, Ántonia, might become an iconic figure in the memory of a man far removed from her in place and status (*My Ántonia*). A young man might flare in the imagination of an older man, and remain there as an embodiment of values lost in a tawdry age of commercialism (*The Professor's House*). A morally "fallen" woman, the cynosure for rumormongering, sustains an idealized allure for a younger man (*A Lost Lady*). Two Catholic priests move through a terrain where Christian and secular icons, and the iconic places of indigenous religion, present a varied and complex pilgrim's progress (*Death Comes for the Archbishop*). A female artist dies tragically and young, but resonates in the imagination of the man who loved her (*Lucy Gayheart*). Again and again, Cather's texts center on dynamic relationships between an onlooker (or secret sharer) and the object of fascination who achieves, for the viewer, the status of an icon.

The final proof of Cather's status, of course, is her steady movement to the center of the twentieth-century U.S. literary canon. This volume diagnoses a cultural transformation of which it itself is a symptom. But even here there are characteristically Catherian twists to the story. Cather is an icon for a good number of literary scholars (many of them represented in these pages), but she has achieved a status that extends beyond the immediate community that works on her texts. A commentary by poet laureate Robert Pinsky begins our book; Pinsky's poem *An Explanation of America* (1979) extensively meditated on Cather's work as the major artistic representation of the so-called frontier experience. In a further turning of the iconic circuit, Cather's texts now insert themselves into the works of a future generation of writers, becoming part of an evolving American iconography.

A Commentary on *An Explanation of America*

ROBERT PINSKY

I tried to make *An Explanation of America* a long poem somewhat in the old, premodernist way: a compendious, heuristic tour of a subject, with many an allusion and submerged quotation. I had in mind a way of allusion (the root of that word is "to play," as in *ludicrous*!) far more like the eccentric adventuring of Lucretius or Burton's *Anatomy of Melancholy* than the fragmentary modernist manners of *The Cantos* or *The Wasteland*. ("Postmodernism" was not quite yet a slogan when I was working on the poem.)

After Walt Whitman, the author I found myself raiding most for the poem was Willa Cather. Her brilliant phrase "obliterating strangeness" renders the oceanic prairie into the sea crossed not only by Homeric heroes but by the European immigrants who in their own way challenged Poseidon, taking heavy losses, on their journey that ended in places like a crossroads in Nebraska.

In Jim Burden's garden encounter, early after his own immigration to the Plains, the obliterating smallness and vastness of his new world are an American, urgent redaction of Keats's romance with death in "Ode to a Nightingale." Alan Shapiro, in his book *In Praise of the Impure*, writes with great insight about the ways I use Cather's garden scene. His descriptions of the tense and person changes in my versified adaptation have been instructive to me.

The wanderer who leaps into the harvest machinery embodies a terrifying, literal negative side to our forgetful national abundance. His suicide echoes the darkest vaults of "obliterating strangeness," as reflected by his vaguely xenophobic remarks. Some such cultural and social line I try to trace by borrowing the strength of Cather's great words and images, trying to see into them and, by their light, into our history.

What Happens to Criticism When the Artist Becomes an Icon?

ELSA NETTELS

Critics by themselves do not make writers into literary icons. But the iconic status of writers often owes much to the critics and scholars who edit the anthologies read in schools and colleges, write books and articles that teachers read in preparing their literature classes, and write introductions to texts published for students and general readers. In turn, the emergence of a writer as a literary icon may have powerful effects on criticism. Recent studies of Willa Cather show with particular clarity the many ways that Cather's presence as a cultural icon has made an impact on her critics.

The ever-increasing volume of scholarship and critical attention devoted to Cather in itself attests to her prominent place in American literary history. The MLA Bibliographies from 1997 through 2001 cite 230 books and essays on Cather. During an earlier five-year period, from 1970 through 1974, only 63 citations to published Cather scholarship appear. Scholarly papers on Cather's life and work are regularly presented at the annual meetings of the American Literature Association and the Western Literature Association and at the annual spring conference in Red Cloud, Nebraska. Between 1999 and 2003 five volumes of essays were published based on papers presented at conferences on Cather in New York City, Mesa Verde, Quebec City, Winchester, Virginia, and Nebraska City. Cather's place in anthologies of American literature is now as secure as Hemingway's or Faulkner's. So many high school and college students are reading Cather's novels and stories that a biannual journal, *Teaching*

Cather, sponsored by Northwest Missouri State University, was inaugurated to aid teachers from middle schools to graduate seminars.

Undergirding Cather scholarship is the Willa Cather Scholarly Edition, published by the University of Nebraska Press, which issued its first volume (*O Pioneers!*) in 1992 and its eighth (*One of Ours*) in 2006. *Alexander's Bridge* is scheduled for publication in 2007. Each volume contains the text of Cather's work, extensive notes, and a detailed historical essay about the sources, composition, publication, and critical reception of the work.

The burgeoning interest in Cather has revived interest in other artists whom Cather knew or who were in some way important to her. Papers presented at the International Cather Seminar in 2003 at Bread Loaf, Vermont, brought a number of figures—some little known or forgotten until now—into the critical spotlight: Edward Abbey, Dorothy Canfield Fisher, Louise Guiney, Burton J. Hendrick, Margaret Matzenauer, Ole Rolvaag, and Edward Steichen, among others.

Another sign of the transformation of author into icon is the interest of critics in the process by which Cather as a cultural icon has been constructed. In particular, Joan Acocella, Michael Schueth, Janis Stout, Joseph Urgo, and Deborah Williams have examined how Cather herself acted to create her public image—through interviews, biographical sketches for her publishers, and public letters. In the winter/spring 2003 issue of the *Willa Cather Newsletter and Review*, David Porter analyzes the typescript, recently acquired by Drew University, of an interview, published in the *Nebraska State Journal* as a genuine interview, that Cather herself wrote. (One thinks of Whitman writing laudatory reviews of his own poetry.) Stephanie Thompson, in *Influencing America's Tastes: Realism in the Works of Wharton, Cather, and Hurst* (2000), analyzes the ways Cather created her "ideal audience" within her novels (127).

It might seem paradoxical that a writer whose protection of her privacy has become almost legendary should have cared so intensely about the way she presented herself and was presented to the public. But as Michael Schueth has astutely observed, Cather created a public image of herself shaped by her childhood, which gave her readers "a sense of personal relationship" with her and at the same time protected her privacy by diverting attention from other parts of her life. Making a similar point, Deborah Williams has developed a compelling analogy between Cather's creation of a "marketable image" for S. S. McClure in her writing of his autobiography and her own "construction of a public surface" by which she controlled the kind and extent of the public's knowledge of her life.

Interviews, reviews, memoirs, and reminiscences have combined to create the icon that still endures—Cather, the celebrant of the western pioneers' heroic strength and courage: "the straightforward prairie writer" in Deborah Williams's words. The amount of truth in this image and Cather's success in conveying it are evident in Sharon Hoover's 2002 book, *Willa Cather Remembered*. Almost without exception, the memories and impressions of Cather written by acquaintances and friends present a writer of resolute strength, determination, and conviction, self-confident and self-possessed, a writer of "clear-eyed, unquestioning certainty," as her friend Fanny Butcher described her (qtd. in Hoover 109). Such words as *strong*, *sturdy*, *vigorous*, *steadfast*, *fresh-colored*, and *clear* appear repeatedly in their accounts. To these observers, Cather did not seem to have a "mania for privacy" (Acocella's phrase); rather, she merely seemed determined to protect her time and energies, to save herself for her work.

The image of Cather as the forthright novelist of the plains is reflected and reinforced by photographs, most notably Edward Steichen's famous photograph of Cather, age fifty-three, wearing a middy blouse and looking directly at the viewer. Films inspired by Cather's work are based on those novels—*O Pioneers!*, *The Song of the Lark*, and *My Ántonia*—that portray the triumph of the protagonist over the hardships and privations of frontier life. The program on Cather filmed in Red Cloud in 2001 and shown on CSPAN in the American Writers series captures the spirit of Cather's "Biographical Sketch" (1926), in which the novelist refers to Nebraska as "home" and her love of the "open plains" as "the great passion of my life" (54).

The potency of the iconic image has moved many critics in the past twenty-five years to resist it, attack it, or speculate about what it might conceal. For instance, Judith Fetterley's reference to "the official story" in her 1998 essay on *Sapphira and the Slave Girl* implies that the popular view somehow falsifies the realities of Cather's life and work. The assumption that Cather was a lesbian (however that term is defined) encouraged a number of critics in the 1970s and 1980s to conclude that the limpid surface of Cather's fiction concealed homosexual desires that could not be openly expressed and must be hidden in a subtext. Few phrases in literary history have borne so heavy a burden of argument as "the inexplicable presence of the thing not named" in Cather's essay "The Novel Démeublé" (50). Few critics would now insist that the "thing not named" must be homoerotic desire—the phrase so clearly refers to aesthetics, to the art of evocation and suggestion. Moreover, influential critics such as Joan Acocella, Janis Stout, and Cynthia Griffin Wolff have effectively rebutted claims that Cather's fervent letters to Louise Pound and her assumption of masculine dress and haircut in adolescence are themselves indisputable proofs of lesbianism. But there is no going back to the time when biographers could write about Cather without any reference to gender and sexuality. As Joseph Urgo has stated, "Iconic status opens inquiries into all of Cather" (327).

Whether or not critics see "sexual orientation" as a determining source of Cather's art, they have dispelled the idea of Cather as an uncomplicated "plainspoken prairie writer." Words such as *ambivalence*, *anxiety*, *conflict*, and *ambiguity* have replaced the earlier vocabulary. The premise of Janis Stout's biography (2000) is that Cather—far from being a calm and confident person of unwavering convictions—was a "deeply conflicted writer" (xi) with ambivalent views about race, gender, immigration, and America's destiny. Marilee Lindemann, in her 1999 book, *Willa Cather: Queering America*, perceives in Cather's fiction "an uneasy movement between ecstatic optimism and sometimes deadly anxiety" (4), evident in the portrayal of "queer" characters such as Thea Kronborg and Claude Wheeler, who rebel against a system that would enforce conformity to the dominant ideology of race and gender roles.

Whether or not Cather was a "deeply conflicted writer," it

is indisputable that her fiction has inspired conflicting views among her critics. The reader of recent criticism is struck by how sharply critics disagree about the meaning of her novels, how differently they interpret characters (e.g., St. Peter and Ántonia), and how differently they perceive Cather's attitude toward them. Whether or not Cather gives greater power to men or to women in the prairie novels remains a subject of debate. Does Cather endorse or reject the values, ambitions, and desires of St. Peter in *The Professor's House*? John Swift concludes that we cannot know for certain where she stands: "We cannot tell; the multiple ironies . . . make any single perspective untenable" (19). We will continue to analyze and criticize Cather's novels precisely because she is unfathomable, because scenes and characters may "offer a proliferation of meanings" that cannot be comprehended in one interpretation, as Richard Millington has observed (77).

Critics have mounted a strong challenge to the familiar literary icon, but they have not replaced it with another. When Richard Schickel wrote the script for the celebratory *"Into the Morning": Willa Cather's America* (1988) for the Films for Humanities series, he chose passages from the novels expressing characters' aspirations and ideals to accompany the famous photographs and beautiful images of western prairies and mountains. In describing Alexandra Bergson as the embodiment of "all the pioneer virtues—patience, courage, imagination," he undoubtedly believed that he was presenting Cather's heroine as most readers see her, or should see her.

Several critics, most recently Jonathan Goldberg and Christopher Nealon, have proposed to make Cather an icon for gay writers—in Nealon's words, "a lesbian forebear," to be claimed through "identification with an ancestor" (94, 96). I am told that a photograph of Cather hangs in one of the rooms of the Pride Institute at Minneapolis. But the recent criticism shows that Cather is a compelling subject for almost every kind of critic—feminist, queer theorist, new historicist, ecocritic, ethnographer, structuralist, deconstructionist, reader-response critic, and psychoanalyst. There is no critical consensus that Cather belongs in any one literary tradition. John Murphy and Amy Ahearn have established her affinities with the naturalists;

John Anders places her in the tradition of male homosexual literature, to which Plato, Walter Pater, and Walt Whitman belong. The winter 2001 issue of *American Literary Realism* is devoted to Cather as a realist. Jo Ann Middleton, Guy Reynolds, Phyllis Rose, Janis Stout, and Steven Trout have persuasively defined her as a modernist, but Cather remains a unique, original writer who resists being categorized or definitively analyzed. What Edmund Morgan says of Benjamin Franklin in his 2002 biography—"he kept a kind of inner core of himself intact and unapproachable" (30)—is also true of Cather.

But writers do not become literary icons because they seem unapproachable or create characters who inspire controversy. Writers become icons when they come to embody or are recognized as literary creators of an era, a region, a city, a culture, or a way of life that we recognize as an essential part of a nation's history and character.

Cather's ambition to be a literary creator is revealed most clearly in her best-known novel, *My Ántonia*, itself an icon, now in print in more than twenty-five editions, chosen in 2002 for the third installment of the citywide reading program One Book, One Chicago. Within the novel itself, Cather, through her narrators, Jim Burden and the unnamed "I" of the introduction, creates Ántonia as an icon. The narrator of the introduction states: "More than any other person we remembered, this girl seemed to mean to us the country, the conditions, the whole adventure of our childhood" (x–xi). When Jim Burden returns to the scenes of his childhood after twenty years and sees Ántonia again, he reflects that she "had always been one to leave images in the mind that did not fade—that grew stronger with time. . . . She lent herself to immemorial human attitudes which we recognize by instinct as universal and true" (397–98).

This view of Ántonia has provoked much controversy, very much like the controversy surrounding the familiar iconic image of Cather herself. Many early readers and reviewers saw Ántonia as the embodiment of vitality and indomitable strength, a triumphant, heroic figure, a "symbol of calm and faithful endurance" (Acocella 33). Such readers saw Jim's vision of Ántonia at the end as the fitting climax to a novel "unique in its serenity," "a glorious celebration of life" (qtd. in Murphy 18, 13). Recent critics, however, have dwelled on the darker sides of the novel—the scenes of violence, attempted rape, and suicide, the melancholy sense of exile and loss, Ántonia's endurance, above all, of the exploitation, rejection, and betrayal of her by most of the male characters.

For every critic like Stephanie Thompson, who perceives Jim as the "ideal narrator" who best "realizes what [Ántonia's] powers are over others" (144), a dozen are skeptical of Jim's celebratory vision of Ántonia and regard his making of the woman into an icon as an attempt to control her, to make her "safe" by turning her into a fixed symbol. No doubt many of the novel's early readers saw Jim as Elizabeth Shepley Sergeant saw him, "in some sort an incarnation of the author" (qtd. in Hoover 73). That many readers still see Jim in this way is suggested by Schickel, who refers in his film to Jim Burden, "who is in fact Willa Cather." But by the 1970s Jim had become a suspect figure—an unreliable narrator, a mask to hide the author's presumed lesbian desires, an androgynous figure, more feminine than masculine, a romantic mythmaker, "a more disingenuous and self-deluded narrator than we supposed," according to Blanche Gelfant (79). The degree of irony with which Cather viewed her narrator has not yet been established.

Surely Cather was aware that she was creating in Jim Burden a character who often failed in charity and compassion. One may well feel that he has not earned his ecstatic vision of Ántonia after his absence of twenty years, that his celebration of her at the end therefore seems sentimental and self-indulgent. But the power that Jim invests in Ántonia is the power that Cather wanted her own novel to have. She wanted her novel, like Ántonia, to "leave images in the mind that did not fade—that grew stronger with time." To convey her purpose, she needed a narrator with a "romantic disposition," which the narrator of the introduction ascribes to Jim Burden (x). She needed a narrator who feels the vast emptiness of the prairie as Jim feels it: "nothing but land: not a country at all, but the material out of which countries are made" (8).

Cather's ambition to be the maker of a country is expressed indirectly, in the words from book 3 of the *Georgics*, in the lecture on Virgil given by Jim's teacher, Gaston Cleric, as recalled by Jim in book 3 of the novel: "for I shall be the first, if I live, to bring the Muse into my country." Jim remembers Cleric's reading of the passage in the *Georgics*: "This was not a boast, but a hope, at once bold and devoutly humble, that he might bring the Muse (but lately come to Italy from her cloudy Grecian mountains), not to the capital, the *palatia Romana*, but to his own little 'country'; to his father's fields, 'sloping down to the river and to the old beech trees with broken tops'" (299).

Cather sets between herself and Virgil two figures—Jim Burden and Gaston Cleric. Thus she avoids presuming to identify herself with the Latin poet, or to compare her novel to the work praised by Dryden as "the best poem of the best poet." But the parallels are there for the reader who cares to draw them. Both the *Georgics* and Cather's novel were completed in the authors' prime years of middle age, in their forties. Both writers celebrated a *patria* from which they had for years been separated (Virgil having lived near Naples for many years before finishing the *Georgics*). The following observation by Gilbert Highet could apply to the author of *My Ántonia* as well as to Virgil, who would bring the Muses "in triumph from the Aonian peak": "Roman civilization . . . was to Greece as the culture of America, North and South, is to that of Europe—a new variety, formed and strengthened by transplantation" (66).

That Cather has become a cultural icon is evidence that she succeeded in her ambition. In bringing the Muse into her own country, she did for the frontier prairies and plains what Hawthorne did for the Puritans, what Mark Twain did for the Mississippi River, what Fitzgerald did for the Jazz Age. And in doing so, she, like them, inspired readers to look beyond the famous images, the icons, to seek the depths and mysteries that give to the images the power they continue to have for us.

WORKS CITED

Acocella, Joan. *Willa Cather and the Politics of Criticism*. Lincoln: U of Nebraska P, 2000.

Ahearn, Amy. "Full Blooded Writing and Journalistic Fictions: Naturalism, the Female Artist, and Willa Cather's *The Song of the Lark*." *American Literary Realism* 33 (Winter 2001): 143–56.

Anders, John P. *Willa Cather's Sexual Aesthetics and the Male Homosexual Tradition*. Lincoln: U of Nebraska P, 1999.

Cather, Willa. "A Biographical Sketch." *Willa Cather Newsletter and Review* 46 (2003): 53–54.

———. *My Ántonia*. 1918. Willa Cather Scholarly Edition. Ed. Charles W. Mignon with Kari A. Ronning. Historical essay James Woodress. Lincoln: U of Nebraska P, 1994.

———. "The Novel Démeublé." *Not Under Forty*. New York: Knopf, 1936. 43–51.

Fetterley, Judith. "Willa Cather and the Question of Sympathy: An Unofficial Story." Romines 20–21.

Gelfant, Blanche H. "The Forgotten Reaping-Hook: Sex in *My Ántonia*." *American Literature* 43 (March 1971): 60–82. Rpt. in *Willa Cather's* My Ántonia. Ed. Harold Bloom. New York: Chelsea, 1987. 79–97.

Goldberg, Jonathan. *Willa Cather and Others*. Durham NC: Duke UP, 2001.

Highet, Gilbert. *Poets in a Landscape*. New York: Knopf, 1957.

Hoover, Sharon, ed. *Willa Cather Remembered*. Lincoln: U of Nebraska P, 2002.

Lindemann, Marilee. *Willa Cather: Queering America*. New York: Columbia UP, 1999.

Middleton, JoAnn. *Willa Cather's Modernism: A Study of Style and Technique*. Rutherford NJ: Fairleigh Dickinson UP, 1990.

Millington, Richard H. "The Experience of Meaning in *The Professor's House*." Swift and Urgo 71–88.

Morgan, Edmund S. *Benjamin Franklin*. New Haven: Yale UP, 2002.

Murphy, John J. *My Ántonia: The Road Home*. Boston: Twayne, 1989.

Nealon, Christopher. *Foundlings: Lesbian and Gay Historical Emotion Before Stonewall*. Durham NC: Duke UP, 2001.

Porter, David H. "Cather on Cather II: Two Recent Acquisitions at Drew University." *Willa Cather Newsletter and Review* 46 (2003): 49–58.

Reynolds, Guy. *Willa Cather in Context: Progress, Race, Empire*. New York: St. Martin's, 1996.

Romines, Ann, ed. *Willa Cather's Southern Connections: New Essays on Cather and the South*. Charlottesville: UP of Virginia, 2000.

Rose, Phyllis. "Modernism: the Case of Willa Cather." *Modernism Reconsidered*. Ed. Robert Kiely. Cambridge: Harvard UP, 1983. 123–45.

Schickel, Richard, dir. *"Into the Morning": Willa Cather's America*. Films for the Humanities, 1988.

Schueth, Michael. "Cather and Her Stars: Negotiating a Culture of Celebrity in the 1890s." *Willa Cather Newsletter and Review* 45 (2001): 33–37.

Stout, Janis P. *Willa Cather: The Writer and Her World*. Charlottesville: UP of Virginia, 2000.

Swift, John N. "Unwrapping the Mummy: Cather's Mother Eve and the Business of Desire." Swift and Urgo 12–31.

Swift, John N., and Joseph R. Urgo, eds. *Willa Cather and the American Southwest*. Lincoln: U of Nebraska P, 2002.

Thompson, Stephanie Lewis. *Influencing America's Tastes: Realism in the Works of Wharton, Cather, and Hurst*. Gainesville: UP of Florida, 2002.

Urgo, Joseph R. "The Iconic Willa Cather." *Modernism/Modernity* 9 (2002): 327–33.

Williams, Deborah Lindsay. "Hiding in Plain Sight: Willa Cather and Ghostwriting." *Willa Cather Newsletter and Review* 43 (1999): 25–31.

Wolff, Cynthia Griffin. "Dressing for the Part: [What's] The Matter with Clothes." Romines 198–220.

Advertising Cather during the Transition Years (1914–1922)

ERIKA HAMILTON

On 12 January 1921, Willa Cather wrote to Ferris Greenslet, her editor at Houghton Mifflin, to report that "Claude," later to become *One of Ours*, would be published by Alfred Knopf. Although she had voiced numerous complaints about Houghton Mifflin's handling of *My Ántonia*, she claimed that her main reason for switching to Knopf was advertising.[1] She had been studying Knopf's advertisements, including his successful publicity for *Youth and the Bright Medusa*, and concluded that his endorsements were more spirited, sincere, and enthusiastic than Houghton Mifflin's. She refused at first to commit to a permanent break from Houghton Mifflin—she wanted the option of offering them future novels for publication—but she firmly believed Knopf would do the best publicity work for "Claude."

Differences in advertising strategies are evident in issues of the *New York Times Book Review*, *Publishers Weekly*, and the *New Republic* from 1914 through 1922. If Cather perused issues of the *New Republic*, as she likely did, she would have seen differences between Houghton Mifflin's book lists and Alfred Knopf's signed letters.[2] Houghton Mifflin's full-page advertisements often listed and briefly described ten to thirty books, sometimes including excerpts from positive reviews. The company's few exceptions to this strategy included a December 1914 full-page advertisement devoted to Emerson's journals and a July 1921 back-cover quarter-page for an Amy Lowell novel. Houghton Mifflin occasionally promoted poetry collections and Lowell's fiction in the *New Republic*, but its advertisements focused primarily on nonfiction, such as biographies and histories, to reflect the periodical's attention to domestic and international affairs. Alfred Knopf also placed book lists in the *New Republic*, but his offered more enthusiasm and substance. Within a short description of a book, either nonfiction or fiction, Knopf included a mixture of subject and plot synopses, excerpts from reviews, and his own recommendations. Adolph Kroch recalls in his essay "To Alfred Knopf from a Bookseller" that Knopf's lists were "not sales talks, but literary dissertations and elucidations of a publishing program that was clear, incisive, uncompromising" (41). Some Knopf advertisements did not look like lists at all, but like personal letters to a friend complete with paragraphs and his signature in script. In these, Knopf marketed himself as a publisher who was more concerned with literary quality than market demand.

Houghton Mifflin anticipated Knopf's letter-style technique in a 3 October 1915, quarter-page advertisement for *The Song of the Lark* in the *New York Times Book Review*. Unlike Knopf's, Houghton Mifflin's "letter" does not end with a personal signature in script. It also fails to announce the book's title in large, bold type. To discover what the advertisement promotes, one must read through its first four lines. Readers who scan the page for bold titles and headlines may miss it altogether. The first lines are elegantly formal: "Messrs. Houghton Mifflin Company take pleasure in announcing a new and impotant [*sic*] novel." This is not a personal, enthusiastic announcement, like when a friend rushes to the table, pushes a book forward, and gushes, "You've got to read this! It is so good!" Instead, the advertisement reads like a black-tie event where guests stand and politely applaud as the book is escorted to the stage for a prepared introduction—an impressive formality quickly forgotten when the book is mistakenly called impotent by the host rather than important. Cather scorned this black-tie event when she expressed dissatisfaction with Houghton Mifflin's formal introductions of her books (Cather to Greenslet, 19 May 1919).

Cather wanted advertisements to exude sincere enthusiasm and excitement (Cather to Scaife, 30 October 1915). Instead, the announcement for *The Song of the Lark* exudes detachment. It classifies the novel as a "study" and "panorama," terms that sound heavy and academic. Except for the word "glorious" in the first paragraph, the synopsis reads like a vague book report. The second paragraph indicates that Cather handles her theme "in a big way" but does not explain what that means. Does it mean *The Song of the Lark* is a long novel (which it is), or does it mean something else? The advertisement's last sentence finally shows some enthusiasm: "*The Song of the Lark* will stand high among the really worth while novels of the year." While this statement promotes Cather's work as important and worthwhile, it is overshadowed by the misspelled word in the first sentence. Houghton Mifflin had a company rule that advertising layouts "were to be studied with the same painstaking attention" given to advance copies of books (Ballou 426). The poor copyediting of this advertisement suggests that it did not receive the proper "painstaking attention" and that *The Song of the Lark* was not as important to Houghton Mifflin as it wished to indicate.

Earlier, in March 1915, Cather had expressed jealousy over Doubleday's publicity methods, which she said made her feel wistful (Cather to Greenslet, 28 March 1915). She may have seen Doubleday's advertisement for Joseph Conrad in the 13 March 1915 issue of *Publishers Weekly*. This eye-catching announcement, with its headless statue and fearless predictions, exudes a bold confidence and enthusiasm that are lacking in Houghton Mifflin's announcement for *The Song of the Lark*. Unlike the tucked-away title in Houghton Mifflin's advertisement, Doubleday prominently displays Conrad's title, *Victory*, in large, bold letters that are difficult to overlook. The bottom corners advise that Conrad's *Chance* was voted "the Best Novel of 1914" and that Doubleday predicts "double the sales of *Chance*" for *Victory*, a prediction repeated in the second paragraph of the announcement's text. The text praises *Victory* for the "directness of its narrative" and the "extraordinary power and swiftness of its action," but it also claims that *Victory* has more "popular elements" than Conrad's previous novels. The first paragraph clears up possible confusion over the title. *Victory* is not a war novel, as the title suggests, but a "romance of Axel Heyst and Lena, the girl from a travelling Ladies' Orchestra, and their strange life on the deserted South Sea island of Samburan." The novel addresses an individual's isolation from other individuals, not a nation's conflict with other nations.

Besides the bold title, optimistic predictions, and enthusiastic praises for *Victory*, Doubleday's advertisement does something else that appealed to Cather. It includes a quotation from H. L. Mencken: "a tale indeed!" Cather often prodded Greenslet and R. L. Scaife, Houghton Mifflin's advertising director, to take advantage of positive comments her work received. She suggested review excerpts and rewrote advertising copy to include quotations. On 19 October 1915, more than two weeks after publication of *The Song of the Lark*, Scaife wrote to Cather, enclosing an advertisement proof to be printed in *The Transcript*. He remarked that "the reviews which are appearing are stunning, and any further announcement must include the *Nation*, which I have just seen this morning, and which is the best yet." Cather responded to Scaife on 30 October and said *The Transcript* advertisement was uninspiring. She considered it damning to promote a book with empty phrases such as "an uncommonly interesting novel" or "unquestionably a novel of distinction." She believed a review's enthusiastic tone was more important and influential than words of commendation. Along with her letter to Scaife, Cather sent a revised advertisement that included review excerpts from the *Nation*, the *New York Commercial Advertiser*, the *New York Tribune*, and the *Chicago Tribune*. Two days later, she wrote to Greenslet and asked him to let Scaife know about quotable reviews in the *Boston Advertiser* and *New Bedford Standard* (Cather to Greenslet, 1 November 1915).

When an advertisement for *The Song of the Lark* appeared in the 20 November 1915 issue of *Publishers Weekly*, it included a review quotation. The excerpt, however, ignores all of Cather's suggestions, including her disdain for empty commendations. It praises *The Song of the Lark* as "a distinct improvement on her previous novels, 'O Pioneers,' [*sic*] and 'Alexander's Bridge.' It is unquestionably a novel of distinction."[3] This excerpt, which includes a phrase Cather condemned in her letter to Scaife, seems to say that *The Song of the Lark* is a "novel of distinction" because it is "a distinct improvement," implying that Cather's previous novels were inferior in one or more unnamed ways. This ambiguous advertisement is overshadowed by the "glorious romance" of *The Fortunes of Garin*, "a brilliant story" in *K*, and the "brightness, sparkle, vivacity, rollicking humor" of *Little Miss Grouch* (as praised by the *Boston Advertiser*). A better, more exciting quotation would have described *The Song of the Lark* and Cather's previous novels with clear, positive, enthusiastic adjectives rather than obscure praise.

Three years later, a December 1918 article in *Publishers Weekly* announced the winners of their Book-Ad Contest and explained that every advertisement should impress a book upon the reader's mind. The article stated that the advertising director's job "is not merely to prepare a series of striking announcements, but to see to it that the idea behind the advertising, the point of view of his house in publishing the books, penetrates the minds" of all booksellers and buyers ("Award" 1963). The director must "present the facts attractively; he must place this knowledge before the public in such a way that they are impressed." A successful advertisement "attracts, creates interest, kindles desire, convinces and impels action." That action, of course, is to buy the book being advertised. Although this article was not published until 1918, its ideas can be applied to advertisements from 1915. Does the 20 November 1915 advertisement for *The Song of the Lark* impress? Does it create interest in the story or kindle a desire to buy the book? Sadly, no.

The Book-Ad Contest asked all booksellers to select their three favorite advertisements and explain why they were the best that appeared in *Publishers Weekly* from 14 September to 16 November 1918. The judges weighed each nomination against three "fundamental principles" of advertising—phraseology, pictorial construction, and typographical display ("Award" 1963). An honorable mention was awarded to a Houghton Mifflin advertisement nominated by a bookseller who explained that she had never seen a bad advertisement from the company. Houghton Mifflin's advertisements in general were not of poor quality, but the company's low expectations and budget for Cather's novels did not encourage them to do their best when advertising her work.

At least one Houghton Mifflin advertisement for Cather, an advertisement for *My Ántonia*, managed to impress. It was so well done that it attracted the attention of the man who would later publish *One of Ours*. Alfred Knopf, in his "Miss Cather" essay, describes "an oddly dignified advertisement" for *My Ántonia* that he saw in the fall of 1918 (205). Perhaps he saw the 29 September 1918 advertisement in the *New York Times Book Review*. While this quarter page does not include review quotations, it does show more enthusiasm. The title immediately catches the eye with bold type and is followed by a list of Cather's previous works: *The Song of the Lark* and *O Pioneers!* "etc., etc." This list not only invokes the memory of past novels to help sell the new novel but also indicates that Cather has written more than three books. She is a prolific novelist with an established and growing reputation. The paragraph that follows praises Cather's "rare quality of being able to put into her books the flame and driving force of unconquerable youth." While *The Song of the Lark* was classified as a study or panorama, *My Ántonia* is "a love story of profound human appeal." In the last few lines, Houghton Mifflin describes the book as "one of the really notable American novels of recent years. We unreservedly recommend it to every lover of good fiction." The very bottom is signed in script: "Houghton Mifflin Company." This advertisement is no longer a black-tie event but rather a fancy dinner party where a guest wishes to gush about the new book, but must do so within the manners of polite society.

Despite the improved enthusiasm in Houghton Mifflin's advertisements, Cather continued to be dissatisfied. In her five-page grievance letter to Greenslet, she expressed admiration for Knopf's advertising of Joseph Hergesheimer's *Java Head*, noting that Knopf's splendid publicity work had improved Hergesheimer's reputation and career, even if it did little to increase sales (Cather to Greenslet, 19 May 1919). Throughout 1919, Cather peppered her letters with references to Knopf's advertising strategies and requests for Houghton Mifflin to follow Knopf's lead.[4]

Cather might have seen the *Java Head* advertisement in the 12 January 1919 issue of the *New York Times Book Review*. Unlike Scaife, Knopf did not wait long to include review excerpts in his advertisements. By 12 January, *Java Head* had been on store shelves for only one week, yet it was "an instantaneous success." This advertisement includes five enthusiastic reviews. The first says that *Java Head* is "a strange, most unusual, beautiful, intriguing story," and another calls Hergesheimer "one of the great novelists of the period." This was what Cather wanted in her advertisements—instantaneous and enthusiastic review excerpts.

While Cather appealed for better advertisements, Houghton Mifflin decreased its advertising budget for her novels. The firm distrusted any link between advertising and sales (Mignon 512). In May 1919, Greenslet indicated to Cather that he was unsure if more advertising would help sell her novel. "Possibly more advertising of 'My Ántonia' would have resulted in larger sales," he said, "but for whatever reason, it did not react as it should" (Greenslet to Cather, 23 May 1919). Despite this distrust, the firm awarded higher allocations to books whose authors had proven to be profitable. If a previous book was a best-seller, the company was confident that the author's new book would repay advertising costs in high sales. In 1914, Houghton Mifflin allotted over $6,000 to advertise Henry Harrison's novel *V. V.'s Eyes* because his first novel, *Queed*, had done so well (Ballou 558).[5] Eleanor Porter's *Just David* received an allocation of $4,000. The novel accumulated 100,000 advance orders and became a best-seller in 1916. Next to these generous sums, the allocations for Cather's books were minuscule. *The Song of the Lark* received an advertising budget of $1,000 (Crane 48), while *My Ántonia* received only $300 (58). These figures, especially the $300, demonstrate Houghton Mifflin's lack of confidence in the selling power of Cather's novels.

Cather explains her switch from Houghton Mifflin and "the manufacture of stories for which there is a market demand" to the "search for something for which there is no market demand" in her 1920 essay "On the Art of Fiction" (8). She explains that, "in the beginning, the artist, like his public, is wedded to old forms, old ideals, and his vision is blurred by the memory of old delights he would like to recapture" (8). As a new novelist, Cather was "wedded" to old literary ideals (particularly noticeable in her Jamesian novel, *Alexander's Bridge*). She was therefore well matched with the old-form, long-established, market-minded Houghton Mifflin. In her 1922 essay "The Novel Démeublé," however, Cather refuses to write novels "manufactured to entertain great multitudes of people," because "fine quality is a distinct disadvantage in articles made for great numbers of people who do not want quality but quantity" (36). Cather's insistence on literary quality required a publisher who not only valued quality and experimentation but gladly spent money to advertise it.

Accounts vary regarding Cather's first meeting with Alfred Knopf, but he offers similar versions in "Miss Cather" and a paper he presented to the Massachusetts Historical Society. During the presentation, Knopf said:

> I think it was in 1919 that there happened to me the sort of thing a publisher dreams about but doesn't often experience. A lady named Willa Cather walked unannounced into our small offices on West 42nd Street. . . . She expressed surprise to learn that I knew who she was, and you must remember she had already published *My Ántonia*, so I didn't think I was very clever. She liked the kind of advertising we were doing (it must have been on a very small scale because we were very small publishers in those days). ("Random" 99)

In her 1940 essay honoring Knopf, Cather explains that she was impressed in 1919 (and afterward) by Knopf's sincere enthusiasm for his authors and his willingness to "take any amount of pains with a book" despite a lack of funds ("Portrait" 12). He did not reserve generous advertising budgets for only his profitable authors, as Houghton Mifflin did, but was generous with all of his authors. Knopf's approach inspired Cather to allow him to publish and advertise a collection of her short stories in 1920 as a trial run. The collection was *Youth and the Bright Medusa*.

There is plenty of enthusiasm and praise in Knopf's 29 September 1920 advertisement for *Youth and the Bright Medusa*. Although Houghton Mifflin rarely advertised fiction in the *New Republic*—mostly because of the journal's "somewhat limited field of critical endeavor" (Greenslet to Cather, 23 May 1919)—

Knopf chose that periodical to advertise Cather's newest collection. He displayed confidence and faith in her work by listing her collection at the top of a full-page book list in a medium that printed more advertisements for nonfiction than fiction. Above the collection's title is the announcement: "A new Book by the author of 'My Antonia' [*sic*], etc."[6] This is a bold statement by Knopf, especially since Cather had not yet broken from Houghton Mifflin. By referring to *My Ántonia*, Knopf draws on the popularity of the Houghton Mifflin book to help increase sales of the Knopf book.

The advertisement's first sentence establishes Cather as an important author who should be noticed: "There are not many living writers from whom a new book commands the attention with which each successive volume of Miss Cather's is now awaited. There seems to be no disputing the fact that she is our foremost living woman novelist." Knopf teases readers by implying that a new book is forthcoming but not saying what it is. One must read on: "In the stories in the present volume she deals with youth's adventures with the many-colored Medusa of art." This sentence does two things. First, it answers the question, "What is the next book about?" Second, it explains the book's unusual title so that confusion over its meaning will not decrease sales. Fanny Butcher, a book reviewer and friend of Cather's, explains in her memoir that "a title has often made the difference between a winner in the literary horse race and the forgotten nag" (363). By explaining the title, Knopf tries to keep the book from being forgotten. The third sentence explains Cather's unique style with strong words: "Each tale is marked by the amazing ardor and restless energy of imagination which is peculiarly Miss Cather's; by a quick, bold cutting into the tissues of human experience and emotion that makes each of them a new discovery about character and life." Cather accused Houghton Mifflin's advertising of being timid, but Knopf's aggressive technique includes forceful imagery of cutting human tissue.

Knopf did not wait for *Youth and the Bright Medusa* to be reviewed before he included quotations in the advertisement. Instead, he found reviews of Cather's past work and used those, again drawing on the reputation she had established with

Houghton Mifflin. He even included a review excerpt from a periodical in Sweden, proving that Cather's work was not only read nationally but internationally as well.

Almost two weeks after the *New Republic* advertisement for *Youth and the Bright Medusa*, a different advertisement appeared in the *New York Times Book Review*. It is a short book list with interesting contrasts to Houghton Mifflin's list from five years earlier. While *The Song of the Lark* is promoted in the bottom corner of Houghton Mifflin's advertisement—overshadowed by the intriguing, central panel advertising *K* as "The Novel That Has Swept The Country"—*Youth and the Bright Medusa* appears at the top of Knopf's. The Houghton Mifflin book list does not refer to any of Cather's previous works, but the Knopf list immediately refers to Cather as "Author of 'My Antonia' [*sic*]." Houghton Mifflin offers a simple description of *The Song of the Lark*, "the story of a prima donna's life, from childhood on a Western ranch to international fame—a story of ambition, of triumph and of love," but Knopf offers a review excerpt from the *Nation* about *Youth and the Bright Medusa*, "one of the most poetical interpretations of American life that we possess." While *The Song of the Lark* struggles to compete with the fascinating books surrounding it, *Youth and the Bright Medusa* leaps off the page with its announcement of "eight distinguished stories!"

With *One of Ours*, Knopf continued to invest in enthusiastic advertising that took advantage of Cather's reputation. An announcement in the 10 September 1922 issue of the *New York Times Book Review* takes full advantage of her visibility, something she said Houghton Mifflin did not do. It includes a photograph of Cather, mentions *My Ántonia* (again without the accented "Á"), and proclaims that "Miss Cather was the only woman in the list of five leading American writers who have emerged in this decade." This statement, coupled with Burton Rascoe's comment that "Miss Cather is the one woman of indubitable genius that we have," elevates Cather as an important American novelist. Knopf goes on to introduce *One of Ours* as "an authentic masterpiece—a novel to rank with the finest of this or any age." If this is not enough to send readers to bookstores, Knopf continues his push by describing Claude Wheeler as "a sort of American Hamlet" and praising Cather's "daring, impatient mind, her subtle and flexible style." This advertisement is careful to not mention the book's war aspect, but hints of the war are present in references to "the final adventure which releases the baffled energy of his [Claude's] nature" and "the ever deepening sense of national drama, of national character." These references conceal without misleading. Anyone surprised by the last half of *One of Ours* could return to these and recognize their subtle overtones of war.

While some critics were surprised by the novel's war aspect and wrote negative reviews, it did not adversely affect sales. Cather had hoped to receive 10,000 advance orders for *One of Ours* (Lewis 115); instead, Knopf's aggressive advertising led to 12,000 advance orders. He printed 15,000 copies at first, but immediately printed another 10,000 to meet demand. In contrast, *My Ántonia* did not sell well until *One of Ours* won the Pulitzer Prize and boosted sales of all Cather titles. Houghton Mifflin's first printing of *My Ántonia* ran 3,500 copies (Crane 58). Cather's longtime companion, Edith Lewis, reports that "the initial sale of *My Ántonia* was small—in the first year it brought about $1,300, and not quite $400 in the second year" (108).[7] The combined royalties for *Youth and the Bright Medusa* and *One of Ours* were approximately $19,000 (115).

One thing about Knopf that appealed to Cather from the beginning was his strong interest in establishing long-term reputations for his authors. Knopf, who began his firm in 1915 at the age of twenty-three, was still establishing his own reputation as a New York publisher in 1919 and 1920. His fortune was linked with the fortunes of every one of his authors. His success depended on theirs, and he referred to his publishing business as a "personal affair" ("Random" 101). Knopf admired his authors, a fact Cather appreciated. Edith Lewis states that Knopf "made evident, not only to her [Cather] but to the world in general, his great admiration and belief in her" (116). This was an important contrast to Cather's claim that Houghton Mifflin showed little faith in her work.

In response to Cather's grievance letter in 1919, Ferris Greenslet voiced his belief that, if Cather were to switch publishers, she "would, in the end, fare worse" (Greenslet to Cather, 23 May 1919). Instead, she fared better. In 1940, Cather wrote the following: "I have always been proud that I asked young Mr. Knopf to take me over, with not so much as a hint from him that he would like to have me. It was a rather sudden decision. Did it work? The answer is, twenty years" ("Portrait" 26). Her decision to switch publishers—her move away from publicity devoted to formality and market demand in favor of publicity devoted to enthusiasm and literary quality—finally helped establish Cather as a prominent author and American icon.

NOTES

I am grateful to Susan J. Rosowski for reading and commenting on various stages of this article.

1. Charles Mignon, in his textual commentary for *My Ántonia*, suggests that Houghton Mifflin's timid publicity for Cather's novels "may very well have had an effect on her move to Alfred A. Knopf" (512). Here I argue that advertising played a prominent role in her decision to switch publishers. Differences in the advertisements of Houghton Mifflin and Alfred Knopf are also discussed in Susan J. Rosowski's historical essay in the Willa Cather Scholarly Edition of *A Lost Lady*. That essay offers insight into what Cather saw as major differences between advertising strategies; Cather's transition to Knopf so that "Claude" would receive better advertising; and the effect of Cather's Pulitzer Prize on book sales. A two-page spread in the Scholarly Edition includes a copy of Knopf's advance pamphlet advertising *One of Ours*.

2. The information in this paragraph was gathered by studying several issues of the *New Republic* from 1914 through 1922. The descriptions of advertising techniques are summaries of the many advertisements studied.

3. The absence of the exclamation mark from *O Pioneers!* again suggests that Houghton Mifflin's advertisements for Cather did not receive proper attention or care before they were printed.

4. See Cather to Greenslet, Saturday [May 1919], 7 October [1919], and 17 November 1919.

5. Greenslet often referred to the success of *Queed* in his letters to Cather. On 30 March 1915 he wrote about "the historic case of 'Queed' which went in the front door of the Doubleday shop and left by the back and led the six best sellers for nearly a year under our imprint." On 1

November 1915, while discussing strategies for advertising *The Song of the Lark* in women's colleges, Greenslet commented: "Something like this was used very successfully in launching 'Queed' while Harrison was still unknown." Houghton Mifflin was proud of its success with Harrison's first novel, and that pride carried over into the advertising of his next.

6. The majority of advertisements studied for this article, regardless of whether they were from Houghton Mifflin or Alfred Knopf, do not include the accented "Á" in Ántonia's name. A notable exception is a Houghton Mifflin advertisement in the 28 September 1918 issue of *Publishers Weekly*. Subsequent *Publishers Weekly* advertisements printed "Ántonia" without the accent.

7. These sales figures were compared with Houghton Mifflin's production records and confirmed during research for the Willa Cather Scholarly Edition of *My Ántonia*. See James Woodress's historical essay in that edition.

WORKS CITED

Alfred A. Knopf. Advertisement for Joseph Hergesheimer's *Java Head*. *New York Times Book Review* 12 Jan. 1919: 15.

———. Advertisement for *One of Ours*. *New York Times Book Review* 10 Sept. 1922: 25.

———. Advertisement for *Youth and the Bright Medusa* and other titles. *New Republic* 29 Sept. 1920: back cover.

———. Advertisement for *Youth and the Bright Medusa* and other titles. *New York Times Book Review* 10 Oct. 1920: 23.

"The Award of Prizes in the Publishers Weekly Book-Ad Contest." *Publishers Weekly* 21 Dec. 1918: 1963–65.

Ballou, Ellen B. *The Building of the House: Houghton Mifflin's Formative Years*. Boston: Houghton, 1970.

Butcher, Fanny. *Many Lives—One Love*. New York: Harper, 1972.

Cather, Willa. Letters to Ferris Greenslet and Roger L. Scaife. Houghton Library, Harvard U.

———. "The Novel Démeublé." *New Republic* 12 Apr. 1922, suppl.: 5–6. Reprinted in *Not Under Forty*. New York: Knopf, 1936. 43–51.

———. "On the Art of Fiction." *The Borzoi 1920*. Ed. Alfred Knopf. New York: Knopf, 1920. 7–8. Reprinted in *Willa Cather on Writing*. New York: Knopf, 1949. 101–4.

———. "Portrait of the Publisher as a Young Man." *Alfred A. Knopf: Quarter Century*. Ed. Bruce Rogers. New York: Plimpton, 1940. 9–26.

Crane, Joan. *Willa Cather: A Bibliography*. Lincoln: U of Nebraska P, 1982.

Doubleday, Page & Co. Advertisement for Joseph Conrad's *Victory*. *Publishers Weekly* 13 Mar. 1915: 757.

Greenslet, Ferris. Letters to Willa Cather. Houghton Library, Harvard U.

Houghton Mifflin Co. Advertisement for an Amy Lowell novel. *New Republic* 27 July 1921: back cover.

———. Advertisement for Emerson's journals. *New Republic* 12 Dec. 1914: back cover.

———. Advertisement for *My Ántonia*. *New York Times Book Review* 29 Sept. 1918: 414.

———. Advertisement for *My Ántonia* and other titles. *Publishers Weekly* 28 Sept. 1918: 886.

———. Advertisement for *The Song of the Lark*. *New York Times Book Review* 3 Oct. 1915: 360.

———. Advertisement for *The Song of the Lark* and other titles. *New York Times Book Review* 10 Oct. 1915: 362, 385.

———. Advertisement for *The Song of the Lark* and other titles. *Publishers Weekly* 20 Nov. 1915: 4.

Knopf, Alfred A. "Miss Cather." *The Art of Willa Cather*. Ed. Bernice Slote and Virginia Faulkner. Lincoln: U of Nebraska P, 1974. 205–24.

———. "Random Recollections of a Publisher." *Proceedings of the Massachusetts Historical Society* 74 (1961): 92–103.

Kroch, Adolph. "To Alfred Knopf from a Bookseller." *Alfred A. Knopf: Quarter Century*. Ed. Bruce Rogers. New York: Plimpton, 1940. 39–46.

Lewis, Edith. *Willa Cather Living: A Personal Record*. 1953. Lincoln: U of Nebraska P, 1976.

Mignon, Charles W., with Kari A. Ronning. Textual Commentary. *My Ántonia*. By Willa Cather. Willa Cather Scholarly Edition. Lincoln: U of Nebraska P, 1994. 481–521.

Rosowski, Susan J., with Kari A. Ronning. Historical Essay. *A Lost Lady*. By Willa Cather. Willa Cather Scholarly Edition. Lincoln: U of Nebraska P, 1997. 177–233.

Scaife, Roger L. Letter to Willa Cather. 19 Oct. 1915. Huntington Library, San Marino CA.

Woodress, James. Historical Essay. *My Ántonia*. By Willa Cather. Willa Cather Scholarly Edition. Lincoln: U of Nebraska P, 1994. 369–401.

Willa Cather and Her Public in 1922

JANIS P. STOUT

Recent scholarship has substantially displaced the once widely accepted image of Willa Cather as an otherworldly aesthete, withdrawn from society in general (though with a few selected intimates) and unconcerned with material matters. Such a view of her was fostered in the memoir published by Edith Lewis, her devoted and protective companion, in 1953, six years after Cather's death. There, Lewis emphasized Cather's single-minded devotion to her literary discipline, insisting that although her response to people was naturally warm, she was compelled to "withdraw more and more from the world" for "self-preservation" as an artist (135–37). Similarly, but with somewhat different emphasis, both James Woodress and Hermione Lee maintained in their late-1980s biographies that Cather had an "obsession with privacy" (Lee 72 and 185; Woodress, *Literary Life* 141 and 475). A great deal of evidence supports such a view, to be sure, and the understanding of Cather as withdrawn, uncommunicative, and uninterested in the trappings of success has in some measure persisted. But the obsession Woodress and Lee refer to was primarily a characteristic of her later years, not her years of busy career building.[1] We now recognize that the Cather of the early 1920s was not yet the unapproachable person, wrapped in disapproval of social realities, that she later became.

One of the most important challenges to the convention of Cather's reclusiveness was Brent Bohlke's invaluable 1986 collection of interviews and other public statements, *Willa Cather in Person*. The materials in this volume compel us to recognize Cather's interest in public issues and her at least sporadic availability to the public media. Indeed, it has recently been demonstrated that on at least one occasion her desire for publicity was such that what appears to be an interview was in fact "an autobiographical fiction created by Cather herself," in effect a press release for which she wrote "both her own words and those of her interlocutor" (Porter 55).[2] In addition to the documents he collected, Bohlke presented an incisive introductory argument that Cather suffered a "civil war" in her personality: "Willa Cather courted and enjoyed public notice, yet she loved anonymity and seclusion. She was enamored of the notice of the press and deeply resentful of the intrusions the press made upon her time and energies. She sought fame but disliked attention" (xxi). Sixteen years later, in 2002, Sharon Hoover extended Bohlke's work by completing and editing his compilation of published and unpublished reminiscences of Cather in *Willa Cather Remembered*, a volume that demonstrates the breadth and liveliness of her various acquaintances and public roles beginning with her college days. The notion of Cather as a withdrawn aesthete jealously guarding her privacy has also been effectively belied by various elements of the Scholarly Editions of her works, notably essays by Charles Mignon (on *My Ántonia*) and Susan J. Rosowski (on *A Lost Lady*). Both of these essays trace Cather's negotiations with her publishers, allowing us to see quite clearly how knowledgeable Cather was about the business of publishing and how deeply involved she was in decisions affecting the publication and advertising of her work.

My purpose here is to extend this revisionist challenge of the once-standard image of Cather by taking, as a case study, her professional activities during a single year, 1922, as they relate to her involvement in the construction of her public reputation. In discussing a different but related case study, Cather's change of publisher from Houghton Mifflin to Knopf, Rosowski emphasizes her desire to "protect her books as well as herself from commercial pressures" (178). My emphasis is instead on her desire to enhance her commercial success and public standing. Yet it is important to recognize that the two efforts existed side by side—dramatically so in this year when Cather was working on *A Lost Lady* (as Rosowski points out, "the first novel Cather conceived and wrote knowing that Knopf would publish it" [Historical Essay 177–78]) and at the same time engaging in the savvy business dealings I will trace here. Primarily I will do so by reading two specific sequences of letters—those relating to arrangements for her summer lecturing at the Bread Loaf School of English in Vermont, and those relating to the publication and reception of *One of Ours*, which appeared in September 1922. In both sequences we see her engaged in what Bohlke refers to as "court[ing] and enjoy[ing] public notice," and we see that she not only sought the public aspects of success but demonstrated considerable skill as a businesswoman and self-publicist.

My choice of 1922 for this case study is by no means arbitrary or incidental. Cather herself singled it out in the prefatory note to her 1936 volume of essays, *Not Under Forty*: "The world broke in two in 1922 or thereabouts." This much-scrutinized statement has generated a persistent scholarly debate. Interpretations have emphasized the near proximity of World War I (Michael North calls 1922 "the first real postwar year" [5] for England) and the social changes that followed, but have also included such biographical factors as the hostile critical reception of *One of Ours*, a novel that had occupied her for four years, and her 1923 visit to Isabelle McClung Hambourg in France (1923 being covered by the "thereabouts").[3] But as Michael North and Marc Manganaro have recently pointed out in books devoted to 1922, it was also a year of great significance for modernism generally—a fact by no means unrelated to the question of what Cather meant in her cryptic prefatory note. The year 1922 saw the publication of *The Waste Land* and *Ulysses* as well as a number of other notable modernist texts, including *One of Ours*. Indeed, North argues that Cather's choice of 1922 as the year when the world broke in two was made for essentially literary reasons—both because of the experimental texts published in that year and because of the new writers' misogynistic association of the old-fashioned with the feminine. James Joyce, for example, stated that *The Waste Land* "ends [the] idea of poetry for ladies" (North 174).

The significance of 1922 for Cather studies becomes all the

greater when we note that she taught at the Bread Loaf School in that year. A graduate program operated by Middlebury College, the School of English and American Literature was then in its third year of operation, having held its inaugural session in 1920. The land and buildings used by the school had been willed to Middlebury in 1915. In later years the same facilities would house the Bread Loaf Writers' Conference, convening in late summers after the School of English finished its six-week session. At the time Cather lectured at Bread Loaf, the Writers' Conference did not yet exist; it would be established four years later, largely through the advocacy of Robert Frost, seconded by Cather and two other summer lecturers of 1922, Katherine Lee Bates and the respected critic Louis Untermeyer.[4] Already, however, the Bread Loaf School must have achieved some measure of prestige, having attracted Frost to its faculty in 1921. Cather's invitation to teach there in 1922 was a significant recognition of her status as a literary artist whose words could command the same interest on the part of highly qualified and intent students as those of Frost and Untermeyer.

Although my emphasis here is on the ways in which the events of 1922 bore an impact on Cather's status as a public figure, her 1936 statement about the world's breaking in two holds direct pertinence if we take the sentence in its entirety rather than stopping with its familiar first clause: "The world broke in two in 1922 or thereabouts, and the persons and prejudices recalled in these sketches slid back into yesterday's seven thousand years" (O'Brien 811). Why did the persons she referred to in her essays (Annie Fields, Sarah Orne Jewett, Thomas Mann, Katherine Mansfield) slide back?—assuming, for the moment, that she was correct in saying that they did. The explanation would seem to be that they and their public grew apart. This was precisely what, in 1922, Cather was trying to see to it did *not* happen to her.

Setting aside for the moment the larger literary context and the matter of her ongoing distress over World War I, we can see that 1922 was a significant year for Cather personally as well:

— During January, though she had begun reading proofs of *One of Ours*, she was living a life of social gaiety, attending parties and enjoying the guests at her Friday afternoons at home, as well as the friendly attention of a number of younger writers (Stout, *Calendar* no. 576).[5]

— In February she fell ill with influenza, from which she had difficulty recovering. Her correspondence during this month included negotiations with Wilfred Davison regarding the possibility of lecturing at Bread Loaf and the beginning of a lengthy exchange with Dorothy Canfield Fisher in which Cather revealed her uneasiness about *One of Ours* (*Calendar* no. 578).

— In March or early April she underwent a tonsillectomy and was sent to a sanatorium, where she continued to work on proofs of *One of Ours*.

— On 12 April "The Novel Démeublé" was published in the *New Republic*.

— In July she taught for three weeks at the Bread Loaf School, lecturing to aspiring writers.

— In August she vacationed on Grand Manan Island, which she liked for its "beauty and isolation," affording her a quiet place to work (Woodress, *Literary Life* 323).

— On 8 September *One of Ours* was released. Reviews began to appear within a week, most of them unfavorable. On the other hand, the popular reception, as indicated by sales figures and by letters from ordinary readers, indicated success.

— On 4 November "The House on Charles Street" (which became "148 Charles Street" in *Not Under Forty*)—a memoir of Annie Adams Fields, widow of the noted Boston publisher James G. Fields—was published in the *New York Evening Post Literary Review*.

— On 29 November Cather left for a lengthy visit with her parents in Nebraska, and on 22 December she and they were confirmed in the Episcopal Church.

All of these factors relate, in various ways, to the shifting fortunes of Cather's standing as a public figure. When 1922 dawned Cather was a person who had once been a successful magazine editor but whose achievements in that field would soon be a decade in the past, and a writer whose latest novel was soon to be four years past: not exactly someone in the limelight. True, she had made a name for herself, but the dearth of recent publications was putting it at risk of slipping.[6] By the end of the year, the attention attracted by *One of Ours* had made her controversial. By mid-1923, as the author of a novel that had sold well and had been awarded the Pulitzer Prize, she would be indisputably a public figure—one sign of that status being that she had her portrait painted by a well-established artist at the behest of the city of Omaha.[7] The question is, what happened in 1922 to move her from a state of relative obscurity to the status of public figure? And what did she do to promote this change?

Cather's correspondence in 1922 reveals that she was working hard to consolidate her standing and shape her public image. In particular, the relatively brief sequence of letters relating to her lecturing at Bread Loaf and the more extensive series relating to the public reception of *One of Ours* provide considerable evidence that the once-accepted conception of Cather as an intensely private person, zealously guarding that privacy and indifferent or even hostile to public attention, is only partially accurate. At minimum, they show that she was exerting considerable effort to shape the terms on which her public image would be formed. Given the length of time that had passed since she last published a major work, it was clearly a crucial year for her in terms of her position in the world of letters. Her 1922 letters show that she was simultaneously courting and (as her liking for Grand Manan would indicate) fending off the public gaze.

So far as I know, the existing record of correspondence relating to Cather's invitation to teach at Bread Loaf consists of just six letters: three addressed to Wilfred E. Davison, director of the school, and three to her fellow writer and old friend from college days Dorothy Canfield Fisher. Unfortunately, the Canfield Fisher Papers at the University of Vermont hold only the letters written by Cather, not the other side (or rather, sides) of the correspondence. The letters written by Canfield Fisher and Davison might provide valuable insight into what Cather knew about Bread Loaf or learned about it in the course of her negotiations, and thus clues to her motivation and expectations when she accepted the invitation. Even without their context of responses, however, the letters provide an illuminating window on Cather's skills as a businessperson and a writer still building her career. She positions herself as a desirable but reluctant lecturer—perhaps the more desirable because reluctant.

The first of the six letters, dated 26 January 1922 (*Calendar* no. 574), is addressed to Canfield Fisher, with whom Cather had initiated a renewal of communications in March of the previous year. At that time she had tactfully solicited Canfield Fisher's advice about the difficult last quarter of *One of Ours*. Now she continues that topic and also, apparently in response to an overture by Canfield Fisher, takes up the idea of lecturing at Bread Loaf.[8] Her response is measured; she seems, indeed, rather indifferent, saying that her plans for the summer are unclear, though she will probably make a trip to Nebraska at some point. Expressing a guarded willingness to give three or four lectures, she adds that she had never heard of Bread Loaf until now—an entirely plausible statement since the school was preparing for only its third session.

On 6 February (*Calendar* no. 578) Cather again wrote to Dorothy, indicating that Wilfred Davison had written to her in the meantime extending a formal invitation to lecture at Bread Loaf for six weeks. He had not, however, indicated either the exact dates or how much he was offering as payment. How hard, she asked, should she negotiate? Here, especially, we would like to have Canfield Fisher's reply. Whatever it was, on the basis of that reply Cather wrote to Davison on 15 February, replying to his invitation in what strike me as remarkably temporizing terms (*Calendar* no. 580). In effect stringing him along, she says that she thinks she can come to Bread Loaf, or at any rate does not know of any reason why she cannot, though she might have to go to Nebraska on short notice if her mother's health should worsen. If she does come, she thinks she can give four or five sessions, which she goes on to describe in ways that would surely have been very attractive to Davison or to the director or any such school. Referring to the fact that most of the students in attendance would be hoping to breaking into writing careers by way of magazines, she explains that she had been an editor at *McClure's* in its glory years, when it fostered the development of young writers. She then names her price, claiming it is a bargain rate that she is willing to accept only because of the special nature of Bread Loaf—an enterprise that less than three weeks earlier she had (according to her letter to Dorothy) never heard of.

The fee Cather named was $200 plus hotel expenses. As I read the letter, this seems to mean $200 for the whole, plus expenses. Woodress reads it as $200 per lecture (*Literary Life* 322). But according to what she then goes on to say in the letter, that would not be a bargain rate at all. She begs Davison to keep the amount a secret because she usually demands that much *per lecture* from colleges and even more from clubs, in order to avoid those who are not genuinely avid to get her. That is, in what appears to be an effort to enhance her value in Davison's eyes or to convince him that the price she has quoted is indeed a bargain, she positions herself as a writer being pursued by people intent on having her come talk to their groups and usually reluctant to agree.

It was quite true that Cather was being pursued as a speaker. She had lectured in Lincoln and in Chicago the previous fall, and in the month following her letter to Davison she would decline an invitation from Mary Austin to be a luncheon guest of the Query Club. (Whether Austin wanted her to be a speaker or simply attend the luncheon is not clear.) Apparently she settled on a slightly later date with the Query Club, but then missed it due to her tonsillectomy. Perhaps she did not clearly tell them she was not coming; a note to Austin dated 21 April asks her to apologize to the secretary of the club. A few months later (on 19 November; *Calendar* no. 645) she would decline Ida Tarbell's invitation to the Pen and Brush Club on grounds that she was going to be away in Nebraska. The terms in which she declined are remarkably gentle ones that could not possibly have offended the club's members—whom she may well have thought of as readers she did not wish to alienate. She made a tentative commitment to speak to Tarbell's club on the first Sunday in February—that is, 4 February 1923. There is no record of her having given such a talk, however, and her correspondence indicates that she was absent from New York from 2 through 9 February 1923. With respect to clubs as well, then, Cather seems to have both invited and fended off attention.

The fourth of the six letters relating to arrangements for coming to Bread Loaf is dated 18 February, three days after the letter to Davison (*Calendar* no. 579, incorrectly shown there as 11 February). She reports to Canfield Fisher that she has specified terms for going to Bread Loaf and has constructed an out for herself by giving advance warning that she might have to back out for reasons of her parents' health. Contrary to Woodress's statement that she made a firm commitment early in the year and then regretted it after she fell ill (*Literary Life* 322), it does not sound as if her commitment was very firm. Indeed, she goes on to tell Dorothy explicitly that she has put in this part about her parents' health so that Bread Loaf will have no basis for a breach-of-promise suit if she should change her mind.

Cather's presence at Bread Loaf actually remained in doubt up into July. Davison must have been getting worried when she wrote him on 2 July (*Calendar* no. 608) that both her health and business matters with Knopf have detained her in New York and kept her plans uncertain. She still believes she can probably come to Bread Loaf by mid-month, but she does not sound very sure of it. Assuming she does, she asks, may she bring Edith Lewis along? He must have replied with haste, because only a week later, on 9 July, she writes again to confirm her expectations of a suite of rooms in Maple Cottage and transportation from the train station.

It is clear that once Cather finally fulfilled her commitment to Bread Loaf, she enjoyed her stay. In a note written in August from Grand Manan she exclaimed what a nice group of people there had been there (*Calendar* no. 612). On 1 September (*Calendar* no. 615) she wrote Canfield Fisher that her three weeks at Bread Loaf had been marvelous. And indeed a familiar snapshot of her taken while there shows her with a big smile, looking wonderfully relaxed. We might note, too, that for all her disclaimer about her lecture rate, the $200 apparently came in handy. On 2 May, while negotiations with Bread Loaf were still going on, she had been writing to Ferris Greenslet (*Calendar* no. 593) asking for an advance on royalties to help pay her medical bills. Yet when Davison asked her to return two years later, she gracefully declined and indicated that she would probably never come back. What factors went into her thinking we do not know; perhaps, as Woodress writes, she had found the experience "exhausting" (*Literary Life* 322). But we do know that in the meantime *One of Ours* had stabilized her income.

A parallel process of self-positioning vis-à-vis her public was carried out more elaborately and at greater length in Cather's numerous letters of 1922 relating to the reception of *One of Ours*.

In the letter of 26 January with which we began our survey of the Bread Loaf letters, she returns to the conversation about the novel that she had initiated with Dorothy Canfield Fisher the previous spring. After expressing concern that the last part will not be as well achieved as the first, she says that when Dorothy reads it she will understand what a difficult undertaking it was. This idea of the difficulty of what she had undertaken in *One of Ours* would be a recurrent note in the veritable campaign she launched in its behalf. On 6 February (*Calendar* no. 578) she asks Dorothy to read the proofs, and if so, to read simply as a general reader might, in order to spot errors or false notes in the section set in France. Clearly, her desire to produce a sound text was very strong. In early April, perhaps on the eighth (*Calendar* no. 588), after Canfield Fisher had begun her reading of the existing draft, Cather conceded that the book would be called a war novel and attempted to define how it did or did not fit that category.[9] Much as in the Bread Loaf negotiations, she here adopts a posture of reluctance. Claiming that she had not voluntarily undertaken to write such a book, she solicits Dorothy's sympathy by confiding the personal associations that compelled her to do so. In preparation for Canfield Fisher's reading of the rest of the manuscript, she explains the effects she intended.

Cather continued her discussion of the novel with Canfield Fisher throughout the spring and into the summer in a series of letters that shape her friend's response to *One of Ours* both in words and by arranging for her to meet Alfred Knopf. The result, whether this was Cather's half-conscious intention or not, was that Canfield Fisher became a singularly well informed reader and wrote a positive review.

Dorothy Canfield Fisher was not, however, the only literary

colleague whose response to *One of Ours* Cather was attempting to shape as its release date drew near, through a series of communications that Steven Trout refers to as a "prepublication campaign to secure positive notices"—a campaign that demonstrates how well she understood that she had broken "literary taboos," hence her need to try to influence reviewers' responses (Trout 109). An innocuous note to Carl Van Doren on 2 January 1922, inviting him to tea (*Calendar* no. 570), might be regarded as a first step in this campaign. However sincere her impulse to friendliness, and however sincere she was in saying that she wanted to talk with Van Doren about his comments on Henry James, we have to recognize that here was a writer who had not published a novel in four years, who had published only three new short stories in that four-year period (since *Youth and the Bright Medusa* consisted mostly of stories not only previously published but previously collected), a writer who knew she would have a novel coming out before the end of the year and was implicitly cultivating a member of the literary establishment that would be responding to her work. But if the note to Van Doren was connected to her campaign in behalf of *One of Ours*, it was an indirect connection. Far more direct ones would follow.

On 6 February (*Calendar* no. 577), the same day she wrote to Dorothy about Davison's invitation to Bread Loaf, Cather wrote to H. L. Mencken, a powerful arbiter of taste and a critic whose favorable review of *My Ántonia* had been important, whose favorable attention she naturally wished to retain. Engagingly reviewing her career to date, she asks Mencken to read an advance copy of the new novel. It is because this book is so unlike her others, she claims, that she especially wants to get his opinion—as if she regards this as a strictly private exchange! Adding a note of flattery, she says that she realizes how difficult he is to convince, and if he likes it and regards her character's feelings as valid she will know she has succeeded in spite of the difficulty of what she has undertaken. That is, she says that Mencken will be the acid test; he is a harder audience than any other, and if he is pleased she will know she has achieved her intentions. As with Canfield Fisher, she then goes on to try to shape his response by telling him in advance why Claude reacts to the war as he does and how thoroughly she understands him. She and Claude were and continue to be part of each other, she says; so there can be no question of guesswork as to his feelings about the war and his emotions generally. She closes by asking Mencken to keep her letter to reread when he reads the novel. Then, she says, if he judges that she has written an insipid, womanish book, let him tell her so bluntly, as if man to man.

And so he did. She had attempted to disarm the very criticism to which she knew she was most vulnerable by naming it herself before her critic had a chance to do so, but her strategy did not work.

In May, Cather continued her campaign by using a routine social occasion, the writing of a thank-you note, as an opportunity to tell Carl Van Doren about the new novel (*Calendar* no. 594). As she had with Mencken, she here seems to try to construct a response in advance by describing the intensity of her own involvement with the story. Van Doren, too, was someone who might be reviewing it.

On 22 June (*Calendar* no. 603) she wrote to William Allen White, the influential editor of the Emporia, Kansas, *Gazette*, stating, after an elaborately apologetic introduction, that she was going to have an advance copy of *One of Ours* sent to him in August and hoped he would review it. Reminding him that he had reviewed *My Ántonia* favorably, she attempts, as she had with the others, to shape his response to the new book in advance. First, after mentioning his acquaintance Dorothy Canfield Fisher and intimating that she was helping promote the book, she tactfully flatters White by telling him she knows he has a great deal of influence among people in the Midwest. She then states that the new novel is much more substantial than *My Ántonia* and confesses how much she cares about whether people in the plains states, her own place, read the book and understand it. These were, of course, the very people who were White's primary audience.

As we know, Cather's efforts were to little avail. Late September brought a storm of negative reviews. White himself joked with her at a party (as she reported in a letter to Canfield Fisher on

3 October, *Calendar* no. 624) that when her own literary clique forsook her the Lord Himself would have to be her rescue. She wrote to White on 19 October (*Calendar* no. 629) praising his witticism and thanking him for his support and encouragement, and took the opportunity to reiterate her view of the novel's strengths—that is, her thorough understanding of Claude and the soundness of the presentation. White was still in a position to be influential, and she wanted to shape the terms in which he might speak of the book.

Cather was severely hurt, and would remain hurt, by the critical reception of *One of Ours*, but she consoled herself that sales were strong—that is, that a different and more general public was affirming her. Having earlier conceded to Canfield Fisher that *her* sales were always stronger, Cather was now able to claim 16,000 sold in two weeks (*Calendar* no. 621). To Elizabeth Sergeant she complained of the insulting reviews and the fact that the *New Republic* gave her only a single paragraph. At the same time, she gloried that the book had sold ahead of Sinclair Lewis's *Babbitt* in Chicago and Minneapolis (*Calendar* no. 625). On 26 October (*Calendar* no. 638) she wrote to Canfield Fisher again, reporting that 17,000 copies had been sold, though Knopf was claiming 35,000; then wrote to her again on 28 November (*Calendar* no. 651) saying that sales had truly now passed 30,000. Whatever the correct number, the book was indeed selling well, and Cather was delighted. The next day, 29 November, she left for Red Cloud for the extended visit that would include her confirmation, along with her parents, in the Episcopal Church. If lecturing at Bread Loaf had signaled her recognition as a member of the *literary* establishment, this event at the very end of 1922 (as I have argued more fully elsewhere) signaled her arrival in the *social* establishment.[10]

My intention here has not been to debunk Cather or to deny her obviously very strong commitment to high standards in literary art. Rather, I have wanted to point out that she was also, and quite reasonably so, engaged in managing her career and the way in which she would be thought of by her public. Throughout 1922, despite her heavy involvement in textual corrections of

One of Ours and in the writing of *A Lost Lady*, often regarded as the most perfectly crafted of her works,[11] she found time to try to cajole the favorable reactions of influential critics. In parallel to this campaign of letter writing, she published, in April, "The Novel Démeublé," attempting to shape how members of the liberal intelligentsia, those who read the *New Republic*, would read her work. We might even say that "The House on Charles Street," published in November, was an attempt to specify the company she would keep in literary history—that is, the circle within whose context she would be viewed.[12]

Although I have taken 1922 as my example year for purposes of this essay—partly because of its singular importance in Cather studies and the history of modernism, partly because by meeting at Bread Loaf in 2003 the Cather International Seminar invited attention to this year in which Cather herself came to Bread Loaf—it is scarcely unique. The letters of 1922 continue an involvement in publicity and details of book production (paper, design) that was already well established. Such an involvement was clearly evident, for example, in Cather's letters to Ferris Greenslet in connection with publicity for *The Song of the Lark* and *My Ántonia*. Indeed, she began 1922, in January, by writing to Greenslet to complain that *My Ántonia* was out of stock at Omaha bookshops and to continue a discussion about a pasteup of press clippings that she had made for display purposes (*Calendar* no. 571). On numerous occasions, not just during this one year, she demonstrated a keen interest in how her books were publicized, complained when she did not think Houghton Mifflin was pushing them or using excerpts from reviews to advantage in its advertising, and commented on techniques being used to publicize other writers. Like Mary Austin, whose publicity skills she admired, Cather became rather adept at self-promotion. Even so, she continued to chafe when her public got too close. Liking some aspects of her status as a public figure but lamenting others, she remained conflicted about the public role that had come to her as an inseparable aspect of the success—commercial as well as artistic—that she had sought.

Cather's relationship to her public was complex, not only with respect to her business dealings and her participation in publicity efforts but also in ways that go beyond the scope of this essay. An at least equally important question is the extent to which she spoke as part of the social and political establishment of her time or as a resister to it. Here, too, the answer is not a matter of simple either/or but of degrees or of simultaneously existing levels or impulses that were sometimes in conflict. This is a question directly pertinent to the novel whose fate before the public was of such concern to Cather during 1922. *One of Ours* must be a central text in any attempt to answer larger questions of her stance vis-à-vis public culture and public issues. Derided both publicly and privately for having glorified the nation's military involvement despite, as a woman, knowing nothing about it, she stubbornly insisted that the romanticizing of the war in *One of Ours* was Claude's alone and that his responses to his experience in the war should not be generalized or taken to represent her own. Yet a public person cannot speak on a public issue and expect to hide behind narrative point of view. And a public person was what Cather had become.

We may be able to conclude, at this distance of time, that Cather is a writer of complexity, ambiguity, and conflict and leave it at that. But in 1922, when she was complaining with mock humor that the pacifists were after her for what they saw as her militaristic bombast in *One of Ours*, the issue was not one from which serious readers could so easily distance themselves. She had touched a public nerve. With the United States consolidating its position as world power, with membership in the League of Nations having so recently gone down to defeat, with proponents of American military power and a navy second to none already being challenged by antimilitarists (as they would be more stringently in the 1930s), a novel seemingly written in celebration of the glories of warfare could not be the expression of a writer who shunned public response. It may be that her denials of an intention to characterize more than the one soldier she happened to know very well were prompted, in part, by misgivings over the likelihood that she would be entering a public debate in which she was little qualified to hold her own—even, perhaps, one in which she was not sure where she stood.

All of this lies beyond the issue I have examined here, but

is not unrelated, especially in that it touches on what Bohlke calls Cather's inner "civil war." In illustration of that inner conflict, we can return once more to the 26 January 1922 letter to Dorothy Canfield Fisher in which Cather first intimated that she might lecture at Bread Loaf. In the closing paragraph, in an aside curiously parallel to the mixed nature of her comments on Bread Loaf itself, she made another revelation of her ambivalence about being a public figure. She had recently attended a number of public dinners among the literary circle in New York, she wrote, and the experience had given her a feeling of keen dislike for her own kind (i.e., for writers) to the point that she would like to steal into her den and sleep for months. Maybe so. But we note that she *did* attend the dinners. Here, as at other points in her correspondence during 1922, we see Cather at once seeking and rejecting the public role that accompanied her chosen identity as successful writer.

NOTES

1. In his first biography of Cather, in 1970, Woodress points out that her obsession with privacy became increasingly strong after about 1933 (*Life and Art* 244).

2. Porter's argument that the supposed interview published in the *Nebraska State Journal* on 5 September 1926 (Bohlke 89–91) is Cather's own creation which she was able to get published in the newspaper is based on his study of a typescript with holograph emendations recently donated to Drew University. From this and from a corrected typescript of the 1926 promotional brochure issued by Knopf, Porter judges her to have been a "PR maven" (57).

3. For an indication of the variousness of readings of Cather's statement about 1922, see Reynolds, arguing Cather's disaffection from "the spirit of modern America" (1); Skaggs, arguing the devastating impact of the reviews of *One of Ours* (5); Stout, "Autobiography," arguing the significance of her trip to France; and Woodress, 473, and Rosowski, *Voyage* 130, arguing the waning of respected traditions. Given Cather's habit of drawing on phrases in her letters in later writings, it is possible that she specified 1922 as the year in which the world broke in two not so much because of any distinctiveness in the year itself as because it was in 1922 that she wrote, in a letter to Dorothy Canfield Fisher, that

they "seem[ed] to be living in a different world than the one they used to know" (Stout, *Calendar* no. 601). That is, 1922 may have been simply a good-enough date for the alienation she felt and the sea change she sensed in the world about her because she happened to have remarked on it in her letter in that year. If so, it was a surprisingly fortuitous selection, given the importance of 1922 in the history of modernism. At bottom, the primary source of Cather's (and others') sense of facing a world "jarred loose from all its moorings—intellectual, moral, and aesthetic" (Stout, *Cather* 186) must be seen as World War I and the great collection of related changes. Samuel Hynes emphasizes the prevalence of a sense that "the years after the war" were "discontinuous from the years before" (xi).

4. Information on the history of Bread Loaf is available at web sites for the Bread Loaf Conference and the Bread Loaf School. Katherine Lee Bates (1859–1929) was a prolific poet as well as a Shakespeare scholar, best known as the author of the lyrics to "America the Beautiful." She taught at Wellesley College from 1886 until her retirement in 1925; thus her presence at Bread Loaf in 1922 would have been a sound academic anchor to the enterprise. Another faculty member in the summer of 1922 was George Whicher, a professor of English at Amherst. The Whichers and Cather became fast friends.

5. Since Cather's letters are still protected by copyright and quotation from them is prohibited, I must necessarily follow the summaries in my own volume *A Calendar of the Letters of Willa Cather*, supplemented by additional paraphrases from the letters themselves. References to the *Calendar* by letter number will direct readers to the archival location of the original, where material that could not be included in the necessarily brief *Calendar* listings can be found. We might note that the restriction on scholarly use of the letters that Cather's will initiated serves, in itself, as an illustration of her mixed signals with respect to her status as a public figure. When we do get access to the 1922 letters (and others), what we find is a Willa Cather who *wanted* publicity, *wanted* to be regarded as a public figure, but also wanted to be able to limit public access so that it would occur solely on her own terms.

6. My view of Cather's professional standing at the beginning of 1922 differs markedly from Skaggs's statement that "by New Year's Day of 1922 . . . Cather had reached a professional high point" (1).

7. Hermione Lee (185) recognizes this significance of the portrait. We might recall that the Pulitzer was given not solely for literary merit but for work expressing solidarity with its national public. In Ferris Greenslet's summary when he was explaining to Cather in January 1919 why he wanted to nominate *My Ántonia* for the first awarding of the

prize, it was to be given for work best presenting "the wholesome atmosphere of American life, and the highest standard of American manners and manhood"; Greenslet to Cather, 14 January 1919, Houghton Library, Harvard, bMS Am 1925 (341) folder 31 of 45.

8. It is apparently on the evidence of this letter that Woodress states Canfield Fisher served as "the go-between to recruit her" for Bread Loaf (*Literary Life* 322).

9. Notes in the file at the University of Vermont place this undated letter a month earlier, on 8 March.

10. If we look at what Cather has to say in her letters about her so-called conversion to the Episcopal Church, we see—nothing at all! I have not found a single instance of her speaking of the event *at the time*. Twenty years later, in letters to Bishop Beecher, yes. It is this absence of any expression of religious renewal in any letters to any of her closest friends that leads me to regard her joining the church in 1922 as an event more connected to social status than to inward conviction. For a fuller argument of the point, see my "Faith Statements and Nonstatements."

11. Rosowski reports that Cather was deeply involved in work on *A Lost Lady* in the summer of 1922 when she lectured at Bread Loaf. Having made two distinct starts on the novel, one in third-person point of view refracted through Niel Herbert as observer and one in first person, she was carefully considering the technical choice of narrative technique (Historical Essay 191).

12. Rosowski similarly discusses "The Novel Démeublé" and the earlier essay "On the Art of Fiction" as attempts at "educating her readers about her ideas of fiction and, at the same time, refining the principles according to which she would write *A Lost Lady*" and according to which she wanted to be read (Historical Essay 185–88).

WORKS CITED

Bohlke, L. Brent, ed. *Willa Cather in Person: Interviews, Speeches, and Letters*. Lincoln: U of Nebraska P, 1986.

Bread Loaf School of English. 9 Feb. 2004. http://www.middlebury.edu/blse.

Bread Loaf Writers' Conference. 9 Feb. 2004. http://www.middlebury.edu/blwc.

Hoover, Sharon, ed. *Willa Cather Remembered*. Comp. L. Brent Bohlke and Sharon Hoover. Lincoln: U of Nebraska P, 2002.

Hynes, Samuel. *A War Imagined: The First World War and English Culture*. New York: Atheneum, 1991.

Lee, Hermione. *Willa Cather: Double Lives*. New York: Pantheon, 1989.

Lewis, Edith. *Willa Cather Living*. New York: Knopf, 1953.

Manganaro, Mark. *Culture, 1922: The Emergence of a Concept*. Princeton: Princeton UP, 2002.

Mignon, Charles. Textual Commentary. *My Ántonia*. By Willa Cather. Willa Cather Scholarly Edition. Lincoln: U of Nebraska P, 1994. 481–522.

North, Michael. *Reading 1922: A Return to the Scene of the Modern*. New York: Oxford UP, 1999.

O'Brien, Sharon, ed. *Willa Cather: Stories, Poems, and Other Writings*. New York: The Library of America, 1992.

Porter, David H. "Cather on Cather II: Two Recent Acquisitions at Drew University." *Willa Cather Newsletter and Review* 46.3 (2003): 49, 53–58.

Reynolds, Guy. *Willa Cather in Context: Progress, Race, Empire*. New York: St. Martin's, 1996.

Rosowski, Susan J. Historical Essay. *A Lost Lady*. By Willa Cather. Willa Cather Scholarly Edition. Lincoln: U of Nebraska P, 1997. 177–234.

———. *The Voyage Perilous: Willa Cather's Romanticism*. Lincoln: U of Nebraska P, 1986.

Skaggs, Merrill Maguire. *After the World Broke in Two: The Later Novels of Willa Cather*. Charlottesville: UP of Virginia, 1990.

Stout, Janis P. "Autobiography as Journey in *The Professor's House*." *Studies in American Fiction* 19 (1991): 203–15.

———, ed. *A Calendar of the Letters of Willa Cather*. Lincoln: U of Nebraska P, 2002.

———. "Faith Statements and Nonstatements in Willa Cather's Personal Letters." *Willa Cather and the Culture of Belief*. Ed. John J. Murphy. Provo UT: Brigham Young UP, 2002. 7–28.

———. *Willa Cather: The Writer and Her World*. Charlottesville: UP of Virginia, 2000.

Trout, Steven. *Memorial Fictions: Willa Cather and the First World War*. Lincoln: U of Nebraska P, 2002.

Woodress, James. *Willa Cather: A Literary Life*. Lincoln: U of Nebraska P, 1987.

———. *Willa Cather: Her Life and Art*. New York: Pegasus, 1970.

A Portrait of an Artist as a Cultural Icon
Edward Steichen, *Vanity Fair*, and Willa Cather

MICHAEL SCHUETH

The spectacle is not a collection of images; rather, it is a social relationship between people that is mediated by images.
—Guy Debord, The Society of the Spectacle

Photography . . . began, historically, as an art of the Person: of identity, of civil status, of what we might call, in all senses of the term, the body's formality.
—Roland Barthes, Camera Lucida

The twentieth-century phenomenon of the icon celebrity has a fundamental relationship to the photographic image. The invention of the camera led to the increasing presence of the visual image in American culture. As Catharine R. Stimpson contends in her foreword to Brenda Silver's *Virginia Woolf: Icon*, the twentieth-century icon "is unthinkable without the presence of the camera." Photography, she explains, "accelerates and reaffirms the process of iconization and celebrity making" through modern modes of mass production (xii). Consider the images of Albert Einstein sitting at his desk with his tousled white hair, Marilyn Monroe standing above the subway grate, or Madonna in her cone-shaped bustier. These images have become infamous portraits, functioning as visual shorthand for each personality in particular and the cultural era each represents in general.

While we recognize the powerful role the iconic figure plays within our culture to create powerful signifiers of ideas, attitudes, historical frameworks, and personal identities, how does one go about *becoming* an icon? In the case of Willa Cather, her image is documented through her legacy of photographic portraits and her selection of artists Leon Bakst and Nikolai Fechin to paint her portraits. In each of these cases, Cather collaborated with other artists to shape her public image. In the case of the Bakst portrait, she wrote in a letter that after the disappointing result of the portrait, she had resolved to work with other artists only if she could have complete control over the final result. The fireplace, she explained, was the place for images that did not please her (Cather to Duncan M. Vinsonhaler, 13 January 1924). Cather's frank talk about her public image allows us insights into how she managed her career in the increasingly celebrity-driven literary marketplace. Even in the face of her disappointment with Bakst's portrait, Cather followed her own advice and became more careful in her management of her public image. Like other celebrity actors, sports figures, and artists, Cather acknowledged the degree to which celebrity had become a series of collaborations with other artists and celebrity-driven mechanisms. She collaborated throughout her career in a variety of ways, most centrally by working closely with the publicity department at her publishing houses (Houghton and then Knopf), sending out photographs for magazine and newspaper profiles, and joining forces with key image makers within her contemporary celebrity culture. In this essay I place Cather within the context of one such collaboration with top celebrity photographer Edward Steichen, arguing that his 1927 *Vanity Fair* portrait of Cather was a key moment in defining Cather's iconic status within American culture. Embedded in this argument is the notion that Cather's literary celebrity was established within a larger cultural machine that had, in many ways, already begun to mechanize the creation of celebrities—or at least exploited celebrity through new, sophisticated marketing strategies. Although Cather did much to obfuscate her relationship to that celebrity machinery through her persona, which seemed antagonistic to modernization, my study reveals her shrewd ability to fit that persona into her contemporary celebrity culture. To follow the lines of this argument, I will take a historical approach to link the development of celebrity culture within the technological development of modern image making. In so doing I hope to place Cather's image in context to reveal the importance of Steichen's image and the specific ways in which photographic images of celebrities were created to "speak" in specific ways to viewers. I then turn to a discussion of the celebrity-driven magazine *Vanity Fair* and the role Steichen had in turning the magazine into a celebrity-making tool through his iconic images of famous writers, actors, and sports figures. Finally, my analysis concludes with a discussion of Cather's public persona, her western image, and the relationships among her clothing, sexuality, and identity as a western writer.

PHOTOGRAPHY AND THE INVENTION OF MODERN CELEBRITY

Willa Cather came of age in the formative period of modern American celebrity culture. Cultural historian Neil Harris calls the period between 1885 and 1910 the "iconographical revolution," a time when photographs became deeply entrenched in American print, advertising, business, and personal life (199). As Guy Reynolds has noted, "Technologies were changing what 'writing' and being 'a writer' might mean . . . photography and recording equipment would mean that writers would now be more than their words, would have an image and a spoken voice" (4). The introduction of Kodak's box camera, for example, brought picture taking and the consumption of image to a new, personal level. With a simple and effective design, Kodak advertised its new camera to the masses: "Anybody can use the Kodak. Press the button—we do the rest" (Collins 56). Further, the increasing refinement of halftone printing processes beginning in the 1880s meant that magazines and newspapers could cheaply mass-produce photographic-quality images. During her editorial years at *McClure's*, Cather would have had control in positioning photographs and other images with text—a value she understood well because the magazine touted its visual appeal. When ghostwriting S. S. McClure's autobiography, she included his reflection that "[t]he development of photo-engraving made such a publication [as *McClure's*] more than possible" (*Autobiography* 207). Magazine historian David Reed notes from his study of *McClure's* that photographs played a "prominent role" in the development of the magazine's visual look, since nearly half of the illustrations were in photographic form (49).

Among many early pioneers of American photography, Matthew Brady brought the budding field into the realm of public spectacle. Brady's high-profile celebrity portrait studio capitalized on the public's curiosity about photography by exploiting its even greater curiosity about, as Brady termed them, "illustrious figures." Brady photographed such prominent men and women as Abraham Lincoln, General Robert E. Lee, Jenny Lind, Thomas Cole, Clara Barton, Jefferson Davis, Walt Whitman, and P. T. Barnum ("Matthew Brady's Portraits"). The public flocked to Brady's galleries, paying admission to gaze at images of public figures whose appearances were, aside from engraved portraits in books and newspapers, wholly unknown to them unless they had been lucky enough to see them in person on the street or stage. Brady's celebrity pictures had a larger cultural effect than merely enabling him to profit from the public's desire to see famous faces. Leo Braudy, in his extensive study of fame, suggests that Brady's portraits brought about a shift in the "emotional intimacy" between public figures and their audiences; that is, Brady's photographs were suggestive of the underlying humanity of his subjects.

The larger entertainment world quickly took advantage of the promise Brady demonstrated in capturing the public's curiosity of public figures. Specifically, photography played a key role in propelling actors and actresses into new, unprecedented states of fame. When Jenny Lind, a relatively unknown singer in the United States, toured American cities under the management of P. T. Barnum beginning in 1851, she had her photograph taken in virtually every city she visited and quickly became one of the best-known personalities in the country (Taft 81). Photography allowed for the relatively inexpensive dissemination of actors' and actresses' images through *cartes de visite* (small picture calling cards) as well as regular picture postcards. By manipulating this new medium, Sarah Bernhardt, one of Cather's favorite stars, significantly changed how the public interacted with famous theatrical actors. Bernhardt, according to Heather McPherson, was part of a "new paradigm of the modern mass-media star" who used photography to "simulate and re-create the visual and emotional dynamics of her performance"; and as a "genius" of publicity, she made sure that newspapers in Europe, England, and the United States carried full-page picture stories related to her every role (78).

During the time of this graphic revolution, Cather was a university student in Lincoln working on her degree and supplementing her income by reviewing touring theatrical productions. In these reviews, Cather distinguished herself by noting the developing role of the star in relation to art; that is, while the stage magazines of the age were full of publicity and gossip, Cather was most interested in those actresses to whom "truth is necessary and all important" (*World and Parish* 209). Cather lauds actress Mary Anderson in one review, for example, when she turns her back on "fame and flattery," the "most intoxicating of all successes" (*World and Parish* 202). Cather's reviews during these years demonstrate a sustained interest in the negotiation between the public stage and the private life of the artist. They also show a young woman fascinated by the ways in which celebrity figures threw themselves into the spotlight. In another review, Cather notes her disapproval of "methods of advertising" such as recommending "complexion soap" or having an "agent distribute [an actress's] pictures and press notices" (*World and Parish* 213). While Cather shows an early preference for those actresses who shy away from self-advertising, she nevertheless paid attention to these facets of her culture.

As American photographers, illustrious figures, and actresses were shaping new cultural modes of celebrity, so too were writers placing themselves within celebrity culture. No figure in American literature represents this shift from the older, genteel model of the writer and the new, image-driven construction of the American author better than Walt Whitman. In the early 1850s, as he made his transition from journalism to the literary world, Whitman brought with him his previous experience in newspapers and printing, in which he would have seen firsthand the "vastly" expanding role of advertising in American culture (Newbury 160). One of the most effective ways Whitman chose to disseminate his public self was by publishing illustrations of himself in his books. Since, as Whitman states in his preface to the 1855 edition of *Leaves of Grass*, "the great poet is the equable man," the visual illustration of himself as "one of the roughs" (50) simultaneously served to illustrate his aesthetic principles and increase his public recognition. So the image of Whitman with an open collar, posing casually with his hand on his hip, was, according to Ed Folsom, "in sharp contrast to the expected iconography of poets' portraits, portraits that conventionally emphasized formality and the face instead of this rough informality, where we see arms, legs, and body" (140). Folsom further notes that Whitman's use of his image in *Leaves of Grass* had a "highly influential" effect on "the way most American poets portrayed themselves on their book jackets and frontispieces" (135). Kenneth Price recognizes that Whitman "set a new precedent for how a literary project could be advanced through photography, demonstrating photography's power to contribute to celebrity status" (39). The crucial aspect Whitman brought to modern understandings of celebrity authorship is the visual connection between the construction of his appearance and the construction of his poetic project. Text and image work recursively to construct the author's persona, and the public dissemination of the writer's image also guides the public's expectation of that literary project—it necessarily commits the writer to a particular channel of literary output. By incorporating Whitman's poem into the title of her second novel, *O Pioneers!*, Cather placed her literary project in Whitman's tradition. She further aligned herself, as we will see, through her 1927 Steichen portrait to Whitman's 1855 iconic frontispiece.

While duties such as buying fiction and poetry, writing the personality-driven Mary Baker G. Eddy series, and managing the magazine's content at *McClure's* gave Cather the critical experience to manage her own image, when she began her professional writing career she had to build a persona to sell to the public. Her correspondence with her editors at Houghton Mifflin reveals her sensitivity to the crucial role of photographs in book publicity. She often complained that her photographs were not sent out to newspapers and magazines to be published with reviews (Cather to Ferris Greenslet, 20 January 1920); she bemoaned the practice of publishing images of authors at all; she explained that seeing the picture of the author of a book she had meant to read made her decide otherwise, for she found the woman ugly (Cather to Van Tuyll, 24 May [1915]). Some in the public might hold the same prejudice against her, Cather wrote, but authors were different from performers, and while it was important for actresses and singers to be beautiful, authors could not (and should not, judging by the looks of most authors) depend on looks to sell their books (Cather to Van Tuyll, 24 May [1915]). The distinctions Cather made here between publicity and book design were ones she implemented: her picture never appeared on her dust jackets or frontispieces. However, she did approve photographs for use in those materials less connected to her actual work, such as sales booklets, posters, and other promotional materials.

Along with her correspondence, Cather's writing during the mid-1910s documents her concerns over issues of publicity in an image-driven market. In her 1916 short story "The Diamond Mine," written between the publication of *The Song of the Lark* and *My Ántonia*, Cather tells the story of a diva deeply concerned with her image. Cather opens her story with the diva, Cressida Garnet, surrounded by "young men with cameras." She stands "good-naturedly posing for them" because "she was too much an American not to believe in publicity." We further are told that she believed "All advertising was good. If it was good for breakfast foods, it was good for a prima donna,—especially for a prima donna who would never be any younger and who had just announced her intention of marrying a fourth time" (67). Cather's larger-than-life representation of her heroine in this story highlights her awareness of the ways in which artists were increasingly flattened into pure product—art and advertising threatened to become one and the same.

The pressure for artists like Cather and her fictional character Cressida Garnet to become public personalities was fueled, in part, by the emergence of the motion picture industry. The "movie star" became a new phenomenon that tied magazines, Hollywood, and advertising together, giving rise to a public personality much different from that of the nineteenth century; that is, these stars could generate significant public interest and fascination not so much by what they did but by the sheer fact of who they were (Susman 223). Richard Schickel argues that the movie celebrity forever altered the expectations the public had toward *all* public persons: politicians, writers, artists, intellectuals, and even scientists became "performers so that they may become celebrities so that in turn they may exert genuine influence on the general public" (9). This transformation of the public figure into celebrity figure resulted in two competing realities: on the one hand, there was the individual's everyday common life; on the other, there was the life one lived through newspapers and magazines, by which celebrities could be "as familiar to us, in some ways, as our friends and neighbors." The celebrity-as-familiar dominated "enormous amounts" of the public's "psychic energy and attention," even though the closest the average person would ever come to knowing these celebrities was in a halftone photographic image—literally, ink on paper (8).

Celebrity culture formulated itself most powerfully in the pages of popular magazines, and no magazine between the world wars better expressed that celebrity culture than *Vanity Fair*, a gem in publisher Condé Nast's crown, which included best-selling *Vogue* and, later, *Home and Garden*. *Vanity Fair* was founded in 1914 as a competitor to H. L. Mencken's *Smart Set*, and *Vogue*'s success allowed Condé Nast to make *Vanity Fair* a "slick" magazine that incorporated all the costly elements that the financially rocky *Smart Set* was unable to give its readers: high-quality paper, graphic design, and a plethora of images. Editor Frank Crowninshield had bought *Vanity Fair* (then a small New York "peekaboo" magazine) in 1913 with a short-lived intention to reincarnate it into a *Vogue*-like fashion magazine. In 1914, however, he decided that he wanted *Vanity Fair* to be a magazine "read by people you meet at lunches and dinners" covering "the things people talk about at parties—the arts, sports, theatre, humor, and so forth" (qtd. in Douglas 96). Crowninshield's main strategy for setting the magazine apart from its competitors was to publish stories by European and American avant-garde writers and artists. In particular, *Vanity Fair* printed some of the first images of Picasso and Matisse, ran poems by Dorothy Parker, and published articles by Robert Benchley. According to magazine historian George Douglas, *Vanity Fair* "was as appealing to the eye as it was to the tastes of its intended readers . . . it always had substance and it always had guts" (94). With style and substance, *Vanity Fair* attracted the attention of New York's rich, educated elite, and while it never attained mass-market appeal (circulation hovered below 100,000), the high advertising rates *Vanity Fair* charged its select advertisers gave Condé Nast a profitable income.

The magazine hit its stride after World War I, when its identity folded perfectly into the mood of the Jazz Age's appetite for style, entertainment, and refinement. Readers of *Vanity Fair* are said to have conspicuously read the magazine in public and placed copies of the magazine on coffee tables before parties. The magazine's popularity suggests how it so masterfully captured the spirit of the postwar era—witty, playful, experimental, and rich. As John Russell says in his introduction to *Vanity Fair: Photographs of an Age*, "*Vanity Fair* was not in the business of aesthetics. It was in the business of getting people talked about" (xvii). Those talked about included the obvious group of Hollywood and Broadway celebrities such as Charlie Chaplin and Gloria Swanson, but also included a surprisingly eclectic group of personalities including scientists, professional tennis players, golfers, boxers, conductors, composers, writers, critics, and even dog breeders. This construction of celebrity within *Vanity Fair* intermixed full-page portraits of well-known Hollywood and Broadway stars with the less well recognized, putting a glamorous face to writers, intellectuals, and composers while at the same time giving an intellectual flair to the Hollywood celebrity.

Vanity Fair, I suggest, defined celebrity in much more inclusive and even intellectual terms than did other popular magazines of its time. Crowninshield told his readers they were "people of discrimination, clever, and full of a wide and varied culture," and so he assumed that such readers would naturally be interested in the people he and his friends were interested in, from the stage actor to writer to sportswoman (qtd. in Russell xii). One could be a celebrity outside the narrow definition of the "movie star" in the magazine, which invited readers to place themselves imaginatively into celebrity culture through their consumption of the magazine.

THE IMAGE MAKER

A key aspect to the popularity of *Vanity Fair* stemmed from its use of photography. Crowninshield's belief that fine fashion photography could be elevated to an art form had helped *Vogue* become one of the most popular fashion magazines of the time, and he had similar revolutionary plans for photography in *Vanity Fair*. Hiring portrait artists such as Edward Steichen and Man Ray, relative unknowns in the world of high art, Crowninshield gave these photographers "privacy, discretion, unstressed commitment," and paid Steichen (at least) an annual salary of $35,000 (Russell x).

Steichen had been in the art world for more than twenty years by the time he signed onto *Vanity Fair*. Only six years younger than Cather, by the early 1900s he had become became involved with Alfred Stieglitz's circle as a founding member of "291" and Photo-Secession galleries. During World War I, Steichen helped develop aerial photography, and during this period he also began evaluating his aesthetics. Moving from the early photographic style of soft-focus pictorialism, Steichen's work with aerial photography began to pique his interest in sharp lines and clean detail—the fundamental aesthetic qualities he used to transform portrait photography. By the early 1920s Steichen had attained fame for avant-garde work, yet, according to Joanna Steichen, his "photography brought Steichen more fame than income" (xx). That all changed in 1923 when Steichen accepted his position with *Vanity Fair* and *Vogue*. His high Condé Nast salary raised eyebrows among Stieglitz's crowd, who saw Steichen's venture into commercial photography as selling out on their quest to improve the stature of photography in the art world. But according to Joanna Steichen, he believed in "the photograph's potential as a medium for mass communication," viewing his work with magazines as an artistic and aesthetic challenge to raise the everyday, pedestrian magazine photo into an artistic object (xx). No doubt Steichen's knowledge of mass communication directly led to his ability to produce what we now recognize as iconic photographs of his subjects.

A critical aspect of *Vanity Fair*'s attractiveness to both literary and visual artists of the period was its ability to feature new, emerging artists and promote their name recognition within the art world in particular and in highbrow culture in general. This was certainly the case for Cather, who first appeared in a 1922 *Vanity Fair* article titled "American Novelists Who Have Set Art above Popularity: A Group of Authors Who Have Consistently Stood Out against Philistia." This group included Theodore Dreiser ("among the most extraordinary phenomena of American letters"), James Branch Cabell ("quite unlike anything else in American fiction"), Edith Wharton ("The greatest living American novelist"), Sherwood Anderson ("Foremost among those who are using the novel as a means of criticizing American civilization"), and Cather ("*My Ántonia* is the best novel ever written by an American woman writer") (Cleveland and Bradlee 58). The magazine's title for this page suggests some critical tensions with its own view of celebrity culture, as it highlights the fact that this group of authors put "Art above Popularity" even though the magazine itself gravitated around celebrity culture. Perhaps the key here is the magazine's reference to the "Philistia," or the lowbrow common reader who did not read *Vanity Fair* and thereby confirmed the intellectual superiority of those who did. Yet no matter how *Vanity Fair* positioned these writers to its readers, the fact remains that this first mention in *Vanity Fair* marked Cather's entrée into the developing celebrity culture of the 1920s. Cather fits into the larger celebrity model Philip Fisher has outlined, in which writers need to place themselves into "a high cultural form of celebrity" while at the same time maintaining "a personal hold on [their] audience" (156). This becomes, then, a balancing act of sorts as authors maintain a dual hold on highbrow and middlebrow audiences.

Although Cather had been a well-known and best-selling writer since her Pulitzer Prize award in 1923, her inclusion into celebrity culture came to fruition in 1927 when her portrait by Steichen was featured in *Vanity Fair*. A Cather letter reveals that she had dinner plans with Steichen in February 1927, presumably before or just after the sitting (Cather to Mary Virginia Auld, 19 February 1927). Steichen and Cather shared common interests, and his work, which included portraits of Cather's early heroes Eleonora Duse and Sarah Bernhardt, must have fascinated her. There is little documentation detailing Cather's participation in and reaction to the *Vanity Fair* issue, although what we do have suggests that she was proud of the picture. Blanche Knopf, who worked closely with Cather throughout the 1920s, was so impressed with it she sent a telegram to Cather in Wyoming, writing, "HAVE JUST SEEN STEICHEN PHOTOGRAPH IN VANITY FAIR SIMPLY SUPERB DON'T YOU THINK WOULD LIKE TO USE IT TOO IF THEY PERMIT AND YOU APPROVE WITH MY LOVE" (17 June 1927). Cather replied that by contract the photo belonged to Condé Nast, and so it could not be used for publicity (19 June 1927).

In the *Vanity Fair* portrait, Cather is featured seated, as Steichen captured most of his writers. She sits as though the viewer is sitting across from her in an intimate discussion, her right hand resting on the armrest of her chair. Cather looks comfortable and self-assured. Titled "An American Pioneer—Willa Cather," the profile employs Cather's most popular and well-known subject matter, the pioneer West. While the title plays up Cather's public persona as a western writer, the subhead explains, "The Noted Novelist Has Just Completed Her New Work 'Death Comes for the Archbishop.'" This profile, then, extended Cather's western image toward her new subject matter, the Southwest.

30 VANITY FAIR

STEICHEN

An American Pioneer—Willa Cather

The Noted Novelist Has Just Completed Her New Work "Death Comes for the Archbishop"

SINCE the publication in 1915 of *The Song of the Lark*, each new story by Willa Cather has won an increasing recognition as a picture and an evaluation of the American landscape. Today, after twenty-four years of scrupulous craftsmanship she is the heir apparent to Edith Wharton's lonely eminence among America's women novelists. Her contradictory avocations include landlord-farming in Nevada and a one-time editorship on *McClure's Magazine*. Daughter of pioneers, graduate of a prairie farm and the University of Nebraska, her position in American letters is an absolute one by right of sheer artistic stature, beyond the categories of literary schools or *genres*. She writes in a way that seems utterly transparent and forthright but that conceals in its overtones a vast and subtle interplay of ironical intelligence. The depth and variety of her understanding is implicit in a swift, muscular style, wrought with an economy that discovers the inevitable word and the inevitable idea. No one else has so well expressed the new philosophy, the urge "to live out our potentialities", because no other novelist has so deeply felt the need of it, yet so vividly seen that such a philosophy should not mark a break with our past but an enrichment. Miss Cather's intellectual roots go deep into the soil of early America yet her spare, beautiful style has the poise and elegance inherent in the great tradition of English prose

Fig. 1. Steichen's portrait of Cather as it appeared in *Vanity Fair*. Courtesy of Michael Schueth.

Cather's image in the Steichen photograph corresponds to an image of Cather as a western writer, yet the picture showcases her in other critical ways as well. Her loose-fitting middy blouse and tie together with her gently rolled cuffs suggest an informal moment—as if we have just found the writer in the midst of her work. Like Whitman, whose illustrations and photographs communicated a general attitude that corresponded to his literary work, Cather visually communicates a sense of her "forthright" style. Cather, this photograph suggests, is not regal like Edith Wharton, nor is she so stylish and "fast" as the younger Jazz Age writers such as F. Scott Fitzgerald. Through this informal, forthright style, the Cather we see in the pages of *Vanity Fair* corresponds to the larger literary project she was building. As she laid out her aesthetics in her 1922 essay "The Novel Démeublé": "Whatever is felt upon the page without being specifically named there" informs "the emotional aura of the fact or the thing or the deed that gives high quality to the novel or the drama, as well as to poetry itself" (48–49, 50). Cather believed that art "crowded with physical sensations is no less a catalogue than one crowded with furniture" (50). That there is no visible background or foreground in the picture suggests that Cather's artistic aesthetic informs Steichen's composition. The viewer, then, is given a sense of intimacy with the author because there is nothing intruding between the subject and the viewer. Rather than ridding herself of the pioneer image she had built in advertising and interviews, Cather deepened the iconic resonance of the middy blouse and tie to encompass the entire West. This expansion of place beyond region would not have surprised avid readers of Cather, since the Southwest setting is critical in novels as early as *The Song of the Lark* (1915) and as recent as *The Professor's House* (1925).

The text accompanying Cather's photograph adds another level of complexity to the portrait as it positions Cather well at the top of American literature. As "the heir apparent to Edith Wharton's lonely eminence among America's women novelists," Cather, as *Vanity Fair* saw her, should be regarded as a literary giant, not just as a regionalist. The text ties Cather's aesthetic to the Steichen image: "The depth and variety of her understanding is implicit in a swift, muscular style, wrought with an economy that discovers the inevitable word and the inevitable idea." Yet the magazine writer is also savvy enough to note that Cather's "utterly transparent and forthright" style "conceals in its overtones a vast and subtle interplay of ironical intelligence."

While the photograph generally plays with Cather as western writer, it also resists placing her into categories. Cather's image in this photograph blurs distinctions of feminine/masculine and urban/regional; as the writer of the *Vanity Fair* article concludes, Cather is "beyond the categories of literary schools or genres." This resistance to classification begs readers to ask, just who is the Willa Cather presented in this photograph? Patricia Johnson counters Joanna Steichen's argument that Steichen captured the "private character in the public faces he photographed" (89–90), arguing that Steichen was a "master of illusion" who "concentrated on the sitter's looks rather than character": "His images of celebrities are chiefly publicity photographs: they extract and polish the public persona much as his advertising photographs create an image for the product. Thus they shaped the sitter's public identity or synthesized an established image. Audiences could feel that by reading a celebrity's image they knew the person beneath the surface" (200–201).

This leads us to ask, how much does the Steichen portrait reflect a deeper sense of the author herself? As the anonymously written text accompanying the portrait notes, while Cather's prose "seems utterly transparent," it also "conceals." Arguably, so too does Steichen's photograph conceal, or perhaps better yet, signify, a host of possible meanings to the viewer. Specifically, I draw on emerging scholarship that places modern women artists in the tradition of the dandy figure. Susan Fillin-Yeh argues that twentieth-century female dandies "took up and deliberately altered that dandy's image inherited from the nineteenth century, refashioning it to their own needs and a new avant-garde art" (130). Fillin-Yeh points to such diverse modernist figures as Georgia O'Keeffe and Coco Chanel as "glimpses of female dandies" we can recognize "through a refocused lens of theory and history," and she suggests that these artists responded to the struggle "to assert individuality with what was still *male* avant-garde culture" (133). Female dandies of the 1920s challenged the tradition of the male dandy, who was "a creature perfect in externals and careless of anything below the surface, a man dedicated solely to his own perfection through a ritual of taste," who was the "epitome of selfish irresponsibility . . . free from all human commitments that conflict with taste: passions, moralities, ambitions, politics or occupations" (13). But as for the eighteenth- and nineteenth-century male dandy, costume for the early-twentieth-century female dandy was also a source of sexual transgression, especially since male dandyism rejected traditional familial attachments such as marriage and children in favor of showing refinement through the cut of clothing (Moers 18).

Fillin-Yeh points to Greenwich Village as a critical space for early-twentieth-century female dandy figures in the United States. Specifically within the world of Greenwich Village, Cather's home for twenty years, women could seek "distance from bourgeois life and conventional politics" by further distancing themselves from the either/or binaries that had historically limited women's artistic careers (131). By playing with masculinity, women artists simultaneously usurped the guise of traditional male artistic power and exposed that guise as a performance, blurring the line between male and female and ultimately allowing women artists to find power through ambiguity. As with the traditional dandy figure clad in costume, women's take on dandyism continued to operate as a "'social hieroglyphic' that hides, even as it reveals, class and social status and our expectations about them" (2). Fillin-Yeh suggests that such "ambiguities encourage dandies," who are "constantly" and "irrepressibly" drawn to reinvent their appearance (2). Yet the dandy's particular power comes not from clothing alone but moreover from a mysterious sexual *je ne sais quoi* quality that resides in the figure him or herself. In the case of the female dandy, and unlike the apolitical male dandy, Fillin-Yeh suggests that the performance of masculinity asserts that "the better man is (also) a woman" (14).

The construction of the dandy figure is especially well suited to Cather, because she had long played with the gendered quality of her dress. Going by the ambiguous nickname "Willie," and even less ambiguously signing her name "William Cather, Jr." and "Wm. Cather, M.D.," Cather was, as biographer James

Woodress suggests, stymied by her personal ambitions toward a professional career and the cultural limitations of late-nineteenth-century American culture that restricted women's professional opportunities (55–56). Photographs from the late 1880s and early 1890s suggest Cather's playful invention with self-image. Janis P. Stout notes that while photographs of Cather in the early 1890s do evoke a boyish appearance, her clothing nevertheless kept within women's contemporary fashion (*Cather* 20). The critical point here for this discussion is not whether Cather was cross-dressing but whether from a young age she showed an uncanny ability to experiment with her outward appearance. Even after Cather abandoned her overtly "mannish" style midway through her university years in Lincoln, her softened professional look nevertheless retained hints of the "mannish." Photographs reveal that Cather had a fondness for waist shirts, middy blouses, and a variety of tie styles, including the masculine straight tie. While Cather may have been participating with other female modernists in revising the dandy figure, as with the boyish cross-dressing of her youth, her fashion once again fell in line with contemporary women's fashion. So while the dandified figure Cather represents was subtle, it was, nevertheless, readily available to readers "in the know."

Those "in the know" readers of the *Vanity Fair* portrait, then, had access to an entirely different reading of this portrait. Perhaps it is this quality of layered meaning that powers the iconic potential of Steichen's Cather portrait. Those who read this photograph within the specific context of the modern dandy figure could read Cather as a specifically urban, New York writer; Cather's middy blouse and tie, which draw attention to aspects of masculine dress, may have offered suggestions about Cather's sexuality. Subtly, this one portrait communicates all of the aspects of Cather's professional and private life that scholars still wrestle with—her play between New York and Nebraska identities, her ambiguity between masculine and feminine, and her aesthetic qualities. The brilliance of the photographic image in this case is that the portrait suggests Cather but does not contain her.

Edward Steichen had the power to build celebrities into iconic figures, and Cather worked to build her post-1927 public image as a reflection of his *Vanity Fair* portrait. In 1933 and 1940 newspaper features on Cather, for example, she reappears in her middy blouse and tie, affirming the iconic image she created years before. While the Steichen photograph highlights the celebrity culture and image of the 1920s, the outdoorsy, snapshot style of the newspaper photographs presents the same Cather in nature. Regardless of Cather's changes in her subject matter (most notably in *Death Comes for the Archbishop* and *Shadows on the Rock*), her public appearance remained the same. The authors of both newspaper features pick up on Cather's well-known image as a writer of the prairie and tie her physical appearance to her literary style. For example, in Dorothy Canfield Fisher's 1933 essay on Cather the subhead reads, "Willa Cather Lived Her Books before She Wrote Them. Her Girlhood Was Spent on the Unfenced Prairie; She Knew the Trials and Triumphs of the Pioneer." In the *New York Herald Tribune*, Stephen Vincent and Rosemary Benet similarly describe Cather as a real, unaffected person, having "no ivory tower about" her, since "she is too hearty for that." They further describe her appearance as "Of medium height, with clear blue eyes, she gives an impression of great intellectual vitality and serenity combined, calm strength and lively independence" (ix). Cather's photographs along with the writers' descriptions of her in the newspaper profiles strongly suggest the degree to which her "middy blouse image" became iconic to her audience. After twenty-five years of maintaining a particular stylish image, Cather did not allow that image to overtake her writing, but used it to complement her writing.

American icons such as Whitman, Twain, and Chaplin reveal the degree to which dress empowers a particular image of a celebrity to the public, what Sarah Burns calls "key markers of the public self" (223). Although Cather never developed a costume as strict as Twain's post-1906 white suit ensemble, she did develop and maintain a visual look that the public could easily recognize after her break with *McClure's*. In doing so, Cather built her iconic image in a subtle, but nevertheless effective, visual manner through her white middy blouse with loose-fitting tie. The look, much in the tradition of Whitman, ties Cather to her middle- and working-class readers, since the look was popular, comfortable, and relaxed. Snapshot pictures reveal that this look was an expression of her everyday style.

THE LEGACY OF IMAGES

Cather's public image was further complicated by Cather herself. During 1937 and 1938, Knopf was working with Cather on the Autograph Editions of her collected works. Unlike her other novels, each edition in this collection was personalized with a different Cather portrait in its frontispiece. During this time Cather carefully defined her image through her selection process. Notably, she chose not to use the Steichen photograph in the edition (Stout, *Calendar* no. 208). Perhaps the reason lies in her growing ambivalence toward celebrity culture at the end of her career. Much like the experience Hemingway would later face, Cather found the price of fame too high to let her work be compromised by Hollywood movies like the disastrous 1934 adaptation of *A Lost Lady*. Leonard J. Leff argues that Hemingway's participation in his celebrity culture eventually became a "cancer" that "devoured the private person within." The iconic Hemingway could "spark sales and make publisher and author wealthy" simply using his photographs "on reprints, magazine stories, and book club advertisements," but those results came at a high price to the man who wanted to be taken seriously as an artist (198–99). Unfortunately, the literary market that made Cather retreat from public life in the late 1930s was only a sign of growing pressures on writers to serve as larger-than-life personalities first and artists second.

Despite this later ambivalence, Cather was an iconic figure of her culture by the end of the 1930s. Carefully balancing her image with reviews to sell books, maintaining a "style" through her middy blouse and tie that echoed back to Whitman's 1855 portrait, and getting her photograph in *Vanity Fair* at a critical moment in her career, Cather demonstrated an ability to read her culture's dependency on image to sell books. Beyond her lifetime, images such as Steichen's *Vanity Fair* portrait have come to stand as powerful evocations of Cather and her West. The University of Nebraska, for example, continues to promote the university and recruit students through photographs taken from Steichen's photo shoot with Cather. In this way, photographs live with us. Celebrity promises a chance for mortal humans to live beyond their years, through cultural memory and history.

WORKS CITED

Amory, Cleveland, and Frederic Bradlee. *Vanity Fair: Selections from America's Most Memorable Magazine*. New York: Viking, 1960.

Barthes, Roland. *Camera Lucida: Reflections on Photography*. Trans. Richard Howard. New York: Hill and Wang, 1982.

Braudy, Leo. *The Frenzy of Renown: Fame and Its History*. New York: Vintage, 1997.

Burns, Sarah. *Inventing the Modern Artist: Art and Culture in Gilded Age America*. New Haven: Yale UP, 1996.

Cather, Willa. *The Autobiography of S. S. McClure (My Autobiography)*. Lincoln: U of Nebraska P, 1997.

———. "The Diamond Mine." *Youth and the Bright Medusa*. New York: Knopf, 1920. 67–120.

———. Letter to Duncan M. Vinsonhaler. Sunday [13 Jan. 1924]. Alderman Library, University of Virginia, Charlottesville.

———. Letter to Ferris Greenslet. 20 Jan. 1920. Houghton Library, Harvard U.

———. Letter to Mary Virginia Auld, Saturday [19 Feb. 1927]. University Archives and Special Collections, The University of Nebraska–Lincoln, copy, not original.

———. Letter to Miss Van Tuyll. 24 May [1915], from New York. Houghton Library, Harvard U.

———. "The Novel Démeublé." *Not Under Forty*. New York: Knopf, 1936. 43–51.

———. Telegram to Blanche Knopf. 19 June 1927. Alfred A. Knopf, Inc. Collection. Harry Ransom Research Center, U of Texas–Austin.

———. *The World and the Parish: Willa Cather's Articles and Reviews, 1893–1902*. Ed. William M. Curtin. Lincoln: U of Nebraska P, 1970.

Collins, Douglas. *The Story of Kodak*. New York: H. N. Abrams, 1990.

Debord, Guy. *The Society of the Spectacle*. New York: Zone Books, 1994.

Douglas, George H. *The Smart Magazines*. Hamden CT: Archon P, 1991.

Fillin-Yeh, Susan, ed. *Dandies: Fashion and Finesse in Arts and Culture*. New York: New York UP, 2001.

Fisher, Dorothy Canfield. "Daughter of the Frontier." Clipping dated Sunday, 28 May 1933, from the Alfred A. Knopf Archives at the Harry Ransom Center, U of Texas–Austin.

Fisher, Philip. "Appearing and Disappearing in Public: Social Space in Late Nineteenth Century Literature and Culture." *Reconstructing American Literary History*. Ed. Sacvan Bercovitch. Cambridge: Harvard UP, 1986. 155–88.

Folsom, Ed. "Appearing in Print: Illustrations of the Self in *Leaves of Grass*." *The Cambridge Companion to Walt Whitman*. Ed. Ezra Greenspan. Cambridge: Cambridge UP, 1995. 135–65.

Harris, Neil. "Iconography and Intellectual History: The Half-Tone Effect." *New Directions in American Intellectual History*. Ed. John Higham and Paul K. Conkin. Baltimore: Johns Hopkins University Press, 1979. 196–211.

Johnson, Patricia. *Real Fantasies: Edward Steichen's Advertising Photography*. Berkeley: U of California P, 1997.

Knopf, Blanche. Telegram to Willa Cather. 17 June 1927. Alfred A. Knopf, Inc. Collection. Harry Ransom Research Center, U of Texas–Austin.

Leff, Leonard J. *Hemingway and His Conspirators: Hollywood, Scribners, and the Making of American Celebrity Culture*. Lanham MD: Rowman & Littlefield, 1997.

"Matthew Brady's Portraits." National Portrait Gallery. Washington DC: Smithsonian Institution. http://www.npg.si.edu/exh/brady.

McPherson, Heather. *The Modern Portrait in Nineteenth-Century France*. Cambridge: Cambridge UP, 2001.

Moers, Ellen. *The Dandy: Brummell to Beerbohm*. Lincoln: U of Nebraska P, 1978.

Newbury, Michael. "Eaten Alive: Slavery and Celebrity in Antebellum America." *ELH* 61 (1994): 159–87.

Price, Kenneth M. "Walt Whitman and the Politics of Desire." *Whitman East and West: New Contexts for Reading Walt Whitman*. Ed. Ed Folsom. Iowa City: U of Iowa P, 2002. 36–70.

Reed, David. *The Popular Magazine in Britain and the United States, 1880–1930*. Toronto: U of Toronto P, 1997.

Reynolds, Guy. "Cather as Equivocal Icon." *Digital Commons*. Lincoln: U of Nebraska–Lincoln Libraries. 10 Apr. 2006. http://digitalcommons.unl.edu/englishtalks/2.

Russell, John. Introduction. *Vanity Fair: Photographs of an Age: 1914–1936*. Ed. Diana Edkins Richardson. New York: Clarkson N. Potter, 1982. ix–xx.
Schickel, Richard. *His Picture in the Papers*. New York: Charterhouse, 1973.
Silver, Brenda. *Virginia Woolf: Icon*. Chicago: U of Chicago P, 2000.
Steichen, Joanna. *Steichen's Legacy*. New York: Knopf, 2000.
Stimpson, Catherine R. Foreword. Silver xi–xiv.
Stout, Janis P., ed. *A Calendar of Letters of Willa Cather*. Lincoln: U of Nebraska P, 2002.
———. *Willa Cather: The Writer and Her World*. Charlottesville: Virginia UP, 2000.
Susman, Warren I. "'Personality' and the Making of Twentieth-Century Culture." *New Directions in American Intellectual History*. Ed. John Higham and Paul K. Conkin. Baltimore: Johns Hopkins UP, 1979. 212–26.
Taft, Robert. *Photography and the American Scene: A Social History, 1839–1889*. New York: Dover, 1938.
Vincent, Stephen, and Rosemary Benet. "Willa Cather: Civilized and Very American." *New York Herald Tribune* 15 Dec. 1940: IX.
Whitman, Walt. *Complete Poetry and Collected Prose*. New York: Library of America, 1982.
Woodress, James. *Willa Cather: A Literary Life*. Lincoln: U of Nebraska P, 1987.

Willa Cather and the Book-of-the-Month Club

MARK J. MADIGAN

As if set against ever becoming a "cultural icon," Willa Cather refused to allow her work to be issued in paperback, forbade its cinematic adaptation, and for several years opposed its distribution through book clubs. Nevertheless, at the urging of her friend Dorothy Canfield Fisher, who was a Book-of-the-Month Club (BOMC) judge, Cather granted permission for *Shadows on the Rock* to be designated as a main selection, or "book of the month," in 1931. She would do the same for *Sapphira and the Slave Girl* ten years later. This much has been documented by Cather's biographers. What has not been recognized until now is the extent and significance of Cather's association with the BOMC, which began in 1926, the club's first year of operation. In addition to the two main selections, *My Mortal Enemy*, *Death Comes for the Archbishop*, *Obscure Destinies*, *Lucy Gayheart*, *Not Under Forty*, and *The Old Beauty and Others* were all reviewed in the *Book-of-the-Month Club News* and were made available to subscribers as substitute selections for the book of the month. *My Ántonia* was featured as "An Outstanding Older Book" in the April 1929 issue of the *News* as well.

The role of the BOMC in Cather's career has drawn little attention from those who write about her. Save for that of *Sapphira and the Slave Girl*, the reviews discussed here have neither been republished nor properly recorded in any bibliographies.[1] Focusing on these reviews and related documents, this article will investigate the ways in which Cather's work served the BOMC and how the BOMC served Cather, helping to make her a "cultural icon." The club sold thousands of her books to its members, and its reviews provided those early subscribers, many of whom were first-time readers of Cather, with a lens through which to read her work. At the same time, her association with the club did nothing to aid her reputation with critics who regarded her work as being old-fashioned in subject matter and form—in their view, perfectly suited for the BOMC.

Because the records have not survived, the demographic makeup of the BOMC's early membership cannot be precisely determined; however, some important details can be established from anecdotal evidence and oral-history interviews with club officials.[2] Although these sources suggest that the majority of members were women, the business did not explicitly market itself to them. Rather, the chair of the club's Committee of Selection, Henry Seidel Canby, referred to the club's target market as the "general reader," which he defined as "the average intelligent reader, who has passed through the usual formal education in literature, who reads books as well as newspapers and magazines, who, without calling himself a litterateur, would be willing to assert that he was fairly well read and reasonably fond of good reading" (qtd. in Radway 296). What Canby referred to as the general reader, others have called "the middlebrow."[3] Canby's definition suggests (and other sources confirm) that a significant percentage of the BOMC's middlebrow readers were college-educated members of the professional-managerial class (Radway 295–96). Janice Radway has asserted in *A Feeling for Books: The Book-of-the-Month Club, Literary Taste, and Middle-Class Desire* that "the club's particular selections may have helped to consolidate their faith in a specific set of values and assumptions about the world. . . . Their reading may have assured them that their world was still centered—and centered in a way that they understood" (298). Radway contends that the BOMC also functioned to "promote identification with the point of view of the professional-managerial class among individuals poised at the outer reaches of that group" (297). As we will see, reviews of Cather's work in the BOMC *News* made distinct appeals to both of these middlebrow constituencies. To appreciate Cather's fiction, they implied, was a marker of aesthetic sophistication, a step up in the cultural hierarchy; and in her work, subscribers were promised a safe harbor from modernist literary experiments in style and form.

The BOMC was founded in February 1926 by Harry Scherman, a onetime writer turned advertising executive, and publisher Robert K. Haas. Prior to the BOMC, they had worked together at the Little Leather Library Corporation, which produced and marketed inexpensive editions of literary classics. As president of the Little Leather Library from 1916 to 1925, Scherman contended with a lack of bookstores outside major U.S. cities and turned to then-unconventional methods of distribution, such as selling books in department stores and packaging small editions of individual Shakespeare plays in boxes of candy. Following a successful attempt at selling sets of the "Thirty World's Greatest Masterpieces" by mail, he settled upon the idea for the BOMC with financial backing from Haas (Lee 22–29). The business was the first of its kind, predating its main rival, the Literary Guild, by one year.

Scherman envisioned a mail-order business that would distribute newly published books chosen by a panel of literary experts in whom middlebrow readers would have confidence. The inaugural operating principles were straightforward: members agreed to buy the monthly selection at a price of no more than three dollars plus postage for twelve months. Soon after, readers were asked to buy only four books per year and allowed to substitute one of several alternate choices reviewed in the *News* for the month's main selection before shipping. The club's policies evolved to include price reductions, publication of BOMC editions, and distribution of "free" books as "dividends" (Lee 33, 37). The Book-of-the-Month Club was an immediate success; the initial subscriber list in February 1926 was 4,750 and grew to 60,000 within a year. In the midst of the Depression, in 1935, the number reached 137,000, and by the end of the decade it surpassed 362,000 (Lee 30).

For the first Committee of Selection, Scherman chose Heywood Broun, Canby, Fisher, Christopher Morley, and William Allen White. Broun was a popular critic widely published in newspapers and magazines. Canby was the editor of the *Saturday Review of Literature* and a former Yale English professor. Fisher and Morley were best-selling novelists. White was a fiction writer and the Pulitzer Prize–winning editor of the *Emporia Gazette*, a Kansas daily. The five judges were charged with the task of reading a prescreened group of forthcoming books and meeting once a month in New York to agree upon a "main selection."

There is no evidence that Cather had met Broun or Morley, but she did have personal connections to the rest of the committee. White had published in *McClure's* during Cather's editorial tenure at the magazine and had made her acquaintance. When H. L. Mencken gave *One of Ours* a bad notice, it was White who consoled Cather by saying, "If thy Mencken and thy Nathan desert thee then the Lord will take thee by" (qtd. in Woodress 334). Canby had been a friend of Cather's since 1916, when he frequented the Friday-afternoon social gatherings at her Bank Street apartment in Greenwich Village (Woodress 281). As Rubin has noted, the list of works Canby was most proud of having selected for the BOMC revealed his taste for "older writers and established forms" (121). He viewed Cather as a traditionalist whose work contrasted sharply against the moral and stylistic excesses of her modernist contemporaries (*Seven Years' Harvest* 287). She was, in his words, the "most skillful" American novelist of the 1910s and 1920s and a writer "worthy of any [nation's] literature" (*American Memoir* 266).

Fisher first met Cather in 1891 in Lincoln, Nebraska. Cather was then a student at the state university, of which Fisher's father was chancellor. The two grew close and maintained their friendship through visits and letters after leaving Nebraska to pursue their literary careers. Their relationship was strained by a dispute over one of Cather's early short stories, but by the time the BOMC opened for business, the two had reconciled and held each other in high regard.[4] For Fisher the BOMC represented more than a promising financial opportunity or vehicle for self-promotion. With a family background in education, she was raised to believe that books were vital to the development of healthy individuals and societies. She saw her role on the selection committee as a form of public service and was its "most conscientious" reader

(Rubin 130). She and Canby were Cather's strongest supporters on the selection committee.

The BOMC *News* was edited by Scherman and received by subscribers no fewer than three weeks before the main selection was mailed. The twelve-page, eight-by-eleven-inch booklet was typically composed of a three-page lead review, six pages of "Other New Books Recommended" capsule reviews (two hundred to five hundred words each), an occasional one-page "Outstanding Older Book" review, and two pages listing approximately sixty "Books Recommended in the Past." Included in the publication was a "Substitution Request" form, which subscribers could fill in to receive one of the "Other New Books Recommended" or the "Outstanding Older Book" instead of the main selection. The substitution books were chosen by either the selection committee or the BOMC's team of first readers. When subscribers were first offered alternate selections in April 1926, Fisher was especially pleased. She remarked, "The position which this booklet plays in the BOMC distribution of books is for me literally all important, because it represents the vital fact that nobody is obliged to accept the book picked by our Committee of Selection" (Lee 145). As Radway has written, Fisher "worried that promotion of a single title would obscure all the other worthy books published at the same time. . . . [She] conceived of her role at the club as a kind of scout on behalf of a variety of readers. She was attempting to match prospective readers with titles that would appropriately and effectively address their needs" (264). Exchanges, substitutions, and separate purchases were not only allowed but encouraged, according to a statement published under the "Other New Books Recommended" heading in the *News*:[5] "The Committee does not set itself up as a censor of taste; its job is a practical one—to choose an outstanding book each month, a book which it considers *most people* would not care to miss. If the choice in any one month does not meet your own tastes, which should be sacred to you, get one of the books described below—or one of the many books recommended previously by the Committee" (3).

The selection committee wasted little time in making Cather's work available to its subscribers, choosing *My Mortal Enemy* as one of its "Other New Books Recommended" in 1926.[6] The unsigned review in the *News* acknowledged that critics had disagreed about Cather's latest novel, "some placing it above and others below the standard of her previous performance." The reviewer hastened to add that this standard was "exceptionally high," for Cather was "unquestionably one of the most skillful, one of the most significant writers of fiction of our day, both in this country and in Europe." To summarize the plot of *My Mortal Enemy* would be an injustice, the review continued, since "the value of it—as with any high piece of work—is wholly in the manner of its telling." What is most significant about this notice is not so much its limited commentary on *My Mortal Enemy* as its final sentence, which urged "those who have not yet become acquainted with the character of Miss Cather's work" to purchase the novel. Recognizing that her core readership could be counted upon to buy her latest offering under almost any circumstance, the BOMC endorsement was aimed at expanding her audience.

In the absence of records, it is impossible to determine how many copies of *My Mortal Enemy* were sold as a result of its designation as one of the BOMC's recommended books. It is safe to say, however, that the number was significant. Fisher once noted that "about half of the enormous number of subscribers do not accept our choice but do take the trouble to specify some other book or none at all" (Lee 145). Furthermore, a listing in the "Other New Books Recommended" section of the *News* led not only to sales directly through the club but also to sales in bookstores. In 1927, Scherman commented, "it is a conservative estimate that whenever we list a book and describe it, in what we call our supplementary list, it is good for at least an indirect sale of from five hundred to a thousand copies of that book in the bookstores" (Lee 144).

In a 15 August 1927 letter, Fisher wrote to Cather's publisher Alfred A. Knopf about the forthcoming *Death Comes for the Archbishop* to see if there was anything she could do to "help the distribution of that exquisitely beautiful book." She expressed disappointment that the selection committee had not chosen it as the book of the month for September. Other committee members had appreciated its "loveliness," she explained, but felt it was "too contemplative and had too little 'action' (whatever that means!) to appeal to a very large and very miscellaneous audience."

Fisher was chagrined that *Death Comes for the Archbishop* was not sent out as a main selection, but it was offered to subscribers in the "Other New Books Recommended" section of the *News* in September 1927. The unsigned review began, "To an ever-increasing host of discriminating readers each new novel by Willa Cather is a gala event" (3). The remainder mainly quoted from the report of one of the selection committee members, most likely Canby or Fisher. The reviewer acknowledged the "problem" of scant plotting cited by the rest of the committee but asserted that "if there is no story there is a hero . . . perhaps two heroes . . . two French priests, one of them fine, cultivated, and sensitive, the other of rougher, sturdier stuff" (3). Any deficiency of plot was additionally compensated for by Cather's vivid descriptions of the "magnificent Southwest country" (3). To be an admirer of Cather's novels, the review implied, was to join a cadre of readers—as opposed to a "very large and very miscellaneous audience"—for whom plot or "story" was not a primary concern. Appreciation of character, setting, and the formal qualities of Cather's writing, then, identified one as a "discriminating" reader capable of enjoying *Death Comes for the Archbishop* on its own terms. This appeal to the intellectual aspirations of the club's subscribers paralleled that of its advertising slogan, "Handed to You by the Postman, the New Books You Intend to Read" (Lee 28).

Rebuffed over *Death Comes for the Archbishop*, Fisher promoted *My Ántonia* as an "Outstanding Older Book" in April 1929. Suggesting that readers should not merely rely upon the recommendations of the selection committee, Fisher wondered in the full-page review "if there is a life-experienced person who has not acquired a comprehensive scepticism of what is told him by other persons' reports" (10). Regarding books, she wrote, one might instead enter a public library to see which had been borrowed most often. She observed, "If the binding looks weary, if the edges of the book have lost their raw crispness and are blurred by the thumbing over of human fingers, if the dates of lending are stamped thickly all over the card at the back—there is no doubt about it, that is a book which is part of the food on which America is feeding its heart and mind" (10). Fisher claimed to put *My Ántonia* to this test whenever she visited a public library. "By this time I know beforehand that it will bear witness to long and hard use," she wrote. The "worn and shabby" copies of the novel in public libraries testified to "the lasting love of our people for that beautiful book" (10).

Turning to reasons for buying and not just borrowing *My Ántonia*, Fisher wrote, "The next step should be to move it from the public library shelf to the home shelf, to see it in every American's house as part of the stuff of life" (10). She posited that *My Ántonia* was a book to be owned, even if one did not have time for a cover-to-cover rereading. Its episodic structure and descriptive scenes made it perfect for skimming. "A glance at any page of it as it falls open in your hand brings golden reward, something to beautify or deepen any mood," she asserted (10). Addressing subscribers who might have been reticent to buy a book they had already read, she concluded that the novel was not only one to "live with" but also a book to "grow up to." Cather's story of "a lovable, deep-hearted, natural Bohemian girl" would enrich any home with "more understanding and more love of life" (10).

In *Shadows on the Rock* the selection committee found a Cather novel upon which it could agree to endorse as a book of the month. The author and her publisher, though, needed to be convinced that selling it through the BOMC was a good idea. Cather had expressed doubts about the BOMC as early as 1928 in a letter to her Houghton Mifflin editor, Ferris Greenslet (Stout 140). According to Knopf, she was opposed to offering her work to book clubs because she did not want anyone to be forced to buy it. He worried that booksellers would object to the selection of *Shadows on the Rock* on the basis that it would hurt in-store sales. Knopf reports that Fisher alleviated Cather's concerns by explaining the club's policies and procedures in a "very long" letter, the whereabouts of which are now unknown (138). In a 26 June 1931 letter to Canby, Cather wrote that she had left the matter of the book club up to her publisher (Stout 157). Knopf asked his salespeople to survey their most important accounts regarding whether he should sell the novel through the BOMC. He was surprised to hear that the booksellers echoed Scherman's claim about the positive effect of a club selection on sales in stores (138). With Cather's and Knopf's approval, the BOMC made the novel its main selection for August 1931.

The club played a major part in making *Shadows on the Rock* Cather's best-selling novel. Scherman once pointed out that before 1931, *Death Comes for the Archbishop* had been Cather's best-selling book, taking four years to reach the 100,000 sales mark. By contrast, *Shadows on the Rock* sold 120,000 copies, not including the club's distribution of nearly 45,000 copies, within six months of its being selected as a book of the month (Lee 164–65). The only best-seller of Cather's career, it finished second in sales for the year, trailing only Pearl Buck's *The Good Earth* (Hackett 143).

Canby's lead review in the *News* referred to Cather as one of the few living novelists "from whom a new book is an event" (1).[7] He wrote, "The plot is—Quebec, the rock to which the ships come once a year across the seas, and from which the canoes go down the lakes. It is enough. The simplicity of this chronicle is the simplicity of art. To recreate such a culture and animate it with such personalities is not simple" (2). He continued: "*Shadows on the Rock* seems at first reading to be a quieter chronicle than *Death Comes for the Archbishop*, but, to speak technically, the texture of the narrative is even finer, the emergent characters more varied, the story as a whole more completely knit into an imaginative reconstruction, so perfect that for English readers at least this book is likely to become the classic of French civilization in North America" (2). Canby not only described Cather's latest novel but also implicitly spoke to the cultural desires of the BOMC's middlebrow subscribers. To appreciate the "simplicity" of Cather's work, he suggested, required an ability to divine the "finer" qualities of literary art, an ability for which highbrow critics gave the public little credit.

Obscure Destinies was Cather's first collection of short stories to appear since the BOMC's inception. One of the "Other

New Books Recommended" for August 1932, it was reviewed by Fisher, whose opening remark was, "I am confessedly a Willa Cather fan" (7). Of the volume's three stories, "Old Mrs. Harris" and "Neighbour Rosicky" received Fisher's highest praise. Both were "miracles of effortless condensation . . . packed with minutely realistic, perfectly painted details as any Van Eyck canvas" (7). The former was compared to Cather's poem "Poor Marty," a tribute to Marjorie Anderson, a domestic worker in the author's Virginia childhood home (Woodress 24); the latter was called "neighbor and kin" to *My Ántonia*. About the third story, "Two Friends," Fisher wrote that the protagonists "probably lifted their hats high to *A Lost Lady*, silently devoted to her charm" (7). By linking the new volume to the autobiographical poem, as well as two of Cather's most successful Nebraska novels, the review made clear to readers who preferred her earlier work that her foray into historical fiction in *Death Comes for the Archbishop* and *Shadows on the Rock* was over.

Cather's next book, *Lucy Gayheart*, was considered for main selection status as it was going to press in 1935. This novel did not fare so well as *Shadows on the Rock*. In a five-page letter to Fisher dated 28 April 1935, Scherman defended the club's decision not to select *Lucy Gayheart* as a book of the month. On the selection committee, White had detected "crudities" in the prose and opposed Fisher and Canby, who had argued in the novel's favor. Scherman agreed with White and could not see the "absence of sophistication" as a "*deliberate* imitation of the story-telling of that day," which he took to be Fisher's "theory" about the novel. His view was that Cather had not been living in the present for some years. She was a realist, but of the past. In *Death Comes for the Archbishop* and *Shadows on the Rock*, for example, she wrote of the historical past, which she had to work hard to make real to herself. Cather wrote of an "imagined actuality" in both, according to Scherman. The lack of "polish and finish" in *Lucy Gayheart* was attributable to the fact that she had "experienced the past she was writing about" and, thus, did not refine and revise to the extent that she had in her two previous novels.

Unable to persuade her colleagues that *Lucy Gayheart* was

worthy of main selection status, Fisher reviewed the novel in the "Other New Books Recommended" section of the August 1935 *News*. There she called Cather "a poet if there ever was one" and *Lucy Gayheart* "a poem, rather than a novel" (4). Fisher located the work in the tradition of poetry concerned with "the death of youth" by either "rough material accident" or "the ruthless hands of the fleeting years" (4). Cather, like the great poets before her, was adept at making "something lovely out of telling melancholy stories of [youth's] inevitable end," according to Fisher (4). *Lucy Gayheart* revealed another of its author's strengths, she wrote, which was "her magical ability for tender reconstruction of times gone by." The novel had a "golden patina of the past" and "a wistful charm of the irrevocably lived through and left behind" (4). With these latter comments, Fisher may have done her friend an unintentional disservice. The Depression era had brought Cather criticism for being disconnected from the crises of contemporary life. In "The Case Against Willa Cather," the influential critic Granville Hicks had made such an argument, and the term "escapist" was being increasingly applied to her fiction. The "golden patina" and "wistful charm" of which Fisher wrote admiringly were being cited as the principal deficiencies of Cather's work. As one critic wrote of *Lucy Gayheart*, it seemed as if the author "had decided that the mood and methods of the genteel tradition in novel writing were enough" (O'Connor 464).

In his "Other New Books Recommended" review of *Not Under Forty* in December 1936, Canby offered a positive gloss on the generational divide announced in its title. He declared, "Under forty could not have written them; but under forty will read!" In his view, the literary reminiscences and critical essays collected therein were "done with the sure grip of character and the significance of details which distinguish Miss Cather's art as a novelist" (4). Her final demonstration of that novelistic art, *Sapphira and the Slave Girl*, was a BOMC dual main selection (with William Saroyan's *My Name Is Aram*) for January 1941. Accompanied by a biographical sketch of Cather by Elizabeth Sergeant, Fisher's lead review situated the novel in the context of the "human slavery" then spreading across Nazi-dominated Europe (2). In the face of "calamity almost beyond human imagining," Fisher wrote, readers might be skeptical about a novel with a happy ending. Nevertheless, she stated, Cather's latest book presented "a lovely story of escape from slavery, which is not only literally and factually true, but deeply and symbolically the truth" (2). The author was credited for her depiction of the Virginia setting and for capturing the difference between "the language used by house servants when speaking to their white masters and when talking together in their own cabins." Fisher also drew comparisons to Faulkner and Hemingway, placing Cather above them both. Mrs. Colbert would have been portrayed by Faulkner in "livid purples and bloody reds," leaving the reader "shouting for help," she contended. Hemingway would have tried to produce a "physical shudder" in dramatizing the threat that Nancy faced, as opposed to Cather's more subtle approach. Returning to her opening theme, Fisher concluded that the "golden human values" of *Sapphira and the Slave Girl* were "consoling and comforting" at a moment marked by "recurring, ever-nearer dangers to our own freedom" (3).

In a 13 December 1940 letter, Cather asked Fisher to send her a copy of the *Sapphira* review. She was probably pleased by the comment about the authenticity of the novel's slave dialect, since she had unabashedly called Fisher's attention to this attribute in a 14 October 1940 letter. The review was clever in some regards and problematic in others. Fisher argued for the relevance of *Sapphira and the Slave Girl* to its time but was apparently left untroubled by its problems with race, as have since been explicated most notably by Toni Morrison (18–28).[8] In positioning Cather against Faulkner and Hemingway, the review would have appealed to conservative members of the BOMC.[9] Yet statements such as these situated Cather's work outside the main current of literary modernism. Middlebrow readers might have turned to a novel to find consolation, comfort, and "golden human values," but the country's most influential critics valued hard-edged, ironical fiction more highly.

Cather's final volume of fiction, the short-story collection *The Old Beauty and Others*, was reviewed by BOMC first reader Amy Loveman in September 1948. She began with praise for the formal attributes of the work: "Whatever Willa Cather wrote had the stamp of the artist upon it, and this posthumous volume reveals again her simplicity and elegance of style and the dexterous manipulation of her material" (8). Yet Loveman would offer only a conditional recommendation to subscribers, for despite the "charm" of the stories, *The Old Beauty and Others* was a "minor work." The volume was one that "Cather's admirers will want to read, and collectors of her writings will wish to own," she concluded (8). The uninitiated were, then, implicitly forewarned of its narrow appeal.

In the aggregate, reviews of Cather's work in the *News* conjure competing images of the author. During Cather's lifetime, the BOMC promoted her as a literary artist of the highest order, a cultural icon. The "Miss Cather" constructed in the pages of the *News* was wholly devoted to her work, seemingly uninterested in artistic trends, topical issues, and commercial concerns. Her greatest literary asset was her prose style, which was characterized by simplicity and lyricism. Her fiction emphasized character and setting over plot and incident and was marked by emotional austerity. All of these characterizations were intended as plaudits and to make Cather appealing to the BOMC's middlebrow membership.

Seen from another angle, however, the club's sympathetic representation of Cather's work reinforced some of the notions of her harshest critics from the late 1920s onward. Its reviewers mediated her texts, highlighting their formal qualities and characterization, while ignoring their tantalizing problems and complexities. This "Miss Cather" was a highly skilled but conventional novelist who was out of touch with her time. She was indeed a writer of lyrical prose, but in the midcentury marketplace of literary reputation, prose stylists and midwestern regionalists did not rank with narrative experimentalists and more cosmopolitan authors on the literary vanguard.[10] As John Chamberlain wrote dismissively of *Shadows on the Rock* in the *New York Times Book Review*, "Superbly written, with that sensitivity to sunset and afterglow that has always been Miss Cather's, it still shows that good prose is not enough" (O'Connor 364).

As the theme of Cather as "cultural icon" suggests, Cather has since come to be routinely included among the first rank of twentieth-century American writers. Her work has continued to be popular with general readers and sought after by book clubs. I will conclude with but one example. In announcing the choice of a novel for its "One Book, One Chicago" program—part of a nationwide initiative in which entire cities are encouraged to function as book clubs—Mayor Richard Daley confirmed in August 2002 what Dorothy Canfield Fisher had written in the *Book-of-the-Month Club News* several decades previous. The mayor said that although the Chicago selection had been published more than eighty years earlier, it had retained its thematic relevance and dealt with contemporary issues such as class, religion, and immigration. He invited citizens to participate in discussions, lectures, and film screenings; three thousand copies of the novel were ordered for the city's libraries, including translations in Spanish and Korean. That novel, *My Ántonia*, had proven to be an "Outstanding Older Book" indeed (Reardon 38).

NOTES

1. Fisher's *My Ántonia* review is listed in Marilyn Arnold's indispensable *Willa Cather: A Reference Guide* as an "unidentified newspaper clipping" (62).

2. The interviews, conducted by Louis M. Starr in 1955, are housed in the Columbia University Oral History Collection, Butler Library, Columbia University, New York.

3. Cultural historian Lawrence W. Levine points out in *Highbrow/Lowbrow* that this term originated from the pseudoscience of phrenology, which correlated the height of the brow with one's intelligence. By the 1880s, "highbrow" was used to describe "intellectual or aesthetic superiority"; shortly after the turn of the century, "lowbrow" had come to be equated with vulgarity (221–22). In *The Making of Middlebrow Culture*, Joan Shelley Rubin surmises that the term "middlebrow" was coined by Margaret Widdemer in a 1933 *Saturday Review* essay titled "Message and Middlebrow," where Widdemer wrote that middlebrow readers were "men and women, fairly civilized, fairly literate, who support the critics and lecturers and publishers by purchasing their wares" (Rubin xii). The "middlebrow" label has acquired a more negative connotation since then, as writers and critics from Virginia Woolf to Dwight Macdonald to Allan Bloom have associated the middlebrow

with the diminishment of aesthetic taste and the decline of artistic standards (Rubin xiii–xiv).

4. The disputed story was "The Profile," the protagonist of which is a woman with a grotesque facial scar who was modeled after one of Fisher's friends. Fisher protested that the story would psychologically damage her friend if published, but Cather refused to drop it. Finally, whatever measure of victory either side could claim was provisional. "The Profile" was not published in the *Troll Garden* in 1905, but it did appear in *McClure's Magazine* two years later, following the death of the real-life prototype. Bitter feelings between the two persisted for many years. The impasse was broken in the early 1920s, when Cather asked Fisher to help edit the sections of *One of Ours* set in France. Cather's letters from that point forward document their renewed friendship. For in-depth discussions of this controversial story, see my "Willa Cather and Dorothy Canfield Fisher: Rift, Reconciliation, and *One of Ours*" and "Regarding Willa Cather's 'The Profile' and Evelyn Osborne."

5. These books were obtained by the BOMC directly from the publisher. Special club editions were issued only for main selections.

6. I am unable to provide a full bibliographic citation for the *My Mortal Enemy* review, since the only extant copy I am aware of is neither dated nor paginated. This photocopy is housed in box 24, folder 9, of the Dorothy Canfield Fisher Collection at the University of Vermont's Bailey/Howe Library.

7. The review was accompanied by a "Biographical Sketch" that is widely believed to have been written by Cather herself in 1926 (Crane 314–15).

8. Fisher's failure to recognize the novel's racial problems does not suggest that she was insensitive to racism. Fisher was a strong advocate for African American civil rights in both her fiction (see her novel *The Brimming Cup*) and her charitable activities. On the selection committee she argued persuasively that Richard Wright's novel *Native Son* should be a main selection. In April 1940 it became the first book of the month by an African American author. Its introduction was written by Fisher.

9. The only work by either Faulkner or Hemingway ever to be sent out as a main selection was the latter's *The Old Man and the Sea* in September 1952.

10. Following Cather's death in April 1947, Bernardine Kielty, wife of Harry Scherman and a BOMC first reader, wrote a eulogy for the author that reinforced some of these ideas about Cather's work. Published in the June issue of the *News*, it read, in part:

> Willa Cather is such a hallowed name, and she herself was such an almost legendary figure within her own time, that it was a shock to

> learn, with her death, that she had been living in New York—even as you and I; that she strolled up Park Avenue in the sun to her apartment in the 60s, and gone perhaps to the same butcher and the same movies. If posterity ever localizes Willa Cather it will be as a Middle Westerner, because of *My Ántonia* and *The Lost Lady* [*sic*] and *O Pioneers* [*sic*] and *The Song of the Lark*. . . . Her beautiful prose was her glory, and she came by that only by dint of hard work and self-abnegation. Like Flaubert she toiled for clarity and exactness, and like him, achieved timelessness. (Kielty 24)

Kielty's piece also gets book titles wrong and strikes false biographical notes. It is indeed difficult to imagine Cather in a butcher's shop or movie theater; grocery shopping was left to her housekeeper, and she disdained movies as an inferior relative of stage plays.

WORKS CITED

Arnold, Marilyn. *Willa Cather: A Reference Guide*. Boston: G. K. Hall, 1986.

Canby, Henry Seidel. *American Memoir*. Boston: Houghton Mifflin, 1947.

———. Rev. of *Not Under Forty*, by Willa Cather. *Book–of–the–Month Club News* December 1936: 4.

———. Rev. of *Shadows on the Rock*, by Willa Cather. *Book–of–the–Month Club News* July 1931: 1-2.

———. *Seven Years' Harvest: Notes on Contemporary Literature*. New York: Holt, Rinehart, and Winston, 1936.

Cather, Willa. Letters to Dorothy Canfield Fisher. Dorothy Canfield Fisher Collection. Special Collections Department. Bailey/Howe Library. U of Vermont, Burlington.

———. "Willa Cather: A Biographical Sketch." *Book-of-the Month Club News* July 1931: 3–4.

Crane, Joan. *Willa Cather: A Bibliography*. Lincoln: U of Nebraska P, 1982.

Fisher, Dorothy Canfield. Letters to Willa Cather. Letter to Alfred Knopf. Dorothy Canfield Fisher Collection. Special Collections Department. Bailey/Howe Library. U of Vermont, Burlington.

———. Rev. of *Lucy Gayheart*, by Willa Cather. *Book-of-the-Month Club News* Aug. 1935: 4.

———. Rev. of *My Ántonia*, by Willa Cather. *Book-of-the-Month Club News* Apr. 1929: 10.

———. Rev. of *Obscure Destinies*, by Willa Cather. *Book-of-the-Month Club News* Aug. 1932: 7.

———. Rev. of *Sapphira and the Slave Girl*, by Willa Cather. *Book-of-the-Month Club News* Dec. 1940: 2–3.

Hackett, Alice Payne. *Seventy Years of Best Sellers, 1895–1965*. New York: Bowker, 1967.

Kielty, Bernardine. "Authors between Books." *Book-of-the-Month Club News* June 1947: 24.

Knopf, Alfred A. "Publishing Willa Cather." *Willa Cather Remembered*. Ed. Sharon Hoover. Lincoln: U of Nebraska P, 2002. 136–39.

Lee, Charles. *The Hidden Public: The Story of the Book-of-the-Month Club*. Garden City: Doubleday, 1958.

Levine, Lawrence W. *Highbrow/Lowbrow: The Emergence of Cultural Hierarchy in American Culture*. Cambridge: Harvard UP, 1988.

Loveman, Amy. Rev. of *The Old Beauty and Others*, by Willa Cather. *Book-of-the-Month Club News* Sept. 1948: 8.

Madigan, Mark J. "Regarding Cather's 'The Profile' and Evelyn Osborne." *Willa Cather Newsletter and Review* 44 (spring 2000): 1–5.

———. "Willa Cather and Dorothy Canfield Fisher: Rift, Reconciliation, and *One of Ours*." *Cather Studies* 1 (1990): 115–29.

Morrison, Toni. *Playing in the Dark: Whiteness and the Literary Imagination*. New York: Vintage, 1993.

O'Connor, Margaret Anne, ed. *Willa Cather: The Contemporary Reviews*. Cambridge: Cambridge UP, 2001.

Radway, Janice A. *A Feeling for Books: The Book-of-the-Month Club, Literary Taste, and Middle-Class Desire*. Chapel Hill: U of North Carolina P, 1997.

Reardon, Patrick T. "*My Ántonia* Selected for City-wide Reading Program." *Chicago Tribune*, date unknown. *Willa Cather Newsletter and Review* 46 (fall 2002): 38.

Rev. of *Death Comes for the Archbishop*, by Willa Cather. *Book-of-the-Month Club News* Sept. 1927: 3.

Rev. of *My Mortal Enemy*, by Willa Cather. *Book-of-the-Month Club News* 1926.

Rubin, Joan Shelley. *The Making of Middlebrow Culture*. Chapel Hill: U of North Carolina P, 1992.

Scherman, Harry S. Letter to Dorothy Canfield Fisher. Dorothy Canfield Fisher Collection. Special Collections Department. Bailey/Howe Library. U of Vermont, Burlington.

Silverman, Al, ed. *The Book of the Month: Sixty Years of Books in American Life*. Boston: Little, Brown, 1986.
Stout, Janis, ed. *A Calendar of Letters of Willa Cather*. Lincoln: U of Nebraska P, 2002.
Woodress, James. *Willa Cather: A Literary Life*. Lincoln: U of Nebraska P, 1987.

"Two or Three Human Stories"
O Pioneers! and the Old Testament

JESSICA G. RABIN

INTRODUCTION: BECOMING A GIVEN

Scholarship on canon construction suggests that texts become literary icons in much the same way that symbols accrue meanings, that is, through association. If a *canonical* work is "authoritative in our culture" (Bloom 1), then an *iconic* work might be emblematic or representative of certain ideas in a generally recognized way. In the case of both canon formation and iconography, intertextuality, or the ability to tap into a recognized tradition while still making a unique contribution, would seem essential. Sometimes canonicity and iconography collapse into one, rendering a literary text (or an author) both an icon and the cornerstone of a canon. The Old Testament, for example, occupies such a place in our culture and literature. Harold Bloom establishes this centrality of the Old Testament to the canon of Western literature by describing it as "such a given that we are blinded to its idiosyncrasies" (4). Many writers since have both adopted and adapted the biblical tradition as part of their own journey to canonical and iconic status. While Willa Cather's literary corpus has by now earned an indisputable place in the canon of American literature, her status as an icon is only beginning to be systematically investigated. One step toward understanding Cather as cultural icon might involve beginning to explicate an iconography of Cather. Therefore it would seem that the powerful undercurrent of the Old Testament in Cather's texts, in terms of both content (particularly themes and motifs) and techniques (style and genres), would provide significant insights into Cather's emergent status as literary and cultural icon.

Explication of these undercurrents should not, however, be confused with engaging in the often fascinating but ultimately meaningless process of enumerating correspondences. A major flaw in such delineations is the necessity of establishing intentionality on the author's part (otherwise we are just talking about coincidence). As familiar as Cather was with the Old Testament, it is safe to assume that she did not have access to (or perhaps even interest in) a wealth of biblical criticism and traditional rabbinic scholarship. But positing influence does not require intentionality. The likelihood that consciously created parallels and unconscious similarities coexist in Cather's work does not detract from the importance of these Old Testament echoes. Quite the contrary, as Cather herself might point out. In fact, it seems plausible to argue that given Cather's knowledge of the Old Testament, the elements that recur throughout Cather's novels serve as another manifestation of "the thing that teases the mind over and over for years, and at last gets itself put down rightly on paper" (*Not Under Forty* 76).

"A FADED TAPESTRY DEEP IN THE CONSCIOUSNESS"

Cather's knowledge of the Bible and its lifelong influence on her sensibilities have been well established: the Bible was among her earliest reading materials, and at least one prominent critic "can imagine her enjoying the sonorous phrases of the King James Bible" at her own funeral (Hoover 192).[1] Furthermore, Cather habitually read from the Bible before writing, according to Malcolm Cowley, who speculates "that it did involve a touch of piety" (188) despite Cather's avowal that she was only interested in quality prose. The rhythms and devices of that prose certainly made their mark. And although, as Thornton Wilder reports, Cather "regretted that she had formed this habit, for the prose rhythms of 1611 were not those she was in search of" (qtd. in Cowley 188), her disclaimer should only serve to pique our interest, particularly since in other places she accepts this influence as a matter of course.

Cather's admiration for the Old Testament as a literary text with far-reaching canonical influence is apparent in her review of Thomas Mann's *Joseph and His Brothers*, in which she proclaims the ubiquitous character of the Old Testament for herself and her contemporaries:

> We have all been there before, even if we have never crossed salt water. . . . The Bible countries along the Mediterranean shore were very familiar to most of us in our childhood. Whether we were born in New Hampshire or Virginia or California, Palestine lay behind us. We took it in unconsciously and unthinkingly perhaps, but we could not escape it. It was all about us, in the pictures on the walls, in the songs we sang in Sunday school, in the "opening exercises" at day school, in the talk of the old people, wherever we lived. And it was in our language—fixed, indelibly. The effect of the King James translation of the Bible upon English prose has been repeated down through the generations, leaving its mark on the minds of all children who had any but the most sluggish emotional nature. . . . The Book of Genesis lies like a faded tapestry deep in the consciousness of almost every individual who is more than forty years of age. (*Not Under Forty* 101–2)

Further, much of what Cather says about Mann's text could also be said of her first Nebraska novel, *O Pioneers!* For example, Cather praises Mann's decision to write from the inside instead of using structure to produce distance. In *O Pioneers!* she dramatizes the universal through the particular by using Alexandra to show how "the history of every country begins in the heart of a man or a woman" (64). Cather also praises Mann's "tempo, the deliberate, sustained pace" (*Not Under Forty* 99), which she finds particularly appropriate to his subject. When writing *O Pioneers!*, Cather similarly allowed the text itself to dictate its form. James Woodress explains that she "worked out a form that was loosely episodic and let the tale pace itself" (*Life and Art* 156); this ultimately produced, in Cather's words, "a slow-moving story" (*Willa Cather on Writing* 94).[2] Ultimately, what Cather proves in *O Pioneers!* is precisely that which she credits Mann with knowing: "what we most love is not bizarre invention, but to have the old story brought home to us closer than ever before, enriched by all that the right man could draw from it and, by sympathetic insight, put into it" (*Not Under Forty* 119). Hence by adapting the content and cadences of the Old Testament to the story of Swedes in Nebraska, Cather creates a novel that reaches back to the foundation of Western literature (the Old Testament) while simultaneously setting its author on the path to the immortality of iconic status.

"A RIDE THROUGH A FAMILIAR COUNTRY"

Critical examinations of Cather and the Bible thus far have generally fallen into two categories: explications of allusions and attempts to link biblical influence with spiritual or religious identification.[3] Building on the groundwork laid by these former explorations, this article quickly moves beyond the parallels to early Genesis to considerations of some of the less-often-noted books of the Old Testament. Even more fundamentally, it probes the way the literary techniques by which the Bible conveys its message similarly operate in *O Pioneers!*, emphasizing embedded structures as well as content-level comparisons.

While biblical style and influence is apparent throughout Cather's canon, many critics have used words like "archetypal" (Butterworth) and "iconic" (Urgo 44) specifically in reference to *O Pioneers!* The text that Ferris Greenslet said would establish Cather as "a novelist of the first rank" (qtd. in Woodress, *Life and Art* 159), *O Pioneers!* initiates the sequence of Nebraska novels that in turn made Cather a Nebraskan icon. In both lay and academic circles, Cather is equated with Nebraska in an iconographic way that belies the facts—she was not born there, she spent very little of her adult life there, and she is not buried there. And yet Cather is not connected with New York City (where she lived for more than forty years), Virginia (her birthplace), New Hampshire (where she is buried), or the Southwest (a prominent setting in *Song of the Lark*, *The Professor's House* and *Death Comes for the Archbishop*) in the way that she and Nebraska have become identified with each other. "Willa Cather" brings to mind the image (or icon) of a plow magnified against the sun, not a pub in Greenwich Village or even a turquoise set in dull silver. While it is arguable that someone like Gertrude Stein became an icon as much for how she lived as for what she wrote (particularly early in her literary career when she had trouble finding a publisher), it would seem that the private and reserved Cather became a cultural icon primarily through her literature. Cather describes writing *O Pioneers!* as a sort of homecoming: "this was like taking a ride through a familiar country on a horse that knew the way, on a fine morning when you felt like riding" (*Willa Cather on Writing* 92–93). She similarly places the idea of homecoming at the thematic center of the Old Testament, which she calls "that greatest record of the orphan soul trying to find its kin somewhere in the universe" (*Not Under Forty* 97).

Indeed, *O Pioneers!* serves as a foundational text in Cather's canon and one that sets the stage for Cather's use of the characters, devices, and worldview of the Old Testament in subsequent texts. As Granville Hicks observes, "*O Pioneers!* contains all the elements that, in varying proportions, were to enter into her later novels" (139). While critics have already laid essential groundwork by analyzing the role of Genesis in the text (esp. Creation and the Fall),[4] an expanded overview of some of the Old Testament echoes and parallels can further elucidate the iconography of this novel and thereby help to situate Cather herself within an iconographic tradition. A careful look at structure, characterization, theme, motif, and genre in *O Pioneers!* reveals that the Old Testament is, to a large extent, that which "is felt upon the page without being specifically named there" (*Not Under Forty* 50).

STRUCTURAL PARALLELS

Like the Pentateuch, *O Pioneers!* consists of five books, and like the book of Deuteronomy (literally a "second [telling of the] law"), "Alexandra" serves as a sort of reprise for the main action that takes place in the first four books. In addition, Cather utilizes the technique of envelope structure, prominent in the Psalms and much other biblical prose, defined by Robert Alter and Frank Kermode as "a formal organizing device frequently used by biblical writers in which the borders of a poetic or narrative unit are marked by repetition, at the end, of salient terms, phrases or clauses that appear at the beginning" (669). While it is significant that *O Pioneers!* begins and ends with Alexandra and Carl on the land, it is equally important that two of the main figures introduced at the beginning of the novel, Marie and Emil, are absent from the final scene, an illustration of another significant biblical pattern: repetition with a difference. This technique is also apparent in repeated references to the white mulberry tree, roses, ducks, and journeys (especially the comings and goings of Emil and Carl). Using repetition as a structuring device is a hallmark of Cather's modernism, and it is equally characteristic of biblical prose. Furthermore, Alter's assertion that in biblical narrative "there is never leisurely description for its own sake; scene setting is accomplished with the barest economy of means" (22) could be taken word-for-word from Cather's philosophy of the novel démeublé: "How wonderful it would be if we could throw all the furniture out of the window; and . . . leave the room as bare as the stage of a Greek theatre" (*Not Under Forty* 51).

Finally, even the composite structure of *O Pioneers!* is consistent with the composition of much biblical prose. As Keen Butterworth explains, Cather wrote "Alexandra" and "The White Mulberry Tree" and then "realized [the two] could be merged . . . to make a novel." David Stouck elaborates that the process took place over a period of several months and that the poem in the beginning, "Prairie Spring"—itself further evidence of genre blending—was part of Cather's writing process as well (Historical Essay 284–85). Rather than viewing composite structure as a flaw, biblical critics such as Alter liken it to other composite art, for example, the construction of great cathedrals, in which the presence of multiple artists does not take away from the greatness of the whole (25). Thus in both composition and form, Cather's iconic first Nebraska novel reveals a kinship with the Old Testament; the characters of the Old Testament resonate within Cather's text as well.

CHARACTERIZATION: IVAR AS OLD WORLD/ OLD TESTAMENT PROPHET

Crazy Ivar has been read variously as a religious mystic (Rosowski, *Voyage* 50), an embodiment of discomfort with sexual difference (Lindemann 37), a latter-day representation of the biblical Noah (Murphy, "Comprehensive" 115), an "early monastic desert Christian" (Schubnell 41), and one of a series of literary "wise fools." In addition to these comparisons, Ivar's emphasis on holiness through separateness echoes the ways of the Levitical priests. At the same time, the "spells" that periodically come upon Ivar, making him unlike himself and causing Alexandra's brothers to fear for her safety, further suggest the madness of Saul, the ill-fated warrior-king whose hybrid religio-political position is reflected bodily in his mysterious malady (Rosenberg 128). An "old-time" person (*O Pioneers!* 91) out of place in the New World and displaced from his property by an inability to manage it effectively, Ivar also bears a distinct resemblance to Old Testament prophets such as Jeremiah, Ezekiel, and Joel, all post-Exilic prophets who personally experience displacement and alienation.

To begin with, Jeremiah offers a precedent for the difficulties Ivar encounters in the New World, time and again facing a hostile audience and living under the ongoing threat of imprisonment. When Jeremiah prophesies doom to the Israelites, they respond on several occasions by having him beaten and imprisoned (Jeremiah 20:2, 26:8).[5] In Cather's novel, Lou and Oscar, who have neither honored Ivar's requests nor heeded his warnings, advise Alexandra to institutionalize Ivar herself before the neighbors complain and Ivar is "taken up by force" (95), a thinly veiled threat that Alexandra recognizes but refuses to be intimidated by.

In addition to sharing aspects of Jeremiah's fate, Ivar joins Jeremiah and Ezekiel in the practice of prophecy as performance, living, as well as speaking, his prophecies. While both Jeremiah and Ezekiel symbolically act out aspects of the nation's fate, Ezekiel in particular undergoes symbolic sufferings, including having to lie on his side for 430 days and eat coarse bread cooked on coals of animal dung in order to teach and heal his wayward people (Ezekiel 4:4–17). Ivar seems to have a similar approach to healing, as Oscar reports: "They say when horses have distemper he takes the medicine himself, then prays over the horses" (37). Carl confirms that when Ivar helped his family with a sick horse, "he kept patting her and groaning as if he had the pain himself" (36). Further, Ezekiel is frequently referred to in the biblical text as *Ben Adam*, variously translated as "Mortal," "Son of Man," or "Son of Earth." The third translation suggests a particular kinship with Ivar, who goes barefoot and "dislikes human habitations" (84). While Ezekiel is particularly known for his visions (e.g., the flaming chariot and the dead bones resurrected), Ivar believes that he is "despised . . . because I have visions" (88).

Although Ivar's visions alienate him from his neighbors, he reports that where he came from, he was not unusual: "At home, in the old country, there were many like me, who had been touched by God. . . . But here, if a man is different in his feet or in his head, they put him in the asylum" (88). Such was the case in biblical times as well, according to the Hebrew sages, who teach that there were many more prophets than the twenty or so recorded in the Old Testament, but that only those whose prophecies transcend their context and have relevance for later generations are recorded and passed on. Another biblical precedent for Ivar's attitudes and experiences comes from the book of Joel, which proclaims "a radical democratization of spiritual authority" (Marks 230): "After that, / I will pour out My spirit on all flesh; Your sons and daughters shall prophesy; / Your old men shall dream dreams, / and your young men shall see visions" (Joel 3:1). Also like Joel, Ivar accepts prophecy but not necessarily all of the aspects of law and ritual: "he had a peculiar religion of his own and could not get on with any of the denominations" (40). Hence, some of Ivar's difficulties spring from the disjuncture between the individualist approach he takes toward religion and the conformity insisted upon by most of his neighbors.

While Ivar shares Jeremiah's experiences, Ezekiel's media, and

Joel's attitudes, another important similarity between Ivar and the post-Exilic prophets is the shift in the role that each takes on after tragedy strikes and the concomitant shift in the tone of his message: condemnation to comfort. Once the great temple in Jerusalem has been destroyed, the prophets cease prophesying doom for the Israelites and instead speak of return to the Promised Land, reunification of the tribes of Israel, renewal of the covenant between God and his people, and rebuilding of the sanctuary. Ivar shares this role, for after he discovers "sin and death for the young ones" (242), he serves as Alexandra's caretaker and comforter. He looks after both her physical well-being and her psychological needs, fetching her by wagon from the graveyard during a storm and using biblical tones as he urges Signa: "When the eyes of the flesh are shut, the eyes of the spirit are open. She will have a message from those who are gone, and that will bring her peace. Until then we must bear with her" (246–47). In fact, the need for rebuilding and moving on in the face of tragedy is just one important thematic echo of the Old Testament in *O Pioneers!*

THEMATIC ECHOES

While the book of Genesis gives us the Creation story, the Garden of Eden, and paradise lost, it also introduces thematic elements such as the wanderings and generations of the forefathers, the tension between continuity and crisis, the necessity of sacrifice, the ties of brotherhood, and the destructive capacity of jealousy; *O Pioneers!* resonates with these themes, as well. For example, in Cather's novel, Lou's and Oscar's fear that Alexandra's accumulated wealth will go outside the family prompts them to run off her only suitor. Even her suspicions of their plans—later confirmed by Carl himself—cannot prevent Carl from being driven away. Furthermore, we learn that Frank is "jealous about everything, his farm and his horses and his pretty wife" (111). The harm caused by jealously permeates the Pentateuch from Cain's murderous jealously of Abel to the envy that prompts Joseph's brothers to stage his death and sell him into bondage, and it wreaks havoc on Cather's Divide, as well.

Looking beyond Genesis, the book of Numbers presents the wilderness as a testing ground, a theme that finds analogue in "The Wild Land" of *O Pioneers!* Indeed, while the fourth book of the Pentateuch does begin with a census and contain many numbers, this is not an accurate translation from the Hebrew. Rather, *Bamidbar* translates as "In the Wilderness," a much more fitting name for the biblical book and a clear parallel to the testing ground of the prairie's "Wild Land." While wandering in the desert and relying on God to provide for them, some Israelites repeatedly grumble about leaving the ills of Egypt for another, less certain set of ills in the desert, saying, "Oh, why did we ever leave Egypt!" (Numbers 11:20). Such grumbling usually provokes rebuke from Moses and yet another sign of God's omnipotence. The wanderings are full of tests—no food here, no water there—but the most important test involves spying out the Promised Land, a test that all but two of the spies (Joshua and Caleb) fail. The spies report: "The country that we traversed and scouted is one that devours its settlers. All the people that we saw in it are men of great size . . . and we looked like grasshoppers to ourselves, and so we must have looked to them" (Numbers 13:32–33). Hearing this account, the community directs its backlash to Moses and Aaron: "If only we had died in the land of Egypt . . . or if only we might die in this wilderness! Why is the Lord taking us to that land to fall by the sword? Our wives and children will be carried off! It would be better for us to go back to Egypt! . . . Let us head back for Egypt" (Numbers 14:2–4). Only Joshua and Caleb respond: "The land that we traversed and scouted is an exceedingly good land. If the Lord is pleased with us, he will bring us into that land, a land that flows with milk and honey, and give it to us; only you must not rebel against the Lord" (Numbers 14:8–9). As a result of the spies' lack of faith, the entire wilderness generation, save Joshua and Caleb, is fated to die outside the Promised Land.

The Divide in *O Pioneers!* tests its inhabitants, as well. It has "its little joke," as Alexandra calmly remarks in retrospect, but while it was "pretend[ing] to be poor" (108), it required sacrifice and faith from the farmers, and Alexandra's belief in the land is gauged in precisely these terms. Like the Israelites who grumbled in the desert, the pioneers on Cather's Divide have second thoughts about coming "to the end of the earth" (23), first leaving the Old Country and then abandoning steady jobs in the city for the unknowns of the frontier. For example, when the Linstrums give up on the land and return to St. Louis, where Mr. Linstrum will return to his factory job, Lou tries to convince Alexandra that "everybody who can crawl out is going away" (57). While Lou and Oscar contend that "it's too high to farm up here," Alexandra insists that "the land itself will be worth more than all we can ever raise on it" (58). Having gone to spy out the river farms, Alexandra tells Emil, "we must have faith in the high land" (63), the land of their father, and she transmits this attitude to Lou and Oscar. And when Lou demands a sign, asking "how do you *know* that land is going to go up enough to pay the mortgages," Alexandra can only offer him faith: "I can't explain that, Lou. You'll have to take my word for it. I *know*, that's all" (66). Lou objects that Alexandra's idea "must be crazy or everybody would be doing it," but Alexandra realizes that "the right thing is usually just what everybody doesn't do" (67). Like the Israelites who have a special destiny, Cather's epic farmers must chart their own path, trust their fathers, and show faith during difficult times.

Looking beyond the themes of the Pentateuch, the book of Isaiah provides additional prototypes of farming and fecundity motifs and a miraculous journey, echoed in Alexandra's trip to the river farms. Butterworth notes that "the land which at first seemed flat and monotonous proved to furnish endless variations on the theme of fertility." In Isaiah, "The future emerges as a seed shooting forth and opens for itself a way upward" (Schokel 178). Isaiah further prophesies that "The arid desert shall be glad, the wilderness shall rejoice and shall blossom like a rose" (35:1), while in Nebraska, "under the long shaggy ridges, [Alexandra] felt the future stirring" (69). Similarly, Isaiah later reports that "Truly the Lord has comforted Zion, comforted all her ruins; He has made her wilderness like Eden, Her desert like the Garden of the Lord" (51:3). Sixteen years after the opening of Cather's novel, the once-poor Divide has been transformed into a new Eden of rich farmland: "there is something frank and joyous and young in the open face of the country" (74). Clearly, the motif of seasonal renewal in *O Pioneers!* extends well beyond that of initial Creation.

Moving from the Prophets to *Ketuvim*, or the other collected writings of the Old Testament, the book of Ecclesiastes, which reminds us "to everything there is a season and a time to every purpose under the heaven" (3:1), also provides important thematic precedents for Cather's novel. Ecclesiastes stands out in the Old Testament for its basic secularity: the locus of authority is not God or tradition but individual experience. Indeed, its emphasis on realism, experimentation, and cyclical patterns suggests that everyone must struggle to find his or her own answers: try out, build up, destroy, and move on. The Hebrew sages explain that the paired lines that make up the famous third chapter[6] do not fall into a predictable pattern—for example, stating the good and then the bad—because life itself has no order. Instead, Ecclesiastes offers a realistic outlook on life, suggesting that the key to happiness is not to avoid difficult times but to know how to handle them when they come. Furthermore, the cycles put things in perspective, reminding us that the pendulum will come back around. These are lessons that Alexandra learns firsthand. The opening words of Ecclesiastes, *Hevel hevalim*, have been variously translated as "vanity of vanities" or "utter futility," but they also connote that which is ephemeral or fleeting, suggesting that everything in this world is constantly changing and short-lived and that therefore we must make the most of our time here. Certainly Alexandra senses the basic ephemerality that forms the backbone of Ecclesiastes when she tells Carl, "the land belongs to the future. . . . We come and go, but the land is always here. And the people who love it and understand it are the people who own it—for a little while" (272–73).

MOTIF: THE PROMISED LAND

The land is "the great fact" (*O Pioneers!* 11) in Nebraska, in Cather's writing, and in the Old Testament. And once the pioneers learn to farm the land productively, it becomes, as Carl notes, a land of "milk and honey" (110). In *O Pioneers!* the land takes on a special status; as Butterworth observes, "the sacredness of landscape is evoked with spiritual intensity." Cather's novel chronicles the creation and ordering of the land,[7] but it also records the conquering and settling of land, the focus of the biblical book of Joshua. Indeed, the book of Joshua is divided into two nearly equal sections: chapters 1–12 recount the conquering of the land, while chapters 13–22 focus on the Israelites' efforts to become a people in the land.[8] Further, the promise of the land, preparation for entering the land, attaining and conquering the land, becoming a people in the land, and striving to retain and then to regain the land form the crux of the bulk of the Pentateuch and the Prophets (from Genesis to Malachi). Because the Promised Land is a special inheritance that God has set aside for his chosen people, the books of Numbers, Deuteronomy, and Joshua contain numerous injunctions to the Israelites to separate themselves from the practices and beliefs of the nations who currently occupy it: "When the Lord your God has cut down before you the nations that you are about to enter and dispossess, and you have dispossessed them and settled in their land, beware of being lured into their ways after they have been wiped out before you! Do not inquire about their gods, saying 'How did those nations worship their gods? I too will follow those practices'" (Deuteronomy 12:29–30). Although Alexandra is willing to listen to college graduates, the land itself, and her own heart, her conservative brothers resist doing anything that might make them stand out: "they hated experiments and . . . disliked to do anything different from their neighbors" (47). Not surprisingly, it is to Alexandra that the "Genius of the Divide . . . bent lower than it ever bent to a human will before" (64).

Alexandra's success is not unmitigated, however. She links her success on the land with that of her "tended-hearted" boy (55), Emil, and she reflects: "Yes, . . . it had been worth while; both Emil and the country had become what she had hoped. Out of her father's children there was one who was fit to cope with the world, who had not been tied to the plow, and who had a personality apart from the soil. And that, she reflected, was what she had worked for. She felt well satisfied with her life" (191). It is at precisely this moment that the Nebraskan landscape exacts its toll. Alexandra's efforts toward continuity and freedom are cut off by Emil's death. The very best (Emil, Marie, and even Amedee) do not live to enjoy the land's fruits, seemingly singled out because they are the best, as Carl surmises: "he was the best there was, I suppose. They were both the best you had here" (271). In the Old Testament, Moses was a prophet like no other, as Deuteronomy relates: "never again did there arise in Israel a prophet like Moses—whom the Lord singled out, face to face" (34:10). He sees God's face, leads his people out of Egypt, shepherds them through forty years of wandering in the desert, and brings them to the brink of the Jordan only to be condemned to die on the far side. And while Alexandra has a special relationship with the prairie, she cannot foresee or prevent the events that occur under the white mulberry tree, events that threaten to negate everything she has accomplished. Just as Moses is credited with delivering the tablets from Sinai and recording the Pentateuch but cannot make the crossing himself, Alexandra realizes that the story of the Divide is written "with the best we have" (272).

GENRE: SONG OF SONGS AND "THE WHITE MULBERRY TREE"

While what happens under "The White Mulberry Tree" contains elements of the Garden of Eden motif (Murphy, "Comprehensive" 113–17; Rosowski, *Voyage* 54) and draws on the Greek pastoral tradition (Rosowski, *Voyage* 54), this section of *O Pioneers!* also has important connections to the biblical pastoral, Song of Songs, a love poem that uses juxtaposition of images (especially red and white) to explore the tension between unity and disunity and the dual-edged nature of love. Narrative cannot be the point of "The White Mulberry Tree," as Elizabeth Janeway observes: the story itself is "ancient" and "often told" (xii). Along similar lines, Francis Landy argues that Song of Songs offers "no 'story' . . . , no truth, only a set of anecdotes, hovering between reality and dream, that exemplify the relationships of lovers" (316). Cather's novel and the biblical pastoral also share a prevalent image pattern: "the interplay of white and red evokes a powerful symbolic contrast (purity versus sexuality)" (Landy 309). This juxtaposition recurs throughout *O Pioneers!* whenever the mulberry tree and the orchard are mentioned: when Alexandra brings Carl to visit Marie, we are told that "wild roses were flaming in the tufts of bunchgrass along the fence," immediately followed by information about the "white mulberry tree" (124). When Emil agrees to mow the orchard for Marie, he finishes to find her "sitting under her white mulberry tree, the pailful of cherries beside her" (138). Finally, Ivar discovers "white mulberries . . . covered with dark stain" (240); this image is paralleled by a scene that tells the other half of the story: "two white butterflies from Frank's alfalfa field were fluttering in and out among the interlacing shadows . . . and in the long grass by the fence the last wild roses of the year opened their pink hearts to die" (241).

Thematically, the warning of Song of Songs, "For love is fierce as death, Passion is mighty as Sheol" (8:6),[9] is embodied in Frank's jealous rage and the subsequent death of the lovers. Landy further reminds us that love "is the bond of a vital society" but can "also threaten . . . social order" (318). Lack of awareness of this potential threat to the social order is precisely what blinds Alexandra to the developing passion between Emil and Marie: "she wondered at herself now, but she had never thought of danger in that direction. If Marie had been unmarried,—oh yes. Then she would have kept her eyes open. But the mere fact that she was Shabata's wife, for Alexandra, settled everything. . . . Now, Alexandra could in a measure realize that Marie was, after all Marie; not merely a 'married woman'" (253). Marie's heroic last act of dragging herself to her beloved, "his brows . . . drawn in a frown," and her "look of ineffable content" (241) suggest another central theme of Song of Songs, as Landy explains: "the disunity is also that of the lovers, whose work of integration can never be completed" (316). It is perhaps on the strength of the ideals of Song of Songs that Alexandra chooses to visit Frank and work to have him pardoned. For the biblical pastoral is ultimately a love story about relationships—between a lover and a beloved, between God and the Israelites, and between the sometimes contradictory impulses within a single human heart.

CONCLUSION: FIERCE REPETITION

As perhaps the most enduring and influential text in Western literature, the Bible serves as a crucial foundation for Cather's work, and one that goes far beyond the interesting and important echoes of early Genesis to encompass structure, characterization, theme, motif, and genre across a number of biblical texts. Understanding how the various iconic elements of the Old Testament have been employed and transformed in *O Pioneers!* is an important first step that can only enhance our appreciation for Cather's literary accomplishments and their enduring qualities. Indeed, the Old Testament is a prime source of those "two or three human stories [that] go on repeating themselves as fiercely as if they had never happened before" (110).

Such stories recur throughout Cather's canon; in subsequent texts she will use the elements that she establishes centrally in *O Pioneers!* in iconographic ways, reassembling them to create new variations on familiar themes. As Merrill Skaggs explains, Cather "relied from the beginning through the end of her career on a repertory of trusted devices to get her to her desired new goals" (12). Thus, it would seem possible and indeed essential to systematically explore an iconography of Cather, highlighting other such broadly based biblical techniques as type-scenes, leitwort, and sequence-of-action repetitions across Cather's corpus. Through tapping into an iconographic biblical tradition and creating her own literary iconography, Cather lays the groundwork for becoming a cultural icon herself, fulfilling her own oft-quoted pronouncement: "every artist makes himself born" (*Song of the Lark* 153). Cather's journey and our investigation begin with the Old Testament echoes in *O Pioneers!*

NOTES

1. Arnold believes that Cather's early exposure to the Bible had a formative effect: "I find in Cather's work biblical echoes that suggest an important source, or at least a confirmation, of her values. Her grandfather Cather was a devoted reader of the King James Bible, and her grandmother Boak regularly read to young Willa from the Bible"

("After All" 230–31). Stout confirms that Cather's "early reading, directed largely by her maternal grandmother, Rachel Boak, included such religious standards as *Pilgrim's Progress* and the Protestant Bible" (9). Woodress further contends that Cather "absorbed [the Bible] so thoroughly that her writing throughout her life is loaded with biblical quotations and allusions" (*Literary Life* 23). In terms of the influence of the Bible on the texts Cather produced, Rosowski identifies a "biblical vision" in Cather's early story "Lou, the Prophet" ("Subverted Endings"), while Giannone sees biblical echoes extending all the way to Cather's last novel, *Sapphira and the Slave Girl*.

2. In his 1913 review, Frederic Taber Cooper similarly calls the novel a "slow-moving . . . tale," an observation admittedly not meant as a compliment in this case.

3. Studies that explore Cather's use of biblical allusions include Arnold, "The Allusive Cather"; Giannone; Murphy, "Comprehensive"; Rosowski, "Subverted Endings"; and Stouck, *Imagination*. *Willa Cather and the Culture of Belief* (ed. Murphy) offers fifteen essays that emphasize religious implications of Cather's biblical references; most of these essays focus their attention mainly on Christian scripture rather than the Old Testament. Murphy's "Biblical and Religious Dimensions of *My Ántonia*" both charts biblical allusions and explores religious ramifications.

4. Murphy's analytical overview of *O Pioneers!* includes a section titled "The Genesis Dimension," in which he traces several important biblical motifs in Cather's text. These include creation of order and light from chaos, the blind Isaac's deathbed instructions to his feuding sons, Noah's relationship to the animals, and sin and death in the Garden of Eden ("Comprehensive" 114–17). Rosowski argues that "the biblical Garden of Eden is evoked in the general setting of the Shabata orchard, where Maria and Emil play in apparent childlike innocence and where danger takes the form of a snake," but she notes that Cather's story goes on to introduce "enormous differences . . . mak[ing] a 'fit' between characters and myth impossible" (*Voyage* 54, 56). Stouck notes that the novel employs two important Genesis motifs: "Alexandra's is the story of creation . . . [while] Emil and Marie's is the story of lovers cast from the earth's Garden through sin" (*Imagination* 31).

5. All biblical citations come from *Tanakh: The Holy Scriptures* (Philadelphia: Jewish Publication Society, 1985), except for the quotation of Ecclesiastes 3:1–8 in note 6, which is reproduced in its best-known translation, the King James Version.

6. The section reads as follows:

> To everything there is a season, and a time to every purpose
> under the heaven:

a time to be born, and a time to die;
a time to plant, and a time to pluck up that which is planted;
a time to kill, and a time to heal;
a time to break down, and a time to build up;
a time to weep, and a time to laugh;
a time to mourn, and a time to dance;
a time to cast away stones, and a time to gather stones together;
a time to embrace, and a time to refrain from embracing;
a time to get, and a time to lose;
a time to keep, and a time to cast away;
a time to rend, and a time to sew;
a time to keep silence, and a time to speak;
a time to love, and a time to hate;
a time of war, and a time of peace.
—*(Ecclesiastes 3:1–8)*

7. Murphy argues that "In part 2, 'Neighboring Fields,' set thirteen years later, order has indeed come to the wild land—creation is complete and the earth fruitful" ("Comprehensive" 116).

8. Gunn finds a thematic message in this formal division: "the taking of Jericho and Ai and the other campaigns dramatically recounted in chapters 1–12 sweep us along in a vision of easy success. Chapters 13–21 implicitly suggest that occupation involves much more. They also establish a sense of ambivalence which will not readily be resolved" (103).

9. The Hebrew word *Sheol* is sometimes translated as "the grave" or "the netherworld," but it expresses a concept that cannot readily be translated into English. Hence, many translations use the transliteration of the Hebrew instead of trying to come up with an English equivalent.

WORKS CITED

Ackerman, James. "Numbers." Alter and Kermode. 78–91.

Alter, Robert. "Introduction to the Old Testament." Alter and Kermode. 11–35.

Alter, Robert, and Frank Kermode, eds. *The Literary Guide to the Bible*. Cambridge MA: Belknap P, 1987.

Arnold, Marilyn. "The Allusive Cather." *Cather Studies* 3 (1996): 137–48. *The Willa Cather Archive*. 4 Mar. 2004. http://www.cather.unl.edu.

———. "Willa Cather after All." *Willa Cather and the Culture of Belief*. Ed. John Murphy. Provo UT: Brigham Young UP, 2002. 229–38.

Bloom, Harold. *The Western Canon*. New York: Riverhead Books, 1994.

Butterworth, Keen. Rev. of *O Pioneers! Scholarly Edition*, by Willa Cather. 4 Dec. 2002. http://www.msstate.edu/Archives/TEXT/vol9/cather.html.

Cather, Willa. *Not Under Forty*. 1922. Lincoln: U of Nebraska P, 1988.

———. *O Pioneers!* 1913. Willa Cather Scholarly Edition. Ed. Susan J. Rosowski and Charles W. Mignon with Kathleen Danker. Historical essay and explanatory notes David Stouck. Lincoln: U of Nebraska P, 1992.

———. *The Song of the Lark*. 1915. New York: Signet, 1991.

———. *Willa Cather on Writing*. 1920. Lincoln: U of Nebraska P, 1988.

Cooper, Frederic Taber. Rev. of *O Pioneers! Bookman* 37.6 (1913): 666–67. Rpt. in *Twentieth-Century Literary Criticism*, vol 11. The Gale Group, 2004. *Literature Resource Center*. 4 Mar. 2004. http://galenet.galegroup.com/servlet/LitRC.

Cowley, Malcolm. *And I Worked at the Writer's Trade*. New York: Viking P, 1978.

Giannone, Richard. "Willa Cather and the Unfinished Drama of Deliverance." *Prairie Schooner* 52 (spring 1978): 25–46.

Gunn, David. "Joshua and Judges." Alter and Kermode 102–21.

Hicks, Granville. "The Case against Willa Cather." *Willa Cather and Her Critics*. Ed. James Schroeter. Ithaca: Cornell UP, 1967. 139–47.

Hoover, Sharon, ed. *Willa Cather Remembered*. Lincoln: U of Nebraska P, 2002.

Janeway, Elizabeth. Introduction. *O Pioneers!* By Willa Cather. 1913. New York: Signet, 1989. ix–xxi.

Landy, Francis. "The Song of Songs." Alter and Kermode. 305–19.

Lindemann, Marilee. *Willa Cather: Queering America*. New York: Columbia UP, 1999.

Marks, Herbert. "The Twelve Prophets." Alter and Kermode. 207–33.

Murphy, John J. "Biblical and Religious Dimensions of *My Ántonia*." *Approaches to Teaching Cather's* My Ántonia. Ed. Susan Rosowski. New York: Modern Language Association of America, 1989. 77–82.

———. "A Comprehensive View of Cather's *O Pioneers!*" *Critical Essays on Willa Cather*. Ed. John J. Murphy. Boston: G. K. Hall, 1984. 113–27.

———, ed. *Willa Cather and the Culture of Belief*. Provo UT: Brigham Young UP, 2002.

Rosenberg, Joel. "1 and 2 Samuel." Alter and Kermode. 122–45.

Rosowski, Susan J. *The Voyage Perilous: Willa Cather's Romanticism.* Lincoln: U of Nebraska P, 1986.

———. "Willa Cather's Subverted Endings and Gendered Time." *Cather Studies* 1 (1990): 68–88. *The Willa Cather Archive.* 4 Mar. 2004. http://www.cather.unl.edu.

Schokel, Luis Alonso. "Isaiah." Alter and Kermode. 165–83.

Schubnell, Matthias. "Religion and Ecology on the Divide: Ivar's Monasticism in *O Pioneers!*" *Willa Cather and the Culture of Belief.* Ed. John Murphy. Provo UT: Brigham Young UP, 2002. 41–49.

Skaggs, Merrill. *After the World Broke in Two: The Later Novels of Willa Cather.* Charlottesville: U of Virginia P, 1990.

Stouck, David. Historical Essay. *O Pioneers!* By Willa Cather. 1913. Willa Cather Scholarly Edition. Lincoln: U of Nebraska P, 1992.

———. *Willa Cather's Imagination.* Lincoln: U of Nebraska P, 1975.

Stout, Janis P. "Faith Statements and Nonstatements in Willa Cather's Personal Letters." *Willa Cather and the Culture of Belief.* Ed. John Murphy. Provo UT: Brigham Young UP, 2002. 7–27.

Urgo, Joseph R. *Willa Cather and the Myth of American Migration.* Urbana: U of Illinois P, 1995.

Woodress, James. *Willa Cather: A Literary Life.* Lincoln: U of Nebraska P, 1987.

———. *Willa Cather: Her Life and Art.* Lincoln: U of Nebraska P, 1970.

Barbusse's *L'enfer*
A Source for "Coming, Aphrodite!" and "The Novel Démeublé"

RICHARD C. HARRIS

Anyone who has read a great deal of Willa Cather's work cannot help but realize that she was an ardent Francophile. Whether it was painting or literature—or cooking—Cather from an early age was convinced that the French had developed the arts to the highest degree. In an 1895 article written for the *Nebraska State Journal* she declared that if that "very little country" should someday slide into the English Channel "there would not be much creative power of any sort left in the world" ("Dumas" 223).

In 1933 Dorothy Canfield Fisher remembered that while she and Cather were students at the University of Nebraska in the 1890s, Cather "amazed and sometimes abashed some of her professors by caring more for their subjects than they did. Especially French. There seemed to be a natural affinity between her mind and French forms of art. During her undergraduate years she made it a loving duty to read every French literary masterpiece she could lay her hands on" (9). Moreover, George Seibel, recounting his experience reading French masterpieces with Cather during her Pittsburgh years, said that their reading "covered a vast territory" (196). In his assessment of Cather's French connections, Michel Gervaud declared in 1974 that Cather's "imbibing of French literature was to be intense and prolonged until her last years" (72). And James Woodress noted in his 1993 article on Cather and Alphonse Daudet that in the index to his biography of Cather he found the names of twenty-six French writers whom she had read (156).

As would be expected, Woodress's list includes the nineteenth-century giants, among them Balzac, Daudet (Cather's favorite), Dumas (*pére* and *fils*), Flaubert, Hugo, Maupassant, Merrimée, Musset, Sand, Verlaine, and Zola. To that list we must add the name of the twentieth-century journalist, short-story writer, novelist, biographer, and essayist Henri Barbusse (1873–1935). It was probably through his war novel *Le feu* (*Under Fire*) that Cather came to know of Barbusse, and she may well have found some useful background information for her own "war novel," *One of Ours*, in that book. Barbusse's novel *L'enfer* (*The Inferno*), however, was almost certainly an even more important source, providing what Henry James called the "germ" for Cather's 1920 short story "Coming, Aphrodite!" and suggesting some of the central ideas in her 1922 essay "The Novel Démeublé."

Le feu, originally published in French in 1916 and then in English under the title *Under Fire* in 1917, came out of Barbusse's firsthand experience in World War I. Having joined the French army filled with patriotic spirit and moral fervor, Barbusse suffered a terrible sense of disillusionment in the face of that apocalyptic horror which would lead him to become one of France's most outspoken pacifists in the postwar period. In *Under Fire* he describes the brutal dilemma of the common soldier as no one before him had. In the late 1910s and early 1920s the novel was generally considered the greatest European account of the war, and it was certainly the most popular such account until the publication of Remarque's much shorter *All Quiet on the Western Front* in 1929.

Contemporary reviewers were struck by the awful truthfulness of *Under Fire*. Francis Hackett, writing in the *New Republic*, asserted, "No description of bombardment surpasses M. Barbusse's, even in translation. And no description of going forward, so it seems to me, can equal his chapter Under Fire" (358). Another reviewer found the novel a powerful indictment of modern war, "a grim book with a vengeance" (Gwynn 805). Robert Herrick, in his comment in the *Dial*, titled "Unromantic War," called *Under Fire* "the most searching, the most revealing statement of what modern war means both morally and physically" (133). In his 1926 essay, Brian Rhys stated, "The conviction comes that *Under Fire* will remain on record as the greatest novel of its kind" (xii); a half century later, in the 1976 article "Henri Barbusse: 'Le feu' and the Crisis of Social Realism," Jonathan King argued that *Under Fire* was not merely a major war novel but that its publication marked "a key moment" in the history of social realist fiction (46).

It was not merely the literary establishment or a European audience that read the book, however. In his 1919 *New Republic* review of Barbusse's volume of short stories *We Others*, John Manning Booker observed, "Americans consumed *Under Fire* by the tens of thousands; thrilled, throbbed, and ached over it" (146). Willa Cather must certainly have been one of those readers. She very likely looked at Barbusse's *Under Fire* in doing the research—what she called the "gathering" of materials—for *One of Ours*, which she began writing in late 1918. In *Memorial Fictions: Willa Cather and the First World War*, Steven Trout notes not only that Barbusse's novel likely was one of Cather's sources for information on the war but also that there are striking similarities between macabre descriptions of bodies of the dead in Barbusse's chapter "The Doorway" and Cather's description of bodies found by Claude Wheeler and David Gerhardt in the Boar's Head trench in book 5 of *One of Ours*.

Having noted this likely connection between Cather and Barbusse's *Under Fire*, let us focus on two other connections with Barbusse that are even more obvious. They involve another extremely popular Barbusse novel, *L'enfer*, originally published in France in 1908, and published in English under the title *The Inferno* in 1918. Although, as Woodress points out, Cather read French with ease, an English translation, published in New York by Boni and Liveright in 1918, would have been readily available to her. The title page of that edition reads: "The Inferno, by Henri Barbusse, Author of Under Fire; Translated from the *100th* [emphasis mine] French Edition with an Introduction by Edward J. O'Brien."

O'Brien's opening remarks include the following statement: "'L'Enfer' has been more widely read and discussed in France than any other realistic study since the days of Zola. The French sales of the volume, in 1917 alone, exceeded a hundred thousand copies, a popularity made all the more remarkable from the fact that its appeal is based as much on its philosophical substance as on the story it tells" (9). While there is no recorded mention of Barbusse in Cather's letters, Elizabeth Sergeant, recalling the period of the late 1910s, says, "Willa was always happy to know of new French authors, whom she preferred to new American authors" (157). Given the widespread interest in Barbusse's novel, Cather as an avid reader of French literature would hardly have been unaware of, or unfamiliar with, *The Inferno*. And given her attempts to hide or disguise her sources, it is understandable that references to Barbusse do not appear in her correspondence.

By the winter of 1919–20 Cather felt she needed a break from work on *One of Ours*, which she later told Fisher had become an obsession with her. As Woodress puts it, "During the Christmas season of 1919 Cather took a break from her novel and wrote a long story just for fun, an uncharacteristic act but one that turned out well" (*A Literary Life* 309). By this time Cather had become dissatisfied with her publisher, Houghton Mifflin, and was considering offers from several New York publishers who seemed to like her work more, chief among them Alfred A. Knopf. Knopf, at twenty-three (and as he put, "full of *chutzpah*"), had founded his own publishing company in New York in the late spring of 1915, and in the late 1910s he was aggressively pursuing writers to add to his list. He wooed Cather with offers to publish a volume of short stories—in fact, to reprint a number of stories from the earlier volume *The Troll Garden* (1905) while she completed her novel. On 1 February 1920, Cather and Knopf agreed to a contract for the volume of short stories, a move that changed the course of Cather's whole artistic career.

Youth and the Bright Medusa was published in September 1920, with four stories from the earlier volume ("Paul's Case," "A Wagner Matinée," "The Sculptor's Funeral," and "'A Death in the Desert'"); three more recent stories, previously published in magazines ("The Diamond Mine," "A Gold Slipper," and "Scandal"); and one new story, "Coming, Aphrodite!" The gem, without a doubt, was "Coming, Aphrodite!," which had been published in the *Smart Set* in August as "Coming, Eden Bower!" Critics simply raved about the story. The reviewer for the *Nation* said that Cather here had completely achieved the effect she was after; another said the story had been written with "the utmost skill, and the deftest effects of descriptive incident." H. L. Mencken declared that "Coming, Aphrodite!" showed "utterly competent workmanship in every line." The reviewer for the *New York Times* called the publication of *Youth and the Bright Medusa* "decidedly a literary event" and said that if Cather had written nothing except "Coming, Aphrodite!" "there could be no doubt of her right to rank beside the greatest creative artists of the day" (O'Connor 99–104).

Certainly one of the most striking elements in the story is the embedded narrative, "The Forty Lovers of the Queen," a violent Aztec fertility tale that Don Hedger tells Eden Bower. As Cather scholars have long known, Cather wrote Sergeant in 1912 that the story had been told to her by a young Mexican singer during Cather's visit to her brother Douglass in Winslow, Arizona, in the summer of that year. The other particularly fascinating detail of "Coming, Aphrodite!," the premise of the story, the Jamesian *donné*, involves Don Hedger's discovering a hole in the wall of a closet in his apartment, which enables him to look into the room next door and observe its occupants. The incident has long fascinated Cather readers. Woodress calls the account of discovery "one of the most remarkable scenes Cather ever wrote" (*A Literary Life* 313).

Cather did write a remarkable story, but she clearly did not invent the remarkable scene. That scene, as well as other details in "Coming, Aphrodite!," in fact, almost certainly came right out of Barbusse's *The Inferno*. Barbusse's novel begins with a thirty-year-old unnamed narrator alone in a room he has just taken in a Paris boardinghouse. Cather's Don Hedger is twenty-six years old. Both men have been on their own for years: Barbusse's character had lost his mother and father "eighteen or twenty years before" (19), and Cather's character had been a foundling and "had grown up in a school for homeless boys" (17). Reflecting on his life, Barbusse's narrator notes, "I was unmarried. I had no children and shall have none" (19). Cather's Don Hedger is "singularly unencumbered; he had no family ties, no social ties, no obligations" (17).

In "Coming, Aphrodite!" Don Hedger has lived for four years on the top floor of an old house on Washington Square. Like that of Barbusse's narrator, his room is dark, "very cheerless, since he never got a ray of direct sunlight" (11). In Barbusse's novel, the door between the narrator's room and the room next door is "always kept locked" (30); in Cather's story, Hedger's apartment is separated from the one next door by "bolted double doors" (13).

Early in Barbusse's novel, his narrator, looking over some notes after a long day of travel, says, "I heard a song hummed quite close to my ear. . . . The singing came from the room next to mine." Barbusse continues:

> Why was it so pure, so strangely near? Why did it touch me so? I looked at the wall between the two rooms, and stifled a cry of surprise.
>
> High up, near the ceiling above the door, always kept locked, there was a light. The song fell from that star.
>
> There was a crack in the partition at that spot, through which the light of the next room entered the night of mine.
>
> I climbed up on the bed, and my face was on a level with the crack. Rotten woodwork, two loose bricks. The plaster gave way and an opening appeared as large as my hand, but invisible from below, because of the moulding.
>
> I looked. I beheld. The next room presented itself to my sight freely. (30–31)

In Cather's story, Don Hedger makes a remarkably similar discovery. One afternoon shortly after a new neighbor has moved into the apartment next door, Hedger is cleaning out his clothes closet. Cather tells us,

> When he took his overcoat from its place against the partition [between the two rooms], a long ray of yellow light shot across the dark enclosure,—a knot hole, evidently, in the high wainscoating [*sic*] of the west room. He had never noticed it before, and without realizing what he was doing, he stooped and squinted through it.

> Yonder in a pool of sunlight, stood his new neighbour, wholly unclad, doing exercises of some sort before a long gilt mirror. (26)

Both men are stunned by their views into the adjoining rooms—Hedger, obviously, more so. For both, peering through the hole becomes an obsession. Barbusse's narrator says that he "could not tear his eyes from" the room next door (53). For Cather's character, "the pull of that aperture was stronger than his will. . . . This thing . . . drank him up" (30). What happens in the two narratives after this initial shock and fascination, however, is quite different.

Over a period of several weeks Barbusse's narrator observes a number of different individuals and couples in the room next door: a hotel maid who reads and kisses a letter, apparently from her lover; an adolescent boy and girl who have discovered the thrill of first love and have sneaked into the room to be alone together; a frustrated young woman trapped in an empty and monotonous marriage, who has escaped there with her lover; another woman, pregnant, who is there with her terminally ill husband.

While there is a voyeuristic element to the book, Barbusse's real interest is not in the prurient possibilities of the narrator's situation but rather in the opportunity to observe the truths behind the lives of those who enter the room. Of his glimpse of the maid, his speaker says, "And that simple gesture of kissing the paper, that gesture buried in a room, stripped bare by the dark, had something sublime and awesome in it" (34). Realizing the essential differences between the young married woman and her lover, he remarks, "And suddenly the veil fell from my eyes, and reality lay stripped before me. I saw that between these two people there was an immense difference, like an infinite discord, sublime to behold because of its depths, but so painful that it bruised my heart" (70).

Barbusse's characters all suffer a modern malaise in a contemporary Dantean inferno, a world without God. They are painfully alienated from each other, they desperately cling to the false hope that relationships—love—can free them from their loneliness, and they are overwhelmed by a terrible awareness of their mortality. Malcolm Cowley said in 1922 that the books Barbusse wrote before 1914 (*The Inferno* was originally published in 1908) were "so blackly pessimistic that Schopenhauer beside them seems a booster for the Rotary Club" (180). As Colin Wilson has noted, Barbusse's unnamed narrator is the Outsider, the modern man alienated by his vision of the truth and his insistence on confronting it. In a word, *Under Fire* is a remarkable early existential text.

While it seems clear that Cather "borrowed" (T. S. Eliot said, "Young writers imitate; mature writers steal") the defining event from Barbusse's novel, her story has a much different tone and takes a much different direction after Don Hedger discovers the hole in the wainscoting of his room. Hedger is sexually aroused by the vision of the woman next door, becomes infatuated with the young diva Eden Bower, and carries on a brief affair with her that ends in a dispute over the relationship between artistic integrity and popular success. When Hedger insists that he, like any other real artist, works only for himself, Eden asks incredulously, "You mean you could make money and don't? That you don't try to get a public?" (66). Days after the disagreement, Eden leaves New York to pursue her ambitions. After years of "spectacular success" in Paris, she returns in triumph to New York. Curious about what had happened to Hedger, she looks up the art dealer M. Jules, who reveals that Hedger is a highly respected though not wealthy artist, and remarks, "But Madame, there are many kinds of success" (77).

Marilyn Arnold has surmised that the newer stories in *Youth and the Bright Medusa*, "like *The Song of the Lark*, probably had their genesis in Cather's meeting and subsequent friendship with [the Swedish-born opera singer] Olive Fremstad" (106), and Woodress speculates that "Coming, Aphrodite!" must have given Cather the idea for the volume as a whole. With her earlier success as editor of *McClure's* magazine and particularly with the very recent triumph of *My Ántonia*, Cather at this point in her life, circa 1920, was clearly pondering the causes, consequences, and meaning of fame and fortune; in finally coming to know the pleasures of success (though real financial success would only come in the next couple of years), she also no doubt had developed a heightened awareness of the dangers of same to the serious artist. A reading of *The Inferno* certainly would have provided additional food for thought.

Toward the end of *The Inferno*, the narrator enters a large restaurant. In the room he is saddened by overheard bits of conversation that surprise him with their "persiflage" and "consistent irony" (234). Amid the "general hubbub," he is particularly interested in a M. Villiers, a famous writer, who is holding court, and in Villiers's claim that he is currently writing a novel the theme of which is Truth, "a succession of human beings caught just as they are" (235). The novel begins, Villiers relates, with the following event: "A man pierces a hole in the wall of a boarding-house room, and watches what is going on in the next room" (236).

Initially astonished by the coincidence between the experiences he has actually had for the last month and the scenario the author describes, Barbusse's narrator is then angered by the glibness with which the popular writer describes what he has written thus far: "he retailed a lot of amusing oddities, described comical persons and things, heaped up picturesque and piquant details, coined typical and witty proper names, and invented complicated and ingenious situations. He succeeded in producing irresistible effects, and the whole was in the latest style" (237). The crowd in the restaurant responds with "Ahs" and "Ohs" and cries of "Bravo" as the writer, in the narrator's words, continues "to travesty the truth" (238). "Thank God," Villiers exclaims, "I am a writer, and not a thinker" (237).

Returning to his room and once again drawn irresistibly to look into the adjoining room, Barbusse's narrator hears the lover of the frustrated young married woman describing a meeting he had had with a poor woman and her baby on the street earlier that evening. The young man, who had been deeply touched and inspired by the divine beauty of that woman in rags and had written a poem about her and the child, "seemed to be searching for something, to be seeing things, and believing infinitely. He was in another world where everything we see is true and everything we say is unforgettable" (241). Is not the contrast established in these two characters—the popular, glib writer who superficially sees the tales of those characters in his novel merely as "amusements" to be used to gain literary success and popularity, and the truly sensitive, unknown poet who recognizes the essential human tragedy and artistic possibility in that poor woman's smile—very similar to that which Cather establishes between Eden Bower and Don Hedger in "Coming, Aphrodite!"? Might Barbusse's novel perhaps have provided not only the *donné* for the first story in *Youth and the Bright Medusa* but also solidified a fundamental theme for the volume as a whole?

Finally, there is a possible connection between Barbusse's *The Inferno* and Cather's 1922 essay "The Novel Démeublé." There Cather declares, "In any discussion of the novel, one must make it clear whether one is talking about the novel as a form of amusement, or as a form of art" (35), and she deplores the cheapness of the novel "manufactured to entertain great multitudes of people" (36), much as Barbusse's narrator deplores the work of the facile, popular author in the restaurant, who finds the lives of his characters merely "amusing" (237). The narrator of *The Inferno* is dedicated to an ideal, Truth. His observations through the peephole as an unknown observer have given him insights into what is "real," the tragic dilemma of the human condition, which almost defies expression.

The lover-poet describing the profound significance of his meeting with the simple woman on the street has been overwhelmed by what he has experienced. He tells his mistress that the experience with the poor woman has "pierced [his] heart" (241) and revealed to him a higher truth. In "The Novel Démeublé" Cather asserts that "realism" is not merely a matter of "cataloguing" details but rather is "an attitude of mind on the part of the writer toward his material, a vague indication of the sympathy and candour with which he accepts, rather than chooses, his theme" (37). "The higher processes of art," she continues, "are all processes of simplification" that lead to "a higher and truer effect" (40).

Barbusse's narrator has come to understand the truths to be discovered by those individuals and true artists who honestly seek or are open to them, and who understand that realization of them often challenges or defies expression. "I have such respect for the actual truth," Barbusse's narrator tells us, "that there are moments when I do not dare to call things by their name" (244). "Whatever is felt upon the page without being specifically named there," Cather says in "The Novel Démeublé," "that one might say, is created. It is the inexplicable presence of the thing not named, of the overtone divined by the ear but not heard by it, the verbal mood, the emotional aura of the fact or the thing or the deed, that gives high quality to the novel or the drama, as well as to poetry itself" (41–42). The similarities in both phrasing and meaning are striking.

Finally, might Barbusse's novel even have suggested the title for Cather's essay? What dark but beautiful truths emerge from that room, "stripped bare by the dark" (*The Inferno* 34), into which Barbusse's narrator peers. That room, figuratively "unfurnished," now unseen, is exactly what Cather describes at the end of her essay: a scene left "bare for the play of emotions, great and little" (43).

Henri Barbusse, then, seems to have been another very important French connection in Willa Cather's literary career. In his novel *Under Fire* Cather most likely found some information that proved useful in writing *One of Ours*. *The Inferno*, however, appears to have had an even more significant influence on her. Interestingly, Cather ends "The Novel Démeublé" by noting the elder Dumas's opinion that to make a drama all a writer needed was one passion and four walls. There is good reason to accept Dumas's assertion, but Barbusse seems to have given Cather not only four walls and a passion but also a peephole, and thus the "germ" for one of her very best short stories. In addition, Barbusse's room "stripped bare by the dark" and his assertion that there are moments when one dare not "call things by their name" almost certainly provided Cather with the inspiration for one of her most important statements about the art of fiction.

WORKS CITED

Arnold, Marilyn. *Willa Cather's Short Fiction*. Athens: Ohio UP, 1986.

Barbusse, Henri. *The Inferno*. Trans. Edward J. O'Brien. New York: Boni and Liveright, 1918.

———. *L'enfer*. Édition definitive. Paris: Éditions Albin Michel, 1949.

———. *Under Fire: The Story of a Squad*. Trans. Fitzwater Wray. New York: Dutton, 1917.

Booker, John Manning. "Barbusse in Peace and War." Rev. of *We Others*, by Henri Barbusse. *New Republic* 3 Sept. 1919: 146–48.

Cather, Willa. "Alexandre Dumas *fils*." *The World and the Parish: Willa Cather's Articles and Reviews, 1893–1902*. Ed. William M. Curtin. Lincoln: University of Nebraska Press, 1970. 1: 222–23.

———. "Coming, Aphrodite!" *Youth and the Bright Medusa*. New York: Knopf, 1920. 11–78.

———. "The Novel Démeublé." *Willa Cather on Writing: Critical Studies on Writing as an Art*. Bison Books Edition. Lincoln: U of Nebraska P, 1988. 35–43.

Cowley, Malcolm. "Henri Barbusse." *Bookman* Oct. 1922: 180–82.

Fisher, Dorothy Canfield. "Daughter of the Frontier." *New York Herald-Tribune* 28 May 1933, sec. 11: 7, 9.

Gervaud, Michel. "Willa Cather and France: Elective Affinities." *The Art of Willa Cather*. Ed. Bernice Slote and Virginia Faulkner. Lincoln: U of Nebraska P, 1974. 65–83.

Gwynn, Stephen. "The Man on the Firestep." *Nineteenth Century* Oct. 1917: 803–17.

Hackett, Francis. "A War of Men." *New Republic* 27 Oct. 1917: 358–59.

Herrick, Robert. "Unromantic War." *Dial* 14 Feb. 1918: 133–34.

King, Jonathan. "Henri Barbusse: 'Le feu' and the Crisis of Social Realism." *The First World War in Fiction: A Collection of Critical Essays*. Ed. Holger Klein. New York: Macmillan, 1976. 43–52.

O'Brien, Edward J. Introduction. *The Inferno*. New York: Boni and Liveright, 1918. 9–15.

O'Connor, Margaret Anne, ed. *Willa Cather: The Contemporary Reviews*. Cambridge: Cambridge UP, 2001.

Rhys, Brian. Introduction. *Under Fire*. By Henri Barbusse. New York: J. M. Dent, 1947. vii–xii.

Seibel, George. "Willa Cather from Nebraska." *Colophon* Sept. 1949: 195–208.

Sergeant, Elizabeth Shepley. *Willa Cather: A Memoir*. Bison Books Edition. Lincoln: U of Nebraska P, 1963.

Trout, Steven. *Memorial Fictions: Willa Cather and the First World War*. Lincoln: U of Nebraska P, 2002.
Wilson, Colin. "The Country of the Blind." *The Outsider*. Boston: Houghton Mifflin, 1956. 11–26.
Woodress, James. *Willa Cather: A Literary Life*. Lincoln: U of Nebraska P, 1987.
———. "Willa Cather and Alphonse Daudet." *Cather Studies*. Vol. 2. Ed. Susan J. Rosowski. Lincoln: U of Nebraska P, 1993. 156–66.

Recollecting Emotion in Tranquility

Wordsworth and Byron in Cather's *My Ántonia* and *Lucy Gayheart*

JONATHAN D. GROSS

Matthew Arnold judged Wordsworth and Byron "first and pre-eminent in actual performance, a glorious pair, among the English poets of this century. . . . When the year 1900 is turned," he added, "and our nation comes to recount her poetic glories in the century which has then just ended, the first names with her will be these" ("Byron" 236–37). Arnold's influential preface to *Poetry of Byron* (1881) helped create icons, literary figures who would become touchstones for future generations. For Arnold, Wordsworth and Byron operated as emotional shorthand: the reflective Wordsworth contrasting with the tempestuous Byron. By creating characters who are by turns Wordsworthian and Byronic in *My Ántonia* and *Lucy Gayheart*, Willa Cather engaged in a dialogue with the British icons who preceded her.

My Ántonia exemplifies this engagement, for Cather portrays Jim Burden as a man who has closed his Byron and opened his Wordsworth.[1] *My Ántonia* celebrates Wordsworth's values as expressed in "Lines Written a Few Miles above Tintern Abbey," though the theme of nature never betraying the heart that loved her is colored, curiously enough, by allusions to Byron's "When We Two Parted." In *Lucy Gayheart*, Cather turned to the theme of Byronic pessimism, and this particular lyric, in earnest. She showed just what can happen when someone gives way to Byronic passions without the sustaining influence of the land (Clement Sebastian) and what can happen when he does not (Harry Gordon). *My Ántonia* ends on a note of Wordsworthian hope, with Jim Burden exalted by the picture of Ántonia that revives again, much as Wordsworth drew sustenance from the "wild eyes" of his sister, Dorothy. *Lucy Gayheart* ends with the heroine's drowning and Harry Gordon's meditation on the meaning of her death and his own, quite passionless, life. For Jim Burden and for Lucy Gayheart, as for many in the nineteenth century, Byronism is both an inspiration and a disease. If the Wordsworthian impulse is centrifugal, inclined toward *nostos* (home-bound), the Byronic is centripetal, marked by nomadic wandering. Lucy Gayheart summarizes these twin impulses as she contemplates the Byronic influence of Clement Sebastian on her life: "she had lost it as one can lose a ravishing melody, remembering the mood of it, the kind of joy it gave but unable to recall precisely the air itself," Cather's narrator notes. "If only one could lose one's life and one's body and be nothing but one's desire; if the rest could melt away and that could float with the gulls, out yonder where the blue and green were changing!" (103). Cather's characters express a similar wish to cast off restrictions on their artistic vision, an allegory, perhaps, for Cather's own literary career in which she achieved iconic status, in part, by rejecting American forms of parochialism.

WORDSWORTH AND BYRON IN *MY ÁNTONIA*

In his preface to *Lyrical Ballads*, Wordsworth wrote that "poetry is the spontaneous overflow of powerful feelings: it takes its origin from emotion recollected in tranquility" (126). Five years had passed since he first visited the Wye valley in 1793, and "Tintern Abbey" begins by recording this fact: "Five years have passed; five summers, with the length / Of five long winters!" (ll. 1–2). Wordsworth contrasts chronological time (clock time) with felt time. In the year 1793 (five years before 1798), he stood with his sister and Annette Vallon in Calais, having visited France shortly before the outbreak of the French Revolution. England declared war on France in February 1793, and in January of that month Louis XVI was beheaded. So important is the passage of time for Wordsworth that he includes the date of July 13, 1798, in the very title of the poem, using the word "again" ("Once again / . . . again repose") in order to chart his mental development from what he once was to what he now is, to what he will one day become.[2] Specifically, Wordsworth charts his movement from a childish experience of nature, to adolescence, to adulthood (ll. 66–88). Through Dorothy's eyes, the speaker learns to look on nature

> . . . not as in the hour
> Of thoughtless youth; but hearing oftentimes
> The still, sad music of humanity,
> Nor harsh nor grating, though of ample power
> To chasten and subdue. (ll. 89–93)

The barometer of Wordsworth's changes is his sister, Dorothy, the unseen presence who inspires the poem itself. The poet clearly prefers the loyalty of nature ("Nature never did betray / The heart that loved her"), which he finds exemplified in Dorothy, to the fickleness of the French Revolution (July 14, 1789), to which he indirectly alludes (Johnston 13).

In her introduction to *My Ántonia*, Cather depicts a special understanding between reader and listener, one fused by the landscape they shared and by their sensitivity to Nature (x). Wordsworth depends upon Dorothy to maintain his relationship to nature and his better self. Jim Burden lives imaginatively as long as Ántonia is alive in his mind. The land becomes "more dear both for itself and for thy sake," the Wordsworthian speaker says.

As writers, both Jim Burden and Wordsworth consider women as muses, forces that connect them to the earth. Part of this connection is linguistic; it helps to explain the simple, unadorned language one finds in Wordsworth and Cather. Like the narrator of *My Ántonia*, Wordsworth lived in a time that threatened to "blunt the discriminating powers of the mind . . . unfitting it for all voluntary exertion to reduce it to a state of almost savage torpor" ("Preface" 128). Cather's narrator in *My Ántonia* notes how Jim's marriage has been unfortunate; his wife does not appreciate his "quiet tastes"[3] any more than Wordsworth's audience was prepared to appreciate "Lines Written a Few Miles above Tintern Abbey." Just as Wordsworth attacked the "sickly and stupid German Tragedies" that pandered to a vulgar taste created by "the encreasing accumulation of men in cities" ("Preface" 128) such as London, Burden's wife patronizes a group of young poets and painters of advanced ideas and mediocre ability" in New York (x). Wordsworth's purpose, by contrast, was to "adopt the very language of men" ("Preface" 130); to include "no personifications of abstract ideas" (130) such as appear in the poetry of Pope; to avoid artificial diction and allegorical language such as appears in the poetry of Thomas Gray; to deny any "essential difference between the language of prose and metrical composition" (134). These are very much akin to Burden's simple tastes, scorned by his urban and sophisticated wife, and form another "kind of freemasonry" (x).[4] The public for both Cather and Wordsworth is led astray by the "gaudiness and inane phraseology" (Wordsworth, "Advertisement" 116) of modern writers, by the assault on the senses that is characteristic of urban life.

In *My Ántonia*, the heroine speaks a language of the heart not unlike the diction Wordsworth defended in the preface to *Lyrical Ballads*. Jim is attracted to Tony because her language is as striking and vivid as her personality. She conveys an emotional and physical warmth that contrasts strikingly with his mother's patronizing attitude toward the Shimerdas.

> Tony slipped under his arm. "It is very cold on the floor, and this is warm like the badger hole. I like for sleep there," she insisted eagerly. . . . As we rose to go, she opened her wooden chest and brought out a bag made of bed-ticking. . . . At sight of it, the crazy boy began to smack his lips. When Mrs. Shimerda opened the bag and stirred the contents with her hand, it gave out a salty, earthy smell, very pungent, even among the other odors of that cave. She measured a teacup full, tied it up in a bit of sacking, and presented it ceremoniously to grandmother.
>
> "For cook," she announced. "Little now; be very much when cook," spreading out her hands as if to indicate that the pint would swell to a gallon. (73, 75)

Cather takes up the mantle that Wordsworth threw down for this passage, which includes its own idiot boy "smack[ing] his lips." At the same time, the passage points out Grandmother Burden's spiritual limitations, the way in which a decorous language keeps her from conveying the spiritual warmth Ántonia exudes. "All the way home, Grandmother and Jake talked about how easily good Christian people could forget they were their brothers' keepers" (75–76), she says rather too piously.

Cather's obvious respect for the Shimerdas, immigrants from Bohemia, plays itself out as a competition between two countries, even two types of bread ("I prefer our bread to yours, myself" [75]), and ultimately two forms of Christianity (Protestant and Catholic). One might even argue that the novel is about two ways of speaking. As Wordsworth wrote, in a preface meant to explain his own aesthetic purpose in including such poems as "The Idiot Boy" and "Lines Written a Few Miles above Tintern Abbey" in a single collection: "Low and rustic life was chosen because in that situation the essential passions of the heart find a better soil in which they can attain their maturity; are less under restraint, and speak a plainer and more emphatic language" ("Preface" 124). Cather was as committed as Wordsworth to conveying "feelings and notions in simple and unelaborated expressions" ("Preface" 124). In recalling Ántonia, Jim Burden speaks the "emphatic" ("Preface" 124) language of the heart, for the "introduction" presents his manuscript as a continuation of a conversation he has on a "burning day when we were crossing Iowa" (xi). Throughout his text, Jim Burden succeeds in recapturing his heroine through an attention to the language of everyday life.

PICTORIAL METAPHORS IN WORDSWORTH AND CATHER

As Cather continues her introduction, pictorial metaphors like those employed by Wordsworth in "Tintern Abbey" emphasize the theme of recollection that is such an important part of his novel. "I had lost sight of her altogether, but Jim had found her again after long years, and had renewed a friendship that meant a great deal to him," the frame narrator notes. "He made me see her again, feel her presence, revived all my old affection for her" (xi–xii). Wordsworth's reliance on pictorial metaphors in "Tintern Abbey"—the picture in the mind that revives again—recalls Burden's gift: "He made me see her again" (xii). Burden fulfills Wordsworth's dictum that poetry is the "spontaneous overflow of powerful feelings recollected in tranquility" ("Preface" 126), for he writes Ántonia's history long after his most passionate feelings for her have subsided, giving the manuscript to a friend.

At the very moment when Cather is most Wordsworthian, she inevitably alludes to Byron. In the introduction, her narrator notes that Jim "had found her again after long years," recalling Byron's lyric "When We Two Parted" ("If I should meet thee / After long years"). Cather then repeats this grace note two more times at key points in the novel, to heighten the dramatic encounter between her central characters and provide both pathos and historic, even poetic, *gravitas*.

> The next afternoon I walked over to the Shimerdas' . . . Ántonia was shocking wheat . . . I went down across the fields, and Tony saw me from a long way off.
>
> She stood still by her shocks, leaning on her pitchfork, watching me as I came. We met like the people in the old song, in silence, if not in tears. (310)

The emphasis on perspective ("Tony saw me from a long way off") is Wordsworthian ("Tintern Abbey" is written "a few miles *above* Tintern Abbey" and also emphasizes perspective), but the "old song" refers to a Byron lyric, "When We Two Parted," alluded to in the introduction.

> When we two parted,
> In silence and tears,
> Half broken-hearted
> To sever for years,
> Pale grew thy cheek and cold,
> Colder thy kiss;

> Truly that hour foretold
> Sorrow to this . . .
> If I should meet thee
> After long years,
> How should I greet thee!—
> With silence and tears.
> —(*Complete Poetical Works* [CPW] 3: 320)

Cather successfully connects the Wordsworthian introduction to the body of the text through a single prepositional phrase: "after long years." Byron's rather conventionally romantic, if moving, lyric speaks of a secret shame that trails the woman Byron once loved, much as Ántonia's illegitimate child by Larry Donovan leads Burden to "hear thy name spoken, and share in its shame" (CPW 3: 320). Byron's poem most likely alludes to Lady Caroline Lamb and Lady Frances Webster, with whom he had erotic and platonic affairs, respectively, between 1812 and 1813. Both Lamb and Webster later flirted with the Duke of Wellington in 1815, inspiring Byron's caustic line, repeated in several different works, "the once fallen woman forever must fall" (CPW 3: 475).

In Cather's novel, animosities and sexual jealousy are kept at a lower temperature than in Byron's letters to Lady Melbourne describing these relationships. The next meeting between Ántonia and Burden, more than twenty years later, reflects Cather's method of mixing recollection and erotic passion, for it strikes both Wordsworthian and Byronic notes, though the former predominate (321). The echo of a romantic, Byronic moment, "It always is [a shock] to meet people after long years," competes with the Wordsworthian tone of this passage. Burden sees "the full vigour of her personality, battered but not diminished, looking at me, speaking to me in the husky, breathy voice I remembered so well" (321). Wordsworth was interested in the courage it takes to face life with fortitude: many of his figures—the Old Cumberland Beggar, the leech gatherer in "Resolution and Independence," Michael—become heroes or heroines because of their endurance. For Cather, raising a large family requires a heroism (as she suggests in *Song of the Lark*) tantamount to those acts rewarded by nations in paintings by Delacroix or pensions granted to war heroes. *My Ántonia* is emphatically not a story of the boy getting the girl "after long years," of becoming disappointed with her or sharing in her shame. Rather, it is about a boy attaining the "philosophic mind" to appreciate Ántonia's human dignity (her "grizzled" hair) despite all the hardship she has been through and to accept her unconventionality in the best Byronic, Wordsworthian, and romantic spirit.

What Jim Burden values in Ántonia is precisely her capacity to bring pictures before the mind, a quality Wordsworth attributes to his sister, Dorothy. Both Dorothy and Ántonia serve as an *amanuensis*: an inspirational force that helped the poet visualize nature in his mind's eye. Wordsworth wrote that "Tintern Abbey" has not been "As is a landscape to a blind man's eye" (l. 25); "Ántonia had always been one to leave images in the mind that did not fade, that grew stronger with time," Jim Burden writes of her after this final encounter (342).

> In my memory there was a succession of such pictures, fixed there like the old woodcuts of one's first primer: Ántonia kicking her bare legs against the sides of my pony when we came home in triumph with our snake; Ántonia in her black shawl and fur cap, as she stood by her father's grave in the snowstorm; Ántonia coming in with her work-team along the evening sky-line. She lent herself to immemorial human attitudes which we recognize by instinct as universal and true. I had not been mistaken. She was a battered woman now, not a lovely girl; but she still had that something which fires the imagination, could still stop one's breath for a moment by a look or gesture that somehow revealed the meaning in common things. (342)

What could be more Wordsworthian than this final phrase? After all, Wordsworth wrote that his task in such poems as "Tintern Abbey" was to show the extraordinary in the ordinary ("whereby ordinary things should be presented to the mind in an unusual way" ["Preface" 124]). Cather's portrait of Ántonia with her hand on a crab tree encourages the reader to revisit the Eden myth: there is no fall now, but only a solitary reaper who "makes you feel the goodness of planting and tending and harvesting" (342). Both Burden and Wordsworth celebrate their own countries, their own land, and the women who inhabit them. They write their prose poems and their lyrics for these women. Lena Lingard's laughter "gave a favourable interpretation to everything," Burden writes of his Norwegian lover. An image of the beautiful, alliteratively named Lena Lingard floats before him on the page like a picture, and underneath it stood the mournful line from Virgil's *Georgics* that so moved Samuel Johnson and which serves as epigraph to *My Ántonia*: "Optima dies . . . Prima fugit," "the best days are the first to flee" (iii). It is worth thinking about how Wordsworth's poem, Cather's novel, and W. T. Benda's illustrations create pictures in the mind that "revive again." Which are the most precious? Which are the first to flee? And which ones, ultimately, will we remember?

WORDSWORTH AND BYRON IN *LUCY GAYHEART*

But *My Ántonia* was not the last novel in which Cather posed such questions or attempted to reconcile Wordsworth and Byron through allusions to their verse. Lucy Gayheart's very name recalls Wordsworth's Lucy poems and the blithe possibilities of rural life. Leaving the town of Haverford, Nebraska, is Lucy's undoing and her fulfillment, for in Chicago she meets the great egotist Clement Sebastian, whose strange marriage and curiously intimate relationship with his lame piano player, James Mockford, recalls both Byron's satiric wit and his disability. Mockford's disability, after all, is precisely Byron's: a club foot, dragged "across the stage" (30) with due melodrama. Critics have noted that Sebastian feeds like a vampire on Lucy's youth (Rosowski 225): as such he recalls Dr. Polidori, Byron's physician, who wrote a sketch inspired by that famous night in Switzerland when Mary Shelley began *Frankenstein*. Polidori's "The Vampyre" was attributed, falsely, to Byron, and so the war of egos that ensued (Marchand, *Biography* 2: 787),[5] with Byron denying his authorship, sets the stage for Mockford's uncomfortable rivalry with Sebastian and Lucy's mistrust of him (39).

Thrown in for good measure is Giuseppe, the Italian footman, who recalls Byron's adventure in Italy and the Italian circle that would soon surround him in Geneva and Pisa, near the Bay of Spezia where Shelley drowned.

Cather's allusions to Byron as icon work in at least two ways. The first is literary, through direct references to Byron's lyric "When We Two Parted"; the second is biographical, with references to Shelley's near-drowning, Byron's funeral cortege, and other incidental features of Byron's life: his Scottishness (which is compared to Gordon's), his friendship with Larry MacGowan (which resembles Byron's with Leigh Hunt), his homoerotic friendships with young men and boys like Mockford, MacGowan, and Marius, the adopted son he acquires (all of which recall Don Juan's adoption of Leila and Byron's infatuations with John Edleston, Robert Rushton, Lukas Chalandritsanos, and others). Cather juxtaposes these allusions to Byron's life with Wordsworth's Lucy poems (which explore another Lucy's death) and with the acts of recollection by Harry Gordon, who merges Byronic and Wordsworthian voices by behaving like Byron but recollecting Lucy in Wordsworthian fashion.

I will begin with the allusions to "When We Two Parted." As in *My Ántonia*, they are repeated at least three times. The first occurs when Lucy hears Clement sing. Shortly after her first meeting with Byron in 1812, Caroline Lamb described "That beautiful pale face" as her "fate" (Marchand, *Biography* 1: 331) and summed up Byron as "mad—bad—and dangerous to know" (328). Lucy senses a similar danger when she encounters Clement Sebastian:

> Sebastian walked to the front of the stage in the half-darkness and began to sing an old setting of Byron's *When We Two Parted*; a sad, simple old air which required little from the singer, yet probably no one who heard it that night will ever forget it.
>
> Lucy had come home and up the stairs into this room, tired and frightened, with a feeling that some protecting barrier was gone—a window had been broken that let in the cold and darkness of the night. Sitting here in her cloak,

> shivering, she had whispered over and over the words of that last song:
>
> When we two parted,
> In silence and tears,
> Half broken-hearted,
> To sever for years,
>
> Pale grew thy cheek and cold,
> Colder thy kiss;
> Surely that hour foretold
> Sorrow to this.
>
> It was as if that song were to have some effect upon her own life. She tried to forget it, but it was inescapable. It was with her, like an evil omen. (32)

In a striking transition ("Lucy had come home . . ."), Cather switches the reader from the present tense to Lucy's recollection of the event, as if to combine the Wordsworthian retrospective glance with the adrenaline rush of her heroine's first encounter with a great artist. The poem, cast as a Wordsworthian backward glance, is also an evil Byronic omen predicting the future. (One aspect of this omen is that it is Mockford, not Sebastian, who has the pale, though not beautiful, face.)

The second incident occurs when Sebastian and Lucy part as Sebastian prepares for his continental tour. Sebastian's thoughts are despairing ("It was a parting between two who would never meet again" [126]), and Lucy slowly realizes their love is doomed. "Lucy knew what he was thinking. She felt a kind of hopeless despair in the embrace that tightened about her. As they passed a lamp-post she looked up, and in the flash of light she saw his face. Oh, then it came back to her! The night he sang *When We Two Parted* and she knew he had done something to her life. Presentiments like that one were not meaningless; they came out of the future. *Surely that hour foretold sorrow to this.* They were going to lose something. They were both clinging to it and to each other, but they must lose it" (117). In what amounts to an explication of Byron's poem, Cather stresses key phrases to depict Lucy's and Sebastian's anguish: he notes their "parting between two," and she casts her mind into the future. "Lucy felt the old terror coming back; *to sever for years*" (128). With her sense of "presentiment," Lucy has become "theatrical" (154), as her sister Pauline later regrets: she has caught the Byronic disease, even as her life unfolds in the tripartite time scheme that recalls Wordsworth's description of his life in "Tintern Abbey."

The final allusion to "When We Two Parted" occurs when Harry (Clement's double) abandons Lucy and "share[s] in her shame" by refusing to show her any kindness after Clement's death. When Harry avoids picking up Lucy in his sled during a winter storm, in one of many petty acts—she shouts his name in reproof: "'Harry!' Indignation, amazement, authority, as if she wouldn't allow him to do anything so shameful" (221). The word "shameful" recalls the diction of Byron's lyric, "share in its shame" (and reminds the reader of Larry Donovan's mistreatment of Ántonia in their mock marriage).

If Cather was interested in Byron's "When We Two Parted," as these playful allusions suggest, she was also interested in the male psychology that made such self-serving lyricism possible (evident, perhaps, in Clement and Lucy's willingness to conflate singing a musical setting for Byron's poem with being Byron). In the climax of her novel she rewrites Shelley's boating accident (especially Byron's narration of it) to expose the dangers of Byronic egotism. "The story of Shelley's agitation is true," Byron wrote to John Murray on 15 May 1819,

> I can't tell what seized him—for he don't want courage. He was once with me in a Gale of Wind in a small boat right under the rocks between Meillerie & St. Gingo—we were five in the boat—a servant—two boatmen—& ourselves. The Sail was mismanaged & the boat was filling fast—he can't swim.—I stripped off my coat—made him strip off his—& take hold of an oar—telling him that *I thought (being myself an expert swimmer) I could save him if he would not struggle when I took hold of him*. (*Letters and Journals* 11: 220; my emphasis)

Cather's novel replays this scene.

> *Mockford could not swim and was apparently terrified; he had locked his arms about Sebastian's neck. Wiertz thought Sebastian would be able to control a man so much slighter, so he swam toward the boats coming out from shore. . . .* Mockford must have fastened himself to his companion with a strangle-hold and dragged him down. The bodies had not yet been recovered. (138; my emphasis)

In a mock inversion of Shelley's relationship to Byron, Mockford clings to life relentlessly, drowning Sebastian in the process. Shelley's romantic selflessness has given way to Mockford's sordid self-interest.

Why allude to this historical event, recounted by Edward Trelawny and others, in such an obvious manner? The implication, I think, is that Cather hopes to make a point about Byron's career. Byron and Byronism could affect lives even in remote villages like Haverford, Nebraska. This could happen through brief exposure to icons, a man singing a musical setting of Byron's poem, or an aged singer demonstrating her commitment to excellence and inspiring Lucy to return to Chicago to pursue a musical career (178). Cather deliberately explores the image of Byron as icon by comparing Lucy's father, Jacob Gayheart, to "an old daguerreotype of a minor German poet" (6). If Jacob has something of the poet in him, it is not surprising that Lucy would be inspired by a poet like Byron, whose image was so connected with his fame (through portraits by George Sanders [*Byron and Robert Rushton*], Thomas Phillips [*Byron in Albanian Dress*], Richard Westall, and George Henry Harlow and busts by Lorenzo Bartolini, Bertel Thorvaldsen, and others [see Peach]). Lucy's exposure to Byronism is through the ear rather than the eye (Clement, after all, is described as "oval" [29]), but her susceptibility to icons is repeatedly shown through her frequent viewings of Clement Sebastian in Byronic postures of brooding (31, 54–55). At the same time, Cather's novel exposes Byronic conduct as dangerously egoistic. Clement's somewhat ungracious refusal to give Mockford equal billing as an accompanist (and Mockford's effrontery in asking for it) well illustrates what one might call the Byronic disease. Clement keeps Mockford in a subordinate position, sometimes ostentatiously so, which is ultimately destructive to both artists. Many people who surround Clement become stunted (Giuseppe, Mockford, Lucy, Clement's wife) because of Sebastian's tendency to use people to arrange his gloves, interpret his moods, and restore his youth. And this too was part of Cather's engagement with Byron's iconic status, her subtle critique of Byronic egotism.

If Cather replays the near-drowning of Shelley through the deaths of Mockford and Sebastian, she alludes to another well-known incident in Byron's life: his dramatic funeral train in England, when his body was transported back to England from Messolonghi, Greece. Byron's casket surprised Caroline Lamb in a similar way: "as I was slowly driving up the hill here, Lord Byron's Hearse was at that moment passing under these very walls, and rested at Welwyn" (Marchand, *Biography* 3: 1261). In Cather's novel, the man, not the woman, observes the cortege. "Why had he been compelled to drive in that procession?" Harry asks himself as he recollects Lucy's death. "He couldn't pass it,—not after he had stopped and asked what was the matter" (183). Lucy's funeral is described in part 2 and repeated, through Harry's Wordsworthian reminiscence, in part 3. Cather plays with subject and object, showing Gordon as both brooding Byronic hero and Wordsworthian recollector, as both Byron and Caroline Lamb! In this way she turns Byronic behavior back on itself, forcing Harry to redeem, and overcome, his previously selfish conduct. Paul Douglass's biography of Caroline Lamb shows how prescient Cather was in her portrait of Lucy Gayheart. Byronism was an infection (Douglass calls it "erotomania") that Caroline Lamb could never overcome. By focusing on the funeral cortege, Cather explores the late-nineteenth-century view, popularized in part by Harriet Beecher Stowe's *Lady Byron Vindicated*, that Byronism was morally destructive. Cather's 1935 novel reflects, and adds nuance to, the critique of Byronism that led to the decline of his reputation, his iconic status, in the first half of the twentieth century.

Where Wordsworthian heroes like Jim Burden believe that feelings deepen with time (for they become spiritualized), Byron suggests the opposite (and Clement echoes the sentiment), because both value erotic over spiritual passion. This becomes clear in their response to the death of friends. When Clement hears of Larry MacGowan's death (77), he reviews his life in Wordsworthian fashion: "He had missed the deepest of all companionships, a relation with the earth itself, with a countryside and a people" (78). If the narrator of "Tintern Abbey" imagines, like Jim Burden, a life sustained by a particular landscape, Clement is forced to confront his own itinerant lifestyle and the toll this has exacted on friendships, such as Wordsworth enjoys with his sister, Dorothy. "Friendships?" Clement queries himself. "Larry was the man he had cared for most. Among women? There was little for sweet reflection in that chapter" (78).

Unlike Burden, who remains content with the philosophic mind that he brings to Ántonia, Clement actually seeks out the empathy of a young girl, Lucy. "Did you happen to notice in the morning paper that Larry MacGowan died yesterday in a sanatorium in Savoy?" he asks Lucy. "Years ago if I had seen that thing in brutal type, I would have lain down and cried like a boy. Things happen to our friendships; that's the worst about living. Young people can't know what it means" (83). Byron wrote in similar terms about the death of John Edleston in a letter to Francis Hodgson on 10 October 1811: "I heard of a death the other day that shocked me more than any of the preceding, . . . yet I had not a tear left for an event which five years ago would have bowed me to the dust" (MacCarthy 145). Larry hiked with Sebastian in the Sullanches (as Hobhouse hiked with Byron in the Simplon pass) and appears to be jealous of Clement's wife when he visits them at their home in Chantilly (70). Having lost Larry, Clement tries to turn Lucy into him. "He had sometimes thought of her as rather boyish, because she was so square" (80). By reinventing her as a boy (he "*thought* of her as rather boyish" [my emphasis]), Clement learns to trust Lucy (though others, such as Fairy Blair, describe her as ridiculously feminine, all curls and coquettishness). His comfort with men, including the French basso who cheers him enthusiastically during one of his concerts, reminds us that Clement has been surrounded by male admirers, even as his estranged wife stays abroad in France. Paul Auerbach, who imagines a conventional life for Lucy with a husband like Harry, considers Clement exceptional—not only in his talent, perhaps, but in his bisexuality.

Clement Sebastian's marriage distances him from Larry Donovan, as surely as his infatuation with Lucy Gayheart compromises his intimate relationship with James Mockford. The air from *Twelfth Night* which Sebastian uses to tease Lucy reinforces this theme of a "concealed love" that dare not speak its name: is it Sebastian's love for Lucy? Or Sebastian's love for other boys and men? Perhaps both, as in the complications that attend Shakespeare's drama. For Byron, as for Clement, enjoyment and passion are the thing. This is the epigraph, after all, of *Don Juan*, also taken from *Twelfth Night*. "Dost thou think, because thou art virtuous, there shall be no more cakes and ale?—Yes, by Saint Anne, and ginger shall be hot i' the mouth, too!" (CPW 5: 6). Byron's—and Clement's—allusions to secret pleasures, captured in Clement's patronizing treatment of Lucy, recalls Byron's taunting of the rather "square" Annabella Milbanke with his exploits with young boys in the East.

If Clement tries to turn Lucy into Larry, he also casts her into roles that recall specific incidents in Byron's life. "Perhaps you will dream that we are both twenty, and are taking a walking trip in the French Alps. And I shall call to you at daybreak from my balcony!" (72). This sentence, almost out of place in *Lucy Gayheart*, recalls details of Leigh Hunt's visit to Byron in Italy. "I was generally at my writing when he came down, and either acknowledged his presence by getting up and saying something from the window," Hunt later remembered, "or he called out 'Leontius!' and came halting up to the window with some joke, or other challenge to conversation" (Marchand, *Portrait* 381). These three details are striking, but no more so than the cumulative effect of their being placed, side by side, near other Byronic passages. For example, Marius (whose name recalls the hero of Walter Pater's *Marius the Epicurean*) comes to live with Clement Sebastian, but his wife objects; he then loses a portion of affection for his wife because of her coldheartedness. Similarly, Annabella Milbanke became cold toward Byron because of his homosexual liaisons with boys in the East, exposed (apparently) by the jilted Caroline Lamb. His Harrow friendships, even the Sanders portrait of him with Robert Rushton, who accompanied him in 1809 and 1816, recall Clement's close friendship with Marius. In the same way that Clement visits the boy and misses him, funding his education, Byron made his will over to the boys he fell in love with, providing an education for Robert Rushton (Marchand, *Biography* 1: 286), an annuity of 7,000 pounds to Nicolas Giraud (1: 286), and a posthumous gift to Lukas Chalandritsanos (3: 1227). For Sebastian and Byron, these passionate friendships with boys interfere with their monogamous marriages.

Like *My Ántonia*, Cather's novel moves away from Byronic emotion to Wordsworthian recollection, modifying one mood by making reference to another. As Harry Gordon strives to make a fitting "recollection" of Lucy, he is struck by his own lack of imagination, the very qualities that make Wordsworth's and Cather's Lucy "gay." Cather suggests the inadequacy of his cement rendering of Lucy's light footprint by implicitly comparing it to the footprints in the snow described in Wordsworth's "Lucy Gray; or, Solitude." In Wordsworth's poem, Lucy's father asks his child to "light / Your mother through the snow" (*CPW* 1: 392, ll. 15–16). The deaths of both heroines take place at dusk on a snowy night; the footsteps of both heroines disappear, though Harry Gordon clumsily, uncomfortably (for Milton Chase) preserves Lucy Gayheart's. In the same way that the search party gets as far as a broken bridge where Lucy's footsteps end (she has put on her skates here), Lucy's footprints disappear precisely where her mother tries to find them.

> Not blither is the mountain roe:
> With many a wanton stroke
> Her feet disperse the powdery snow,
> That rises up like smoke.
>
> The storm came on before its time:
> She wandered up and down;
> And many a hill did Lucy climb:
> But never reached the town. (392, ll. 25–32)

A search party is sent out when the mother spied "The print of Lucy's feet" (392, l. 44). They lead down a "steep hill's edge / They tracked . . . / them on, nor ever lost; / And to the bridge they came" (392–93, ll. 45–52). These footmarks, which recall "She Dwelt among Untrodden Ways," are a literal act of disappearance.

> They followed from the snowy bank
> Those footmarks, one by one,
> Into the middle of the plank;
> And further there were none! (393, ll. 53–56)

The resemblance to the search party that is sent out after Lucy's disappearance is striking.

In *My Ántonia* and *Lucy Gayheart*, men almost obliterate women in the very act of trying to love them. Ántonia survives in Jim Burden's memory as an ideal because Jim never possesses her. He avoids doing so, in part, because he learns the danger of Byronic passion through Wick Cutter, who almost seduces him in a scene worthy of *Don Juan*, mistaking him for Ántonia; Jim's humiliation teaches him that love should elevate, not debase. Harry Gordon's efforts to possess Lucy are similarly doomed, and his penance in Haverford partly teaches him this Wordsworthian lesson. Although he tries to preserve her footsteps in cement, the cement is a poor substitute for the original, who becomes, like Wordsworth's heroine, pure spirit, rolled around with rocks, and stones, and trees.

The best days are the first to flee in "Tintern Abbey" as in "When We Two Parted," in *My Ántonia* and in *Lucy Gayheart*. Art's provenance is to remember this fact, sometimes in tranquility, more often in tears. But there are at least two ways of recollecting emotion in tranquility. By contrasting Wordsworth's and Byron's centripetal and centrifugal treatment of passion in their major works, Cather enters into a conversation with these writers. She does not slavishly depend upon them, as Emerson perhaps mistakenly feared an American writer might. Instead, *My Ántonia* and *Lucy Gayheart* perform an important assessment of icons not unlike that which Mill undertook at a debating society in 1827, when he considered "the immoral tendencies of Byron's poetry, with [Sterling] Roebuck upholding Byron" (1: 153). In 1829, Mill again "discussed for two evenings [with Roebuck] the comparative merits of Byron and Wordsworth, propounding and illustrating by long recitations our respective theories of poetry" (153).

Enough of a romantic to take her subject from the soil of Nebraska, Cather also engaged in a conversation with British culture, comparing the moral tendencies of Wordsworth's and Byron's verse as Arnold and Mill had before her. In doing so she showed how Lord Byron and Percy Shelley were relevant to American fiction, that these figures could influence even a young girl on the Nebraska plains. Some of Cather's heroes brood and regret (Harry Gordon); others become meditative about their loss of the visionary gleam (Jim Burden). Both show the limits of Wordsworthian complacency or Byronic egotism, contrasting unfavorably with women like Ántonia and Lucy, who (at their best moments) face life squarely, despite setbacks. Jim Burden and Ántonia, Harry Gordon and Lucy Gayheart do not always achieve the excellence after which they aspire, but they do salute it "from afar" (*Lucy Gayheart* 12; Arnold, "Function" 285). In this sense, they, like the novelist who created them, become icons who form "the best title to esteem with posterity" (Arnold, "Function" 285).

NOTES

1. One of Cather's favorite works by Carlyle was *Sartor Resartus*, in which he instructed his readers to "close thy Byron, open thy Goethe." For Cather's reading of Byron and Carlyle, see Stout 14, 36.

2. Wordsworth's use of the word "still" and "again" recalls Susan Rosowski's description of Jim Burden's Wordsworthian narration: "This is, after all, the middle-aged Jim Burden's recollection of his childhood, a retrospective Cather recalls by phrases repeated so often they become motifs—'I still remember,' 'they are with me still,' and 'I can see them now'" (81).

3. Jim Burden's "quiet tastes" echoes Mill's description of Wordsworth's appeal: "Compared with the greatest poets, he may be said to be the poet of unpoetical natures, possessed of quiet and contemplative tastes" (153). Cather's echo of Mill, however slight, raises the interesting question of whether she read Mill's *Autobiography*. In any case, Mill's assessment gives us interesting insight into Burden. A

lawyer rather than a poet, Burden might be described as "unpoetical" himself, though alive to the poetic gifts of others, such as Gaston Cleric, his teacher.

4. The narrator's odd reference to freemasonry strikes a Byronic note (Byron joined Masonic lodges in Italy to fight with the Carbonari). For Byron and freemasonry, see my article in *Freemasonry in Enlightenment Europe*.

5. Marchand notes that Byron saw an advertisement in *Galignani's Messenger* "for a tale called *The Vampyre*, with his name attached to that of the author, Dr. Polidori, his erstwhile physician, who had taken a ghost-story idea which Byron had projected at Diodati and written a story of his own on the subject" (*Biography* 2: 787).

WORKS CITED

Arnold, Matthew. "Byron." *The Complete Prose Works of Matthew Arnold*. Ed. R. H. Super. 1879. 11 vols. Ann Arbor: U of Michigan P, 1960. 9: 217–37.

———. "The Function of Criticism at the Present Time." 1865. *The Complete Prose Works of Matthew Arnold* Ed. R. H. Super. 1865. 11 vols. Ann Arbor: U of Michigan P, 1960. 3: 258–85.

Byron, George Gordon, Lord. *Letters and Journals*. Ed. Leslie A. Marchand. 12 vols. London: John Murray, 1973–95.

———. *Lord Byron: The Complete Poetical Works*. Ed. Jerome McGann. 7 vols. Oxford: Clarendon P, 1980–93.

Cather, Willa. *Lucy Gayheart*. 1935. New York: Knopf, 1961.

———. *My Ántonia*. 1918. Willa Cather Scholarly Edition. Ed. Charles Mignon with Kari Ronning. Historical essay James Woodress. Lincoln: U of Nebraska P, 1994.

Douglass, Paul. *Lady Caroline Lamb: A Study in Erotomania*. New York: Palgrave, 2004.

Gross, Jonathan David. "'The Vulgar Must Not Share It': Byron, Freemasonry, and the Carbonari." *Freemasonry in Enlightenment Europe*. Ed. William Weisberger. New York: Columbia UP, 2003. 347–74.

Johnston, Kenneth R. "The Politics of 'Tintern Abbey.'" *Wordsworth Circle* 14.1 (1983): 6–14.

MacCarthy, Fiona. *Byron: Life and Legend*. London: John Murray, 2002.

Marchand, Leslie. *Byron: A Biography*. 3 vols. New York: Knopf, 1957.

———. *Byron: A Portrait*. Chicago: U of Chicago P, 1970.

Mill, John Stuart. *Autobiography and Literary Essays*. 1873. *Collected Works*. Ed. B. John M. Robson and Jack Stillinger. 32 vols. Toronto: U of Toronto P, 1963–90.
Peach, Annette. *Portraits of Byron*. Reprinted from *The Walpole Society* 62 (2000): 1–144.
Rosowski, Susan J. *The Voyage Perilous: Willa Cather's Romanticism*. Lincoln: U of Nebraska P, 1986.
Stout, Janis P. *Willa Cather: The Writer and Her World*. Charlottesville: UP of Virginia, 2000.
Stowe, Harriet Beecher. *Lady Byron Vindicated: A History of the Byron Controversy, from Its Beginning in 1816 to the Present Time*. 1870. New York: Haskell House, 1970.
Trelawny, Edward John. *Recollections of the Last Days of Shelley and Byron*. 1858. New York: Doubleday, 1960.
Wordsworth, William. "Advertisement to *Lyrical Ballads* (1798)." *Prose Works of William Wordsworth*. Ed. W. J. B. Owen and Jane Worthington Smyser. 3 vols. 1798. Oxford: Clarendon P, 1974. 1: 116–17.
———. "Lines Written a Few Miles above Tintern Abbey." 1798. *The Poems*. Ed. John O. Hayden. New Haven: Yale UP, 1977. 357–62.
———. "Lucy Gray; or, Solitude." 1800. *The Poems*. Ed. John O. Hayden. New Haven: Yale UP, 1977. 392–94.
———. "Preface to *Lyrical Ballads* (1800)." *Prose Works of William Wordsworth*. Ed. W. J. B. Owen and Jane Worthington Smyser. 3 vols. 1800. Oxford: Clarendon Press, 1974. 1: 118–58.
———. "She Dwelt among the Untrodden Ways." 1800. *The Poems*. Ed. John O. Hayden. 2 vols. New Haven: Yale UP, 1977. 1: 366.

"Have I Changed So Much?" Jim Burden, Intertextuality, and the Ending of *My Ántonia*

TIMOTHY C. BLACKBURN

Jim Burden's question to an Ántonia who does not recognize him after two decades—"Have I changed so much?" (322)—has had an unintended significance over the past thirty-five years, during which Jim has gone from a quiet, romantic memoir writer to the virtual villain of *My Ántonia*: unreliable, immature, repressed and repressive.[1] Such characterizations hinder recognition of Cather's intertextual structuring of book 5 of *My Ántonia*. Through allusions to the *Odyssey*, Jim's return to Ántonia is placed within mythic contexts of return, suggesting heroic stature even while delineating modernity. Through allusions to "Rip Van Winkle," both in its original form by Washington Irving and its dramatic form by Joseph Jefferson, Jim's return marks a profound change of era. Jim emerges as a restless Odyssean traveler living without despair in an America that has failed its great cultural opportunity.

In Cather's modernist aesthetic, to be "absolutely true" to a subject means much more than providing an accurate account of what happened. It can mean connecting to heroic patterns as well as to a figure from popular culture who resonates as something prototypically American and lost, a genial spirit of another time. Every novel's form cannot help but be unique. Thus, *My Ántonia* is "the other side of the rug, the pattern that is supposed not to count in a story. In it there is no love affair, no courtship, no marriage, no broken heart, no struggle for success. I knew I'd ruin my material if I put it in the usual fictional pattern. I just used it the way I thought absolutely true" (Cather, Interview 77). Readers have sometimes resisted the way Cather made the story or a character rather than resisted the "usual fictional pattern." In *My Ántonia* there is a sense of loss, of something missed, some potential not grasped. While much commentary on Jim Burden in effect locates this disappointment in the lack of romance between Jim and Ántonia, an intertextual reading of the novel finds it in the lost potential of the immigrant contribution to American culture. Unlike the sense of distant loss in many romantic and modernist works, this loss is as close and palpable as the feeling at a performance of Jefferson's immensely popular *Rip Van Winkle*.

In "Cuzak's Boys," Jim Burden writes about himself with less distance than in the rest of the novel, that is, as a man writing about a man rather than the boy he once was, precisely at the time Cather invites readers to consider him in terms of others as remote as Odysseus and Rip Van Winkle. This modernist approach is heightened by Jim's presumed awareness of Odyssean overtones to his return, so that readers participate, in a sense, in the writing and imagining. In the first section of this article I establish Cather's allusive invitations, with particular emphasis on Jefferson's *Rip Van Winkle*. In the second part I read "Cuzak's Boys" in terms of the allusions by comparing and contrasting Jim, Odysseus, and Rip in detail. In the third section I argue that the epilogue to Cather's final novel, *Sapphira and the Slave Girl*, uses the same source material as Jim's return in *My Ántonia*, suggesting a consideration of the children's point of view to separate the adult Jim from the boyish icon Ántonia's family has made him.

THE ALLUSIONS: THE *ODYSSEY* AND "RIP VAN WINKLE"

From the first sentence of book 5 of *My Ántonia*, Cather places Jim's return in the Odyssean tradition, thus making explicit the motif of return in earlier parts of the novel: "I told Ántonia I would come back, but life intervened, and it was twenty years before I kept my promise" (317). Cather's many fictional returners come back at widely varying times; given the *Odyssey*'s ubiquity and cultural resonance and Cather's conspicuous allusiveness, especially to classical literature, Cather's choice of twenty years for this man returning home to a woman emphasizes the Homeric connection.[2] Cather reinforces the allusion four paragraphs later, when Jim sees two boys bent over a dead dog, an unexpected event upon arrival that parallels the *Odyssey*'s dead dog, Argus.[3] Cather fascinatingly invites readers to experience Jim's text as a narrative aware, to some extent, of its own Odyssean resonances. Jim narrative openly discusses classical literature, noting in particular his penchant for transposing classical characters and settings to people and places he knows (254).[4]

In book 5 Cather also invites readers to consider less overt allusions to a mythic character than those to the *Odyssey*. In book 3 Jim and Lena see the play *Rip Van Winkle*; in the final chapter of book 5, after Jim has left the Cuzak farm and returned to town, he sees "strange children" (357), the very phrase Rip uses in Irving's story for his own return to town (36), and like Rip he visits his favorite inn. "Rip Van Winkle" itself so resonates with the *Odyssey* that Joyce, for instance, writing at the same time Cather was writing *My Ántonia*, uses it several times in *Ulysses*. Intertextual in its very origin, Irving's "Rip Van Winkle" is based on Johan Otmar's "Peter Klaus," a German story with strong folk and mythic elements; its own pronounced echoes of the *Odyssey* include a return home after twenty years, a dog incident upon arrival, and reunion with a family member. "Rip Van Winkle" was translated into German (one is tempted to say "*back* into German") in 1819, the year of its appearance, and four more times by 1826.[5] By the time *My Ántonia* was published, a full decade before "talkies," "Rip Van Winkle" had been made into no fewer than eighteen films.[6]

As Cather well knew, "Rip Van Winkle" gained its prominence in American popular culture through performance onstage. The play Jim and Lena see starred Joseph Jefferson, probably the best-known, -admired, and -loved American actor of the second half of the nineteenth century, who played Rip almost exclusively for more than forty years, first in London and then in thousands of performances all over the United States. Small towns closed school on the days *Rip* was performed. *Rip Van Winkle* emerged as a play almost immediately after publication of Irving's story. Using a script written and successively modified by the actors Frederick Yates, James Hackett, and Charles Burke and then revamped once again by the playwright Dion Boucicault, Jefferson made it his own, tuning it to his own voice, theatrical tastes, and view of the world.[7] It follows the main points of Irving's story but adds melodramatic complications about a villain, married to Rip's wife, Gretchen, who plots the destruction of Meenie, the loyal daughter Rip loves. Although Jefferson says in his *Autobiography* that he wanted to avoid making it a "temperance play" (336)—in the play's final gesture Rip breaks his pledge once again—it has a strong temperance tension all too familiar to Cather during the time of *My Ántonia*'s composition. The misogyny of Irving's story is toned down, and the father-daughter reunion is given full-blown emphasis: when Rip sobs "Somebody knows me now! Somebody knows me now!" (313), audiences sobbed too, and critics, including Harriet Beecher Stowe, spoke of Lear (Johnson, "Jefferson's *Rip*" 20).

In her 1896 review for the *Pittsburgh Leader*, the young Willa Cather focused instead on the "weirdly poetic" expressionist scene in the mountains as well as on Jefferson himself. Jefferson shared her enthusiasm for the mountain scene because, like Rip's often-addressed dog that never appears, it kept the play away from the insidious tendency toward realistic staging in American drama. He turned down countless suggestions for realistic elaborations because "so unreal a theme could not have been interwoven with all this realism without marring the play" (*Autobiography* 338). Cather's quite similar views of realism, in their best-known expression, match Jefferson's in more than substance; beginning by saying "the property man" has been busy on the novel's pages, and ending by wishing for a room "as bare as the stage of a Greek theater," "The Novel Démeublé" takes its operating analogies from the stage (43, 51). As an inveterate theatergoer and professional reviewer, Cather judged the "gentle," evenly tempered, poetically romantic Jefferson "one of the noblest geniuses of our time" and his Rip "a character perhaps the greatest which the American stage has yet produced" ("An Open Letter" 684–85). Although Cather made these strong pronouncements some twenty years before composing *My Ántonia*, they strengthen the invitation to consider Jim in terms of Rip Van Winkle.

READING "CUZAK'S BOYS" INTERTEXTUALLY

The way Cather structures book 5 of *My Ántonia* as a kind of coda, that is, part of the story yet not part of it, suggests reading its allusions as modernist nuance, there and not there, like Carroll's Cheshire cat. Jim's return forms a proportionately small part of the novel; "return" sections consume fully half of the *Odyssey* and Irving's "Rip Van Winkle," and two of five acts in Jefferson's play, but just one of five books—only about a tenth of the pages—of *My Ántonia*. The hero's return is integral to the story of the *Odyssey* and "Rip Van Winkle"; *My Ántonia*, because not dependent on plot in the ordinary sense, would make sense without book 5. Cather thus limits the iconography of Jim's return yet at the same time heightens awareness of its exceptional features.

The simplest way to follow the allusive invitations is to compare Jim, Odysseus, and Rip in terms of key elements. Disguise, for instance: Odysseus is consciously disguised; Rip does not realize he is; and Jim Burden is somewhere in between, in the modern condition of not being sure if he is disguised or not. Similarly, Jim's reasons for returning accentuate his modernity. Whereas Odysseus is driven by gods to reclaim what is his, and Rip has no reality outside his village, Jim has simply made a youthful promise he chooses to honor. The promise itself has no urgency. When Jim claims he will return someday, Ántonia responds "perhaps you will," adding, without irony, that it won't make much difference if he doesn't (314). Cather so undramatizes the promise that the reader learns about it only three paragraphs before he actually keeps it. By making Jim's return strictly a matter of choice, however grudgingly made, Cather also confers on it a kind of heroic quality. Irresolute about returning, Jim is often described as being "disillusioned," which, in one sense, he is, as he himself says: "In the course of twenty crowded years one parts with many illusions. I did not wish to lose the early ones" (318). But the word "disillusioned" has negative connotations that do not fit Jim, who is not dispirited. He has straightforwardly stated the condition of the man returning, who would be of considerably less interest if he were illusion-ridden and unchanged. As Homer has Odysseus describe himself in book 15, he is "a man who's weathered many blows and wandered many miles" (332), and as Cather has Jim say, it takes some "courage" to return and risk losing cherished values (321).[8] Jim arrives at the Cuzak farm "a little past midday" (319), a classic time for seeing clearly, without shadows or illusions, as in one of Jim's favorite boyhood books, *Robinson Crusoe*, when Crusoe finds the single footprint on the beach one day "about Noon."[9] In spite of noon's clarity, Jim is unsure which farm is Ántonia's, an uncertainty paralleling Odysseus's confusion about his whereabouts when he awakes on Ithaca, and Rip's confusion about everything.

By placing a dead dog in the path of her returner, Cather participates in what has been, since Argus's happy death, a minor literary game, with players including Pope, Fielding, Byron, Joyce, and of course Irving.[10] The suddenness of Jim's encounter with two boys "bending over a dead dog" (319) matches that of Odysseus's encounter with Argus in book 17, although in the *Odyssey* there has been some subtle preparation (Rose 215–30). Homer's dog is spectacularly loyal, representing a "natural" reaction superior to that of the humans who endanger the returned Odysseus. In Irving's "Rip Van Winkle," the dog, a seeming clone of Rip's Wolf, growls at him, a sign of the more Hobbesian world since the Yankee accession. In Jefferson's play, the dog, Schneider, is often addressed but, thanks to Jefferson's theatrical savvy, never actually appears onstage; when Rip returns, he brings up Schneider three times, saying, with characteristically jocular misogyny, "You call the dog Schneider. He'll know me better than my wife" (313).

Cather's dog is neither iconic nor burdened with meanings or even description, an approach emphasizing the reactions of characters and the dog's allusive function. Jim, who apparently had no dog when a child on his grandparents' farm, mentions no color, breed, size, age, condition, or name—just "dead dog."[11] He notes the boys' concern—"this was evidently a sad afternoon for them" (319)—but does not bring up the dog when he speaks to them. He exhibits no sentimentality and indulges in no judgment, an adult approach mirroring that of Ántonia and her family. After listening to Jan's story, Ántonia tempers his sadness by suggesting a special burial space, a good example of Cather's insight into children and her scrupulous attention to detail in "Cuzak's Boys." She provides no name but takes care of the body, whereas when Homer's Argus dies he is never mentioned again.

By making the return of Jim more focused on "the woman" than is the return of Rip Van Winkle, who dreads seeing his wife, or even that of Odysseus, who seeks both wife and throne, Cather distinguishes the modernity of Jim's heroism: his return is voluntary, even gratuitous. As the maker of his return's meaning, he dreads the destructive potential of mutability: "I did not want to find her aged and broken; I really dreaded it" (318). When Odysseus first sees Penelope, Homer describes her radiance and the lustful thoughts of the suitors for seventy-six lines before mentioning that Odysseus "glowed with joy" (18:282), a joy having more to do with her cunning, and hence constancy, than her beauty. In a "faltering voice" Irving's Rip Van Winkle asks his daughter, before he has revealed who he is, about Dame Van Winkle. The narrator comments, upon Rip's hearing she is dead, "There was a drop of comfort at least in this intelligence" (39). Jefferson, in his stage directions, has Rip react "*with mixed emotions*" (305) when he hears she is still alive, then saying (to a sure laugh) "Poor Derrick!" about the man she has married. When he actually sees Gretchen, he reacts to her aged appearance with another laugh line: "My, my! Is that my wife?" (308).

In contrast to Homer's epic tensions, Cather makes Jim's first sight of Ántonia "one of those quiet moments that clutch the heart, and take more courage than the noisy, excited passages in life" (321). Jim describes Ántonia as "battered but not diminished" (321). Instead of Irving's misogyny or Jefferson's conventional male levity about women's aging, Cather has Jim generalize beyond gender about the "shock" it always is "to meet *people* after long years" (321–22, my emphasis). "Battered" is a strong word Cather uses about people to capture something akin to the sublimity Romantics found in ruins, and of course Jim calls himself "battered" after Wick Cutter beats him (241).[12] Cather shows that Ántonia has aged without being defined by that or losing her allure. Jim can present her as "battered," and show her often-prosaic ideas and conventional values, confident that her vitality will dominate. It is important to stress that he says the most romantic, mythologizing things about Ántonia in this section of the novel—she "had always been one to leave images in the mind that did not fade," "she still had that something which fires the imagination," and "she was a rich mine of life, like the founders of early races" (342)—when he describes himself, reminiscent of Odysseus sleeping in the swineherd's hut or Rip sleeping in the woods, lying in a haymow, thinking while he falls asleep. Ántonia becomes Penelope, that is, the icon, most fully in the returning man's dreams.

The details of the actual moment of encounter are enhanced by the allusive power of Jim as Odyssean in the most positive sense, the "no name" searcher of customs and manners. At Ántonia's door Jim is acutely aware of the kind of seemingly adventitious details—white cats among the yellow pumpkins, a girl dropping her dish towel, the "calm and self-possessed" nature of the girl who asks him to sit down—that keen-eyed Odysseus always notes in a new place. The actual moment of reunion happens so quickly that Jim is awkwardly halfway between standing and sitting—Odysseus for once at a loss. Consciously or not, when he sees Ántonia's eyes he thinks in Homeric fashion, contrasting hers to all the thousands of eyes he has seen since last seeing them (320–21). Ántonia speaks to him without recognition, just as Penelope does not recognize Odysseus or as Rip's village does not recognize him: "My husband's not at home, sir" (322).

Jim's "Have I changed so much?" response has fascinating precursors in Cather's fiction and in *My Ántonia* that show how she reworked this dramatic kind of scene so that Ántonia's plain conventionality—a man she does not recognize must be there for her husband, not her—and the absence of eros actually intensify the impact. Cather's fiction shows a steady movement away from eros and passion for her returners as well as a steady increase in the amount of time they have been gone. In "The Treasure of Far Island" (1902), after a ten-year absence, Douglas Burnham says, "Tell me, is this Margie?" (270); Margie later claims that her wait has been "longer than the waiting of Penelope," and at story's end "the two had become as gods" (282). In "The Bohemian Girl" (1912), after twelve years Nils Ericson asks Clara Vavrika, with whom he runs away, "Aren't you at all surprised to see me?" (16), and his mother, "Don't you know me?" (7), the very question asked in *O Pioneers!* (1913) after sixteen years by the returning Carl Linstrum to the woman he eventually marries: "Don't you know me, Alexandra?" (99). Cather builds to the power of the reuniting scene in *My Ántonia* with a motif of surprise entrances in doorways, Ántonia playfully asking "You ain't forget about me, Jim?" (150) when she comes to the Harlings, Lena asking Ántonia "Don't you know me?" (155) when she comes to Black Hawk, and then making the question a statement in Lincoln, "I expect you hardly know me, Jim" (257). Cather's careful preparation for Jim's more-than-rhetorical "Have I changed so much?" emphasizes the extent to which personal identity, rather than eros or family or any other consideration, is at stake.

Like Homer, Cather shows the male returner rediscovering the unpredictable intensity of the woman. The joy of Ántonia's first response—expressed, significantly, to her daughters rather than to Jim—suddenly turns to alarm just as she catches Jim's hands: "What's happened? Is anybody dead?" This response is not in Jim's vision of the event any more than Odysseus's getting tricked by Penelope is, or Rip's not knowing the date. It is one of those small, never-cited details of *My Ántonia*—five words—that strikingly captures Ántonia's emotional, histrionic, even morbid imagination, just as Jim's short response reveals so much about their relationship; after patting her arm, he says, "No. I didn't come to a funeral this time" (322). *This time*: Jim has come back at least once before, for a funeral; while critics of Jim might point out that he did not seek to meet Ántonia then, it is perhaps more to the point that she apparently did not attend the funeral, presumably for one or both of his grandparents. The connection between Jim and Ántonia is marked by a kind of shorthand to which they have returned with ease: neutral, quick communication, above suspicions or blaming, right back to where they were the last time they were together, when Jim "felt rather than saw her smile" while she commented on his promise to return (314).

Cather uses the limited physical contact between Jim and Ántonia at the moment of reunion to epitomize their lifelong physical relationship, which she places between the extremes of Odysseus's eros and Rip's sexual loathing. Ántonia's reaching for Jim's hands rather than embracing him, feeling alarm at the moment of contact ("She had no sooner caught my hands than she looked alarmed" [322]), and ending contact entirely when she is most passionate all suggest exactly what Ántonia's indignant drawing of her face away from Jim when he kissed her more than two decades before suggests: that Ántonia is at least as much responsible for their nonsexual relationship as Jim. The critical focus on Jim's sexuality, as if that were all that mattered, discounts Ántonia's sexuality and identity. His nonsexualized approach to her contrasts with the Odyssean double standard and the anti-sexual angst of Rip Van Winkle, who in Irving's story is glad to hear his wife has died and in Jefferson's play is relieved she is married to someone else. For Rip, sex equals danger because women are allied with chthonic forces of fury. By contrasting Jim with Odysseus and Rip, and by going as far as describing Jim's teenage erotic dreams, Cather emphasizes that people cannot choose the objects of their sexual desire. Although Jim wants her to, Ántonia does not appeal to him sexually; Lena is the temptress of his dreams. For Cather, sexual attraction arises as randomly and uncontrollably as it does in Ovid, no matter whom one might care for or love.

A reader of critical discussions of *My Ántonia* could easily get the impression that it ends with a combination of Jim's hayloft mythologizing and its final paragraph. In between those, however, the chapters on Cuzak and Black Hawk, through allusions to the *Odyssey* and "Rip Van Winkle," intensify the novel's cultural critique of America at the time of World War I. Cather, like Homer, Irving, and Jefferson, implies a future by including depictions of the generation to follow the returner. The second chapter of "Cuzak's Boys" first contrasts and then links Jim and Cuzak. Jim, who is smoking in the orchard when Cuzak and his son arrive, notes that "Ántonia came running down from the house and hugged the two men as if they had been away for months" (345), a contrast to his own return after twenty years so obvious in its histrionic excess that he makes no comment. Unlike Cuzak, Jim has no desire to be the "the corrective" to Ántonia's "impulse" (347). Jim senses immediately that Cuzak reads him accurately—"his lively, quizzical eyes told me that he knew all about me" (345). Neither of them belongs on a farm. In *My Ántonia* Cather does not make settled agriculture the norm for humans any more than Homer or Irving does. Sharing chores with Ántonia's boys, Jim begins "to feel the loneliness of the farm-boy at evening, when the chores seem everlastingly the same, and the world so far away" (336).[13] Jim and Cuzak are fellow Odyssean wanderers, restless, urban, inclined to play, and fundamentally different from the younger generation, represented by Ántonia's children.

The *Odyssey*'s focus on Telemachus suggests that the generation following Odysseus will be strong, though not heroic on the Odyssean scale, and perhaps a little short on initiative. Irving's "Rip Van Winkle" offers a shiftless namesake of Rip but some hope for a curiously matriarchal future thanks to a responsible daughter; Rip will live with a daughter in both Irving's and Jefferson's versions. In *My Ántonia* childless Jim Burden is impressed with the children. Although Jim gives a delicate, perceptive picture of Ántonia's daughters, particularly the "calm and self-possessed" (321) Anna, who in effect runs this family event and appears to be indispensable, his emphasis is on Cuzak's boys. In a frank, physical way, Jim admires these boys possibly more than readers do; dutiful and positive, like Telemachus and Rip's daughter, they seem at best echoes of others, even as they have been named after others, though not, curiously, after Jim. When Ántonia lists who is named after whom, she does not seem self-conscious about the absence of a Jim; perhaps it is a kind of honor. Regardless, the future, as in Tennyson's "Ulysses," is in good but dull hands, a generational extension of what Jim earlier noted about the younger brothers and sisters of the "hired girls," who, despite such sacrifices and "advantages," "never seem to me, when I meet them now, half as interesting or as well educated" as their less privileged siblings (192). In her 1923 *Nation* article "Nebraska: The End of the First Cycle," Cather contrasts the generation from which she drew Ántonia, "rugged figures in the background which inspire respect, compel admiration" to their children, who focus mainly on consumption and "material comfort." Cather in effect explodes the fallacy of liberalism that history is progress (236–38).[14]

Comparing Jim with Odysseus and Rip underscores how positive Cather makes him about his own future. Odysseus will travel again, probably without the earnestness of Victorian bravado in Tennyson's "Ulysses," but definitely away from home. Rip, on the other hand, will stay at home, finding what he can that is unchanging, turning away from the modern Yankee world toward the romantic ideal of village life, living as a kind of a superannuated child, supported by responsible members of the younger generation. Jim, having "the sense of coming home to myself, and of having found out what a little circle man's experience is" (360), shows no desire to stay in this particular place, because it is the self, not a place, he has come home to. His future includes traveling for his job as well as "playing" with Cuzak's boys. He focuses on the sons both because his society allows few ways for him to play with young women and because the sons, trapped as they are by farming, will apparently need "play" more than the daughters. Jim will function as a liberator who knows the value of playing—that is, expansive human behavior wholly unconnected to work or gain—in an increasingly materialistic culture.[15] When he is done with the sons, he has Cuzak, who, like himself (not to mention Rip Van Winkle), acts "as if he had just wakened up" (356), and whom he knows already understands the value, even the necessity, of play and nondirected wandering, at least for himself. Critics who claim that Jim rejects the present to "retreat into a second childhood" (Tellefsen 241) denigrate childhood, a rich time of playing, as well as Jim and the novel. Jim and Cuzak, adults from the generation who witnessed the age's heroic but now vanished transforming of nature, do not long for the past. They live very much in the present, Cuzak expanding the farm and Jim passionate about new ideas and schemes. They do not reject the present so much as delimit it and not overvalue it.

Cather's allusions to "Rip Van Winkle" are most obvious in the chapter ending *My Ántonia*, a Black Hawk visit Jim finds "disappointing." He sees "strange children," notices trees cut down, and experiences the very emblem of Rip's village day by sitting "under a shady cottonwood tree in the yard behind his saloon" with Jelinek (357). Unlike Rip's Nicholas Vedder, Jelinek has survived and also managed to keep his tree, whereas in Rip's changed village, "instead of the great tree that used to shelter the quiet little Dutch inn of yore, there now was reared a tall naked pole" for the cultural symbol of the American flag (37). Jelinek's saloon—which even the "church people" admitted was "as respectable as a saloon can be" (210)—is not a typical American place, any more than Vedder's was, and with the mounting pressure of the WCTU at the time of Jim's narrative, it is not marked for survival.[16] As in "Rip Van Winkle," transplanted European culture in *My Ántonia* is shown losing, chillingly, to a particularly narrow American culture.

The vestigial culture of Jelinek's notwithstanding, Jim has no desire to remain in Black Hawk. In the afternoon, escaping "the curious depression that hangs over little towns," he finds last traces of the native prairie and has "the good luck to stumble upon" other vestigial remains, "a bit of the first road that went from Black Hawk out to the north country" (358–59)—a narrative development that cannot help but raise the question, What has changed? In the *Odyssey*, Odysseus is back where he was, pursuing the heroic life on domestic terms, with humans still caught between the gods and nature. Homer seems to ask if the Trojan War accomplished anything for the Greeks besides a temporary reestablishment of the past. In "Rip Van Winkle," on the other hand, "the very character of the people had changed," from the archetypal "village" of "phlegm and drowsy tranquility" to the Yankee world, "busy, bustling, disputatious" (37).

Irving in effect asks if America has lost the traditional world of villages nestled within the rhythms of nature.

My Ántonia's focus is on a very narrow part of America's epic history, not the ancient life of the Native Americans, only hinted at in town names and legends, or the "heroic" phases of exploration or of moving the indigenous peoples via warfare, but the first real settlers, opportunists who established what now might be called "infrastructure."[17] It is fascinating that Cather always associated Joseph Jefferson, who spent his entire career playing a man who slept into another era, with the same transition period in America that *My Ántonia* portrays. In praising Jefferson's autobiography as "one of the most engaging and least pretentious works in the literature of the drama," for instance, she recalls his "early wanderings" on the Great Lakes, when its shores "were dotted with Indian villages," across the newly settled Illinois prairie, and then into Mexico behind the army, saying the new generation of actors, bounded by "between Broadway and Fifty-first Street," simply cannot have as rich an experience or imagination ("Open Letter" 683).[18] In Cather's version of romanticism, different qualities flourish in different eras, just as distinct cultures invariably nurture some qualities while suppressing others. The vast creation of prairie infrastructure tantalized the imagination with possibilities for the new culture. Although the hope in *My Ántonia* is clearly for the new culture to be more European than Yankee, that is, one where more human qualities flourish, part of the novel's elegiac tone comes from the recognition that Yankee culture, with its Black Hawk repressions, has won.

THE INTERTEXTUAL PERSPECTIVE FROM *SAPPHIRA*

Jim's question "Have I changed so much?" has another dimension not fully clear until Cather's last novel, whose epilogue, read intertextually as describing source material for "Cuzak's Boys," suggests viewing Jim's return from the children's perspective. *Sapphira*, like *My Mortal Enemy*, features a woman returning after twenty-five years for a reunion witnessed by girls disappointed with the returners' resemblance to the much-told stories of their exciting exits. While it is commonly asserted that with her last novel Cather returned for the first time since her literary apprenticeship to the Virginia material of her childhood,[19] *Sapphira*'s epilogue, in which Cather herself appears as a child, strikingly parallels the reunion scene in *My Ántonia*: a changed world, a "classy" forty-something returner, kitchen settings, reunited pairs talking extensively while being overheard by children, and the returner not matching the stories the children knew so well. The children in both novels thus see a "character" with a process of comparison/contrast not unlike the intertextual experience of readers matching Jim, Odysseus, and Rip Van Winkle.[20]

It takes several pages in *Sapphira* for child Cather to stop being a critic of the returner who did not match "the picture I had carried in my mind."[21] In *My Ántonia* Jim realizes that Ántonia's children believe people from her childhood to be "remarkable" (339); thus it is hard for the children and Ántonia herself to imagine them outside that mythic time. Ántonia includes Jim in the term "you children," followed immediately by "these children"; while in the context understandable, it is still an astonishing thing to say to an adult. In the family mythology, Jim is ever a boy, which gives a subtle ironic impact to Ántonia's telling him "I can't believe it's you" (324). When, by asking how many children he has, she does try to consider him as an adult, she ends up getting "embarrassed" (325). With such expectations, no wonder neither Ántonia nor the children—with the fascinating possible exception of Leo—immediately recognize Jim. As a family icon, he *has* changed "so much."

Leo is the child most keenly aware of how much Jim has changed from the family myths. In this regard and others, Leo strongly resembles child Cather as characterized in *Sapphira*. They are ur-artists and critics, iconoclastic, irrepressible and emotionally autonomous. To the extent that we can also link Leo and Blind d'Arnault, whom he physically resembles, we can, a little, deracialize the portrayal of the black pianist: he and Leo, and implicitly child Cather, heroically exude urges and qualities the prevailing culture cannot succeed in suppressing, a lesson child Cather learns in reverse by studying Nancy, who has clearly flourished by leaving Virginia.[22] So too, the demythologized Jim Burden suggests possibilities available only beyond Nebraska.

Despite giving children special insight in both *My Ántonia* and *Sapphira*, Cather does not privilege the child's point of view. The Wick Cutter story, for instance, delights Ántonia's children—"Hurrah! The murder!" (349)—in the same way the Pavel and Peter wolf story thrilled Ántonia and Jim, but Wick's plan to rape Ántonia is not among the children's stories. One of the most daring treatments of rape in American literature, not least because of Jim's reaction of disgust toward Ántonia and sex, it can be misunderstood because of the fallacy of the false present so frequent in commentary on Jim Burden. The fallacy of the false present involves ignoring the true "present" of the narrative at any given point, in which Jim writes and reflects on long past incidents, in favor of the actual time of the incidents. Many of the most negative responses to Jim build a case on his quite normal childhood behavior, such as his complaining that Ántonia sometimes takes a superior tone with him or his asking Ántonia "What did you jabber Bohunk for?" (44) after the close call with the snake.[23] Ignoring the true narrative present can keep readers from viewing Jim the way Cather made him, as a man writing a document, not merely as a boy or an icon of family myth.[24]

Has Jim Burden changed so much? He has aged, of course, and the world has changed, for the heroic cultural potential he and Ántonia experienced as children has been lost. Yet he has learned that the things lost are part of his very identity; they are present to him the way the connections with the *Odyssey* and "Rip Van Winkle" are present to readers of "Cuzak's Boys." Thanks to his reunion with Ántonia he has come "home" to himself, that is, to the old unrest he shares with Odysseus, to the need for play he shares with Rip, and to the child in himself. In that sense he is very much like the little girl in *Sapphira and the Slave Girl* who watched Nancy's return and then reimagined the experience in *My Ántonia* from the simultaneous perspective of adult returner and child witness. Cather's intertextual dexterity transforms being two things at once from modern indeterminacy to art.

NOTES

I am grateful to the National Endowment for the Humanities Summer Seminar program and Newark Academy for generous research opportunities to work on this project.

1. It would be easier to list studies of Cather that *do not* approach Jim rather negatively—Urgo, for instance—because most studies do. Particularly intense characterizations can be found in the following (in chronological order): Gelfant; Lambert; Schwind; Fetterley; Rosowski; Lee; John J. Murphy; Joseph Murphy; Funda; Peck; Woolley; Ammons; Jones; Lindemann, "'It Ain't My Prairie'"; O'Brien, Introduction; Lindemann, *Willa Cather*; and Stout.

2. Cather explicitly alludes to the *Odyssey* in "The Treasure of Far Island" (282), "Flavia and Her Artists" (27), *One of Ours* (209), and *Death Comes for the Archbishop* (4); her description of the Arctic explorer Nansen as "possessed of an old unrest, the Odysseus fever," might reasonably be used about Jim Burden ("Nansen" 523). The various scholarly editions of her novels, as well as John March's *A Reader's Companion to the Fiction of Willa Cather*, give ample evidence for Cather's allusiveness. See also Arnold, Thomas 76–97, and especially Sutherland.

3. Joan Wylie Hall notes the Homeric connection and hypothesizes an allusion to *Joseph Andrews*.

4. I describe Cather's allusiveness in "Cuzak's Boys" as "invitations" in order to suggest how readers might use them but also to acknowledge that, for readers not noticing them, *My Ántonia* still "works." Theories of allusion, often subsumed under Kristeva's 1969 neologism *l'intertextualité* (which she soon discarded), have posited quite disparate combinations of roles for author, text(s), culture, and reader since *My Ántonia* was published in 1918, and have difficulty defining precisely something so apparent, pervasive, ancient yet so varied. Most theories agree on only one point: the inadequacy of previous theory. Joseph Pucci, despite coining the term *attexuality* to replace *allusion*, and treating everything from 1920 to 1965 as the monolithic New Criticism, provides an insightful discussion and overview of the problems of theorizing allusion. For quite different perspectives, see Brower and also Clayton and Rothstein.

5. Kain lists the five overt references to Rip Van Winkle in *Ulysses* with motifs associated with Bloom (283); Gunn discusses a restored passage with another reference to Rip Van Winkle. The rich mythic and folkloric background of "Rip Van Winkle" is extensively explored in Young's "Fall from Time: The Mythic Rip Van Winkle." Much of Otmar's difficult-to-find "Peter Klaus" is available in Prochmann 489–

94. Irving's story suggests such overt political readings that, as Hulpke points out, the German translators had serious difficulties.

6. Postlewait 163. An 1896 film version, featuring Joseph Jefferson on his farm in New Jersey, is discussed in Johnson, "Evaluating Early Film" 101–22.

7. By 1875 he had already performed the role of Rip more than fourteen hundred times (Hutton 208). See also Quinn 330–32, Scanlan 52–54, and Jefferson, *Autobiography* 341.

8. Cather used "courage" similarly—that is, to describe looking directly into someone's eyes in a moment of great emotion—in her previous novel, *The Song of the Lark* (342, 367).

9. Defoe also puts the footprint exactly in the book's middle (112).

10. In the notes to his translation of the *Odyssey*, Pope rises to Argus's (and Homer's) defense against French neoclassic charges that the Argus episode violates epic decorum: "I do not know any thing more beautiful or more affecting in the whole Poem. . . . In my judgment, *Ulysses* appears more amiable while he weeps over his faithful Dog, than when he drives an army of enemies before him" (Pope 148–49). In 1709 Pope also wrote an eighteen-line poem entitled "Argus." In *Joseph Andrews* Fielding has Joseph, unknowingly returned home to the parents who lost him nearly twenty years before, witness the death of "a little Dog, the Favourite of the eldest Daughter," who came "limping in all bloody, and laid himself at his Mistress's Feet," slain through mere "ill-Nature" by a local tyrant, for whom Joseph and Adams have a few strong words and then forget (III.4.178). In *Don Juan*, Juan eats his spaniel's forepaw and Byron jokes that a returning Ulysses will find "his Argus bites him by the breeches" (II: 70–71; III: 23). Byron claimed personal knowledge: "I had one (half a *wolf* by the she-side) that doted on me at ten years old, and very nearly ate me at twenty. When I thought he was going to enact Argus, he bit away the backside of my breeches" (*Letters* 255). In *Ulysses*, Bloom has a cat rather than a dog, but Joyce does have Bloom recall his father's "infirm" dog Athos, early recognized as an echo of Argus, three times, including once in the "Ithaca" episode; Athos appears in the Hades, Circe, and Ithaca sections (89, 516, 706). See Gilbert 162.

11. When a child, Cather witnessed an Argus-like experience. As her family boarded the train to leave Virginia for Nebraska, Vic, her father's favorite sheepdog, "came running across the fields, dragging her broken chain." It was, according to Edith Lewis, "one of Willa Cather's saddest memories" of that "tragic" time (7–8). Perhaps Cather, a longtime reader of and contributor to the Webster County *Argus* (presumably named after the other famous classical Argus), was especially sensitive to the name *Argus*. Her first surviving writing is an essay praising the

"noble" dog over the "crul" cat (Woodress 48). I owe the observation that farm boy Jim has no dog to Robert Miller.

12. In "A Wagner Matinée," Clark uses "battered" about his aunt and connects it to the "awe and respect" one has for damaged explorers (*Collected Stories* 191); in *The Song of the Lark*, the narrator uses it about Wunsch, a man under the sway of Dionysus, and Mrs. Nathanmeyer uses it about a particularly fragile kind of female beauty (24, 277). In the magazine and *Troll Garden* versions of "A Wagner Matinée," Cather used "misshapen," which she switched to "battered" for the 1920 *Youth and the Bright Medusa* (*The Troll Garden* 163).

13. As the ghostwriter of S. S. McClure's autobiography in 1914, Cather has McClure make this point quite strongly: "I had always hated chores, and I had been a chore-boy since I was eleven years old. Now my patience was exhausted. I detested currying horses, for instance; I hated the dust and the hair and the smell; and now I had come to the place where I simply couldn't take care of stables any more. To this day 'chore' is to me the most hateful word in the English language. I am sure that thousands of country boys share my detestation of it. Chores are to country boys what dish-washing is to country girls—a dreary, drudging routine that hangs over the most cheerful day" (*Autobiography of S. S. McClure* 89–90).

14. Cather further comments that the younger generation "wants to live and die in an automobile." Ántonia's daughter Martha and her husband, Joe, have a Ford; New Yorker Jim arrives at the Cuzak farm in a horse-drawn wagon.

15. In "The Bohemian Girl," Nils Ericson, responding to Clara's comment on their youth that "We knew how to play," makes his case for adult play by commenting that "I can play better than I used to, and harder" and following that with "Last call for play, Mrs. Ericson!" (27).

16. Both "Rip Van Winkle" and *My Ántonia* were written at a time when American per capita consumption of alcohol was beginning to fall precipitously. See Musto.

17. See Fischer 31–44 and Stout 157–59.

18. In the section of the *Autobiography* to which Cather refers, Jefferson himself contrasts the bucolic scenes he witnessed along the Great Lakes with the present, though his conclusion is different from Cather's: "Now as I write in the autumn of my life these once quiet shores are covered with busy cities; the furnaces glow with melted iron, the locomotive screams and whistles along the road where once the ox-teams used to carry the mail, and corner lots and real-estate agents 'fill the air.' When we think that all these wonderful changes have taken place within the last fifty years, it is startling to speculate upon what the next half century may bring about" (21).

19. For example, Woodress says the 1902 poem "The Namesake" makes the last "direct use of Virginia" until *Sapphira* (30), and O'Brien asserts that "in 'The Elopement of Allen Poole' (1893) Cather drew on her memories of Back Creek, a source of fictional material to which she did not return until *Sapphira and the Slave Girl* (1940)" (*Willa Cather* 195).

20. Stout's phrase about Cather establishing in *Sapphira* a modernist "fundamental multiplicity of vision" is particularly apt (293).

21. The child's difficulty distinguishing between life and art accentuates a kind of wisdom Cather often gives to children, who bypass the impenetrable barriers between people by in effect witnessing them aesthetically and getting pleasure, even awe, from what child Cather calls "the spell" (288). The childish first responses of a self irritated to find reality divergent from its own picture give way to an "artistic" experience that enriches the child. Rather than whites finding their emotion in blacks, as Morrison charges (27–28), this scene shows children, especially creative children, doing what they always do. Cather's absolute pronouncement on this occurs in "The Treasure of Far Island," in a long paragraph that begins "A child's normal attitude toward the world is that of the artist, pure and simple" and ends "To these two children the entire world, like the people who dwelt in it, had been valued solely for what they suggested to the imagination, and people and places alike were merely stage properties, contributing more or less to the intensity of their inner life" (275–76).

22. O'Brien discusses the reunion scene in *Sapphira* in the context of another Cather childhood incident, when young Willa shocks her mother by proclaiming "I'se a dang'ous nigger, I is!" in the presence of a judge (*Willa Cather* 43–46). This can be seen as reinforcing the connection of child Cather with both Leo and Blind d'Arnault, especially considering O'Brien's reading of Cather's relationship with her mother: Cather has Blind d'Arnault's mother both love him "devotedly" yet be "ashamed" (185) of him, and she makes Leo, unlike herself, his mother's favorite, even though Ántonia calls him the "worst of all" (325).

23. For a discussion of this passage see Lindemann, "'It Ain't My Prairie'" 122.

24. One of the most influential studies of Jim's flaws, Blanche H. Gelfant's "The Forgotten Reaping Hook: Sex in *My Ántonia*" (1971), argues that Jim fears and represses sexuality. Yet the key evidence cited in its title misleads: the reaping hook is not "forgotten" because, clearly, many years after having had the dream Jim recalls its details perfectly and puts them in his manuscript; how else would Gelfant know he had "forgotten" things? Having once described the dream in its entirety,

he refers to it a second time in a shorter version. Notwithstanding the case to be made about what might better be called "the edited reaping hook," the difference between a blink and a wink is crucial. Gelfant's essay has much value, but many of the other criticisms of Jim, often reliant on the "forgotten" reaping hook, reduce him and thus Cather's novel.

WORKS CITED

Ammons, Elizabeth. "*My Ántonia* and African American Art." O'Brien, *New Essays* 57–84.

Arnold, Marilyn. "The Allusive Cather." *Cather Studies* 3 (1996): 137–48.

Brower, Reuben. *Alexander Pope: The Poetry of Allusion*. Oxford: Oxford UP, 1959.

Byron, George Gordon Byron. *Byron's Letters and Journals*. Vol. 4. Ed. Leslie A. Marchand. Cambridge: Harvard UP, 1978.

———. *Don Juan*. Ed. T. G. Steffan et al. New York: Penguin, 1977.

Cather, Willa. *The Autobiography of S. S. McClure*. Lincoln: U of Nebraska P, 1997. Rpt. of S. S. McClure. *My Autobiography*. New York: Frederick A. Stokes, 1914.

———. "The Bohemian Girl." 1912. *Willa Cather's Collected Short Fiction, 1892–1912*. Ed. Virginia Faulkner. Lincoln: U of Nebraska P, 1970. 3–41.

———. *Collected Stories*. New York: Vintage, 1992.

———. *Death Comes for the Archbishop*. 1927. Willa Cather Scholarly Edition. Ed. Charles W. Mignon with Frederick M. Link and Kari A. Ronning. Historical essay and explanatory notes John J. Murphy. Lincoln: University of Nebraska Press, 1999.

———. "Flavia and Her Artists." 1905. *Collected Stories*. New York: Vintage, 1992. 3–29.

———. Interview with Flora Merrill. "A Short Story Course Can Only Delay." *New York World* 19 Apr. 1925: sec. 3:1+. Rpt. in *Willa Cather in Person: Interviews, Speeches, and Letters*. Sel. and ed. L. Brent Bohlke. Lincoln: U of Nebraska P, 1986. 73–80.

———. "Joseph Jefferson in *Rip Van Winkle*." *The World and the Parish: Willa Cather's Articles and Reviews, 1893–1902*. Sel. and ed. with a commentary by William M. Curtin. Lincoln: U of Nebraska P, 1970. 1: 422–23. Rpt. of rev. of *Rip Van Winkle*, *Pittsburgh Leader* 10 Nov. 1896.

———. *My Ántonia*. 1918. Willa Cather Scholarly Edition. Ed. Charles Mignon with Kari Ronning. Historical essay James

Woodress. Explanatory notes James Woodress with Kari Ronning, Kathleen Danker, and Emily Levine. Lincoln: U of Nebraska P, 1994.
———. "Nansen: 'That Unmistakable Norse Accent.'" *The World and the Parish: Willa Cather's Articles and Reviews, 1893–1902*. Sel. and ed. with a commentary by William M. Curtin. Lincoln: U of Nebraska P, 2004. 2: 521–25. Rpt. of "That Unmistakable Norse Accent," *Pittsburgh Leader* 1 Dec. 1897, and *Lincoln Courier* 18 Dec. 1897: 4–5.
———. "Nebraska: The End of the First Cycle." *Nation* 117 (1923): 236–38.
———. "The Novel Démeublé." 1922. Rpt. in *Not Under Forty*. Lincoln: U of Nebraska P, 1988. 43–51.
———. *One of Ours*. 1922. New York: Vintage, 1971.
———. "An Open Letter to Joseph Jefferson." *The World and the Parish: Willa Cather's Articles and Reviews, 1893–1902*. Sel. and ed. with a commentary by William M. Curtin. Lincoln: U of Nebraska P, 2004. 2: 680–87. Rpt. of *Lincoln Courier* 2 Dec. 1899: 3–4.
———. *O Pioneers!* 1913. Willa Cather Scholarly Edition. Ed. Susan J. Rosowski and Charles W. Mignon with Kathleen Danker. Historical essay and explanatory notes David Stouck. Lincoln: U of Nebraska P, 1992.
———. *Sapphira and the Slave Girl*. New York: Knopf, 1940.
———. *The Song of the Lark*. 1915. Ed. Janet Sharistanian. Oxford: Oxford UP, 2000.
———. "The Treasure of Far Island." 1902. *Willa Cather's Collected Short Fiction, 1892–1912*. Ed. Virginia Faulkner. Lincoln: U of Nebraska P, 1970. 265–82.
———. *The Troll Garden: A Definitive Edition*. Ed. James Woodress. Lincoln: U of Nebraska P, 1983.
———. "A Wagner Matinée. *Collected Stories*. New York: Vintage, 1992. 190–96.
———. *Willa Cather's Collected Short Fiction, 1892–1912*. Ed. Virginia Faulkner. Lincoln: U of Nebraska P, 1970.
———. *The World and the Parish: Willa Cather's Articles and Reviews, 1893–1902*. Ed. William M. Curtin. 2 vols. Lincoln: U of Nebraska P, 1970, 2004.
Clayton, Jay, and Eric Rothstein, ed. *Influence and Intertextuality in Literary History*. Madison: U of Wisconsin P, 1991.
Defoe, Daniel. *Robinson Crusoe*. Ed. Michael Shinagel. 2nd ed. New York: Norton, 1994.
Fetterley, Judith. "*My Ántonia*, Jim Burden, and the Dilemma of the Lesbian Writer." *Gender Studies: New Directions in Feminist*

Criticism. Ed. Judith Spector. Bowling Green OH: Bowling Green State U Popular P, 1986. 43–59.

Fielding, Henry. *Joseph Andrews: With Shamela and Related Writings*. Ed. Homer Goldberg. New York: Norton, 1987.

Fischer, Mike. "Pastoralism and Its Discontents: Willa Cather and the Burden of Imperialism." *Mosaic* 23 (1990): 31–44.

Funda, Evelyn I. "'The Breath Vibrating behind It': Intimacy and the Storytelling of Ántonia Shimerda." *Western American Literature* 29.3 (1994): 195–216.

Gelfant, Blanche H. "The Forgotten Reaping Hook: Sex in *My Ántonia*." *American Literature* 43 (March 1971): 60–82.

Gilbert, Stuart. *James Joyce's* Ulysses: *A Study*. 1930. Rev. ed. New York: Vintage, 1952.

Gunn, Daniel P. "Note." *James Joyce Quarterly* 24.2 (1987): 218–19.

Hall, Joan Wylie. "Dead Dogs at Homecoming: A Homeric Motif in *My Ántonia*." *Willa Cather Pioneer Memorial Newsletter and Review* 33.1 (1989): 5–6.

Homer. *The Odyssey*. Trans. Robert Fagles. New York: Viking Penguin, 1996.

Hulpke, Erika. "Cultural Constraints: A Case of Political Censorship." *Interculturality and the Historical Study of Literary Translations*. Ed. Harald Kittel and Armin Paul Frank. Berlin: Erich Schmidt Verlag, 1991. 71–74.

Hutton, Laurence. *Plays and Players*. New York: Hurd and Houghton, 1875.

Irving, Washington. "Rip Van Winkle." 1819. *The Sketch Book of Geoffrey Crayon, Gent*. Ed. Haskell Springer. Boston: Twayne, 1978. 28–42. Vol. 8 of *The Complete Works of Washington Irving*. 30 vols. 1969–89.

Jefferson, Joseph. *The Autobiography of Joseph Jefferson*. Ed. Alan S. Downer. Cambridge: Harvard UP, 1964.

———. *Rip Van Winkle. The Black Crook and Other Nineteenth-Century American Plays*. Ed. Myron Matlaw. New York: Dutton, 1967.

Johnson, Stephen. "Evaluating Early Film as a Document of Theatre History: The 1896 Footage of Joseph Jefferson's *Rip Van Winkle*." *Nineteenth-Century Theatre* 20.2 (1992): 101–22.

———. "Joseph Jefferson's *Rip Van Winkle*." *Drama Review* 26.1 (1982): 3–20.

Jones, Anne Goodwyn. "Displacing Dixie: The Southern Subtext in *My Ántonia*." O'Brien, *New Essays* 85–110.

Joyce, James. *Ulysses*. 1922. New York: Vintage, 1961.

Kain, Richard M. *Fabulous Voyager: A Study of James Joyce's* Ulysses. New York: Viking, 1959.

Kristeva, Julia. *Semeiotikè*. Paris: Editions du Seuil, 1969.

Lambert, Deborah G. "The Defeat of a Hero: Autonomy and Sexuality in *My Ántonia*." *American Literature* 53.4 (1982): 76–90.

Lee, Hermione. *Willa Cather: A Life Saved Up*. London: Virago, 1989.

Lewis, Edith. *Willa Cather Living: A Personal Record*. 1953. Lincoln: U of Nebraska P, 2000.

Lindemann, Marilee. "'It Ain't My Prairie': Gender, Power, and Narrative in *My Ántonia*." O'Brien, *New Essays* 111–35.

———. *Willa Cather: Queering America*. New York: Columbia UP, 1999.

March, John. *A Reader's Companion to the Fiction of Willa Cather*. Ed. Marilyn Arnold with Debra Lynn Thornton. Westport CT: Greenwood P, 1993.

Morrison, Toni. *Playing in the Dark*. Cambridge: Harvard UP, 1992.

Murphy, John J. My Ántonia: *The Road Home*. Boston: Twayne, 1989.

Murphy, Joseph. "Cather's Re-Vision of American Typology in *My Ántonia*." *Willa Cather: Family, Community, and History*. Ed. John J. Murphy. Provo: Brigham Young U Humanities Publication Center, 1990. 213–19.

Musto, David F. "Alcohol in American History." *Scientific American* 274 (April 1996): 78–83.

O'Brien, Sharon. Introduction. O'Brien, *New Essays* 1–30.

———, ed. *New Essays on* My Ántonia. Cambridge: Cambridge UP, 1999.

———. *Willa Cather: The Emerging Voice*. New York: Oxford UP, 1987.

Peck, Demaree C. *The Imaginative Claims of the Artist in Willa Cather's Fiction*. Selinsgrove PA: Susquehanna UP, 1996.

Pope, Alexander. *The Twickenham Edition of the Poems of Alexander Pope*. Ed. John Butt. Vol. 10. New Haven: Yale UP, 1967.

Postlewait, Thomas. "The Hieroglyphic Stage: American Theatre and Society, Post-Civil War to 1945." *Cambridge History of American Theatre*, vol. 2, *1870–1945*. Ed. Don B. Wilmeth and Christopher Bigsby. Cambridge: Cambridge UP, 1998. 107–95.

Prochmann, Henry A. "Irving's German Sources in *The Sketch Book*." *Studies in Philology* 27 (1930): 477–507.

Pucci, Joseph. *The Full-Knowing Reader: Allusion and the Power of the Reader in the Western Literary Tradition*. New Haven: Yale UP, 1998.

Quinn, Arthur Hobson. *A History of the American Drama, from the Beginning to the Civil War*. 2nd ed. New York: Crofts, 1943.

Rose, Gilbert P. "Odysseus' Barking Heart." *Transactions of the American Philological Association* 109 (1979): 215–30.

Rosowski, Susan J. *The Voyage Perilous: Willa Cather's Romanticism*. Lincoln: U of Nebraska P, 1986.

Scanlan, Tom. "The Domestication of Rip Van Winkle: Joe Jefferson's Play as Prologue to Modern American Drama." *Virginia Quarterly Review* 50 (1974): 51–62.

Schwind, Jean. "The Benda Illustrations to *My Ántonia*: Cather's 'Silent' Supplement to Jim Burden's Narrative." *PMLA* 100 (1985): 51–67.

Stout, Janis P. *Willa Cather: The Writer and Her World*. Charlottesville: UP of Virginia, 2000.

Sutherland, Donald. "Willa Cather: The Classic Voice." *The Art of Willa Cather*. Ed. Bernice Slote and Virginia Faulkner. Lincoln: U of Nebraska P, 1974. 156–79.

Tellefsen, Blythe. "Blood in the Wheat: Willa Cather's *My Ántonia*." *Studies in American Fiction* 27.2 (1999): 229–44.

Thomas, Susie. *Willa Cather*. London: Macmillan, 1990.

Urgo, Joseph R. *Willa Cather and the Myth of American Migration*. Urbana: U of Illinois P, 1995.

Woodress, James. *Willa Cather: A Literary Life*. Lincoln: U of Nebraska P, 1987.

Woolley, Paula. "'Fire and Wit': Storytelling and the American Artist in Cather's *My Ántonia*." *Cather Studies* 3 (1996): 149–81.

Young, Philip. "Fall from Time: The Mythic Rip Van Winkle." *Kenyon Review* 22 (1960): 547–73. Rpt. in *Washington Irving: The Critical Reaction*. Ed. James W. Tuttleton. New York: AMS P, 1993. 67–84.

Shadows on the Rock
Against Interpretation

RICHARD H. MILLINGTON

In an early scene in *Shadows on the Rock*, Cécile Auclair has prevailed upon Mother Juschereau to tell her a story of the exemplary piety of her predecessor, Sister Catherine de Saint-Augustin. As the story comes to an end, Mother Juschereau is preparing to deliver the appropriate moral lesson when she is interrupted by a cry from her young listener: "*N'expliquez pas, chère Mère, je vous en supplie!*" ("Don't explain, dear Mother, I beg you!"). The nun takes this emphatic wish for delivery from interpretation as a sign that Cécile "certainly has no vocation" (39). I hope to use this plea to get at what *Shadows* shows us about the way Cather practiced hers. In my view, the book shares with its main character a resistance to interpretation, and it is in that resistance, I will be arguing, that this unobtrusive novel illuminates the ambitions and values that shape Cather's work.

READING *SHADOWS*

"*N'expliquez pas, cher Monsieur, je vous en supplie!*": Of course, the first thing I am going to do is a little explication. But my goal will be to describe a feature of the experience of reading *Shadows on the Rock*, and to specify and explore the significance of what I take to be the book's dramatized resistance to our customary habits of attention (particularly if we are in the habit of being English professors). Let me begin with some polemical definitions, taken from Susan Sontag's famous 1964 essay, "Against Interpretation":

> Directed to art, interpretation means plucking a set of elements (the X, the Y, the Z, and so forth) from the whole work. The task of interpretation is virtually one of translation. The interpreter says, Look, don't you see that X is really—or, really means—A? That Y is really B? That Z is really C? . . . The modern style of interpretation excavates, and as it excavates, destroys; it digs "behind" the text, to find a sub-text which is the true one. The most celebrated and influential modern doctrines, those of Marx and Freud, actually amount to elaborate systems of hermeneutics, aggressive and impious theories of interpretation. (5, 6–7)

My point about *Shadows on the Rock*—and I would suggest that it is representative of a strong strain or impulse within Cather's fiction as a whole—is that it seems to have been designed, as Cécile's cri de coeur hints, to resist the kind of interpretive, explanatory practice that Sontag describes. To read *Shadows* is to be forced by the text to throw away one's interpreter's shovel, to stifle one's inner Mike Wallace (ever on the lookout for the next stage-managed exposé), and to exchange that habit of mind for a form of responsiveness more descriptive and more observatory: a kind of witnessing. In the realm of character, for instance, what could be more fruitless than to psychoanalyze Cécile or Auclair? What could be more irrelevant than to posit on behalf of this novel's inhabitants elaborate schemes of self-recognition or maturation? Characters in this text do not develop in the manner of characters from traditional novels but instead on occasion make evident or transparent their natures, or come to see their own lives in a definitive or characteristic way. My point is not that readers *want* to treat the book's characters in the customary, explanatory way, but that the book, in its way of attending to its characters, pointedly disaffiliates itself from the "depth" model of character and from the interpretive procedures which that model customarily calls forth from its readers.

Similarly, if we think in terms of plot, the text's key moments or events are not revelatory transformations but quieter acts of heightened or illuminated witnessing: the observation of a particular quality of winter light, say, or the apprehension of a weight of meaning as it is gathered up by an object or a ritual. One of my favorite instances of such a moment of post- or anti-interpretive "taking in" is Cather's rendering of Jacques's regard for Cécile's cup:

> Much as Jacques loved chocolate . . . there was something he cared more about, something that gave him a kind of solemn satisfaction,—Cécile's cup. She had a silver cup with a handle; on the front was engraved a little wreath of roses, and inside that wreath was the name, *Cécile*, cut in the silver. Her Aunt Clothilde had given it to her when she was but a tiny baby, so it had been hers all her life. That was what seemed so wonderful to Jacques. His clothes had always belonged to somebody else before they were made over for him; he slept wherever there was room for him, sometimes with his mother, sometimes on a bench. He had never had anything of his own except his toy beaver,—and now he would have his shoes, made just for him. But to have a cup, with your name on it . . . even if you died, it would still be there, with your name. More than the shop with all the white jars and mysterious implements, more than the carpet and curtains and the red sofa, that cup fixed Cécile as born to security and privileges. . . . Cécile had suggested that he drink his chocolate from it, and she would use another. But he shook his head, unable to explain. That was not at all what her cup meant to him. Indeed, Cécile could not know what it meant to him; she was too fortunate. (86–88)

Although the meaning of the cup has everything to do with economic privilege—with class, as it was manifest in seventeenth-century Quebec—such a restating of the already apparent would hardly qualify as an interpretive claim of any use or moment. Rather, one's attention is drawn to the process by which the cup accrues meaning for Jacques, situated as he is; *that* is what qualifies as a significant event within the plot-logic of *Shadows on the Rock*. This characteristic emphasis—not on the emergence of hidden, explanatory meanings but on the ways meanings are made—is also evident in the text's most dramatically clarifying moment (the climax, one would have to say, of its extremely low-key plot), as Cécile re-sees her own domestic world upon returning from her visit to the Île d'Orléans: "These coppers, big and little, these brooms and clouts and brushes, were tools; and with them one made, not shoes or cabinet-work, but life itself. One made a climate within a climate; one made the days,—the complexion, the special flavour, the special happiness of each day as it passed; one made life" (198).

This is not the whole story on meaning-making in *Shadows*. There are characters who have a different kind of presence in the novel, a different relation to meaning. I am thinking here of Mother Catherine de Saint-Augustin, of the recluse Jeanne Le Ber, of Noël Chabanel, and Chabanel's later, intriguingly urbane imitator, Father St. Cyr—a group of characters I want to call "auto-icons." Unlike the book's other characters, members of this group have an extremely self-conscious relation to their own lives, each firmly in the grip of a teleological narrative of his or her own invention. They are, in a sense, people determined to become icons, to become interpretable in Sontag's sense as something other than, more than, themselves. They are, accordingly, associated with extreme, "hypernarrative" (and, intriguingly, performative) forms of language or action: writing in blood ("I will die in Canada"), the irrevocable vow ("I will be that lamp, that shall be my life," says Jeanne Le Ber), the sacred farce that composes Chabanel's career as the world's lamest missionary. There would be much to say about these figures, and I think the book's treatment of them is complex: contained in the bubble of their iconic self-conception, they nevertheless generate narratives that circulate pleasurably through the larger community. Still, one of their effects—their narrative function, I would argue—is to make evident by contrast, through their narrative extremity, their intense commitment to interpretability, the muted and reticent aesthetic of witnessing that is in effect all around them.

Toward the end of her essay, Sontag sets out to answer the two questions necessarily raised by her attack on the culture of interpretation: What kind of art might free the denizens of that culture from their depth-seeking habit of mind? And (in Sontag's own words) "What kind of criticism, of commentary on the arts, is desirable today?" (12). The great mission of contemporary art, as Sontag saw it in 1964, is the evasion of interpretation. This project or purpose is relatively evident and easy to achieve in some art forms—abstract painting, avant-garde experiments that foreground form—but it is also possible, she hopes, in more ostensibly conventional artistic practice: "Ideally, it is possible to elude the interpreters in another way, by making works of art whose surface is so unified and clean, whose momentum is so rapid, whose address is so direct that the work can be . . . just what it is" (11). (Is there a better brief description of Cather's style?) Or, as she puts it a little later in the essay: "Transparence is the highest, most liberating value in art . . . today" (13). Here is her reciprocal recommendation for those of us who write about art: "Our task is not to find the maximum amount of content in a work of art, much less to squeeze more content out of the work than is already there. Our task is to cut back on content so that we can see the thing at all. The aim of all commentary on art now should be to make works of art—and, by analogy, our own experience—more, rather than less, real to us. The function of criticism should be to show how it is what it is, even that it is what it is, rather than to show what it means" (14).

My point in citing Sontag's essay here is less to celebrate her work than to make a point about Cather's. In its "transparency," in its sustained and wittily dramatized resistance to the interpretive habits we bring to it, *Shadows on the Rock* is already "against" or "beyond" interpretation, making possible for us, through its refusal of our habits of attention, new forms of response and the new possibilities of feeling that attend them: "*N'expliquez pas, cher lecteur, je vous en supplie!*"

SHADOWS AND HISTORY

If I am right about the interpretation-resistant experience of reading that Cather creates and dramatizes in *Shadows on the Rock*, we are left with a question. What is the force of that accomplishment, that recasting of the novel and the attendant reshaping of our affective response to it? Why and how does this experience of redistributed interest, of a different kind of imaginative investment, matter? For Sontag, one must resist interpretation as a guard against some aspects of the experience of modern life, as part of an imaginative practice devoted to recovering sensory experience: "Ours is a culture based on excess, on overproduction; the result is a steady loss of sharpness in our sensory experience. All the conditions of modern life—its material plenitude, its sheer crowdedness—conjoin to dull our sensory faculties" (13). We need interpretation-resistant art and criticism because "What is important now is to recover our senses. We must learn to see more, to hear, more, to feel more" (14).

For Cather, I think, the stakes of the redistribution of readerly emotion her works attempt are different, because, as an "early" modernist, her understanding of the historical pressures on life and on the novel is different from the "late" modernist Sontag's. The resistance to interpretation mounted in Cather's work is less a refuge from the modern than an espousal of it (though *The Professor's House*, with its rendering of a fully formed commodity culture, seems to be an exception to this claim). If Sontag's enemy is a content-saturated modern culture, Cather's enemy is the resilient power of American Victorianism: a resolutely interpretive culture and sponsor of the nineteenth-century novel, whose trajectories of plot and character, whose management and instruction of its readers' responses continue to be the energizing antagonists of Cather's fictive practice.

The cultural force of Cather's enterprise in *Shadows* can be felt by recalling the qualities of that predecessor culture. Here I will be following closely the work of the cultural historian Daniel Joseph Singal. In "Towards a Definition of American Modernism," Singal argues that we should think of modernism not as a collection of compositional techniques or avant-garde ideas about art but as a "full-fledged historical culture" (8)—a set of intellectual, moral, and emotional commitments and attitudes that do indeed find powerful expression in aesthetic strategies. If we do this kind of thinking, we see that "modernism" must be defined in relation to—against, really—what might be called

"American Victorianism," its precursor culture, which was the dominant value system in America from the 1830s into the early twentieth century. Here is Singal's lucid description of it:

> At the core of this . . . culture stood a distinctive set of bedrock assumptions. These included a belief in a predictable universe presided over by a benevolent God and governed by immutable natural laws, a corresponding conviction that humankind was capable of arriving at a unified and fixed set of truths about all aspects of life, and an insistence on preserving absolute standards based on a radical dichotomy between that which was deemed "human" and that regarded as "animal." It was this moral dichotomy above all that constituted the deepest guiding principle of the Victorian outlook. On the "human" and "civilized" side of the dividing line stood everything that served to lift man above the beasts—education, refinement, manners, the arts, religion, and such domesticated emotions as loyalty and family love. The "animal" or "savage" realm, by contrast, contained those instincts and passions that constantly threatened self-control, and which therefore had to be repressed at all cost. (9)

As Singal also points out, this dichotomizing habit of mind applied to people as well as values: "Victorians characterized societies as either civilized or savage, drew a firm line between what they considered superior and inferior classes, . . . divided races unambiguously into black and white," and placed the sexes in "separate spheres" based on a now-familiar set of supposedly "natural" characteristics (9–10).

In Singal's view, then, Victorian culture built its sense of stability upon a set of clear, simplifying oppositions. What I would add to Singal's description is this: the sense of the world just described is implemented and sustained by narratives, by the stories about life that put its interpretations of experience into force and proclaim their explanatory power. That is: this was a profoundly and characteristically *allegorical* culture, committed to grand narratives that reached both out into the social and political world and inward into the self. Such definitive Victorian allegories would include outward-turning story lines like "the march of progress," the benevolent triumph of the civilized, and the noble mission of educating the savage, as well as inward-focused story lines like the narratives of maturation, disciplined self-recognition, and interior enlightenment via difficult experience that are recognizable as the master plots of the Victorian novel. In emphasizing this Victorian commitment to a certain kind of big narrative, I do not want to deny that, in both England and America, this could be an admirably self-critical, self-challenging culture. There was no shortage of Victorian critics of Victorian hypocrisy, or Victorian exclusions, or Victorian injustices. Yet these challengers tend to share the sense of story line, of the allegorical shape belonging to experience, with the culture they criticize. They seek a more enlightened selfhood, a still more elevated cultural life, a more vigorous manhood or womanhood. This last point—that defenders and critics of the Victorian status quo share a sense of "the story," of the goals and end points of their culture's cherished narratives—enables us to see that a differently imagined American culture—an authentic modernism—will need not only to challenge Singal's dichotomies but to reinvent the very shape of its central narratives, its routes toward meaning.

And to see that, finally, is to see the importance and ambitiousness of the kind of radical recasting of narrative—which I tried to demonstrate in the first part of this essay—that Cather is unobtrusively accomplishing in *Shadows on the Rock* and in much of her other work. From a historical point of view, then, the great ambition and the great accomplishment of a book like *Shadows* is its radical act of refraining from the customary pleasures and procedures of the novel and its culture (what Sontag calls "interpretation") and the opportunity it hence affords us to feel differently our encounter with this text. *Shadows on the Rock* is a central book in Cather's oeuvre because it exemplifies the way her fiction aspires to the condition of uninterpretability: to bring its readers to a place where our customary habits of attention, our usual forms of feeling, and our orthodox life narratives might be discarded. Insofar as our own response to this novel and to Cather's fiction generally is "interpretive" in Sontag's sense—insofar as we address it allegorically, seeking out the deeper layers of explanatory meaning it resolutely withholds from us—we ourselves betray what is most interesting and refreshing about it.

WORKS CITED

Cather, Willa. *Shadows on the Rock*. New York: Knopf, 1931. Rpt. New York: Vintage, 1971.

Singal, Daniel Joseph. "Towards a Definition of American Modernism." *American Quarterly* 39 (1987): 7–26.

Sontag, Susan. "Against Interpretation." *Against Interpretation and Other Essays*. New York: Anchor Books, 1990. 3–14. Originally published, 1966.

Cather's *Shadows*
Solid Rock and Sacred Canopy

JOHN J. MURPHY

Willa Cather seemed to have little interest in developing herself into a popular icon beyond encouraging the early image of a girl on a pony riding over vast prairies on her way to butter-making and story-telling immigrant homemakers, and the later one of the natural artist who produced *O Pioneers!* (1913) without "writ[ing] at all" (Carroll interview, Bohlke 21) and has Jim Burden declare in *My Ántonia* (1918) that he "didn't arrange or rearrange," just "simply wrote down" what he recalled without awareness of "form" (xiii). As the Benéts affirm in their 1940 interview, "she does not go in for personal appearances, speech-making, banqueting, public autographing, and the like" (Bohlke 136), activities that make popular icons of people who want to become such icons. But the prefatory note in *Not Under Forty* (1936), that she had ceased to identify with the contemporary world and numbered herself among "the backward" (v), suggests that we consider the kind of icon Cather indeed became, intentionally or not, for those dismayed that a major writer would identify with "the backward," and for those who view her as their champion for so doing.

Perhaps because of patriotism, lack of self-confidence, or fear that a favorite image of Cather as an icon of confident midwestern grandeur (a kind of literary Bess Truman) might topple like the Saddam Hussein bronze in Baghdad, scant attention is given to Cather's argument with Americanization. At Laura Bush's celebration of Cather and some others at the White House in

September 2002, many well-known Cather literary passages were conspicuous for their absence among the celebratory ones that made us feel good about America. I remembered Jim Laird's condemnation of Sand City in "The Sculptor's Funeral" (1905) as "a dung heap" (*Collected Stories* 203) and "place of hatred and bitter waters" (210); Jim Burden's condemnation of Black Hawk as a collection of "flimsy shelters" full of "jealousy and envy and unhappiness," a place under the "tyranny" of gossip in which life is "made up of evasions and negations" and "every natural appetite . . . bridled by caution" (212); and Niel Herbert's lament in *A Lost Lady* (1923) about the passing of the Old West from greathearted dreamers to "shrewd young men, trained to petty economies," who "had never dared anything, never risked anything" (102), as well as the narrator's impetuous comment that Niel "was in a fever of impatience to be gone . . . forever, and was making the final break with everything that had been dear to him in his boyhood" (160). Most of all, I remembered Claude Wheeler's reflection in France in *One of Ours* (1922) that he had "no chance for the kind of life he wanted at home [in Nebraska], where people were always buying and selling, building and pulling down. He had begun to believe that the Americans were a people of shallow emotions" (328).

The insistence of such complaints, in spite of the obvious imperfections of the characters who make them, suggests that they probably were Cather's as well, a suggestion confirmed in "Nebraska: The End of the First Cycle," the 1923 article Cather wrote for *The Nation*. In it she laments the "Americanization" that has "done away with" (237) much of European culture and stamped out the use of other languages through English-only programs; she also condemns the indifference and even closed-mindedness of New England and southern settlers toward their Bohemian and Scandinavian neighbors. After presenting a picture of productive fields, new farmhouses with bathrooms, clean and well-kept towns, and "crowds of happy looking children, well nourished," on their way to school, Cather turns to "the other side of the medal, stamped with the ugly crest of materialism." An overabundance of prosperity, movies, and gaudy fiction has generated "the frenzy to be showy; farmer boys who wish to be spenders before they are earners, girls who try to look like the heroines of the cinema screen; a coming generation which tries to cheat its aesthetic sense by buying things instead of making anything." Then she zeroes in on the University of Nebraska, fearing that her alma mater "may become a gigantic trade school. The men who control its destiny . . . wish their sons and daughters to study machines, mercantile processes, 'the principles of business'; everything that has to do with the game of getting on in the world—and nothing else" (238). In *The Professor's House* (1925) the state university is being "farm[ed] . . . out to athletics, and to the agricultural and commercial schools favored and fostered by the State Legislature" (58), and Cather's criticism in this novel embraces both the nation and contemporary life. As a result of the effects of overabundant prosperity "[t]he world is sad to [Professor] St. Peter," and "everything around him seemed insupportable, as the boat on which he is imprisoned seems to a sea-sick man" (148–49).

How much St. Peter's condition can be applied to Cather herself is debatable; that St. Peter's thoughts echo Cather's is less so. The year *The Professor's House* was published, Cather discovered the biography of Bishop Machebeuf and got the particulars she needed to begin *Death Comes for the Archbishop* (1927), her attempt to depict "the story of the Catholic Church in [the Southwest,] . . . the most interesting of all its stories" (*On Writing* 5), in such a way as to measure "all human experiences . . . against one supreme spiritual experience" (9). The worldview of her priest-protagonist (and first European-bred consciousness filter) is not a private creation like Jim Burden's, Professor St. Peter's, or Tom Outland's but one essentially shared by other faithful believers, by his family back in France, by his scattered flock in New Mexico, and by those with whom he labors. A revealing aspect of her project is that Cather must mine the past to find such an integrated world, one clearly evident in the opening book where Latour gets lost in a chaos of conical red hills, each with its conical junipers: "'*Mais, c'est fantastique*!' he muttered, closing his eyes to rest them from the intrusive omnipresence of the triangle" (17). When he opens them to behold the cruciform tree, order is restored; he dismounts, takes out his breviary, and kneels in prayer. Yet he has never ceased to be surrounded by the order of his belief; as David Stouck observes, the omnipresent triangles "begin to suggest the mystical number of the spirit and the Trinity itself, and they culminate in a tree shaped like a crucifix" (136). Cather's parched missionary is about to be miraculously rescued, senses a change in his mare's body, and below him appears "a green thread of verdure and a running stream" (24). In the settlement of Agua Secreta, Latour will find not only water and food but, more importantly, the basic faith he shares with the Mexican family who, in the aftermath of the recent Mexican War (1846–48), classifies Americans as "infidels" (27). He is greeted in the name of the Virgin by a young woman with a kindly face and finds himself "very much at home" among people who believe the Virgin must have led him there to baptize their children and sanctify their marriages (25–26). The wooden figures of the saints cherished here remind him of the stone carvings on the facades of churches in his native Auvergne.

Cather anticipates the integrated world of the *Archbishop* through two earlier protagonists. Claude Wheeler concludes near the end of *One of Ours* that because "[l]ife was so short . . . it meant nothing at all unless it were continually reinforced by something that endured; unless the *shadows* of individual existence came and went against a background that held together" (328, my emphasis). Then Godfrey St. Peter develops this theme in what he calls his "rambling" (*The Professor's House* 70) on the Middle Ages: "As long as every man and woman who crowded into the cathedrals on Easter Sunday was a principal in a gorgeous drama with God, glittering angels on one side and the *shadows* of evil coming and going on the other, life was a rich thing. The king and the beggar had the same chance at miracles and great temptations and revelations. And that's what makes men happy, believing in the mystery and importance of their own little individual lives" (68, my emphasis). Of course, the thoughts of both protagonists look forward to *Shadows on the Rock* as well (even to its title), and it is to the circumstances surrounding the writing of that 1931 novel that I now turn.

When Cather first visited Quebec City, in June 1928, she had been prepared by experience to respond to it in the creative way she did. Since 1922 she had summered on Grand Manan, the rocky island that had become a sanctuary for her, the "only foothold left on earth" (Lewis 153), a refuge from a disturbing and rapidly changing postwar world. Cather and Edith Lewis were taking a route through Quebec to get to their cottage on the island when Lewis caught the flu and had to convalesce for ten days in Quebec City. Here, in one of North America's most spectacular settings, Cather discovered a sanctuary of significant historical implications. Seeing a French city clinging to a gigantic rock above the St. Lawrence, she was, as Lewis puts it, "overwhelmed by the flood of memory, recognition, surmise it called up" (153). We can guess that Cather remembered Avignon, which she described in 1902 as clinging to its rock above the Rhône; perhaps she remembered Mesa Verde, and certainly she remembered Acoma. Her discovery of Quebec came in the midst of personal difficulties that continued through the writing of *Shadows* and compounded her sense of cultural decline. The Bank Street building where she had her New York apartment had been torn down, her father had recently died, and her mother would soon suffer the stroke that would prove fatal after an illness of more than two years. Consequently, the family home in Red Cloud would be broken up—it would be the end of an era. The rock above the St. Lawrence, like Acoma in Bishop Latour's meditation, became another "expression of human need" and "yearning for something permanent" (*Archbishop* 103).

The faith community that had given Cather so much happiness during the writing of the *Archbishop* she now relocated to the rock of Quebec. Lewis speculates that during those difficult times "it may have been . . . a reluctance to leave that world of Catholic feeling and tradition in which [Cather] had lived so happily so long that led her to embark on this new novel" (155). *Shadows* reflects the human need for meaningful order as protection against chaos and for a cosmos to sustain the values of that order. The novel is a defense of what Peter Berger refers to as the "sacred canopy," "man's ultimate shield against the terror of anomy. To be in a 'right' relationship with the sacred cosmos is to be protected against the nightmare threats of chaos"

(26). Cather herself compares her novel to a canopy in a June 1921 letter to Dorothy Canfield Fisher. Traveling back and forth across the country to see her dying mother meant that Cather had no quiet stretch of time, and she tells Fisher that writing *Shadows* was like working on a tapestry tent she could unfold in hotels and sanatoriums, picking it up and putting it down during her life in transit. The novel's first pages establish Quebec as a sanctuary of order surrounded by the chaos of nature: "the dead, sealed world of . . . interlocking trees, living, dead, half-dead, their roots . . . strangling each other. . . . The forest was suffocation, annihilation; there European man was quickly swallowed up" (5–6). Against this, on the rock, secular and sacred order combine for survival. Madame Auclair carefully instructs her daughter, Cécile, on cuisine, washing, and cleaning—practices basic to Cather's depiction of French civilization in this novel: "Without order our lives would be disgusting, like those of the poor savages," Madame Auclair concludes (20). After Cécile's excursion to an Isle of Orleans farm where domestic order has been distanced from the "kind things" one needed "about one" (159) and then compromised by proximity to nature, housekeeping suddenly seems sacred. Cécile compares herself to the nuns who arrived in Quebec to help establish the sacred order there, and she recognizes that she achieves something as sacred with her coppers, brooms, and brushes, that "[o]ne made a climate within a climate; one made the days . . .; one made life" (160).

The sacred cosmos is emphasized in all seven sections of *Shadows*. In the opening scene, Auclair compares the rock-set town to "one of those little artificial mountains made in the churches at home to present a theatric scene of the Nativity" (4). Later, "he would construct a shelf in front of the window-sill" so their crèche scene "could be arranged," like Quebec itself, "in two terraces, as was customary at home" (86). Quebec thus becomes a new Bethlehem early in *Shadows*, and by the beginning of the fourth book it is the New Jerusalem "gleaming above the river like an altar with many candles, or like a holy city in an old legend, shriven, sinless, washed in gold" (137). The paradigm of the sacred canopy is clarified in the novel's second book, where the cheerfulness of the nuns on All Souls' Day contrasts with the sorrow of those burdened by memories of their homes in France. The sisters are at home everywhere, the narrator explains, because they had distanced and theologized nature and inhabit a

> world of the mind (which for each of us is the only world), and they had the . . . well-ordered universe about them; this all-important earth, created by God for a great purpose, the sun which He made to light it by day, the moon which He made to light it by night,—and the stars, made to beautify the vault of heaven like frescoes, and to be a clock and compass for man. And in this safe, lovingly arranged and ordered universe . . . the drama of man went on at Quebec just as at home, and the Sisters played their accustomed part in it. (78)

Under the sacred canopy, as in Professor St. Peter's fantasy, "every man and woman" has the opportunity to become "a principal in a gorgeous drama with God . . . [and] life [is] a rich thing." In a scene before the Christmas section, when Cecile takes the waif she befriends sledding on a tilted street, she experiences an epiphany. It is not an aesthetic one like Thea Kronborg's in *The Song of the Lark* (1915), nor one of private elation like Tom Outland's; it is, rather, contentment in the order of her life:

> A feeling came over her that there would never be anything better in the world for her than this; to be pulling Jacques on her sled, with the tender, burning sky before her, and on each side, in the dusk, the kindly lights from neighbours' houses. . . . On a foreign shore . . . would not her heart break for just this? For this rock and this winter, this feeling of being in one's own place, for the soft content of pulling Jacques up Holy Family Hill into paler and paler levels of blue air. (83–84)

Her revelation is of a world that, like the world of the nuns, is communal and cosmic—it occurs on Holy Family Hill; it includes her link to the waif and to neighbors as well as to the heavens.

The worldview of *Shadows* represents several challenges for contemporary critics. Cather's modernism must be negotiated around cultural absolutes, as Richard Millington attempts to do in situating the fiction against the work of Franz Boas and in pointing out that Cather's interest in place and history precludes a dogged attachment to such absolutes and demands (and develops) culturally sensitive readers. In *Shadows* the interest is in the making of meaning, continues Millington, and objects and events are juxtaposed to illustrate "the [Quebec] community's ongoing work of constructing its meaning" (33). This is an illuminating way to read Cather, and it would be extremely so if it offered complements rather than chose alternatives. Millington concludes that the subject of *Shadows* "is not the revelation of Meaning but the making of meanings" (35), that Cather "is interested in Catholicism not as a believer . . . but as a cultural observer" (36), and that "what interests [Cather] is neither the content of the belief nor its truth value but the imaginative process of its production" (37). Yet in her 1931 letter to Wilbur Cross, Cather expresses admiration for a "feeling [disposition, understanding] about life and human fate [in Quebec] that I could not accept, *wholly*, but which I could not but admire" (*On Writing* 15, my emphasis). Cather suggests the ambivalence at the heart of belief as well as an interest in the meanings we make of Meaning, in how culture grapples with Truth. While certainly interested in change, she admired, she told Cross, what endured. Her modernism is not compromised by this; it is complicated by it. Millington's final estimate of Cecile is a case in point; his Cecile "emerges not as *la petite vierge* but as *une petite moderniste*, consciously choosing" her cultural "affiliation" (39). But the essence of the Virgin's meaning (indeed, the essence of Cecile's religious tradition) is choice: "And Mary said [to Gabriel], Behold the handmaid of the Lord; be it done unto me according to thy word" (Luke 1:38, King James Version).

The relative nature of Meaning is further nuanced by Joseph Urgo, who defines religion as a cultural response to "the nonmaterial essence of life" (100), a way to explain what the dying Count Frontenac detects as "something in himself and in other men that this world did not explain" (201). Urgo interprets Cather's rock as "stability, immutability, the values without which a civilization will not survive," and the shadows on it as "the shades of meaning cast by those in momentary possession of the rock, the closest that human life can get to something that will not change" (98); he concentrates on such shadows to trace French culture transforming into Canadian. While I have little argument with this, I would prefer exploration of both permanence and change within the system represented by the shadows. To what extent does a belief system possess permanence, and to what extent is it transitory? Just how close do the shadows embrace absolutes? Karl Rahner tries to answer this question in tracing the development of Roman Catholicism beyond Europe, suggesting that the Catholic Church has "in potency" the ability to be more than "an export firm which exported a European religion as a commodity it did not really want to change but sent throughout the world together with the rest of the culture and civilization it considered superior" (717). Rahner challenges the system to make distinctions between culture and belief, for as a theologian he refuses to collapse them. Why, he asks, must canon law be a Western code? Why must the marital morality in East Africa reproduce that of the West? Why must grape wine be required to celebrate the Eucharist in Alaska? I think Cather's rock represents the essentials of belief surviving migration and adaptation to a new continent, and the shadows become the primary approach to these essentials.

Cécile does not "rema[k]e the rock out of indigenous materials" (9), as Urgo argues; nor is Pierre Charron a "relativist existentialis[t]" (110) who "rejects the rock for the wilderness" (106). Pierre's basic belief, like Cécile's, is also Father Hector's and Noël Chabanel's. Pierre tells Cécile that "every autumn, before I start for the woods, I have a mass said at the *paroisse* in Ville-Marie for madame your mother" (141). When Bishop Laval asks him if he has confessed since returning from the woods, "Pierre said respectfully that he had" (142). When he reveals to Auclair his heartbreak over Jeanne Le Ber, he credits her prayers with saving him "three times in the woods [when] my comrades . . . thought it was all over with me" (145). In the epilogue chapters, Auclair informs Bishop Saint-Vallier that Cécile married Pierre, who "has built a commodious house in the Upper Town, beyond the Ursuline convent" (228). What Pierre objects to is the cultural identity of many of the priests, that they are "too French" and "smell . . . of Versailles" (140).

Urgo explains that "[c]losed systems of belief, totalizing worldviews . . . are discredited structures of thought in the contemporary world," that our "migratory culture . . . believes above all else in the mutability of belief" and has lost the "sense of the sacred" necessary for a culture "to survive" (109–10). "Cather," he concludes, "accentuates the distance traveled between the origins of Quebec and modern consciousness" by "projecting a past . . . so remote from the present, so foreign in the mode of thought there" (110–11); "[o]ne does not go back" (109), he adds. I would qualify these generally valid insights: first of all, major systems of belief are never closed if they are open to the mystery that is their raison d'être; second, not all readers find the world of *Shadows* remote—it is far less remote to me than, say, *The Great Gatsby* (1925) or *The Sun Also Rises* (1926); third, Cather did "go back"—*Shadows* is not the end of her medieval journey; in the unfinished Avignon story she went back in the manner of her Ursulines, via the mind.

The rock of Quebec further materializes the light beyond the shadows, the light that suggests transcendent reality, the God Thomas Aquinas defines as "not composed of matter and form" (16). The shadows between—darkness, clouds, whatever obscures—are our realm, our lives. Some Cather scholars at the Quebec seminar in 1995 noticed the wall sundial in the courtyard of Laval Seminary with the Latin inscription *Dies Nostri Quast Umbra*, "Our days as if a shadow." The source of the inscription is a line from 1 Chronicles 29:15, which in the King James Version reads, "our days on the earth are as a shadow." The whole verse resonates in Cather's novel: "for we are strangers before thee, and sojourners, as were our fathers; our days on the earth are as a shadow, and there is none abiding." We catch glimpses through the shadows on the rock: during the afterglow, when the sky throbs with fiery vapors; when the sun makes Quebec gleam like an altar; when Cecile and Jacques light candles and watch holy figures emerge from the darkness of the church. The system is not closed; the comfortable universe of the Ursulines is merely a conceit, a fresco, like the frescoes in

Padua's famous Scrovigni Chapel, on the walls and ceilings of which Giotto painted the entire Christian story from the lives of Joachim and Anne to the Last Judgment. But above that final event Giotto painted two angels in the process of rolling back the sky to reveal an ultimate reality ungraspable to us now in our shadow state.

My favorite photograph of Cather is the one by Carl Van Vechten, taken a few years after the publication of *Shadows*. Enclosed in black hat and black furs, the face broods, is sad; yet the volumes in the bookcase behind it and the icon of an equestrian saint (or perhaps of Christ) suggest a world of the mind shared somewhat with those strained baroque Counter-Reformation devotees Cather wrote about in this novel, who were under attack, as she was, on the barricades in an alien age.

WORKS CITED

Berger, Peter L. *The Sacred Canopy: Elements of a Sociological Theory of Religion*. New York: Anchor, 1990.

Bohlke, L. Brent, ed. *Willa Cather in Person: Interviews, Speeches, and Letters*. Lincoln: U of Nebraska P, 1986.

Cather, Willa. *Collected Stories*. New York: Vintage, 1992.

———. *Death Comes for the Archbishop*. 1927. Willa Cather Scholarly Edition. Ed. Charles W. Mignon with Frederick M. Link and Kari A. Ronning. Historical essay and explanatory notes John J. Murphy. Lincoln: U of Nebraska P, 1999.

———. Letter to Dorothy Canfield Fisher. June 1931. U of Vermont, Burlington.

———. *A Lost Lady*. 1923. Willa Cather Scholarly Edition. Ed. Charles W. Mignon and Frederick M. Link with Kari A. Ronning. Historical essay Susan J. Rosowski with Kari A. Ronning. Explanatory notes Kari A. Ronning. Lincoln: U of Nebraska P, 1997.

———. *My Ántonia*. 1918. Willa Cather Scholarly Edition. Ed. Charles W. Mignon with Kari A. Ronning. Historical essay James Woodress. Lincoln: U of Nebraska P, 1994.

———. "Nebraska: The End of the First Cycle." *Nation* 5 Sept. 1923: 236–38.

———. *Not Under Forty*. 1936. Lincoln: U of Nebraska P, 1988.

———. *One of Ours*. 1922. New York: Vintage, 1991.

———. *On Writing: Critical Studies of Writing as an Art*. New York: Knopf, 1949.
———. *The Professor's House*. 1925. Willa Cather Scholarly Edition. Ed. Frederick M. Link. Historical essay James Woodress. Explanatory notes James Woodress with Kari A. Ronning. Lincoln: U of Nebraska P, 2002.
———. *Shadows on the Rock*. 1931. New York: Vintage, 1995.
Lewis, Edith. *Willa Cather Living*. 1953. Lincoln: U of Nebraska P, 2000.
Millington, Richard. "Where Is Cather's Quebec? Anthropological Modernism in *Shadows on the Rock*." *Cather Studies: Willa Cather's Canadian and Old World Connections* 4 (1999): 23–44.
Rahner, Karl. "Towards a Fundamental Theological Interpretation of Vatican II." *Theological Studies* 40 (1979): 716–27.
Stouck, David. *Willa Cather's Imagination*. Lincoln: U of Nebraska P, 1975.
Thomas Aquinas. "Of the Simplicity of God" (Question 3, Second Article). *Summa Theologica*. Trans. English Dominicans. 5 vols. Westminster MD: Christian Classics, 1981. 1: 15–16.
Urgo, Joseph R. *Willa Cather and the Myth of American Migration*. Urbana: U of Illinois P, 1995.

Cather's Secular Humanism
Writing Anacoluthon and Shooting Out into the Eternities

JOSEPH R. URGO

Traveling lady stay awhile
Until the night is over
I'm just a station on your way
I know I'm not your lover.
—*Leonard Cohen, "Winter Lady," from*
Songs of Leonard Cohen

It is something one has lived through, not a story one has read; less diverting than a story, perhaps, but more inevitable. One is "left with it," in the same way that one is left with a weak heart after certain illnesses. A shadow has come into one's consciousness that will not go out again.
—Willa Cather, "A Chance Meeting"

WINTER LADY

When a writer reaches iconic status, we seek less to find a context through which we may comprehend the author (how and why should she be read?) and begin to contemplate the various contexts made available to us through the author's work. The iconic, in other words, is an intellectual force that shapes consciousness—or, in Cather's language, casts a shadow on our minds. As we scrutinize the words and the meanings, we find we cannot turn any away; and as we encounter new ways of receiving texts, we are not at liberty to refuse the implications they bring. On the contrary, the writer whom we acknowledge as iconic we also acknowledge as having, to an extent we seek to realize, produced the way we think.

Willa Cather possessed a hard-thinking and fierce secular humanism. One is awed by her habitual attraction, in her subject matter, to depictions of strong, enabling systems of belief—so much so that she is often thought to be a "believer." But she was not a believer in any particular theology or political program or cause. It was the phenomenon of belief that fired her imagination, whether manifest as patriotism, Catholicism, racial hierarchy, talent, ambition—whatever it was that moved people to something particularly fine. This fire turned her into what "Canadian of the future" Leonard Cohen calls, in another context, "Winter Lady": traveling from setting to setting seeking out the best that was ever desired, the finest manifestations of ideas that leave shadows on consciousness, and of shadows that result in the very finest of human things. One might see a Catherian spirit in Leonard Cohen's image: "Traveling lady stay awhile / Until the night is over / I'm just a station on your way / I know I'm not your lover."

Cather is a great American liberator, an author who truly understood the potential of American secular and humanistic pluralism to serve art and to advance the human condition by lifting it above the denominational. She wrote into it, out of it, and in 1931, at the very height of her career, structured it into a best-selling novel in the same year she received honorary degrees from Princeton and Berkeley and made the cover of *Time* magazine. The title of the novel, *Shadows on the Rock*, evokes Plato's cave, the chained beings who watch the shadows of reality on the cave wall and never know more than what is called "the visible region," and who pride themselves on being "the quickest to make out the shadows as they pass and best able to remember their customary precedences, sequences, and coexistences." Those who are dragged away from the shadows are able to contemplate the "true nature" of what "it is that provides the seasons and the courses of the year and presides over all things in the visible region, and is in some sort the cause of all these things that they had seen" (Book 7: 514–17).[1] However, those who glimpse the eternities do not easily integrate back among the shadows.

According to this philosophical tableau, human beings are prisoners of their limited perception and their attenuated consciousness, and we are further demarcated by the senses through which we are compelled to experience and contemplate reality. What we normally consider to be *the real* are shadows of ultimate phenomena. Certain intellects, those able to free themselves from sense perception and transcend the shadowy world, those of philosophical capacity, are able to break free of the chains, called "systems of thought," and glimpse the true nature of what controls the visible region. These same people, as one would expect, find it difficult to take seriously the sensory world and may turn to investing themselves in philosophy or, in a subsequent civilization, literature. Millennia later, William James—whose influence on Cather Merrill Skaggs has established definitively[2]—would make the same point in terms perhaps more accessible to domestic life in his civilization. According to James's image, "we stand in much the same relation to the whole of the universe as our canine and feline pets do to the whole of human life. They inhabit our drawing rooms and libraries. They take part in scenes of whose significance they have no inkling. They are merely tangents to curves of history the beginnings and ends and forms of which pass wholly beyond their ken" (144).

Recall Count Frontenac on his deathbed in *Shadows on the Rock*, in book 6, "The Dying Count":

> He would die here, in this room, and his spirit would go before God to be judged. He believed this, because he had been taught it in childhood, and because he knew there was something in himself and in other men that this world did not explain. Even the Indians had to make a story to account for something in their lives that did not come out of their appetites: conceptions of courage, duty, honour. The Indians had these, in their own fashion. These ideas came from some unknown source, and they were not the least part of life. (200–201)

The Count is, in 1698, blasphemous; in 1931 (and still, in the early 2000s), he is one of Cather's spiritual pioneers. The Count knows that what he believes, the shadows trained on his mind—*a shadow that has come into his consciousness and will not go out again*, to paraphrase Cather—are the Christian God, the Trinity, and the Last Judgment. But he knows these beliefs to be the shadows of the real, "because he knew there was something in himself and in other men that this world did not explain," and that other civilizations had come into contact with the same shadows, in their fashion. William James completes his image this way: "So we are tangents to the wider life of things. But, just as many of the dog's and cat's ideals coincide with our ideals, and the dogs and cats have daily living proof of the fact, so we may well believe, on the proofs that religious experience affords, that higher powers exist and are at work to save the world on ideal lines similar to our own" (144). Precisely this is revealed to the dying count, whose experience is the culmination, such as it is, of Cather's novel of liberation. Just as there are many human languages to express the very same physical experiences, there exist numerous human religions, shadows of the "something . . . this world did not explain." Cautiously, James claimed that pragmatism could not prescribe a particular religion, "for we do not yet know certainly which type of religion is going to work best in the long run" (144).

A literary pragmatist, Cather was drawn to ideas that *worked*. Her two great "Catholic novels," *Death Comes for the Archbishop* and *Shadows on the Rock*, explore unlikely areas for human habitation, much less emigration—the arid, barren desert and the wintry, isolated cliff—remote areas transformed into destinations on the strength of a very particular theological technology. We might consider her career as that of an itinerant, missionary writer, traveling around North America (and, at her death, planning her next writing-stop in France) with her message: *desire is truth*, and attracted to its finest examples, such as: How Truth happened in Nebraska; How Truth happened in Taos; and, How Truth happened in Quebec.[3] Truth happens wherever the desire for it is strong enough, wherever the language, the mode of thought, the religious practice, the ideological construction of reality (name your cave, in other words), wherever human effort is concentrated sufficiently to summon the appearance of the Virgin, the construction of a cathedral, or the planting of wheat fields that will feed the world. Janis Stout has argued that Cather's interest in religious experience was *cultural*; that is to say, Cather had "an essentially secular and skeptical cast of mind, a cast of mind keenly responsive to the aesthetic experience of religion and its moral and cultural associations" (26).

To borrow Leonard Cohen's image from 1967, the "stations on [Cather's] way" were myriad, as we know—and included virtually every major region of North America, as she seemed to commit herself to seeking out manifestations of what James calls the "live possibilities" of human beings: "if the complementary conditions come and add themselves, our ideals will become actual things" (137). I sense Cather's close pursuit in James's footsteps when he argues, "the only *real* reason I can think of why anything should ever come is that *someone wishes it to be here*. It is *demanded*. . . . This is the *living reason*, and compared with it material causes and logical necessities are spectral things" (138, emphasis in source). Seeking out these living reasons occupied Cather's literary life. What could enable people to live in dugouts and sod houses in an area known as "the great American desert" for its seeming inhabitable topography? How does an artist "tear [herself] loose" from the hole in the ground that awaits her and shoot herself out into the world of ideas and music? Why did so many young men march willingly, almost gleefully, to their deaths in the Great War? Why live past fifty-two, with the knowledge that age bestows? What was the truth that happened in Virginia before her life began, that enabled her kin to own and to systematically degrade other human beings? The "traveling lady" went to these places and situations, probing the shadows, writing what it was that demanded these things to come into being.

ANACOLUTHON

In a letter to the *Saturday Review of Literature* in October 1931, Cather wrote (in response to a favorable review of *Shadows on the Rock* written by Governor Wilbur Cross of

Connecticut) to explain a few things about her novel. "To me the rock of Quebec is not only a stronghold on which many strange figures have for a little time cast a shadow in the sun; it is the curious endurance of a kind of culture, narrow but definite." She went on to describe the narrative as "more like an old song, incomplete but uncorrupted, than like a legend. The text was mainly anacoluthon" ("On *Shadows*" 15). *Anacoluthon* is a linguistic term to describe a sentence or construction lacking grammatical sequence; the Greek root, *akolouthos*, meaning "following," and the prefix, *an*, negating it; the term is literally translated from its Greek root as "not following" or "it does not follow." According to the OED, the word *anacoluthon* can be traced to the early eighteenth century, coming into use, curiously enough, only a few years after Cather's *La Bonne Espérance* left Quebec in 1697, severing an apothecary from the world and leaving him "on a grey rock in the Canadian wilderness" (*Shadows* 3–4).

SHOOTING OUT INTO THE ETERNITIES

In "Before Breakfast," Henry Grenfell is troubled by two things: the scientific study of his private rock-island and the intrusion of beauty upon his privacy. He works himself up fairly nihilistically: "Why patch up?" he says when he decides against his eye medication. "What was the use . . . of anything? Why tear a man loose from his little rock and shoot him into the eternities?" Cather's narrative advice follows: "All that stuff was inhuman. A man had his little hour, with heat and cold and a time-sense suited to his endurance. If you took that away from him you left him spineless, accidental, unrelated to anything" (148–49). Grenfell does not feel better until he realizes and then experiences a physical rejuvenation. He sees the planet Venus in the morning "serene, terrible, and splendid, looking in at him," and counters the night's nihilism with his sense of "immortal beauty . . . yes, but only when somebody *saw* it, he fiercely answered back!" (158). With this realization in mind he scurries over the rock-island. "He had always known this island . . . must once have been a naked rock," as the scientist-professor had told him. "But that fact had nothing to do with the green surface where men lived and trees lived" (161) and where, as he sees immediately, the scientist's pretty daughters shoot themselves off rocks in the morning. "People are really themselves only when they believe they are absolutely alone and unobserved" (164), Grenfell concludes, as he unobservedly observes the girl who dives unobserved (she believes) into the Atlantic, and (for Grenfell) into the eternities. And because he takes her shadow home to breakfast, his appetite is sharpened for more than just food.[4]

1931: AT THE PINNACLE OF A CAREER

Today, the idea of nonsequential telling is common—it is, as Terence Martin has pointed out, "a provocative (and thoroughly postmodern) trope." However, in 1931, when Cather published *Shadows on the Rock*, it was not. In Fowler and Fowler's *The King's English* (1931), anacoluthon is identified as "the most notorious of all" examples of "grammatical misdemeanors," all too common to writers. "The anacoluthon is a failure to follow on, an unconscious departure from the grammatical scheme with which a sentence was started, the getting switched off, imperceptibly to the writer, very noticeably to his readers, from one syntax track to another. There is little to be said on the matter." Today we are more likely to ask, What does *not* follow? Everything follows. The object is to pry oneself loose from the rock that threatens us with narrated nihilism ("What was the use of anything?") by finding what casts the shadow. Whereas Cather acknowledged the idea that the rock was "the utmost expression of human need," as she has it in *Death Comes for the Archbishop* (97), she saw also beyond this metaphor. In *Sapphira and the Slave Girl* we have "solid rock" that is in the process of being blasted away by "the destroying armament of modern road-building" (170); and in "Before Breakfast" it is modern science that suggests the artificiality of the rock, when the geologist tells Grenfell that "the island was interesting geologically because the two ends of the island belonged to different periods, yet the ice seemed to have brought them both down together" (147). If the rock has a *history*, if it was delivered by ice, if something predates it, then even (to get back to the metaphor) those things that we consider rock-fixed and eternal are in fact contingencies, and we are left "spineless, accidental, unrelated to anything," left, like Grenfell, "sitting in his bathrobe by his washstand, limp!" (761). A man sitting limp beside the washstand holds little promise for the survival of the species. Cather's exclamation point is emphatic, ironic, and outrageous.

Shooting out into the eternities juxtaposes two central Catherian ideas. One's experience of life is mainly and grammatically anacoluthon, in Cather's mind. The rock, which we cling to out of need for Stability and Truth, is the hypothesis on which we live our lives and believe our beliefs, "the green surface where men lived" ("Before Breakfast" 161), the rocks on which faith staged miracles and missionaries carried civilizations. But the rock is an illusion of permanence; it is, before all else, a metaphor, a grammar, an *expression* of need, not the need itself or the answer to the need. Permanence, the experience of eternities, is available only when one is "torn loose" from these rocks to which we cling—those few moments when the geologist's daughter floats between the rocks and Grenfell comes back to life.[5]

Although Cather wrote from this fire throughout her career, it takes coherent shape *as an idea* in her mind in 1931, when, like many other authors at pinnacle, she felt the need to explain herself. In "My First Novels (There Were Two)," written in 1931 and published in *The Colophon* right after *Shadows on the Rock*, Cather disowned her first novel, *Alexander's Bridge*, because it was "made out of 'interesting material'" instead of what she knew, what was familiar to her own experience (91). Her second novel was *O Pioneers!*; it was a much better job, a quality Cather attributes to her familiarity with Nebraska despite its literary and geographical flatness. But in 1931, the year she claimed to value familiarity, she published *Shadows on the Rock*. Why write a novel about something she knew nothing about, researching Quebec because she found in it (to throw her words back at her) "interesting material" that was "more exciting than the familiar" (she made five research trips to Quebec between

June 1928 and September 1930), and then write an essay for *The Colophon* disavowing that method of writing as "the wrong road" to take? ("My First Novels" 91, 96). Why declare in *The Colophon* essay that "too much detail is apt, like any other form of extravagance, to become slightly vulgar" (97) after writing a novel concentrating on what she called "the salad dressing" ("On *Shadows*" 16), a novel, James Woodress observes, that is filled with *things* (432) so much that it seems more about things than characters. *Shadows on the Rock* remains somewhat unheralded[6] in Cather studies not only because we have not quite yet understood the full arc of the career but also because we continue to think she was mainly interested in "the country people and the nuns" for the substance of what they believed. We would do better to see how their households resembled, from the perspective of the eternities, the actions of "ants," as she explained to Governor Cross, ants that "begin to rebuild when you kick their house down" ("On *Shadows*" 16).

Also in this crucial year of 1931, Cather met Flaubert's niece, an event she later recounted in "A Chance Meeting," first published in 1933 and later reprinted in *Not Under Forty* (1936). She tells the niece that she does not want any manuscripts or letters of Flaubert's. "The things of her uncle that were valuable to me I already had, and had had for years" (33), Cather claims. Nonetheless, Mme Franklin-Grout sends Cather one of her uncle's letters, which is somehow removed, lost, or stolen from the envelope. "I wrote to her, quite truthfully, that her wish that I should have one of her uncle's letters meant a great deal more to me than the actual possession of it could mean" (41). Cather gave the same cast of mind to Cécile, who says of the Count's glass fruit that is to be hers one day: "it is quite enough to look at it; one would never forget it. It is much lovelier than real fruit" (*Shadows* 48). By way of describing the effect of a Flaubert's *L'education sentimentale* on her, Cather may have revealed her frame of mind in 1931: "It is something one has lived through, not a story one has read; less diverting than a story, perhaps, but more inevitable. One is 'left with it,' in the same way that one is left with a weak heart after certain illnesses. A shadow has come into one's consciousness that will not go out again" ("A Chance

Meeting" 20). The irrelevance of things never seems far from Cather's sense of value.

Cather seems to have lived and thought in nonlinear patterns, where nothing necessarily follows, and so anything may follow. Her transcontinental and transoceanic travel habits, her life in hotels, inns, and cottages—these were manifestations of a restless, anacoluthonic intellect. Cather's, moreover, was one of the minds that produced the era we live in now, where we cling to the nonsequential as if it were true. Cather's mind contributes to the shadow of our present intellectual ecology. *Shadows on the Rock* is the pinnacle, where it all comes together in a novel about stillness—about the rare and oh-so-temporary experience of standing still. It took a while for Cather to write Nebraska out. It was always her rock. Like Grenfell, she got frantic for it and had to visit it or think about it a lot. But once she let it go, she shot out into the eternities and wrote herself into her most intellectually rigorous work. The world may have broke in two in 1922, but it was back as one in 1931.

CATHER'S WHORES; OR, GOING ON DOWN THE ROCK

The coming of shadows into one's consciousness is a recurring motif in *Shadows on the Rock*, the building of frames of mind, of faith and visions. Consider the two working women in the novel. Because, from another perspective, there is something metaphorically whorish about Cather's itinerant career, spending a night here and there, this pen for hire, dropping into Taos or Quebec and "doing" Catholicism, and "doing" Bohemian girls and "doing" midlife professors. *I'm just a station on your way / I know I'm not your lover.* It is remarkable how Cather slips whores into the world of faith and endurance in *Shadows on the Rock*. Then again, how could Cather miss the fact that there were two main institutions by which women could immigrate to Canada without being wives: as the objects of spiritual salvation, and as the objects of physical satiation; ministers to God or sailors.

Cather's main whore is 'Toinette, a whore descended from a whore, from a long line of whores. Her mother was "one of the worst" of the "several hundred" women sent to Canada by the king to marry the men of a French regiment that had subdued the Iroquois—she was not one of the good girls or the orphans. She was one of those whom Cather identifies as the truly bad girls. The whore-mother gives birth to 'Toinette, "as pretty and as worthless a girl as ever made eyes at the sailors in any seaport town." Antoinette, surely Ántonia's dark twin, falls in love, leaves her whorish ways for about as long as Ántonia leaves her good ways, has a child, and then "returned to her old ways, and her husband disappeared" (41). Antoinette opens a "sailors' lodging house," which takes its place among the institutions clinging to the rock, but down low, where she does a pretty good business for a woman surrounded by piety. The girls attract sailors by advertising "'FROGS' and 'SNAILS'" to the hungry sailors, whether they had these delicacies on hand or not, because, as Cather explains, 'Toinette is "still good to look at" (41). (And, if the sailors cannot eat "frogs and snails," they can have either frog or snail, which are also the nicknames of 'Toinette and her business partner, in another of Cather's forays into suggestive orality.) The whore-bird whom Antoinette conceives during her brief fall into grace is Jacques, whose angelic nature Cécile finds in need of shoes.

'Toinette may be a whore, but she is not unenlightened. When she hears that it was the Governor, not Auclair, who bought the shoes for Jacques, she transcends her station for an instant: "The Governor? Ah, that is different. The Governor is our protector, he owes us something. The King owes something to the children of those poor creatures, like my mother, *whom he sent out here under false pretences*" (71, emphasis added). 'Toinette and her son cast strong shadows on the minds of the saintly rock dwellers. Bishop Laval sees Jacques as "a sign that it was time to return to that rapt and mystical devotion of his early life." And for his part, the apothecary Auclair watches Jacques and wonders why it is a whore "should have a boy like that" (71).

The other berating whore in *Shadows on the Rock* is Marie, in the story Mother Juschereau tells Cécile. Marie is such a whore that she must first be introduced by Cather as a *pécheresse*; the English word for *sinner* is apparently not sinful enough to communicate the extent of Marie's whorishness. "She had been a sinner from her early youth," Cather translates, and continues, in an uncharacteristically tortured sentence, "and was so proof against all counsel that she continued her disorders until an advanced age." Apparently lacking the entrepreneurial spirit of 'Toinette, Marie is banished from her town; "she fell lower and lower, and at last hid herself in a solitary cave" where she "dragged out her shameful life, destitute and consumed by a loathsome disease." She died alone, but apparently not unobserved, because after her death someone came around, removed her from her cave, and threw her body into a ditch where it was "buried like that of some unclean animal" (30). In her "solitary cave," however, Marie, like one of Plato's unchained visionaries, manages to free herself and see the source of her shadowy existence in the appearance of the Virgin Mary. At this point the story ceases to be about Marie and becomes a shadow in the consciousness of Sister Catherine. "One day, while [Sister Catherine] was at prayer," we learn, Marie pays her a visit and chews her out: "You commend to God the souls of all those who die," says the whorish Marie. "I am the only one on whom you have no compassion" (31). Sister Catherine immediately makes amends and has masses said for Marie, who returns, a few days later, with news of her admission to heaven. The story makes Sister Catherine's career, because the shadow of Marie leads her to produce a reputation for "always dedicating herself to the impossible and always achieving it" (34).

And so it follows—does it not follow?—that the colony of Quebec was begun in whoredom, sustained by visions of whores visited upon its saints, and continued by bourgeois whores who accept assistance from the governor and raise respectable sons. To place these two whore stories in the context of Cather's controlling metaphor: when we enter the game of rock/shadows/meaning,[7] we commit to a "disorder" that shall continue "until an advanced age." And what is a whore but the shadow of those sexual and economic desires that inform our more sacred, domestic arrangements? "She used to wear her hair like you," we tell the Winter Lady. In the time of the novel, the term *whore* could be—and was—applied to entire communities that had become corrupt or idolatrous. *That whorish Quebec*, one might say. We are all, in this sense, descendants of whores, whether descended from an eventually secularized Quebec or as Yankee descendants of Puritan saints, on their errand into the wilderness.[8]

Cather's liberationist consciousness moves us away from manifestations and back to origins. Whence the shadows on our minds? The "Winter Lady" who stays a while brings the news that belief and desire are human energies that can make the world a sacred or a whorish place. It is the sense of having been shot out into the eternities, of having been pried loose from the rock for a while, of recognizing the cave we call our sanctuary and knowing briefly that what we hold to most dearly are shadows cast by ineffable sources—or by the eternal sources of our own desires. Cather makes us almost believe we can see that.

Recall the soon-to-be-reformed whore, Tom Outland, right after he "requites faith and friendship" (*The Professor's House* 229) and feels pretty bad about it. He does not pursue his estranged friend, Roddy Blake, immediately. While Blake gets away, Tom lies down and watches the shadows come over the mesa at sundown. As the light fades, he thinks, "It all came together in my understanding," so that "the mesa was no longer an adventure, but a religious emotion." Far from feeling that he had done something wrong in his rude treatment of Blake, Outland "wakened with the feeling that I had found everything, instead of having lost everything" (226–27). Blake had done him a great favor in selling off the *things* he had mistakenly valued, and now he can conjure the forces that produced those pots and vases. "I seemed to get the solar energy in some direct way," he muses. Tom Outland, in the final scene of his narrative, has been torn loose from his little rock and shot out into the eternities. "And that's what makes men happy," St. Peter lectures in *The Professor's House*, "believing in the mystery and importance of their own little individual lives" (55). But what makes humanists giddy is the knowledge that the mystery is no more than another shadow cast to keep them in chains. *We believed this, because we had been taught it in childhood.* It is very much like the days when Cécile "loved her town best": not when her view of things was plain, but when her vision of the physical world was obscured, when "The autumn fog was rolling in from the river" and "Everything else was blotted out by rolling vapours that were constantly changing in density and colour" (50)—liberating her, for the moment, from that God-haunted rock.

And in the end, we see the final liberation of Cécile—not into the convent, but into the wilderness; not within the shadowy world where nothing changes, but into the world of what Cather calls "the future," the ever-receding realm of human salvation. Nowhere to be found in the epilogue, Cécile has been liberated from this particular rock. She has been torn loose and shot out into the eternities, and, to invoke Plato again, no longer "required to contend with [the] perpetual prisoners in 'evaluating' these shadows" (517a)—prisoners such as Jean Le Ber, Bishop Laval, even her father, the rock-bound pharmacist—all terribly good people, but imprisoned nonetheless. Think of all the prisons in this novel—from Blinker's tales of torture to Saint-Vallier's captivity in England—and, of course, the prominence of the religious orders in Quebec. How human beings seem to love their cages! And what beauty is produced by an imprisoned soul. But not Cécile. She moved into "a commodious house in the Upper Town," her father explains, "beyond the Ursuline convent" and out of the novel in the arms of Pierre Charron, namesake of the famous sixteenth-century French skeptic.[9] Jacques, the whore's son, has taken over Cécile's chamber and is filling the apothecary's shop with keepsakes—shells and corals. Meanwhile, Auclair recognizes in the Bishop "a man uncertain," in Cather's final invocation of her title, "a man uncertain, and puzzled, and in the dark like ourselves." But Jacques is not at home in the dark very much; he is a sailor and spends much of his life between the rocks, with visions, no doubt, of pretty girls, diving. We might hear the Canadian singing: "I'm just a station on your way / I know I'm not your lover" as he, like us, navigates within the shadows cast by his creator, Willa Cather.

NOTES

1. John J. Murphy has called attention to Cather's evocation of the cave allegory in the novel: "reality is outside the den most of us inhabit; our world is an unsubstantial one of shadows that the child instinctively appreciates, without understanding" (121).

2. In a study of James's influence on *Death Comes for the Archbishop*, Skaggs establishes that "Cather knew William James's work thoroughly" and had been reading it closely throughout her career. "Cather's appetite for the *artistic* satisfaction of ordering the Church and building its focal cathedral in the Southwest was actually whetted" by her knowledge of James's *Varieties of Religious Experience* (101, 103).

3. The allusion is Jamesian: "The truth of an idea is not a stagnant property inherent in it. Truth *happens* to an idea. It *becomes* true, is *made* true by events. Its verity *is* in fact an event, a process: the process namely of its verifying itself, its veri-*fication*" (97).

4. David Stouck suggests a connection between "Before Breakfast" and *Shadows on the Rock*: "Cather wrote of Quebec that there was a feeling about human life and fate there she could not wholly accept—a feeling of 'pious resignation.' I would argue that in 'Before Breakfast' she accepts in a very positive way the message of the rock and the shadows cast on it so briefly" (20).

5. Because insight into "the eternities" is fleeting, dangerous, and ephemeral, throughout history human beings have sought experience with such ultimate reality through intensive interaction with and knowledge of one metaphoric, philosophical, or religious system. Living one way of spiritual desire thoroughly does not negate the validity of other ways of seeking; neither does an interest in investigating systems of belief imply a challenge to the truth contained in them. It would be a mistake to infer from my argument the suggestion that Cather was hostile or even indifferent to religious experience, in this case, the Catholic faith. On the contrary, she seems to have been intensely interested. Proof is in the effect the novel has had on believers. See, for example, Sister Lucy Schneider, who argues against "the frequently made judgment that the Catholicism Miss Cather here proposed is limited only to culture, aesthetics, and comfortable security and that dogma plays no role whatsoever" (92).

6. However, see the important collection *Willa Cather's Canadian and Old World Connections*, volume 4 of *Cather Studies*.

7. For a more complete explication of meaning-making in the novel, particularly as Cather may have been influenced by contemporary anthropology, see Richard Millington, who argues that Cather was drawn to "the interconnected and particular ways distinct communities

construct meanings for the individual lives that unfold within them" (24). Millington's conclusion is particularly appropriate: "The subject of *Shadows on the Rock* is not the revelation of Meaning but the making of meanings, and the book is best understood not as a nostalgic evocation of a lost stability of meaning but as a modernist meditation upon its construction" (35).

8. John J. Murphy points out the parallel debt to St. Augustine's *City of God* held by Quebec and New England pilgrims, in a fine image of Cather as Winter Lady, the itinerant: "Papists and Puritans in the seventeenth century shared Augustine's model, and if United States history emphasizes the Puritans, Cather did not. As in *Death Comes for the Archbishop*, *My Ántonia*, and other novels, she acquainted her readers with other than Anglo traditions and aspirations. She was not creating a city on a rock to compete with but to complement the city on a hill singled out as America's idiosyncratic one" (133).

9. Richard Harris has examined the philosophy of the historical Pierre Charron (b. 1541). Charron's most famous works are *Treatise on the Three Verities* (1594) and *Treatise on Wisdom* (1601). According to Harris, "The philosopher Charron's great contribution to the development of Western philosophy was his creation of a moral system independent of religion" (72).

WORKS CITED

Cather, Willa. "Before Breakfast." *The Old Beauty and Others*. New York: Vintage Books, 1976. 141–66. Collection originally published in 1948.

———. "A Chance Meeting." *Not Under Forty*. Lincoln: U of Nebraska P, 1988. 3–42. Collection originally published in 1936.

———. *Death Comes for the Archbishop*. 1927. Willa Cather Scholarly Edition. Ed. John J. Murphy. Lincoln: U of Nebraska P, 1999.

———. "My First Novels (There Were Two)." *Willa Cather on Writing*. Lincoln: U of Nebraska P, 1988. 89–98.

———. "On *Shadows on the Rock*." *Willa Cather on Writing*. Lincoln: U of Nebraska P, 1988. 14–17.

———. *The Professor's House*. 1925. New York: Vintage Classics, 1990.

———. *Sapphira and the Slave Girl*. 1940. New York: Vintage Books, 1975.

———. *Shadows on the Rock*. 1931. New York: Vintage Classics, 1995.

Cohen, Leonard. "Winter Lady." *Stranger Music: Selected Poems and Songs*. New York: Vintage Books, 1994. 99. Originally published on the album *Songs of Leonard Cohen*. Columbia Records, 1967.

Fowler, H. W., and F. G. Fowler. *The King's English* (1931). 4 Aug. 2003. http://www.ss.ucalgary.ca/JArchibald/Anacoluthon.htm.

Harris, Richard C. "Willa Cather and Pierre Charron on Wisdom: The Skeptical Philosophy of *Shadows on the Rock*." *Cather Studies 4: Willa Cather's Canadian and Old World Connections* (1999): 66–79.

James, William. *Pragmatism: A New Name for Some Old Ways of Thinking* and *The Meaning of Truth: A Sequel to Pragmatism*. Intro. A. J. Ayer. Cambridge: Harvard UP, 1981.

Martin, Terence. "Grande Communications avec Dieu: The Surrounding Power of *Shadows on the Rock*." *Cather Studies* 3 (1996). 4 Aug. 2003. http://www.unl.edu/Cather/scholarship/cs/vol3/gcad.htm.

Millington, Richard. "Where Is Cather's Quebec? Anthropological Modernism in *Shadows on the Rock*." *Cather Studies 4: Willa Cather's Canadian and Old World Connections* (1999): 23–44.

Murphy, John J. "Willa Cather's City of God: *Shadows on the Rock*." *Literature and Belief* 15 (1995): 119–35.

Plato. *The Republic. The Collected Dialogues of Plato, including the Letters*. Ed. Edith Hamilton and Huntington Cairns. Princeton: Princeton UP, 1961.

Schneider, Sister Lucy. "Permanence and Promise: Cather's *Shadows on the Rock*." *Renascence* 26.1 (1974): 83–94.

Skaggs, Merrill. "*Death Comes for the Archbishop*: Willa Cather's Varieties of Religious Experience." *Willa Cather and the Culture of Belief*. Ed. John J. Murphy. Provo UT: Brigham Young UP, 2002. 101–21.

Stouck, David. "'Willa Cather's Canada': The Border as Fiction." *Cather Studies 4: Willa Cather's Canadian and Old World Connections* (1999): 7–22.

Stout, Janis. "Faith Statements and Nonstatements in Willa Cather's Personal Letters." *Willa Cather and the Culture of Belief*. Ed. John J. Murphy. Provo UT: Brigham Young UP, 2002. 7–28.

Woodress, James. *Willa Cather: A Literary Life*. Lincoln: U of Nebraska P, 1987.

Subsequent Reflections on *Shadows on the Rock*

RICHARD H. MILLINGTON,
JOHN J. MURPHY, AND
JOSEPH R. URGO

The three preceding essays, by Richard H. Millington, John J. Murphy, and Joseph R. Urgo, were originally presented as a triptych of papers at the Ninth International Cather Seminar, "Willa Cather as Cultural Icon" (Bread Loaf, Vermont, 28 May–2 June 2003). The three scholars were then invited to respond to each others' viewpoints and to continue the conversation about Cather's iconicity, first in a roundtable discussion at the conference and then in the reflections that follow.

RICHARD H. MILLINGTON

In the spirited discussion that followed the presentation of these three papers at the Breadloaf Seminar, my argument got translated, I believe, into a version of the time-honored "murder to dissect" debate: Should we be interpreting Cather's works at all? I confess to being at the time somewhat befuddled by this development; let me take this occasion, first, to clarify my claims. Sontag, as I hope my essay makes clear, is not calling for an end to literary criticism; she is, rather, arguing that we desperately need a *descriptive* rather than an *explanatory* (or, in her terms, an *interpretive*) approach to works of art, so that we may experience them—and through their example, the world—freshly and directly. Following Sontag, I set out to provide such a description of *Shadows on the Rock*, emphasizing the kind of experience of reading that Cather's formal choices seemed designed to produce. My argument, though "formalist," is not a- or anti-historical: I then tried to show that the very experience of reading that Cather creates in *Shadows*—the way the book enacts its interests and quietly instructs us in feeling and thinking differently—is, when put in the context of a contest between Victorian and modernist cultures, its most significant historical feature. Or, to put this another way, the affective and aesthetic experience of a text may well be the most interesting thing to "historicize." I would add to Sontag's argument this modification: different works require from their readers different forms of response. It makes all the sense in the world to apply the familiar model of character growth and development to Austen's Emma or George Eliot's Dorothea Brooke; it is the occasion of a profound readerly loss to apply such allegorical interpretive schemes to the work of a writer trying her best to escape them.

Perhaps in the spirit of Sontag, let me bring more to the surface the polemical undercurrent of my essay: I think Cather criticism—of all intellectual varieties—pays and has paid far too little attention to the experience of reading that her books create. Resolutely "interpretive," in Sontag's terms, we have explained all sorts of things about her texts—their themes, their relation to her life, their relation to American ideology—but, having explained so much about her books, we have failed to notice sufficiently what is at once most remarkable and most obvious about them: the way they refuse the novelistic tradition they inherit—and, through that refusal, make possible for their readers new forms of response. (Isn't that what major writers do—exemplify or transform structures of thought and feeling?)

Americanist literary criticism generally wriggles under the thumb of the explanatory, but Cather criticism seems to me to have an especially bad case. Am I alone in especially wishing for a respite from the biographical interpretation of her fiction? Let me be clear: biographical *work* is necessarily valuable; it is always good to know more, and that knowledge can sometimes bolster arguments or save one from interpretive error. For example, Janis Stout's fine biographical essay on Cather and the question of belief, with its convincing demonstration that, for most of her life, her actual religious feeling can*not* be pinned down, has the salutary effect of keeping open the genuinely interpretive question of how "belief" might best be understood within her novels.[1] But biographical *interpretation*, the attempt to explain the qualities of the work by recourse to the life, has seemed to me inconclusive at best and, at worst, dispiritingly reductive, often denying Cather the respect due her as an intellectual and an artist. And in the unlikely event that a biographical interpretation *were* convincing, I am hard pressed to think of a case in which it would not make the text *less* rather than *more* interesting: of what possible use is it to know that Cather was feeling *the same thing* as Godfrey St. Peter when she was writing *The Professor's House*, or that Old Mrs. Harris *is really* Cather's grandmother's left-handed maiden aunt, twice removed? Within Cather studies the biographical urge is the most egregious and prevalent instance of rampant allegorism and the avoidance of engagement with the experience of the text. Frankly, I do not think most historicist readings fare much better in this regard. I have been happy to learn much from recent contextual work, but it is rare to find attention to anything but theme in such studies, and their address to the work is no less allegorical, as they track the trajectory of "real" ideological categories across the dispensable "surface" of the text.[2]

My little polemic raises a question. Why are academics, old-fashioned or new, so drawn to the "interpretive" and the "allegorical"—to moralized narratives, whether uplifting or demystifying, that will reveal the hidden truth about a text? Why have we been so impervious to the modernism of texts like *Shadows on the Rock*? Here is a historical answer: English professors—whether pre- or poststructuralist in their intellectual orientation—are the inheritors, through the university and the liberal arts college, the institutions that train and employ them, of the very ethos—high-minded, allegorizing, moralistic—that Cather's texts work so hard to combat. We have met the Last Victorians, and they are us.

JOHN J. MURPHY

Let me begin by acknowledging my collaborators, whose distinguished work on *Shadows on the Rock* has helped rescue the novel from neglect and recognize it as an essential component of Cather's exploration of culture-making. I have cited their essays in my preceding essay because in exploring this flood subject, they touch upon (if ever so gently) what seems an impasse in contemporary criticism vis-à-vis issues of religion and faith. The primary difficulty concerns objectivity, which in our discipline ranges from truth to matters of taste. C. S. Lewis claims that the modern penchant for ideological relativity stems from regarding the savage as the human norm, that as we turn to developed civilizations we find fewer differences than popularly believed. He denies that there exists "choice between clearly differentiated ethical systems," affirming that "no ethical attack on any of the traditional precepts can be made except on the ground of some other traditional precept." His argument recognizes the Absolute (what Cather's rock symbolizes) and concludes that Christianity presupposes moral truth, which (like God) has no basis: "The ultimate ethical injunctions have always been premises, never conclusions" (55). The contemporary urge to mutilate or expurgate what Lewis calls the "text of the . . . original manuscript" (56) stems not only from our demand for intellectual and moral freedom but from scandalous behavior and inconsistency within religious denominations, violent acts committed under the guise of righteousness, resentment of authority, and growing secularism. Sometimes very personal experiences cause literary critics to dismiss religious issues (unless they are discrediting) in texts with obvious religious intentions.

In Cather's case, religious intentions are underrepresented in the criticism generated by her work. Unlike Flannery O'Connor, Cather never really identified with a religious system, yet she was fascinated by the cultures of such systems, by how they determine vision and values and influence motivation. Sometimes Cather was dismayed by the narrowness of religious communities, but more often the saintly lives, folkways, art, and architecture of religion inspired her. But more than cultural curiosity can be implied from the increasing dominance of religious subjects from *The Professor's House* (1925) to the Avignon story left unfinished at her death in 1947. For example, thoughtful speculation on the existence of God is the subject of a 1936 letter Cather wrote to Edith Lewis from New Hampshire. Cather describes (in my paraphrase) how Jupiter and Venus hang together in the October evening sky "for an hour . . . . then silver Venus slips into the rose-colored twilight to be close to the departed sun, and Jupiter now hangs alone in the sky, going down about 8:30. It surely reminds us of Dante's 'eternal wheels.' I can't believe that all this beauty and majesty, these unfailing and fated arrivals and exits, are nothing more than mathematics and horrible temperatures. If they are, then human beings are the only wonderful things—because they can wonder." Cather would express her own wonder through Father Ambrose in the Avignon fragment, yet here it appears unmasked, personal, a concern of the woman as well as the artist. This letter is important in helping us determine why Cather repeatedly returned to religious subjects and why she chose to be confirmed with her parents in Red Cloud's Grace Episcopal Church in 1922.

That an intelligent woman and artist would have such concerns in modern times need not be viewed as an aberration. Intelligent people may still be as concerned about the existence of the ultimate as Thomas Aquinas was in the thirteenth century. His agenda, too, involved proof of the reality of God, the "idea" which in Bishop Latour's speculation in *Death Comes for the Archbishop* was for the ancient Hebrews "their rock . . . the only thing their conquerors could not take from them" (103). St. Thomas also argued from effects ("Existence of God") that God's existence is proven through motion and causation, the need for primacy and maximum being, and the intelligent direction of the universe (the argument Cather refers to in her letter). More convincing for modern sensibilities (because it addresses our psychological composition) is his argument that the fulfillment we seek through temporary pleasures, riches, fame, and so forth can be satisfied only in God ("What Is Happiness?"); this, indeed, is why we crave it. The struggle to sustain faith in such fulfillment is at the core of religious life. Such is Bishop Latour's struggle in "December Night," Noël Chabanel's and Jeanne Le

Ber's during periods of spiritual aridity, and Myra Henshawe's during her terrible final days. Godfrey St. Peter merely struggles with the emptiness of corruptible things; his faith journey begins beyond the pages of Cather's novel. "[P]eople don't realize . . . how much religion costs," Flannery O'Connor wrote to Louise Abbot in 1959. "They think faith is a big electric blanket, when of course it is the cross. It is much harder to believe than not to believe. If you feel you can't believe, you must at least do this: keep an open mind. Keep it open toward faith, keep wanting it, keep asking for it, and leave the rest to God" (354).

I refuse to concede that such struggles are out of date in the twenty-first century, and I feel that literary critics who are agnostics or atheists should acknowledge the seriousness of such struggles, just as believers should recognize that their version of reality may seem irrelevant to others. It should be noted by critics, for example, that Chabanel made his perpetual vow "in the presence of the Blessed Sacrament exposed" (123)—that is, out of the tabernacle—because in his belief Christ was present in the Sacrament. The critic who is an orthodox Catholic should not use this occasion to declare the real presence as a fact; believers must present matters of faith as personal rather than universal truths. If a critic is an agnostic or atheist, he or she should be aware of the significance of such a specification to the character involved; this should not merely be a matter of courtesy but one of comprehensive reading. Cather herself is a perfect model (perhaps even an icon) of the sensitivity and intelligence needed to recognize the meaning of certain traditions and to respect them. With her kind of sympathy, belief and its object, God, will not be relegated to darker ages and peasantry but recognized as viable components of contemporary life.

JOSEPH R. URGO

Near the end of his essay in this volume, John Murphy states that he "would prefer exploration of both permanence and change within the system represented by the shadows," and follows immediately with the question, "To what extent does a belief system possess permanence, and to what extent is it transitory?" This a very good, and haunting, question. In the question-and-answer portion of the public presentation where these essays originated, Charles Peek raised a similar question, which I will attempt to paraphrase here. Granted Cather's interest in strong manifestations of belief, and granted that Quebec presents a particularly salient example of "truth happening" among the devout, what, in Cather's mind, casts the shadow? If Nebraska pioneers, French missionaries in the Southwest, Catholic settlers in Quebec, and soldiers marching off to the Great War are manifestations of something constant in human nature, some unaccountable predilection, as Cather might have it, what exactly is it that is manifest? It does not necessarily follow that the attempt to know about a great number of such manifestations is preferable, superior, or more intellectually sophisticated than devoting a lifetime to knowing one manifestation thoroughly. The quest is common: we seek access to the eternities, to the source both of meaning and meaning-making. The divide is as old as Western philosophy. In their successive attempts to understand human political arrangements, Plato contemplated one, theoretically perfect state. His student, Aristotle, cataloged every known political system. The desire was constant; the means successive, various, and different.

The purpose of literary criticism is, in the end, to renew our interest in literary texts. The enterprise has a number of auxiliary functions, which spill over into every discipline in the humanities, and into the sphere of public affairs. As literary critics we deal, in essence, in the human imagination. When the three of us—John Murphy, Richard Millington, and myself—began to think about this collaboration, what drove us was the experiment of moving *Shadows on the Rock* to the center, rather than the periphery, of the Cather canon, as if it, and not *My Ántonia*, were considered the main text, the great achievement. There is no formal reason why this should not be so; *Shadows on the Rock* is as technically accomplished as any other Cather novel. If Catholicism, and not geographical pioneers, were the source of so much American ideology, then the content of *Shadows on the Rock* would be compelling, not compulsory.

With the evocation of Plato's allegory of the cave, from *The Republic*, Cather implicitly raises a subsidiary issue. No one in literary studies thinks of *The Republic* without recalling that Plato famously bans poets from his ideal state. The danger that the poet (and today, the novelist) brings to the state comes in the habit of mimesis, producing the demand for interpretation, a demand that divides citizens. At the time Plato was writing, philosophers challenged poets for prominence in matters of state. Was not rationality more to be trusted than the mimetic arts? Philosophers argued logically, and their conclusions could be examined and challenged with even more precise and accurate thinking. Poets, however, were liars. They made things up, aroused emotions, evoked opposed responses. The divide continues today, as it has throughout Western intellectual history, between fact and fancy, science and humanities, critics and poets. Our souls, our training, our institutions are similarly divided between the manipulation of what has been given to us and the creation of what has not.

The question of what Cather meant is not as interesting as the nature of the debate she ignited when she stranded the "philosopher apothecary" and his daughter on the rock. We are attracted to poets who are able to articulate and breathe life into that which remains unsettled. The matter of religious pluralism in the contemporary world, the idea of God, the challenge to coexistence posed by fundamentalist systems—the vital nature of these issues does not depend on our eyes being open to them. And unlike Plato's philosopher-kings, we are not at liberty to ban from our presence the poet who compels us to attend to such matters. As descendants of philosophers and poets, we continue to study the effects on our intellectual situation brought to bear by the philosopher's system and the poet's imagination, the confrontation between our received beliefs and the vision of what else might be there. The question—Which are shadows and which are rocks?—will remain with us until we become something else besides our inherited and imaginable selves.

NOTES

1. See Janis P. Stout, "Faith Statements and Nonstatements in Willa Cather's Personal Letters." Let me be clear about my terms: I would describe the three essays that precede this chapter as, mainly, "inten-

tionalist" rather than biographical. The Cather evoked in my essay and Joe Urgo's (and, for most of the time, in John Murphy's) is the artist-intellectual we infer from the distinctive attributes of the texts she writes; in my view, it is precisely when Murphy's essay veers toward the biographical—when it wants to claim something about Cather's actual beliefs—that its argument becomes unpersuasive (as when Pierre Charron's supposed piety is taken as evidence for Cather's, or when Cécile's quite secular celebration of the pots and pans of civilization is somehow taken as evidence of the book's stake in the "sacred").

2. An exception to this criticism is Chip Rhodes's fine discussion of *The Professor's House* in "American Modernism, Aesthetics, and Man-made Truths: Willa Cather and John Dos Passos," chapter 2 of his *Structures of the Jazz Age*.

WORKS CITED

Cather, Willa. *Death Comes for the Archbishop*. 1927. Willa Cather Scholarly Edition. Ed. Charles W. Mignon with Frederick M. Link and Kari A. Ronning. Historical essay and explanatory notes John J. Murphy. Lincoln: U of Nebraska P, 1999.

———. Letter to Edith Lewis. 4 October 1936. Willa Cather Pioneer Memorial, Red Cloud, Nebraska.

———. *Shadows on the Rock*. 1931. New York: Vintage, 1995.

Lewis, C. S. "On Ethics." *Christian Reflections by C.S. Lewis*. Ed. Walter Hooper. Grand Rapids MI: Eerdmans, 1967. 44–56.

O'Connor, Flannery. *The Habit of Being: Letters of Flannery O'Connor*. Ed. Sally Fitzgerald. New York: Vintage, 1980.

Rhodes, Chip. *Structures of the Jazz Age: Mass Culture, Progressive Education, and Racial Disclosures in American Modernism*. London: Verso, 1998.

Stout, Janis P. "Faith Statements and Nonstatements in Willa Cather's Personal Letters." *Willa Cather and the Culture of Belief*. Ed. John J. Murphy. Provo UT: Brigham Young UP, 2002. 7–27.

Thomas Aquinas. "The Existence of God" (Question 2). *Summa Theologica*. Trans. English Dominicans. 5 vols. Westminster MD: Christian Classics, 1981. 1: 11–14.

———. "What Is Happiness" (Question 3, Eighth article). *Summa Theologica*. Trans. English Dominicans. 5 vols. Westminster MD: Christian Classics, 1981. 2: 601–2.

Cather, Freudianism, and Freud

JOHN N. SWIFT

This essay does not argue for or particularly examine Willa Cather's cultural iconicity. It grew from my personal conviction of the immense significance of Cather's writing, and from my old but unexamined habit of linking her mentally with another writer—Freud—whose status is indeed unquestioned. I wanted here simply to bring together more or less systematically two of the great figures in my own "family romance," two strong voices that have echoed in my thinking for more than twenty years.

To many readers (and certainly to Cather herself) they seem an unlikely pair. Yet they have much in common: children of the provinces who came to see themselves as speaking for high culture itself; professional late bloomers who served long, arduous apprenticeships; in their personal lives aloof, in what Freud called "splendid isolation"; meticulous self-fashioners; lovers of classical antiquity and things archaeological, and of European literature from Virgil through Shakespeare to Anatole France. Each described the collapse of his or her world and lived on past it, sometimes bitter but not defeated, into wise or cynical age. Each was until the end an unrepentant iconoclast: Freud's Virgilian epigraph to *The Interpretation of Dreams* in 1900—"*Flectere si nequeo Superos, Acheronta movebo*," which I translate loosely as "If I can't move heaven, then I'll raise hell"—has always struck me as somehow appropriate to Cather, young or old.

When I first read Cather in 1981, as I will describe below, I immediately and without much thought placed her in my own very small canon of literary icons, and it was hard for me to understand why she was even then still for critics often a minor, regional figure. In what follows, reassured by the compelling arguments of others in this volume, I simply take her iconicity—her inexhaustible cultural suggestiveness—for granted, as I take Freud's.

THE VILLAGE FREUDIANS

It is easy to follow the threads of relationship between Willa Cather and Sigmund Freud: there are almost none. I believe that Freud's name appears exactly once in Cather's published and unpublished writings, in a famous 1936 counterattack on young literary critics incapable of appreciating Sarah Orne Jewett's prose: "Imagine a young man, or woman, born in New York City, educated at a New York university, violently inoculated with Freud, hurried into journalism, knowing no more about New England country people (or country folk anywhere) than he has caught from motor trips or observed from summer hotels: what is there for him in *The Country of the Pointed Firs*?" (*Not Under Forty* 92–93). In a subsequent letter to Zoë Akins she identified her targets as NYU graduates with foreign-sounding names publishing essays about sex-starved New England lady authors (Woodress 474; Stout, *Calendar* 206). I do not know the specific writers who incensed Cather, but they sound like practitioners of criticism-as-diagnosis, an approach pretty common in the enthusiastic youth of literary psychoanalysis, and one encouraged by Freud himself, who saw art (like most behavior) mainly as sublimated expression of the artist's frustrated sexual desires.

Beyond this public outburst (more noted now for its nativism—the young critic is of "German, Jewish, Scandinavian" descent—than for its critique of psychoanalysis) we hear little, even off the record, about Cather's awareness of the strong currents of "Freudianism" that surged in American intellectual culture in the 1910s, 1920s, and 1930s. Elizabeth Shepley Sergeant describes a 1921 dismissal of Freud's work as one instance of Cather's growing rigidity and conservatism: "She was truly skeptical about the post-war world. Take this Viennese Freud: why was everybody reading him? Tolstoy knew as much about psychology—with no isms attached—as any fiction writer needed. I didn't agree. Freud was *here*: I had to try to read him, because I lived in today's world. But Willa . . . looked backward with regret" (173–74). Sergeant also tells a strange story of the late 1920s (probably the spring of 1929), of a depressed Willa Cather toying with entering Jungian analysis to address "the enigma of life and death" that hovered over her, unhappily poised as she was between the death of her father and her mother's illness (247–49). Predictably, she chose against analysis.

These fragments indicate that Cather was well aware of Freudianism and the American psychoanalytic movement: and of course she must have been, as an intellectual and a woman of letters living right at the movement's ground zero, Greenwich Village in the 1910s. Her biographers usually insist that her Bank Street apartment was a calm backwater in the tempest of freethinking that made the Village legendary—"Willa had never, of course, been involved with the vagaries of Greenwich Village in the pre-war days," says Sergeant (211). James Woodress is a little less sure of her isolation, calling her "an observer rather than a participant in the yeasty ferment in Greenwich Village in the years before World War I" and suggesting that, while no evidence links her to radical thinkers like Max Eastman, John Reed, or Margaret Sanger, she certainly did know Floyd Dell and Carl Van Vechten, and "may have attended Mabel Dodge Luhan's famous salon on occasion, as everyone in Greenwich Village" did (236). (Woodress later guesses, I think properly, that "Cather must have met [Luhan] in New York . . . when she was Mabel Dodge, a rich patron of the arts" [363].) And Janis Stout calls "puzzling" Cather's apparently deliberate blind eye to the bohemian or avant-garde aspects of her community (*Writer* 128).

I suspect, in fact, that Cather knew the Village's famous left pretty well—well enough to satirize it accurately in her 1918 portrait of Genevieve Whitney Burden, Jim Burden's wife in *My Ántonia*'s foreword, who "gave one of her town houses for a Suffrage headquarters, produced one of her own plays at the Princess Theater, was arrested for picketing during a garment-makers' strike, etc. . . . [and who] finds it worth while to play the patroness to a group of young poets and painters of advanced ideas and mediocre ability" (x–xi). This composite portrait draws on several of the Village's politically and artistically emancipated women. But Mrs. Burden most strikingly resembles Mabel Dodge Luhan herself, the irrepressible grande dame of 23 Fifth Avenue from 1912 to 1915, and a figure of some importance in the spread of Freudian ideas in the intellectual life of Manhattan in the 1910s. Estranged from her midwestern architect husband, Edwin Dodge, Luhan embarked on a brief bright career as a patroness of the modern, one that led her to assemble in her drawing room, in her words, "Socialists, Trade Unionists, Anarchists, Suffragists, Poets, Relations, Lawyers, Murderers, 'Old Friends,' Psychoanalysts, IWWs, Single Taxers, Birth Controlists, Newspapermen, Artists, Modern Artists, Clubwomen, Woman's-place-is-in-the-home Women, Clergymen, and just plain men. . . . It was not dogs or glass I collected now, it was people, Important People" (*Movers* 83–84). Luhan wrote about Gertrude Stein and the new art of the Armory Show; she militated for the unemployed; she arranged a meeting between Isadora Duncan and the mayor of New York to discuss education for the poor; she was John Reed's lover and (by her own account) his muse for the 1913 IWW Paterson Strike Pageant in Madison Square Garden. It is hard to imagine that Cather did not have this energetic woman in her mind when she created Genevieve Whitney Burden. And it is also not very surprising that the portrait of Mrs. Burden almost disappeared from the revised *My Ántonia* of 1926, when Luhan had become Cather's close southwestern friend and correspondent—and her hostess in Taos for two weeks in the summer of 1925.

Among Cather's documented Greenwich Village acquaintances, both Carl Van Vechten and Floyd Dell dabbled in and wrote about Freudian psychoanalysis (as did almost all of the Greenwich Village Bohemians, who usually saw a direct link between sexual and political freedoms, between repression and oppression). Dell in particular (like Cather a young midwestern transplant to New York) underwent analysis in 1917 with the Village doctor Samuel Tannenbaum, crediting the treatment not only with improving his sex life but also with unleashing his artistic talents.[1] He went on to a reasonably successful career as a writer of sentimental fiction and a popular writer and speaker on topics of mental hygiene (Hale 2: 65–66).

Luhan interests me particularly, in spite of the difficulties involved in identifying her as one of Cather's links to the Freudianism of the 1910s. More than twenty warm letters to her from Cather survive (all from the mid-1920s and later), and the two women seem unlikely friends. Larger than life and a serial marrier, Luhan was one of American Freudianism's most energetic, extravagant purveyors, the visible importer of a trendy new European sexology. In 1916, seeking relief in her spectacularly tangled emotional life, she entered therapy with the eclectic, prescriptive analyst Smith Jelliffe; later she consulted A. A. Brill himself, the Austrian Jewish immigrant who translated Freud into English and headed the American psychoanalytic movement. At Brill's urging, she became in 1917 a syndicated advice columnist for Hearst, dispensing (among other things) brief Freudian, Nietzschean, or vaguely Marxian "cures" to the masses, generally advertising salvific personal freedom and health achieved through the willed lifting of societal repressions, or the liberation of stifled libidinal energies (see Rudnick 129–42; Luhan *Movers* 507–10).

Regardless of whether Cather talked with Dell or Van Vechten of psychoanalysis, or whether her specific friendship with Luhan dates from the 1910s, it seems inevitable that the Freudianism she observed firsthand was the Greenwich Village version that these three (and probably Elsie Sergeant as well) knew and admired: Americanized (and thus highly pragmatic), self-consciously "modern," sexy, rebellious, and highbrow, intertwined in a therapy-hungry public's imagination with other self-help techniques and "mental cures" that drew on sources from occultism to Bergsonian philosophy (with which, as we know, Cather *was* familiar). It was explicitly politically progressive, and it typically addressed, not the specific crippling ailments of hysteria and obsessive behavior that its European counterpart had taken as object, but more general complaints of unhappiness or personal meaninglessness—the famous angst of privileged modernism.

Psychoanalysis offered solace and an anchor in a lonely, bewildering time; it proposed, as Luhan put it, a "new world where I found myself: a world where things fitted into a set of definitions and terms that I had never even dreamt of. It simplified all problems to name them. There was the Electra complex, and the Oedipus complex and there was the Libido with its manifold activities, seeking every chance for outlet, and then all that thing about Power and Money!" (*Movers* 440). Central to American responses to psychoanalysis was what its historian Nathan Hale calls "the first stage of America's moral revolution, the repeal of reticence that occurred roughly from 1911 to 1917" (1: 475). Voluntary, profuse confession—the therapeutic transformation of symptomatic unhappiness into liberating language—was a fundamental tenet of this Freudianism. "Psychoanalysis was apparently a kind of tattletaling," said a delighted Luhan of her discovery of Jelliffe, "an absorbing game to play with one's self" (*Movers* 439). "I have a very bad Oedipus complex," she announced to Brill, arriving at their first meeting (*Movers* 505). In every way, Luhan was an eager analysand, in and out of therapy, determined to confess for herself and everyone else: "The less secrets the better, of my own or anybody else's," she proclaimed at the beginning of her four-volume, sixteen-hundred-page autobiography (entitled *Intimate Memories*): "Need anyone *ever feel ashamed*? I doubt it" (*Background* 10).

Cather herself, as is well known, held some different views. By 1922 she had staked out her own ground (in "The Novel Démeublé")[2] as a champion of classical restraint, control, and suggestion in art, and she extended these values to human relations as well. A few years later, in *The Professor's House* (1926), she would write of Tom Outland's diary with transparent reference to her own prose style as it reached its maturity: "This plain account was almost beautiful, because of the stupidities it avoided and the things it did not say. If words had cost money, Tom couldn't have used them more sparingly. . . . Yet through this austerity one felt the kindling imagination, the ardour and excitement of the boy, like the vibration in a voice when the speaker strives to conceal his emotion by using only conventional phrases" (262–63). And in the same novel Godfrey St.

Peter acknowledges with respectful pleasure the essential opacity and haunting privacy of human psychology, even after a lifetime of conversational "knowledge," as at the opera he considers how little he knows his wife, Lillian: "The heart of another," he finds, "is a dark forest, always, no matter how close it has been to one's own" (95). It is not difficult to see why this reticent minimalist in art and emotion, this admirer of spare Greek theater and critic of "tasteless amplitude" (*Not Under Forty* 51), had no sympathy at all in the early 1920s (in the conversation about Freud that Sergeant recounts) for Freudianism's narcissistic excesses, in its theory or in its practice. The messy and voluble personal psychology that Cather brushed against in Greenwich Village was just what her own aesthetic was leaving behind. But a more interesting problem than Cather's anti-Freudianism, I think, is how she and the amplitudinous Luhan maintained their long and evidently good friendship. Considering this question will lead back to Freud himself, rather than the American social movement that carried his name.

ARTIFICERS OF MEMORY

The two thousand miles that separate Manhattan from Taos probably helped Cather and Luhan to get along. But there was something else the women had in common, a fundamental romanticism neither trendy nor classical, but descending from Rousseau and, more immediately, from Wordsworth and Blake: they believed explicitly in childhood, both as a source of aesthetic or creative energy and as a kind of irretrievable mythic homeland, sometimes glimpsed as empowering fragments behind the dull screen of quotidian adulthood. Thus Cather would frequently publicly couch her artistic method as a process of recollection ("Life began when I stopped admiring and started remembering," she told Sergeant [117]), or she would after forty years describe her encounter at the age of nine with the Nebraska prairie as the "passion that I have never been able to shake. It has been the happiness and the curse of my life" (Woodress 36). When Luhan asked Cather's opinion of draft manuscripts of

Intimate Memories, Cather responded that the early parts were the best, because they drew on early memories—the memories of a child with "the artist's eye that adults lose" (Stout, *Calendar* 281). (Her judgment was apt: despite an occasional awkwardly self-conscious overlay of psychoanalytic theory, as in the strange chapter entitled simply "The Breast," Luhan's fragments of childhood and adolescence are at their best as opaquely haunting as Cather's own.) Luhan in turn began *Intimate Memories* with an epigraph that paraphrased Plotinus evoking memory's creative force—"Memory is not a certain repository of impressions but a power of the soul exciting itself in such a way as to possess that which it had not"—and followed it at once with a complaint that sounds Cather-esque (or St. Peter-esque) in its nostalgia: that in the modern world "there are fewer taboos, fewer fears, and less unhappiness. But there is a corresponding lack of savor and of charm. It almost seems as though to lose the glamour and the intensity that form a large part of the dark ages is too great a price to pay for understanding better how to live. . . . [M]y childhood had a wild, sweet, enthralling zestfulness that seems to be missing from the lives of my grandchildren . . . their present seems to me dim and leveled down to a consciousness that has no high moments such as I knew" (*Background*, n.p.). In short, the friends shared—although in very different ways—a conviction of the glamour and pain of the remembered personal past. In adult life Cather quietly produced great art; Luhan flamboyantly produced herself, in a series of generous but transient passions. Each did so, I think, in a complicated and aware response to passionate childhood's generative pressure, surging up against the structures of diminished adult experience.

I arrive now at Freud himself: not the sexologist or even the therapist, but Freud the artificer of memory, for whom thought drove always relentlessly backward, trying to remember its way out of adulthood's or modernity's crippling repetitions of confusion and guilt. I will not here elaborate much of Freud's theory other than to note that at its center (a constantly receding, ultimately unachievable center) stands the obscured figure of the desiring child, learning life's lessons of loss; and that misunderstood memories of that child and those lessons haunt our adult lives. Thus "therapy," the "Freudian method," was at first a reasonably straightforward process of psychological archaeology, of recollecting in order to reconstruct life as sensible narrative. (For various reasons, but primarily because of the mythic quality of formative origins themselves, this straightforward model did not exactly work, leading Freud increasingly to confront the specter of "interminable analysis"—but its inconclusive endlessness seems to me the mark of his thought's genuine modernity.) In a simple sense, then, it was not modernist Freudianism but Freud himself that offered the common ground on which Cather and Luhan could meet: or rather it was the specifically *anti*modern zeitgeist of nostalgia that he best personified and articulated, and which urged him and other modern writers from Proust to Cather to Nabokov to valorize memory. I doubt that Cather ever read Freud (although she must have read a good deal *about* him and his ideas), and it seems to me possible that Luhan may not have either: but all three, I think, labored at the same project.

Let me continue in more immediate anecdotal terms. I came to Cather's work in the early 1980s, at the end of a period of quite intense scholarly immersion in psychoanalytic thought and its relation to literary interpretation. My first Cather novel was *The Professor's House*, and I felt at once that I had come upon a writer who had both access to the great unconscious world that Freud had disclosed—the kingdom of the irrational, the infantile, the prelinguistic—*and* the power to summon its presence on the page. As I read the rest of her works I encountered at every turn the strange forms and phrasings that Freud found in dreams (his "royal road to the unconscious") or in the rituals of his patients. There were inexplicable alterations of narrative's logical structures, like Tom Outland's ghostly voice intruding into the narrative of *The Professor's House* itself, or the repetitions of *A Lost Lady* (whose love story repeats itself for Niel as more-than-Marxian history: first as tragedy, then perhaps as farce—and finally unendingly as desire). There were also unsettling eruptions of suggestive but mute or opaque images and legends into the reasonable historical world: a plow against the sun, suicidal tramps, a doomed bridal party, shards of pottery, a turquoise set in dull silver, a giant baby-eating snake.

And translating these images (through the laborious technique of creating context that Freud called "free association," and which literary critics just call "close reading") led back frequently enough into deep pasts—the dark forests of the Old Country, or the canyon of the Ancient People, or the Cliff City, or others—where shadowy ancestral or parental figures moved, larger than life. There one could glimpse the psychoanalytic world of infantile fantasies, the child's desires and fears, in (for example) the recurrent figure of the orphan, or the several versions of what Freud called "the family romance," a fantasy in which real parents are replaced by noble ones—"the noblest and strongest of men and . . . the dearest and loveliest of women" ("Family Romances" 241)—as in *A Lost Lady*.

Often these figures were fearsome. As many readers have noted, Cather's landscape of childhood is by no means free of shadows: the story *before* the official "beginning of the story," in *A Lost Lady* as elsewhere, is more often than not one of failure, betrayal, and loss. And this is wholly consonant with Freud's essentially tragic vision of childhood as a state of unrequitable filial desire "doomed to extinction because its wishes are incompatible with reality," which "comes to an end in the most distressing circumstances and to the accompaniment of the most painful feelings" ("Pleasure Principle" 20). Perhaps in this state little Jim Burden, orphaned and lapsing out among his pumpkins, has some kinship with the less-well-known prairie newcomer Edward of "The Best Years," the "pale boy" who wets his pants with anxiety and homesickness, trying to "speak up for his State" before his girl-teacher Lesley Ferguesson (*Old Beauty and Others* 83).[3]

But most important, not only did Cather's work seem to me to *exemplify* the various processes and contents of psychic representation postulated by Freudian psychoanalysis, it also appeared to be *aware* of this in itself. In other words, Cather wrote as if she knew the Freudian precepts without having read them. She clearly understood the expression of "meaning" as a difficult, allusive process, or as an oblique passageway between disparate strata of experience: thus her fiction and nonfiction return *in their descriptions of signification itself* to self-conscious tropes of disjunction, displacement, and distortion in which a narrative can be, for example, like a window opening from an overcrowded room onto a gray sea, or a plow can become a "picture writing on the sun," or an unimaginably old voice can tell an incomprehensible tale through a briefly unstoppered fissure in the rock.

Cather simply assumed the presence and agency of the human unconscious in daily life, no matter how much the Freudian terminology repelled her. Her exchange with Sergeant over the desirability of entering analysis derailed and ended in an odd argument about dramatic technique, in which

> Willa hotly stated that every play that amounted to anything contained secret reactions, inner feelings that diverged from what was actually being said and done by a protagonist on the stage. That could be expressed by action, by facial expression, by tone—it did not need to be inserted in spoken dialogue. . . .
>
> Here she disappeared under water, and I knew she was no subject for psychoanalysis. (Sergeant 249)

What was wrong was not the psychological theory itself, the positing of a divided psyche expressing itself indirectly through oblique signs; any good artist understood that. What was wrong was the bad artistry that robbed this process of its compelling mystery by making it too overt, too mechanical: a clinical specimen.

In her most famous pronouncements on art, Cather acknowledged in terms explicitly psychoanalytic the centrality of repetition and the insistence of the unconscious to her own creativity. She reported that Jewett had told her that "the thing that teases the mind over and over for years, and at last gets itself put down rightly on paper—whether little or great, it belongs to Literature" (*Not Under Forty* 76); but that thing clearly also belonged to Freud's psychoanalysis, where, he said, "a thing which has not been understood inevitably reappears; like an unlaid ghost, it cannot rest until the mystery has been solved and the spell broken" ("Analysis of a Phobia" 122). That "thing" is the speechless desire at the foundation of the unconscious, the child's desire, unrepresentable but unforgotten: the "thing not named" (*Not Under Forty* 50) (and unnamable, because it is prior to the alienating deflections of speech), or perhaps more simply "the precious, the incommunicable past" (*My Ántonia* 419).

CATHER, FREUD, AND THE BURDEN OF CULTURE

My purpose in this essay has been to indicate some fundamental similarities of thought—indeed, of specifically psychological and aesthetic thought—that connect Willa Cather and Sigmund Freud, often by way of the volatile figure of Mabel Dodge Luhan. But what I have said, while plausible enough, may seem to evade one large point of Cather's anti-Freudianism, her critique of the Freudians' reduction of literature to sexuality gone awry, to "an epidemic of 'suppressed desire' plays and novels" (*Not Under Forty* 93).[4] After all, Freud *did* indeed suggest that frustrated sexuality lay somewhere essential among the tangled roots of a great range of human behaviors, including artistic creativity. He *did* build a personality theory around improbable-sounding ideas of incestuous infantile desire and anxieties over genital mutilation, and the result has been a hundred years of easily caricatured (and thus easily dismissed) critical and psychological reductionism, like Luhan's. Moreover, Freud's own theory (not just the American Freudianism represented by Luhan) was clearly limited: in its understanding of gender, for example, where it treated as normative the experience of the little boy, or in its usual blindness to its own historical circumstances: middle class, European, urban.

But to point out the shortcomings of Freudian theory, or to object to the crudities of reductive interpretation to which it can lead, and often has led—"stupidities," Cather would have called them—is not to deny its evocative power. Nor do I want to sanitize or deny its sexual content. In the culture wars that have been fought over psychoanalysis for more than a century, that content remains the source of much quick and anxious critical condemnation of Freud's thought, as if it were improper, wrongheaded even, to consider critically that as a species we may be heavily motivated by sexual desire (the drive toward satisfaction in love, to put it in terms that extend more readily into the pregenital)—or that that desire's form may be laid down for us, consequentially but not unalterably, in childhood, among the crossed loves of our parents, caretakers, and siblings. Cather, who was both intelligent and honest, saw nothing improper in either of these propositions: at all points in her career her art pulses explicitly with sexual longing, chronicles its disguises and strange transformations (sometimes transcendent, sometimes destructively perverse), memorializes its defeats.

I am not even willing to discard as useful tools the much-lampooned sexual symbols of Freudian interpretation. I want rather to recognize them as important unofficial coinage in the discursive currency of Freud's historical culture, which was also Cather's, and by and large our own: a culture of Homer and Virgil, Dante and Milton, of castrated or castrating father-gods and annihilating women, where political power literally passed precariously through the male reproductive organ. (We now call this culture patriarchy.) For example—a well-known example—I do not think it at all far-fetched to invoke the Freudian paradigm of castration (as Sharon O'Brien and others have done) in thinking about Cather's famous concern with bodily mutilation, with severed and maimed hands. Woodress tracks this concern through images from several early stories and in *One of Ours*, *Shadows on the Rock*, *Sapphira and the Slave Girl*, and the final Avignon fragment, and links it to a traumatic event described by Lewis, in which a neighboring "half-witted boy" threatened to cut off the five-year-old Willa Cather's hand (Woodress 27). We cannot assess the historical reality of this event, but its psychological importance seems undeniable.

For Freud, the severing of a hand, like oedipal blinding or the knocking out of teeth, inevitably stood in for castration in the fantasies and dreams of his patients, typically reflecting unconscious but not forgotten threats from parents or caretakers, threats intended to subdue inappropriate sexual behaviors like masturbation or attempted seduction. Does the theme of the severed hand then point us to a "primal scene" (perhaps masked by the fiction of the neighboring boy) in which a very small but irrepressible Willa Cather was threatened with castration by Charles or Jenny Cather? A repressed, unspeakable scene that haunted her for the rest of her career? Frankly, this seems unlikely, and it is probably such theatrically personalized Freudian reading—not so much wrong as wholly unconvincing (and unnecessary)—that makes much Freudianism seem simply strange to its readers.

For castration is not local or personal, but rather cultural, and in a sense foundational to the power relations of patriarchy. Its image, or the softer mutilations that recall it, is the historical emblem of the struggle of fathers and sons, authority and rebellion, from Kronos and Zeus to Oedipus to Stephen Dedalus's fear of blinding. Cather knew this discourse well, and not only in the classics—witness, for example, her love of Howard Pyle's medieval children's fantasy *Otto of the Silver Hand*, whose child protagonist's hand is severed by a brutal surrogate father in order that he be reconciled with his real father, and which she praised as embodying "the precious message of romance" (Woodress 51). I am suggesting, then, that for a probably incalculable number of reasons—reasons that blur the boundaries of personal and cultural, inner and outer—*her own hand*, the writer's hand, became for Willa Cather early the valorized organ of mastery and potency, a symbol of the cultural power—a masculine power—that she desired and acquired. As O'Brien puts it, "the hand which holds the pen is the literal agent of creation" (384). And that organ makes its anxious appearances in all phases of her work: beleaguered, mutilated, under threat, associated with failures of masculine intention, authority, or desire. With a particularly moving and terrible irony, age attacked Cather's hand above all else, forcing her into an orthopedic brace for much of the 1940s as her art's flow diminished.

This analysis may stop here, for my purposes. Like all psychoanalytic examination, it needs to be conducted with much more specificity in the analyses of individual appearances of severed hands or mutilations. I want it simply to begin the illustration of my point: that the ubiquity of culture itself, circulating within and without our individual selves, allows us to use the Freudian symbols intelligently and meaningfully without necessarily falling into the strangeness or apparent absurdity of, in this case, assigning to the five-year-old Willa Cather (of whom we really know almost nothing) a "castration complex" with a single biographical point of traumatic origin in a parental threat.

I will close by reiterating the relation I have proposed for Cather and Freud: not one of influence, clearly, but not one of opposition either, as Cather's few comments on psychoanalysis would suggest. Rather, Willa Cather and Sigmund Freud seem to me oddly similar figures standing not at all comfortably at the gates to modernism: each mistrustful of the present and future, and looking romantically backward to a nobler, stronger past, in childhood or in human history—but each also too honest to accept that past as an unproblematic Golden Age. Although Cather was criticized early for the moral libertinism of "The Bohemian Girl," and Freud to some extent helped unleash the sexual bohemianism of Mabel Dodge Luhan and others, both were essentially, profoundly conservative, valuing the great labor of civilization in taming the unruliness of humankind. Yet each also saw individuals and civilization as finally threatened by the obscuring of their own vital origins. In response, and in different ways, each claimed as his or her own the terrain of half-remembered possibility that Freud called the "unconscious," and that landscape—the place of the bottomless mystery of desire—sustained them, minimally but successfully, deep into the barren modern time that each understood explicitly as a catastrophe, a breaking in two of worlds both personal and global.

NOTES

1. Although this is the subject of another inquiry, it is useful to read the stories of *Youth and the Bright Medusa* (and particularly "Coming, Aphrodite!") against Dell's *Love in Greenwich Village* (1926). To do so is to see Cather in an unfamiliar context: as one well familiar with the romantic radical tradition of young midwesterners in the Village in the 1910s.

2. In the *New Republic*, which, interestingly, was in the 1910s a center for the promulgation of "serious" psychoanalytic theory, mainly conducted by Luhan's good friend the young Walter Lippmann (Hale 2: 60–61).

3. Readers of Freud will recognize here almost exactly the most famous of Freud's various "primal scenes" from the Wolf-Man case history—and from Freud's own boyhood, according to Ernest Jones (16–17): a tragicomic moment that mixes pride, appeal, rejection, and shame. Although I am deliberately trying to resist biographical literalism, it is interesting to realize that little Edward corrects a small autobiographical evasion in *My Ántonia* and denial in her own 1915 biographical sketch for Houghton Mifflin: Cather *did* attend school in her first autumn in Red Cloud, and the Catherton school must have been a school much like Lesley Ferguesson's.

4. As usual, Luhan is useful in providing a simple caricature of the Freudian position on literary creativity, and applying it to herself: "That I have so many pages to write signifies, solely, that I was unlucky in love" (*Movers* 263).

WORKS CITED

Cather, Willa. *My Ántonia*. Boston: Houghton Mifflin, 1918.

———. *Not Under Forty*. 1936. Lincoln: U of Nebraska P, 1988.

———. *The Old Beauty and Others*. New York: Knopf, 1948.

———. *The Professor's House*. New York: Knopf, 1926.

Freud, Sigmund. "Analysis of a Phobia in a Five-Year Old Boy." 1909. *The Complete Psychological Works of Sigmund Freud*. Vol. 10. London: The Hogarth P, 1955. 1–147.

———. "Beyond the Pleasure Principle." 1920. *The Complete Psychological Works of Sigmund Freud*. Vol. 18. London: The Hogarth P, 1955. 1–64.

———. "Family Romances." 1909. *The Complete Psychological Works of Sigmund Freud*. Vol. 9. London: The Hogarth P, 1955. 235–41.

Hale, Nathan G., Jr. *Freud in America*. Vol. 1. *Freud and the Americans: The Beginnings of Psychoanalysis in the United States 1876–1917*. New York: Oxford UP, 1971.

———. *Freud in America*. Vol. 2. *The Rise and Crisis of Psychoanalysis in the United States: Freud and the Americans, 1917–1985*. New York: Oxford UP, 1971.

Jones, Ernest. *The Life and Work of Sigmund Freud*. Vol. 1. New York: Basic Books, 1953.

Luhan, Mabel Dodge. *Intimate Memories: Background*. New York: Harcourt Brace, 1933.

———. *Movers and Shakers: Volume 3 of Intimate Memories*. New York: Harcourt Brace, 1936.

O'Brien, Sharon. *Willa Cather: The Emerging Voice*. New York: Oxford UP, 1987.
Rudnick, Lois Palken. *Mabel Dodge Luhan: New Woman, New Worlds*. Albuquerque: U of New Mexico P, 1984.
Sergeant, Elizabeth Shepley. *Willa Cather: A Memoir*. 1953. Athens: Ohio UP, 1992.
Stout, Janis, ed. *A Calendar of the Letters of Willa Cather*. Lincoln: U of Nebraska P, 2002.
———. *Willa Cather: The Writer and Her World*. Charlottesville: UP of Virginia, 2000.
Woodress, James. *Willa Cather: A Literary Life*. Lincoln: U of Nebraska P, 1987.

Cather's Medical Icon

Euclide Auclair, Healing Art, and the Cultivated Physician

JOSHUA DOLEZAL

Written after the deaths of her parents, amid unstable health, and during her retreats to Grand Manan, *Shadows on the Rock* was a refuge for Willa Cather, perhaps even a synthesis of values she believed to be disappearing from the culture of the 1930s. As consoling as the subject of the novel may have been to her, Cather undertook a grueling combination of travel, research, and writing to strengthen its details, visiting Quebec five times to confirm the setting, drawing heavily on old letters, consulting a number of Francis Parkman's Canadian histories, and studying seventeenth-century artifacts (including old herbals) in both French and American museums (Woodress 422, 431–32).[1] As Edith Lewis notes, "Willa Cather was always very painstaking about her facts—she intensely disliked being careless or inaccurate, and went to the trouble to verify them" (161).[2] In the following discussion I will examine the "facts" of *Shadows on the Rock* that are specific to medicine, arguing that these meticulous historical details reveal one of Cather's most consistent cultural ideals, namely, the commingling of medicine and art evident in the character of Euclide Auclair.[3]

Cather's negotiation of the relationship between medicine and art began in her childhood experiences as a physician's assistant in Red Cloud; was clarified during her tenure at the University of Nebraska, when her interest in botany and medical science took shape; and continued in her lifelong correspondence with

Dr. Julius Tyndale, a Lincoln physician and drama critic. With Tyndale's dual interests in medicine and art in mind, I will explore similar characteristics in Euclide Auclair by tracing Cather's construction of his character as a "philosopher apothecary" with the ability to distinguish himself from typical seventeenth-century apothecaries in his scientific acumen and from specialized physicians in his incorporation of an aesthetic sensibility into the practice of medicine. As a cultivated physician grounded both in science and in art, Auclair is a cultural icon as germane to Cather's early-twentieth-century milieu as to seventeenth-century Quebec.

WILLIAM CATHER, M.D.

Most accounts of Cather's childhood interest in medicine assume that she was drawn to hard science more than to art during this time, but this scientific idealism was balanced by a dual interest in theater. Even though Cather was an ostentatious advocate of science, her flair for the dramatic transformed the office of physician into a theatrical role. Her first experience with medicine, according to biographer Mildred Bennett, came while her family still lived in Virginia, as her "great-grandmother Smith had insisted that she be bled once a month" (117). The surgical instruments (likely lances or scalpels) used for this monthly phlebotomy eventually came into Cather's possession after the family moved to Red Cloud, during which time she assisted local physicians in their rounds and occasionally signed her name "Wm. Cather, M.D." (Woodress 55). In an autobiographical sketch dated 10 October 1888, at age fifteen, Cather lists "slicing toads" as a pastime for summer vacation and alleges that "amputating limbs" is "perfect happiness" (Bennett 112–13). Just a few years earlier, Cather had created a make-believe town with her friends called Sandy Point in which she presided as mayor; she had also performed in local plays, including *Hiawatha* and *Beauty and the Beast* (Woodress 57). Armed with her grandfather's lances and scalpels, the young Willa Cather eagerly awaited a career in surgery, which she envisioned as a dramatic and heroic enterprise.

While the tenor of this early personal sketch is playful, the practice of surgery Cather knew from her experience with Dr. Damerell and Dr. McKeeby in Red Cloud derived from the grim operating rooms of the Civil War, in which most operations were either amputations or ball extractions (Cunningham 15). These procedures demanded scientific precision, the kind practiced in the French clinics and brought to the United States by such well-known physicians as S. Weir Mitchell and Oliver Wendell Holmes (Lovering 20; Browner 141). By 1890, the year of Cather's high school graduation, "slicing toads" represented much more than a summer diversion; consequently, her commencement speech posits vivisection as a medium for rigorous scientific investigation, the polar opposite of superstition ("Superstition" 141). At this point in her life, while her rhetoric seems to privilege science over art, Cather associated superstition with ignorance and scientific investigation with heroic human inquiry, the latter constituting a dramatic plot. Medical science was an aesthetic force to the young Willa Cather, commanding her attention precisely for its heroism and thus for its resonance as a touchstone for art.

The journey from Cather's adamant endorsement of experimental medicine in 1890 to Euclide Auclair's confession to his daughter, Cécile, over forty years later that "medicine is a dark science" can be clarified by acknowledging that Cather's dual interests in medicine and art tempered one another at each stage of her development (*Shadows* 171). Cather's attraction to medicine throughout these years lies less in scientific formulae and more in the artistic idea of investigation culminating in discovery. Her dismissal of Émile Zola as "perverse" in his attempt to apply the scientific method to the "experimental novel" sharpens this distinction, as does her thorough disgust for Lucius Sherman's "scientific" literary criticism at the University of Nebraska, which involved "analysis of sentence length, comparative predication, and ratios of force, with charts, diagrams, formulae, and equations" (Woodress 128, 80). As Edith Lewis notes, Cather held that the "Sherman method . . . reduced all that was great in literature, the noblest flights of the human spirit, to dry-as-dust, arbitrary formulae" (35). More than thirty years after her undergraduate tenure, while still defending scientific investigation against superstition in the character of Euclide Auclair, Cather allows science to balance, rather than dominate, her aesthetic sensibility.

To understand Cather's balanced cultural ideal, one might begin with her long friendship with Dr. Julius Tyndale, whom she met during her university years in Lincoln. Tyndale moved to Lincoln in 1893, primarily to practice medicine, but his influence on Cather also extended to drama criticism, which was one of his hobbies (Woodress 84). Notorious for his vicious articles, which earned him the reputation of a "severe iconoclast," the Lincoln physician served as a model for Cather's own "meatax" reviews in the *Journal* once she began to write professionally (84). Tyndale was a "man of great personal and intellectual force," E. K. Brown notes in his critical biography of Cather, "as keenly interested in music and letters as in medicine and science generally" (63). Tyndale and Cather were in frequent correspondence during her retreats to Grand Manan, and the Lincoln physician was also a prototype for Dr. Engelhardt of "Double Birthday," a short story Cather likely finished in either 1928 or 1929 (Woodress 417). For Cather, Tyndale represented "an atmosphere where the arts and manners of a past time lingered with none of the desiccation of the classroom but with the fragrant natural life that can be maintained only by discriminating affection" (Brown 138). As a man of medicine and a blistering drama critic, he was a "dramatis persona" in her life, embodying the commingling of medicine and art throughout their relationship from her undergraduate tenure in Lincoln during the early 1890s to his death in 1929, the year before *Shadows on the Rock* was completed (Woodress 82). These portraits of Tyndale as a physician who actively commingled medicine and art throughout his life closely resemble Cather's representation of Euclide Auclair.

Exhibiting a complexity of character reminiscent of Tyndale's dual medical and artistic interests, Auclair is both a scientific physician and an artist. His commitment to medical science is revealed in his equipment, including "distilling apparatus, mortars, balances, retorts, and carboys," all common pharmaceutical instruments of his time; additionally, his scientific work makes him an "accomplished cook," as "continual practice in making medicines kept his hand expert in handling glass and earthenware and in regulating heat" (*Shadows* 126). Here, Auclair's technical medical skill directly informs the domestic art of cooking; indeed, it is difficult to pinpoint where one ends and the other begins. Within the opening pages of the novel, the scientific elements of the apothecary shop blur into the aesthetics of a home space: "On entering his door the apothecary found the front shop empty, lit by a single candle. In the living-room behind, which was partly shut off from the shop by a partition made of shelves and cabinets, a fire burned in the fireplace, and the round dining-table was already set with a white cloth, silver candlesticks, glasses, and two clear decanters, one of red wine and one of white" (7). A slight division between shop and home appears in the cabinet partition, but the merging of Auclair's medicine making and cooking skill is mirrored in this simultaneous glimpse of medical cabinets and a dining table. From a reader's introduction to Auclair as the "philosopher apothecary of Quebec" to this snapshot of a shop that fades into a salon, Cather creates a space in which scientific precision does not diminish aesthetic resonance and in which artistry does not compromise science (3). Where a medical character with Zola's or Sherman's aesthetic sensibility might regard the act of eating as a mere physiological necessity, Cather turns Auclair's dinner into a work of art, with firelight washing over an elegantly dressed table in full view of his medicine shop.

Cather's view of the scalpel seems to have shifted in the four decades between her mention of "slicing toads" as a summer pastime and her completion of *Shadows on the Rock*, as Auclair's vehement opposition to phlebotomy distinguishes him from the barber-surgeon in Quebec, who complains that "the meddlesome apothecary took the bread out of his mouth" (*Shadows* 210). Of the two, Auclair is undoubtedly the more sophisticated, not only in his aversion to bloodletting but also in his refusal to slander his dubious colleague. Only in the performance of autopsy, after Count Frontenac's death, when medical practice is reduced to dissection, does Auclair work alongside the barber-surgeon, drawing from a "black bag full of deadly poisons" (211). While her respect for the medical profession had not diminished by the end of her life, Cather may have wished Auclair's character to transcend the connotations of reductive science (and cultural bleakness) that she associated with surgery.

AUCLAIR'S PLACE IN MEDICAL HISTORY

As an apothecary, Auclair occupies a humble position even by seventeenth-century standards, yet Cather reinforces his medical competency by granting him the ability to distinguish science from pseudoscience. Auclair's remedies rest upon empirical bases,[4] including his opposition to bloodletting, which he ably defends to Bishop Saint-Vallier by distinguishing between gout and varicose veins and by referring to previously unsuccessful treatments of phlebotomy on Bishop Laval, the patient in question (*Shadows* 96). Auclair's precise medical knowledge is notable, because for centuries apothecaries have been regarded by licensed practitioners as incompetent. An "informal hierarchy" had materialized among medical practitioners by the fourteenth century, as historian Nancy Siraisi notes, in which "university graduates in medicine occupied the highest place, followed by other skilled medical practitioners, then skilled surgeons, and finally by barber-surgeons and various other practitioners, among them herbalists or apothecaries" (20). Roughly two hundred years later, the College of Physicians actively sought to prevent apothecaries from practicing medicine during the seventeenth century, precisely for their alleged incompetence in comparison to university graduates (18). In spite of his rigorous self-education, it would seem that Euclide Auclair occupies the least prestigious position possible in the profession of medicine.[5]

Cather's decision not to incorporate surgery into Auclair's practice of medicine may derive both from her resistance to specialization and from the fact that phlebotomy, as defended by Saint-Vallier, was considered fashionable during the seventeenth century, a possibility I will discuss later. Surgeons themselves were not as problematic to Cather as the cultural connotations of specialization inherent in the position. In fact, while Cather was writing *Shadows on the Rock*, the "only Grand Manan islander she made friends with was Doctor Macaulay, a cultivated graduate of McGill Medical School, surgeon, and physician of more than ordinary skill" (Woodress 416). Macaulay became "a staunch friend," as Edith Lewis puts it, and "helped [them] out in any emergency" (194); his various interests included producing and directing musical performances on Grand Manan (Ingersoll 34–35). Macaulay's dual interests in medicine and art would have resonated with Cather's vision of Auclair's character while also reinforcing Tyndale's influence on the novel as it was taking shape.

Through her correspondence with a medical professional like Dr. Tyndale and friendship with a cultivated surgeon like Dr. Macaulay during the time she wrote *Shadows on the Rock*, Cather drew upon competent medical sources who were also, by her standards, civilized. Auclair "devoted himself seriously to his profession" as a young man, Cather writes, embedding a concise lesson in medical history into her novel: "Euclide had gone deep into the history of medicine in such old Latin books as were stuffed away in the libraries of Paris. He looked back to the time of Ambroise Paré, and still further back to the thirteenth century, as golden ages in medicine,—and he considered Fagon, the King's physician, a bigoted and heartless quack" (24). Throughout his study, Auclair cultivates an open mind regarding both new ideas and "old ideas that had gone out of fashion because surgeons and doctors were too stupid to see their value" (23). By distinguishing between credible practitioners (Paré) and quacks (Fagon), Auclair demonstrates that he believes in standards of competency and holds himself to those standards while maintaining a refined aesthetic sensibility.

Tracing Cather's steps in creating Auclair's character will help clarify what might initially seem like mixed messages. First, her distinction between Auclair's role and the archaic practice of the barber-surgeon in Quebec seems to be complicated by Cather's direct reference to Ambroise Paré as a credible practitioner, since Paré began his career as a barber-surgeon. Barber-surgeons date back to the twelfth century, when medical training was rare and crude surgery (bleeding, lancing, and amputation) was often performed by uneducated barbers. As a result, barber-surgeons were referred to as "surgeons of the short robe to distinguish them from the educated surgeons of the long robe" (Haggard 159). The position of apothecary dates still further back to the rhizotomists ("root cutters") of ancient Greece and Rome, who collected roots and herbs to sell as medical remedies (81). Like barber-surgeons, apothecaries had little formal education and were thus regarded as healers of the "short robe." At first glance it would seem that Auclair's status as an apothecary would bear little resemblance to medical professionals like Tyndale or Macaulay.

Auclair, like Paré, seems to demand the respect given to healers of the long robe, even though his lack of a formal degree complicates this designation. Paré began as a "rustic" and then gained his education on the battlefield as a surgeon; similarly, Auclair inherits his father's and grandfather's shop in Paris and then delves into medical history on his own, making a "profession" of the apothecary business (Garrison 224; *Shadows* 23).[6] If "change is not always progress," as Auclair tells Saint-Vallaint, then Cather indicates that formal degrees do not always signify genuine healers (97). Paré's use of ligature (reducing blood flow by tourniquet) for surgery during the sixteenth century in place of the conventional practice of cauterization (pouring boiling oil into wounds) proved so influential that he is now regarded by some medical historians as the most influential surgeon of his day (Siraisi 176, 192). His work on amputation and gunshot wounds likely informed the medicine Cather learned during the post–Civil War years in Red Cloud, as ligature was common practice by that time. Paré is regarded by Fielding Garrison as a medical pioneer: "Like Vesalius and Paracelsus, he [Paré] did not hesitate to thrust aside ignorance or superstition of it stood in his way" (224). Replacing cauterization with ligature showed Paré's break from a Galenist tradition that began in the second century and persisted in relative constancy until the 1200s (Camp 42).

Auclair's familiarity with medical history is notably limited to a period beginning with the thirteenth century, precisely the time when Galen's influence began to diminish in Western medicine, suggesting Auclair's affiliation with a tradition of practitioners who advanced scientific discovery by challenging the medical establishment. Tyndale's dual interests in medicine and art similarly deviate from the norms of his time, as Cather's portrait of him as Dr. Engelhardt in "Double Birthday," the short story she wrote while finishing *Shadows on the Rock*, demonstrates: "Even in American cities, which seem so much alike, where people seem all to be living the same lives, striving for the same things, thinking the same thoughts, there are still individuals a little out of tune with the times—there are still survivals of a past more loosely woven, there are disconcerting beginnings of a future yet unforeseen" (41). Historically speaking, Auclair, too, is "a little out of tune" with his time, as was Ambroise Paré. But, as Paré's pioneering vision transformed his age, so Cather's representation of the ideal of a cultivated physician in Auclair's character offers a potentially progressive view of the medical and artistic milieus of her time.

If formal degrees do not always signify genuine healers, the question of medical competency is still a serious one in comparing Auclair to Julius Tyndale. Questions of medical competency would have been familiar to Cather during her childhood, as her relationships with Dr. McKeeby, Dr. Damerell, and Dr. Cook (owner of the Red Cloud Pharmacy) stood in stark contrast to the town homeopath, Dr. Tulleys, who once advised Mary Miner's mother to slice open a red onion and place it in the window, where it would allegedly "absorb all the diphtheria" (Bennett 116–17). Divisions between homeopathy and experimental medicine were stark and polemical, as revealed in Oliver Wendell Holmes's denunciation of homeopathy as a "humbug" of the nineteenth century in an 1842 address (39). Holmes links homeopaths with mesmerists and ancient conjurers, claiming that society always includes "a class of minds much more ready to believe that which is at first sight incredible, and because it is incredible, than what is generally thought reasonable" (33). These sentiments also appear in Cather's 1890 speech, especially in her chastisement of ancient civilizations for emphasizing the "mystical and metaphysical" while "leaving the more practical questions . . . unanswered" ("Superstition" 141). Some forty years later, following the deaths of her parents and amid her own struggles with illness, Cather was no doubt struggling to answer the very practical questions of health while *Shadows on the Rock* was taking shape. The cultural ideal of a cultivated physician, grounded in both science and in art, thus would have appealed to her in both physical and metaphysical ways.

As strong as the temptation might have been to use Auclair's character as a means of satisfying her own yearning for quick and easy cures, however, Cather separates the appeal of the "incredible" (as Holmes puts it) or the fantastical from medical practice. "The people have loved miracles for so many hundred years," she reflects, "not as proof or evidence, but because they are the actual flowering of desire" (*Shadows* 111). While Auclair's character distinguishes between religion and the practice of medicine, he is much less dismissive than Holmes (and perhaps than the Cather of 1890) of the "class of minds" ready to believe in miracles. "The relics of the saints," he tells his daughter, "may work cures at the touch, they may be a protection worn about the neck; those things are outside of my knowledge" (103). What lies *inside* his knowledge is an empirical observation that human bone can prove toxic when ingested. "I am the guardian of the stomach," Auclair maintains, drawing a stark line between the realm of faith and his practice of medicine, "and I would not permit a patient to swallow a morsel of any human remains, not those of Saint Peter himself" (103). Auclair's reticence on even the psychological implications of religion for health implies his alliance with scientific medicine, which, for Cather (in 1890 and in 1930), meant opposition to alternative treatments, including religious cures and homeopathy. The cultivated physician as Cather envisioned him needed firm scientific integrity balanced, but not compromised, by an aesthetic sensibility.

If Auclair's medical proficiency is bolstered by his empiricism, linking him to the experimental tradition Cather learned firsthand from physicians in Red Cloud, his ostensible connections to the tradition of herbalism might seem to compromise his practice of medicine. Herbalism, with its frequent mingling of spiritualism and medical practice, is often interchangeable with folk medicine and figures closely into the "holistic" treatment of patients advocated by Samuel Hahnemann, the founder of homeopathy (Garrison 437–38). However, Auclair demonstrates repeatedly that he is capable of distinguishing between authentic and specious alternatives to scientific medicine.

Auclair's discernment is evident in his rejection of viper broth as a remedy, which distances him from Sir Kenelm Digby, a seventeenth-century figure notorious for his misuse of snake venom. As medical historian Garrison wrote in 1929, when Cather was writing her apothecary novel, Digby may have "poisoned his wife with too-frequent doses of viper's wine, given in aid of preserving her good looks" (289). Viper venom was only one aspect of Digby's quackery, which included applying a secretive ointment to battle weapons rather than wounds, believing that the wound would heal sympathetically (287).

As if responding directly to Digby's fashionable practices, Auclair states that he "detest[s] all medicines made from lizards and serpents, . . . even viper broth" (*Shadows* 171). Cather's familiarity with this medical fad is bolstered by Auclair's following explanation of viper broth to his daughter: "My dear, at the time when we came out to Canada, it was very much the fashion at home."[7] Half the great ladies of France were drinking a broth made from freshly killed vipers every morning, instead of their milk or chocolate, and believed themselves much the better for it. Medicine is a dark science, as I have told you more than once" (171). Such informed skepticism of faddish remedies would have been highly atypical among seventeenth-century apothecaries, most of whom would have immediately identified with Digby, owing either to a shared resentment of censorship at the hands of the College of Physicians or to a common belief in miraculous cures.

As a cultivated physician reminiscent of Julius Tyndale, Auclair further demonstrates by his forfeit of underhanded profits in the apothecary trade that his sophistication includes both scientific and cultural integrity. Other apothecaries and pharmacists in seventeenth-century France made a much better living by working directly with doctors or by taking advantage of the high prices their competitors were charging (Garrison 291).[8] Had Cather included a professional relationship between Auclair and a doctor, she may have invoked swindles like those of the medical faculty at the University of Paris during the sixteenth century, including prescriptions of preposterously expensive remedies for members of the royal family (Siraisi 147). In contrast, Auclair discouraged his patients in Paris from seeing doctors, largely because of the popularity of what he called "indiscriminate blood-letting," a treatment that was as expensive as it was ineffective (*Shadows* 24). Instead, he issued "tisanes and herb-teas and poultices, which at least could do no harm," offering dietary advice and "prescrib[ing] goat's milk for the poorly nourished" (24). Auclair's intentional use of placebo (cures that "could do no harm") and his forfeit of pecuniary gain in favor of his opposition to phlebotomy affirm not only the strength of his convictions but also his medical competency.

As an herbalist, Auclair distinguishes himself from the Digbys and the Tulleys, and his admiration for Paré suggests an association with the iatrochemists, who were scientific pioneers within the tradition of herbalism. Inspired by Paracelsus, a sixteenth-century physician regarded by many medical historians as a pioneer in modern chemistry, the iatrochemists abandoned attempts to change lead into gold, focusing instead on the chemical production of medical remedies (Weeks 28; Shryock 12). Similarly, Auclair's "drugs" and "remedies" are "of his own compounding"; when compared with his extensive experience in "handling glass and earthenware and in regulating heat" while making medicine, Auclair's remedial compounds illustrate the kind of technical skill modeled by the iatrochemical school (*Shadows* 18, 126). His use of "alcohol and borax" to purify the "oleum terroe," which he uses to treat snow blindness, contrasts with the practices of spiritual herbalists like Nicolas Culpeper, who distrusted chemicals and preferred nonchemical means of purification such as drying herbs in the sun (170). Auclair's practice of medicine in the novel gains even more credibility when compared with a seventeenth-century iatrochemist like Jean Baptiste van Helmont, who was respected for his discovery of the physiological significance of ferments and gases, but who also "believed that each material process of the body [was] presided over by a special archaeus or spirit" (Garrison 261). Van Helmont's study of gases led him to believe that what he called a "sensory-motive soul" (a material combination of chemicals and spirit) was located "in the pit of the stomach, since a blow in that region destroys consciousness" (261).

While Auclair's self-proclaimed office as "the guardian of the stomach" differs greatly from van Helmont's study of gases, their mutual emphasis on the stomach's importance calls attention to Cather's phraseology, implying that even if Auclair did not believe in a "sensory-motive soul," as his spiritual ambivalence would suggest, Cather might have derived his specific defense of the stomach from the medical discourse of his time. Cather herself saw the stomach as central to the creative process. "My mind and stomach are one," she quipped in an interview with the *Cleveland Press* in 1925, two years before she began work on *Shadows on the Rock*; "I think and work with whatever it is that digests" (Sumner 88). If guarding the stomach in the seventeenth century meant protecting the seat of consciousness, then Auclair's statement carries much more weight than simple dietary advice would imply. Further, if a university-educated iatrochemist like van Helmont is regarded by medical historians as having practiced good science even while entertaining mystical ideas about ferments and spirits, one might take a second look at the ostensible rank of Auclair's character at the bottom of the "informal hierarchy" among seventeenth-century medical practitioners. As a cultivated physician, his defense of the stomach is a defense of consciousness and of the creative process—of the mind itself.

As a "guardian of the stomach," Auclair places a high value on diet, both as a means of maintaining health and as an art form. "Dinner," Cather observes, "was the important event of the day in the apothecary's household," a ritual that Auclair shares daily with his daughter (*Shadows* 13). Cather herself regarded wholesome food as one of the first priorities of life, employing a French cook whose talent she lauded frequently (Woodress 379, 416).[9] As culinary pleasure was among Cather's dearest cultural ideals, it is fitting that the evening meal provides an aesthetic anchor point in Auclair's life and that this close attention to diet largely influences his practice of medicine.

Household medical remedies and cooking recipes were often found in the same books during the seventeenth century, as "good food, fresh and naturally produced, was then, as now, accepted as necessary for good health, although dietetics was not highly developed" (Knight 237). Auclair's prescription of goat's milk for his patients and the mingling of medicinal remedies with cooking spices in his apothecary's shop, as well as his own delight in carefully prepared meals, partially resemble this folk tradition. His empiricism, however, deviates from the thread of superstition that ran through most folk remedies.[10] Additionally, Auclair nowhere demonstrates any belief in the "doctrine of signatures" common among alternative practitioners, which assumed that visual similarities between plants and symptoms of illness or between plants and organs indicated potential cures; thus, "lungwort, with spotted leaves suggesting pulmonary disease, could be used to cure chest complaints. Plants with yellow flowers, or yellow spices, might be good for jaundice" (Knight 240). The doctrine of signatures further illuminates the polarity between experimental medicine and homeopathy in Red Cloud during Cather's childhood, as Dr. Tulleys's association of a red onion with diphtheria would have been disparaged by McKeeby, Damerell, and Cook, whose treatments addressed specific symptoms with experimentally proven cures.

If Auclair's emphasis on good food can be seen to resemble the folk tradition while avoiding its fantastical elements, his aversion to animal-based remedies is illuminated by a similar distinction. During his discussion of viper broth with Cécile, Auclair admits that "in general he distrusted remedies made of the blood or organs of animals," though he concedes that some have proven efficacious (*Shadows* 171). One of these remedies that he has found to be effective through experience is "a medicinal oil from the fat livers of the codfish," though he avoids lumping himself in with those who harbor "an almost fanatical faith in its benefits" (172). Such a qualification of Auclair's principles shows Cather's awareness of the connotations of medical terms and practice, as Auclair's demonstrates at best a cautious trust in his remedies, contrasting the "fanatical faith" some had in cod-liver oil.

Allowing Auclair to profess a general aversion to animal-based remedies, while conceding an exception, bolsters his credibility and invites a reader to investigate his reasons for distrusting certain remedies. His distrust of viper broth derives from its faddish popularity, but the brutality of other animal remedies might have also given him pause. One such seventeenth-century remedy, allegedly effective for consumption, involved plucking a chicken alive, then disemboweling it through an incision made down the back, after which the bird was "pounded in a mortar" and mixed with wine and milk (Knight 245). Presumably, the chicken mercifully died soon after the mortar pounding began, but the drama leading up to that point was meant to intensify a patient's faith in the power of the cure. Auclair's aversion to the brutality of such cures, as well as to their reliance on superstition, reasonably explains this distrust: as an icon of cultural sophistication and medical integrity, Auclair extends the physician's mandate to do no harm from his human patients to animal life as well.

CULTURAL IDEALS IN A TENUOUS REFUGE

That Cather admired medical science in 1890 as an aspiring surgeon is evident in her claim that "scientific investigation is the hope of [her] age, as it must precede all progress" ("Superstition" 142). By 1930 she qualifies her stance somewhat by giving Auclair the line "Change is not always progress" while discussing his "progressivism" as a medical practitioner with Bishop Saint-Vallier (*Shadows* 97). Cather's general disillusionment with the material culture of the twentieth century remained distinct from her still-solid faith in the kind of scientific investigation modeled by Auclair.[11] Had she entirely lost faith in medical science, she might have changed Auclair's line to something more like "Change is a given, but progress is a myth." Her chosen phraseology, however, suggests that Auclair does quietly believe in the ability of science to build upon its empirical store of knowledge, an implication further reinforced by his aspiration to publish his study of the medicinal properties of Canadian plants.

Furthermore, one might say that the value of medical science, to Cather's mind, depends largely on the cultural sophistication of its practitioner, so evident in Auclair's character and so absent (in Cather's mind) from Lucius Sherman and Émile Zola. Auclair's mild mannerisms, as Lewis notes, may derive from Cather's memory of her father while writing *Shadows on the Rock*, as "her mind often went back to his gentle protectiveness and kindness" (156). As Brienzo and Murphy suggest, these memories, the setting of Quebec, and the composition of the novel itself were all sources of comfort to Cather. By delving into the past, Murphy maintains, Cather went in search of "medieval order and spirituality" (76).

As the previous discussion of Sir Kenhelm Digby and the fad of viper broth demonstrates, however, Auclair's seventeenth-century milieu in Europe was anything but orderly; even in Quebec he must face professional stigmas associated with his title of apothecary, haggling with a barber-surgeon who lacks Auclair's sophistication yet seems to have held equal status in the "informal hierarchy" among medical practitioners of the time. Even in Quebec, Auclair is faced with 'Toinette, Blinker, and Bichet, reminders of the Parisian underworld. 'Toinette's dismissal of Auclair's remedies as "poisons" resonates with irony as she lumps him in with the faddish dealers of viper broth and with apothecaries who peddled poisonous compounds to disgruntled courtiers bent on murder (*Shadows* 71; Garrison 173). Moving to Quebec offers little relief from the doubts about his education and medical authority that Auclair would have faced his whole life as the son of apothecaries. In this light, whatever peace he finds (and, by implication, whatever comfort Cather derives from his character) is no simple escape from disagreeable circumstances, as Sargent Bush alleges in his description of Auclair's "retreatist attitude" (272). Rather, like the recluse Jeanne Le Ber's chilling description of her cell as an "earthly paradise," Auclair's discovery of order in Quebec is also a kind of imprisonment that requires perpetual adaptation to grim circumstances (110).

For Cather, exhausted by visits to her mother in California before her death and by the self-imposed research required by an historical novel like *Shadows on the Rock*, solace had little to do with rest and everything to do with cultivating an active mind. Grand Manan, like Quebec, is merely another setting for work, as Cather's scrupulous verification of historical data for the novel and Auclair's independent compilation of a Canadian herbarium with the novel both demonstrate.[12] The public form of the finished novel, in all of its elegance and grace, belies the backbreaking work involved in the creative process and especially obscures Cather's private resistance to writing "safe" fiction. If Cécile's prudish disgust for Madame Harnois's housekeeping calls attention to itself, Auclair's avoidance of Native American remedies in his methodical study of medicinal Canadian plants similarly invites investigation.

By twenty-first-century standards, even by the standards Cather knew in the late 1920s and early 1930s, Auclair's dismissal of Iroquois medical treatments as "savage" reflects deep prejudice. Cather's reliance on Francis Parkman's French Canadian histories, written in the late nineteenth century, may partially influence her representation of indigenous culture in the novel, as Wilbur Jacobs suggests (259). "Without giving names of chiefs," Jacobs argues, "or attempting to describe cultures and lifestyles of the Huron-Iroquois people, Cather paints them all as cannibal-barbarians. She did these native people a great disservice in neglecting to do her homework" (259). Indeed, Cather's reticence on autochthonous themes in Quebec is conspicuous enough to risk undermining the credibility she has established by her otherwise scrupulous historical details. If Auclair is to be trusted as a competent practitioner of scientific medicine, a contemporary reader must wonder why he entirely avoids Native American treatments, many of which have been added to the Western pharmacopoeia.[13]

Cather must have considered this dilemma while composing the novel, especially since Hawthorne had already set a precedent in *The Scarlet Letter* for adopting Native remedies into medical science with Roger Chillingworth's dual use of chemical compounds and indigenous herbal treatments in seventeenth-century Boston.[14] Cather may have decided that to show Auclair's adoption of Native remedies (which would have been closely tied to spirituality) would present a contradiction in his character. Instead, Auclair's reluctance to comment on religion might extend also to indigenous medicine, as he would have regarded both as "outside of [his] knowledge." After all, Auclair's admission to Cécile that "medicine is a dark science" reveals his recognition of his own limitations even within the profession to which he has devoted himself. Cather qualifies his role at the beginning of the novel, stating that "he was clearly not a man of action, no Indian-fighter or explorer" (6). To Wilbur Jacobs this means that "Cather, in short, oversimplifies. . . . She appears to have selected only the historical episodes, incidents, and facts that would serve her story" (260). But, by taking on the challenge of portraying Auclair as a medically competent seventeenth-century apothecary, it seems that Cather complicates the novel; also, it would have been difficult for her to sustain an accurate historical narrative while avoiding selectivity, especially concerning a shy character like Auclair, who would, under different circumstances, have lived his life exactly as his father and grandfather did in Paris (*Shadows* 6).

Auclair is most himself—functioning most as the cultivated physician—when he adds courtesy (or manners) to his practice of medicine. Sometimes this involves nothing more than listening when Count Frontenac feels lonely or when Blinker needs to talk about his previous position as a torturer (*Shadows* 128, 195). Sometimes this means preserving dinner as a ceremony—a preventative medicine—as his evenings with Cécile demonstrate. Even Auclair's literal remedies are things of beauty, such as the cordial he gives to Antoine Frichette, which is meant to "reach the sorest spot in a sick man"; as Frichette takes the cordial, he holds it up to the firelight and admires the color of the drink ("*C'est jolie, la couleur*") before draining the glass (112). Only a cultivated physician might turn a medical prescription, usually associated with pungent odors and bitter flavors, into a work of art.

Suffusing the business of medicine-making with a sense of beauty, as Frichette observes, adds a dimension of pleasure to the patient/healer relationship. Cécile also notes that everything she does with her father is "a kind of play"—not in a trifling sense, but in the sense that one delights in discovery (47). Where Lucius Sherman might allow formulae to dominate his sense of aesthetics, reducing flights of the human spirit to numbers and charts, Cather holds the bold march of scientific investigation up to the firelight as a thing of beauty, even a source of comfort able to "reach the sorest spot in a sick man." Antoine Frichette is not miraculously healed by the cordial (his rupture is an irrevocable injury, assuaged but not cured by the brace Auclair gives him), but rather empowered to face the long task of adapting to a new lifestyle, as Auclair's practice of medicine might also be seen as providing consolation to Cather while emboldening her to face life without her parents and with her own deteriorating health. *Shadows on the Rock* may be a refuge, but the cultural ideal Euclide Auclair represents does not allow for resting places; rather, the commingling of medicine and art provides an anchor point for the ongoing process of investigation, both scientific and aesthetic. As Grand Manan is more a fresh context for Cather's work than a getaway, so Quebec is a new setting for Auclair's rigorous mind, his self-education (begun in medical history, including Ambroise Paré) continuing in the herbarium of Canadian plants that he collects throughout the novel.

When a reader meets Auclair in the opening pages of the novel, Cather highlights his "warm and interested" eyes, which "had a kindling gleam as if his thoughts were pictures" (6). In 1930, while struggling with her own health, Cather must have wished for a physician gifted with such clarity of mind. Working back through her lifelong relationship with Dr. Julius Tyndale, through her friendship with Dr. John Macaulay in Grand Manan, back through the forty years leading up to *Shadows on the Rock*, one might see a steady thread of clarity in Cather's life, namely the ideal of a cultivated physician who could prepare a cordial and relish its color at the same time. While the recent deaths of her parents weighed on her mind as she wrote *Shadows on the Rock*, there is little doubt that Dr. Tyndale's death in 1929, the year before she finished the novel, also affected her deeply (Woodress 419). Mindful of the active dialogue between medicine and art evident in Tyndale's relationship with Cather, one might find added resonance in Euclide Auclair as an icon of medical and cultural cultivation, so meticulously documented yet still somehow playful—rigorous, but warmed by pleasure. On the gray rock of Quebec and within Cather's bleak inner landscape of the late 1920s and early 1930s, Auclair's salon shop pulses with firelight, animating a mortar and pestle atop a dinner table set for two.

NOTES

1. Merrill Maguire Skaggs's article "Cather's Use of Parkman's Histories in *Shadows on the Rock*" and Gary Brienzo's discussion of Cather's employment of "selective history" in the novel both offer extended analyses of Parkman's influence on Cather.

2. Jo Ann Middleton suggests that Cather's stories resonate deeply with medical residents precisely for her close attention to the human condition and her consistently accurate representation of medical details (90, 97).

3. My view of Auclair contrasts with Nadeane Trowse's argument that "Cather's romantic resistance to the medico-scientific model of human existence and interaction, in conjunction with her putative sexual orientation, suggests the disparate threads—biographical, historical, literary—that can be teased out of her texts and woven into a pattern that coheres" (209). As I will explore at length, scientific integrity and cultural sophistication are equally essential to Auclair's function as a healer, and his multidimensional approach to medicine closely resembles that of the physicians Cather befriended throughout her life.

4. By "empirical" I mean sifted by the scientific method of observation, hypothesis, and experiment. This distinction is necessary, as an "empiric" was thought to be an ignorant practitioner who practiced by trial and error versus experimentation. According to L. G. Kelly, the "Empirick" of the seventeenth century was a "barefoot doctor who combined traditional medical beliefs with garbled professional knowledge" (102). Likewise, Michael G. Kenny's study of Elias Smith (a nineteenth-century American folk healer) includes a reference to an "old root-lady," whom Kenny describes as a "rank empiric; if one thing failed to work, she . . . tried another" (210). As my later discussion of folk medicine will show, Auclair stands in sharp contrast to these alternative practitioners in a number of ways, including his avoidance of exotic and dangerous remedies and his willingness to admit uncertainty when he lacks experience, versus shooting in the dark, as Kenny's definition of a "rank empiric" implies.

5. James I exacerbated this debasement of apothecaries by his mandate in 1618 that the Company of Apothecaries break from the Grocers' Guild. This gave the College of Physicians exclusive control over the pharmacopoeia, allowing them to forbid apothecaries to practice medi-

cine (Kelly 96). Auclair resists this reduction of his office to a mere pharmacist, as he dedicates himself to his profession and acts in many ways as a physician.

6. Sargent Bush further reinforces Auclair's intellectual force with his description of the apothecary as a "rationalistic Frenchman, having much similarity to Enlightenment rationalists" (273). While a philosophical analysis of Auclair invites a separate discussion, it is sufficient to note here that Bush's comparison to rationalism implies the solidity of Auclair's education; a typical seventeenth-century apothecary, one of the "short robe," could hardly expect such a comparison, though Auclair's emotional restraint and Cather's precise descriptions of his education bear it out.

7. Viper broth was listed in the *London Pharmacopoeia* as early as 1618; rumors about Digby's use of the treatment likely circulated during his rise to fame in 1658, when he lectured publicly about the efficacy of his "weapon-salve" (Garrison 287). Although the Auclairs of *Shadows on the Rock* sailed for Quebec in the late 1690s, viper broth may still have been en vogue in Paris.

8. Apothecaries, as advocates of the working class, distrusted Catholic priests and physicians alike for their use of Latin, regarding the classical language as a "mare's nest created by grammarians to keep the lower classes ignorant and in place" (Kelly 100).

9. The "civilized French tradition of food" evident in the Auclair household also owes, as Kathleen Danker indicates, to Cather's early memories of her French Canadian neighbors in the Campbell/Wheatland area, "who took pride in their cooking and, in spite of the hardships of the frontier, cultivated gardens of vegetables and salad greens" (47). Auclair's method of preserving doves in tallow or lard also resembles the method Cather observed her French Canadian neighbors use in Nebraska (45).

10. Auclair's avoidance of extravagant remedies is also noteworthy because it sets him apart from the practice of polypharmacy, or the "inclusion in one prescription of up to twenty different ingredients to make sure that some worked" (Camp 164). As Katherine Knight also observes, "the seventeenth-century rationale must have been that because one herb was good for you, a whole gardenful must be that much better. If one herb did not work, another might" (240).

11. As Gary Brienzo notes, the years following 1922 were a period of "great disillusionment" for Cather (154). Murphy adds that Cather's "bitterness at the materialism that was becoming the world's philosophy of life branded her as a medievalist to . . . Marxist critics . . .; simultaneously, her pessimistic outlook on the cultural fulfillment of her own

country, because of its own general acceptance of materialism, branded her as a snob to the outspoken supporters of Americanism" (76). While Cécile's disdain for the Harnois's lifestyle smacks of snobbery, Auclair's rationalism and Pierre Charron's rusticism both temper her effeteness, calling attention to snobbery and inviting critique of it.

12. Cather's historical documentation was meticulous, as her use of an apothecary's diary from the Louvre to bolster the authenticity of Auclair's remedies shows (Bennett 133). Thus, when a Canadian pharmaceutical company wrote her that one of the drugs she included in *Shadows on the Rock* was not used in the 1600s, she was able to refute this claim by pointing to the archived apothecary's journal (133–34). This kind of scholarly rigor belies assumptions that Cather was seeking a passive refuge in *Shadows on the Rock*; in some ways, her relentless historical details made for a more grueling writing process than her earlier novels, set in Nebraska. Thus, Grand Manan and Quebec are, for Cather and Auclair, respectively, safe places for work, not rest.

13. See Eric Stone's *Clio Medica: Medicine among the American Indians* for a further discussion of Native herbal remedies. According to Stone, fifty-nine drugs have been added to the "modern pharmacopoeia" through the study of Native medicine (121).

14. Dimmesdale sometimes watches Chillingworth at work, "visiting the laboratory, and, for recreation's sake, watching the processes by which weeds were converted into drugs of potency" (Hawthorne 90). Chillingworth also admits to his patients in Boston that he has as much respect for the "simple medicines" used by Native American medicine men as he does for the "European pharmacopoeia" (82).

WORKS CITED

Bennett, Mildred R. *The World of Willa Cather*. Lincoln: U of Nebraska P, 1961.

Brienzo, Gary. "Making an Aristocratic Frontier: Selective History in Willa Cather's *Shadows on the Rock*." *Old West–New West: Centennial Essays*. Ed. Barbara Howard Meldrum. Moscow: U of Idaho P, 1993. 154–62.

Brown, E. K. *Willa Cather: A Critical Biography*. New York: Knopf, 1953.

Browner, Stephanie P. "Authorizing the Body: Scientific Medicine and *The Scarlet Letter*." *Literature and Medicine* 12.2 (1993): 139–60.

Bush, Sargent, Jr. "*Shadows on the Rock* and Willa Cather's View of the Past." *Queen's Quarterly* 76 (1969): 269–85.

Camp, John. *The Healer's Art: The Doctor through History*. New York: Taplinger, 1977.

Cather, Willa. "Double Birthday." *Uncle Valentine and Other Stories: Willa Cather's Uncollected Short Fiction, 1915–1929*. Ed. Bernice Slote. Lincoln: U of Nebraska P, 1973. 41–63.

———. *Shadows on the Rock*. New York: Vintage, 1995.

———. "Superstition vs. Investigation." *Willa Cather in Person: Interviews, Speeches, and Letters*. Ed. L. Brent Bohlke. Lincoln: U of Nebraska P, 1986. 141–43.

Cunningham, Horace H. *Field Medical Services at the Battles of Manassas (Bull Run)*. Athens: U of Georgia P, 1968.

Danker, Kathleen. "The Influence of Willa Cather's French-Canadian Neighbors in Nebraska in *Death Comes for the Archbishop* and *Shadows on the Rock*." *Great Plains Quarterly* 20.1 (2000): 35–54.

Garrison, Fielding H. *An Introduction to the History of Medicine*. 4th ed. Philadelphia: W. B. Saunders, 1929.

Haggard, Howard. *The Doctor in History*. New Haven: Yale UP, 1934.

Hawthorne, Nathaniel. *The Scarlet Letter.* 1850. 3rd ed. Ed. Seymour Gross et al. New York: Norton, 1988.

Holmes, Oliver Wendell. "Homeopathy and Its Kindred Delusions." *Medical Essays: 1842–1882*. Boston: Houghton Mifflin, 1891. 1–102.

Ingersoll, L. K. "M.D. for the Islands: The Life and Times of Dr. John Francis Macaulay (1876–1939)." *Grand Manan Historian* 25 (1993): 1–47.

Jacobs, Wilbur R. "Willa Cather and Francis Parkman: Novelistic Portrayals of Colonial New France." *Willa Cather: Family, Community, and History*. Ed. John J. Murphy, Linda Hunter Adams, and Paul Rawlins. Provo UT: Brigham Young U Humanities Pub. Center, 1990. 253–64.

Kelly, L. G. "Plato, Bacon, and the Puritan Apothecary: The Case of Nicholas Culpeper." *Target* 1.1 (1989): 95–109.

Kenny, Michael G. *The Perfect Law of Liberty: Elias Smith and the Providential History of America*. Washington DC: Smithsonian Institution P, 1994.

Knight, Katherine. "A Precious Medicine: Tradition and Magic in Some Seventeenth Century Remedies." *Folklore* 113.2 (2002): 237–59.

Lewis, Edith. *Willa Cather Living: A Personal Record*. Lincoln: U of Nebraska P, 2000.

Lovering, Joseph P. *S. Weir Mitchell*. New York: Twayne, 1971.

Middleton, Jo Ann. "Willa Cather and Modern Medicine." *Willa Cather's New York: New Essays on Cather in the City*. Ed. Merrill Maguire Skaggs. Madison: Fairleigh Dickinson UP, 2000. 90–102.

Murphy, John J. "*Shadows on the Rock*: Cather's Medieval Refuge." *Renascence: Essays on Value in Literature* 15 (1963): 76–78.

Shryock, Richard Harrison. *The Development of Modern Medicine: An Interpretation of the Social and Scientific Factors Involved*. Madison: U of Wisconsin P, 1979.

Siraisi, Nancy G. *Medieval and Early Renaissance Medicine: An Introduction to Knowledge and Practice*. Chicago: U of Chicago P, 1990.

Skaggs, Merrill Maguire. "Cather's Use of Parkman's Histories in *Shadows on the Rock*." *Cather Studies* 2 (1993): 140–55.

Stone, Eric. *Clio Medica: Medicine among the American Indians*. New York: Hafner, 1962.

Sumner, Allene. "Prize Novelist Finds Writing and Eating Kin." *Willa Cather in Person: Interviews, Speeches, and Letters*. Ed. L. Brent Bohlke. Lincoln: U of Nebraska P, 1986. 86–88.

Trowse, Nadeane. "Willa Cather's Condition: Disease, Doctors, and Diagnoses as Social Action." *Cather Studies* 4 (1999): 205–24.

Weeks, Andrew. *Paracelsus: Speculative Theory and the Crisis of the Early Reformation*. New York: State U of New York P, 1997.

Woodress, James. *Willa Cather: A Literary Life*. Lincoln: U of Nebraska P, 1989.

The Dialectics of Seeing in Cather's Pittsburgh

"Double Birthday" and Urban Allegory

JOSEPH C. MURPHY

Willa Cather's stature as cultural icon is inextricable from the iconography of her settings. Her fiction famously engages the spectacles of the Divide and the Southwest, but it draws equally and fundamentally upon those of the modern city. Cather's modern cities are in a sense anti-iconographic: they resist as well as attract the eye. They instill desire in characters who can weather their anonymity and competition; still, their treasures hide behind walls of concert halls and museums, fog and memory, at times as inaccessible as the dead cities of the Southwest that set them in cultural relief. As Susan J. Rosowski has demonstrated in her essay "Willa Cather as a City Novelist," Cather's urbanites tend to be reluctant sojourners in cities rather than devoted metropolitans. For Anton Rosicky the city is an extended stopover on a life journey that begins and ends on the land; for Jim Burden it is only a practical point on the larger, continental map of his imagination; for Thea Kronborg the city fires the imagination and the will but gives no personal repose; and for Lucy Gayheart it is a deception, a "city of feeling" masking the "city of fact" (24). Surveying this field, one wonders whether it is possible for the "eyes [to drink] in the breadth of" the city as Alexandra Bergson's do the land in *O Pioneers!* (64). Is a radical—that is, rooted—city life possible for Cather? Can one settle in the city as one might settle on the land? Cather's 1929 story "Double Birthday," set in Pittsburgh, offers a response to these questions. "Double Birthday" stands out among her portrayals of modern cities in the way her protagonists, a nephew and uncle both named Albert Engelhardt, define themselves imaginatively in terms of urban geography and history.

Among Cather's fictional representations of Pittsburgh, the one we find in "Double Birthday" is unique for its sophistication and range. "The Professor's Commencement" (1902), "Paul's Case" (1905), and "A Gold Slipper" (1917) each portray an almost unbridgeable gap between art culture and commercial values (although the professor tries to build that bridge). Set on the outskirts of Pittsburgh, "Uncle Valentine" (1925) regards the city furtively as a menacing "black pillar of cloud" (24). By contrast, "Double Birthday" portrays the artist-intellectual trying to domesticate the city by bringing its spatial and historical coordinates into dialogue. In his introduction to *The Best American Short Stories of the Century*, where "Double Birthday" is the Cather selection, John Updike characterizes Cather's Pittsburgh here as "a great city as cozy and inturned as a Southern hamlet" (xvii). The protagonists' relationship to Pittsburgh is not oppositional but rather *dialectical*—in Walter Benjamin's sense that capitalist society can be reimagined by reading its fragmentary forms against the grain of progress.

The Jewish messianic Marxist critic's world might seem remote from Cather's, but Benjamin's life span (1892–1940) falls within her own, and both harshly criticized modernity while drawing vital energy from it. Benjamin loved cities not for what they show but for what they conceal. For him the modern city, the epitome of progress, is lost in an extended dream fueled by its commercial and industrial engines. Awakening requires stepping through the city in syncopated rhythm, distractedly, close-up—the perspective of the flâneur, the walking city observer—to discover dialectical images. Dialectical images juxtapose past and present forms, expose the vanity of what is called progress, and project a possible future invisible to those caught in the machinery of modern life. In his great unfinished work, *The Arcades Project*, Benjamin applies this method of analysis to the Paris arcades: glass and iron commercial passageways that represented modernity to the nineteenth century but lay in ruins by the 1930s. The rise and fall of the arcades epitomizes for Benjamin the transience of capitalism at large. "With the destabilizing of the market economy," he writes, "we begin to recognize the monuments of the bourgeoisie as ruins even before they have crumbled" (*Arcades* 13). This recognition creates a space for imagining "the utopia that has left its trace in a thousand configurations of life, from enduring edifices to passing fashions" (4–5). Benjamin studies this urban phantasmagoria in Baudelaire's depictions of Paris in the era of high capitalism. For Benjamin, Baudelaire is an allegorist who rummages through the fragments of modernity "and tests to see if they fit together—that meaning with this image or this image with that meaning" (368). Each epoch, Benjamin argues, dreams the next in dialectical images. By brooding upon history rather than transcending it, the urban allegorist finds grounds for hope where the city appears most frangible. "[T]here are no periods of decline," Benjamin writes. "[E]very city is beautiful to me" (458).[1]

"Double Birthday" resonates with Benjamin's dialectic because it seeks a realignment of community and values within a city that is in various ways disintegrating. Poised, unconsciously, on the brink of the Great Depression (published in February 1929), looking back to the turn of the century, the story spans the heyday of the industrial affluence that occasioned Cather's arrival in Pittsburgh in 1896 as a young editor.[2] Its unifying event is the shared birthday of uncle and nephew Albert (hereafter "Uncle Albert" and "Albert"), born twenty-five years apart on 1 December. Uncle Albert, at eighty, is a retired throat doctor, and Albert, fifty-five, is the last surviving son of a wealthy glass manufacturer. Albert appears to have styled his life upon Benjamin's premise that industrial capitalism—and paradigmatically, glass—yields meaning only in its ruins. Since his father's death, Albert and four brothers have squandered the family's fortune, liquidating the glass factory and substantial real estate—"all gone, melted away" (42). Structurally, the story requires a dialectical reading through the mutual illumination of points in space and time. Remembering her wide-ranging experiences there as editor, writer and teacher, Cather integrates four sections of Pittsburgh—South Side, Squirrel Hill, Allegheny, and downtown—conventionally separated by forces of class and history. The story also reaches beyond Pittsburgh—to New York, where Uncle Albert's sponsorship of Marguerite Thiesinger's vocal training was cut short by her death, and to Rome, where Albert spent three golden years of youth. These locations exist in a dialectical tension that draws upon but reconfigures the hierarchy of the industrial capitalist city. Each of the four sections of Cather's Pittsburgh is anchored in a house—a house that is divided against itself, yet stands.

The two Alberts now live together "in a queer part of the city, on one of the dingy streets that run uphill off noisy Carson Street" (45). They share "a little two-story brick . . . workingman's house," an overlooked property of Albert's father that has become their last refuge (45). Cather modeled this house on the South Side residence of editor George Seibel and family at 114 South Seventeenth Street, where she found a social and intellectual refuge, far exceeding its modest address, during her Pittsburgh years. Cather read French and German literature at the Seibels, and she brought Dorothy Canfield there for a memorable Christmas visit in 1896 (Byrne and Snyder 18–26; Sullivan 22–23; Bennett 66–69). For their part, Cather's two Alberts have likewise patched together on the South Side an unusual family that defies class definition. They rent the downstairs to a former workman in the glass factory and his wife, who keeps house while Albert goes to work, and their granddaughter, who humors old Uncle Albert. Ashes fall in the yard from neighboring chimneys, while the winds of history and culture blow through Albert's rooms. His writing table, rugs, books and pictures, the piano he still plays daily—"[a]ll the years and the youth which had slipped away from him still clung to these things" (45). For Albert, to be free is to feel the friction of history passing and to reflect upon it: "[H]e had lived to the full all the revolutions in art and music that his period covered" (55). Their fragments collect in his apartment—the fin de siècle decadence of Beardsley, Dowson, and Wilde, "works which, though so recent, were already immensely far away and diminished. The glad, rebellious excitement they had once caused in the world he could recapture only in memory" (45).

Albert moves into the future with his eyes fixed on the accumulating debris of the past, much like the Angel of History, Benjamin's allegorical figure in "Theses on the Philosophy of History" (1940). Benjamin's description of this figure, based upon Paul Klee's painting *Angelus Novus* (1920), warrants full quotation for the light it sheds on Albert's outlook, and on Cather's as well:

> His face is turned toward the past. Where we perceive a chain of events, he sees one single catastrophe which keeps piling wreckage upon wreckage and hurls it in front of his feet. The angel would like to stay, awaken the dead, and make whole what has been smashed. But a storm is blowing from Paradise; it has got caught in his wings with such violence that the angel can no longer close them. This storm irresistibly propels him into the future to which his back is turned, while the pile of debris before him grows skyward. This storm is what we call progress. (*Illuminations* 257–58)

Like Benjamin's Angel, Albert reads history against the grain of progress that pushes him ineluctably into the future. Rejecting progressive history, he incorporates the refuse of that history—the fragmented, the unfinished, the outmoded—into his daily life. Albert lives with memories of his own expended youth, and of the youth of modernism, even as he lives, physically, with a worker his father once employed, long after the factory has shut down. Likewise, he lives with memories of the truncated career of his piano teacher, Rafael Joseffy, while Uncle Albert lives with his "lost Lenore," Marguerite Thiesinger, in a perpetuated state of mourning that carries her severed youth into his old age. From Benjamin's perspective, these mournful fixations—although they do not "awaken the dead" or "make whole what has been smashed"—are hopeful because they militate against the oblivion of progress. Benjamin's urban allegorist is a "brooder" whose "memory ranges over the indiscriminate mass of dead lore. Human knowledge, within his memory, is something piecemeal—in an especially pregnant sense: it is like the jumble of arbitrarily cut pieces from which a puzzle is assembled" (*Arcades* 368). Albert's lifestyle, and Cather's narrative of it, bespeaks an alternative history and an alternative future. Uncle Albert's closing reference to Thomas Gray sounds the note of the entire story: "E'en in our ashes live their wonted fires" (Gray 92).

Judge Hammersley, a friend of Albert's late father, looks down upon Albert from a substantial house on posh Squirrel Hill, the story's second residential coordinate. This house is modeled on the Squirrel Hill residence of Judge Samuel McClung, father of Cather's friend Isabel McClung, at 1180 Murrayhill Avenue, where Cather lived from 1901 through 1906 (Byrne and Snyder 39–40; O'Brien 234–38). Shaded by old oaks, the Judge's house is "comfortable in the old-fashioned way, well appointed," with a library of divinity, philosophy, and early American history (43). The Judge "didn't think highly of what is called success in the world today," but he laments that Albert has "nothing whatever to show" for his fifty-five years (42). Hammersley has his own rightful piece of the show, but Cather subverts it by portraying him in lockstep with "the machinery of life" (43), by viewing Squirrel Hill from Albert's bohemian perspective, and by culminating the action with the joyful visit of the Judge's daughter to the Alberts' South Side home. Walking past the "massive houses" holding "nothing but the heavy domestic routine[,] all the frictions and jealousies and discontents of family life," Albert "felt light and free" (55).

In the dialectic between South Side and Squirrel Hill, Cather at once deploys and undercuts the contrast between "bohemian" and "Presbyterian" Pittsburgh she drew in an 1897 article in the *Nebraska State Journal*: "Now all Pittsburgh is divided into two parts. Presbyteria and Bohemia, and the former is much the larger and more influential kingdom of the two" (*World and Parish* 2: 505). According to Sharon O'Brien, Cather meant by "Presbyteria" "the mutually reinforcing Protestant ethic and spirit of capitalism that denigrated emotion and art." "Bohemia" was "Cather's alternative, marginal world of art and artists who worshipped truth and beauty with aesthetic and emotional fervor rather than mercantile piety." Although Cather knew that the art world depended upon wealth generated by business, she believed Bohemia also depended upon values of "passion, creativity, and spontaneity" antithetical to "Presbyterian" culture

(O'Brien 224–25). Cather, O'Brien argues, passed easily between these two camps during her Pittsburgh years, but gradually she retreated from Bohemia, eventually landing in the house of eminent Presbyterian Samuel McClung. In Albert, Cather portrays a character who moved quite intentionally in the opposite direction—from Presbyteria to Bohemia—but "Double Birthday" is really about the upsetting of such categories.

A third house, where the Engelhardt boys grew up, rises from turn-of-the-century Allegheny in section 3. This house "of many-colored bricks, with gables and turrets," "striped awnings," and "glittering gravel," situated on the Park and near the market, is a fantastic complement to the surrounding industrial city (48, 57). Whereas South Side and Squirrel Hill exemplify the present-day separation of working class and bourgeoisie, here class divisions and mercantile striving are suspended on a kind of Olmstedian middle ground. In its transitivity the house embodies Benjamin's concept of modern urban experience.[3] As in Benjamin's account of Naples, life in the Engelhardt house is "dispersed, porous, commingled. . . . [E]ach private attitude or act is permeated by streams of communal life" (*Reflections* 171). Welcoming to shop boys, to common Marguerite Thiesinger, to the Judge's daughter in her youth—who appreciated that the Engelhardt boys "enjoyed" a woman "aesthetically" rather than "grab[bing]" her "brutally"—the place has now passed into memory (57). Its openness to what Uncle Albert calls "aspiration" rather than "ambition" (51) is symbolized in the large stained-glass window on the west side, "representing a scene on the Grand Canal in Venice, the Church of Santa Maria della Salute in the background, in the foreground a gondola with a slender gondolier" (48). The house opens into Venice, the world city of fluid passageways. As stained glass, the window contrasts with the industrial glass that made the family fortune, glass called "brutal" in Marguerite's deathbed scene in a New York hospital for its teasing combination of transparency and confinement: "*Pourquoi, pourquoi?*" he [Uncle Albert] muttered, staring blindly at that brutal square of glass" (52).[4]

The fourth section of Cather's Pittsburgh (actually the first chronologically) is downtown, and its signature house is the "gray stone Court House" where, as the story opens, Judge Hammersley awkwardly encounters Albert (41). Although the building is not specifically named as such, Cather's faithfulness to the actual cityscape would identify this as the Allegheny County Courthouse, a late, great work of Henry Hobson Richardson, whose bold Romanesque-American architecture, like Cather's art, fashioned modernity from the forms of the past. By beginning at this courthouse Cather, portrays Pittsburgh's public square as one of justice, but Richardson's subtle blending of modernism and tradition, and his multitude of rhythmically interdependent arches—each casting its own trajectory—counsel against simplistic judgments.[5] Indeed, Cather distinguishes her authorial judgment from the ideology of progress by which the Judge sizes up Albert. "Even in American cities, which seem so much alike," she begins, "where people seem all to be living the same lives, striving for the same things, thinking the same thoughts, there are still individuals a little out of tune with the times—there are still survivals of a past more loosely woven, there are disconcerting beginnings of a future yet unforeseen" (41). Cather evaluates Albert's peculiarity according to a dialectical vision of the city: the vestige of the past typifies the future, the "disconcerting" sound strikes the key of a remote harmony. Benjamin writes: "Historical 'understanding' is to be grasped, in principle, as an afterlife of that which is understood" (*Arcades* 460).

Cather's retrospective modernism would have found common cause with the City Beautiful movement embraced by urban planners in the early 1900s. Inspired by the magisterial White City at the 1893 Chicago World's Columbian Exposition, and culminating in Daniel Burnham's *Plan of Chicago* (1909), the City Beautiful sought order and visibility through spectacular civic centers and axial boulevards unifying previously separate urban districts (Rybczynski 127–48). "Double Birthday" resonates with this movement by bridging different urban sections and by interweaving the lives of characters from these sections. Further, by alluding to Venetian and Roman scenes (in the Allegheny stained glass, and in Albert's memories), the story shares the City Beautiful's enthusiasm for what one of its historians calls "the importable architectonic triumphs of Venice and Rome" (Wilson 85). Although in Pittsburgh the ideal of beauty was stymied by industrial priorities, the city did pursue a comprehensive, long-range plan (beginning with recommendations by Frederick Law Olmsted Jr. and others in 1910, and continuing into the 1930s) to knit together its metropolitan area, centralize public buildings, and clean the air and rivers (Lorant 364, 368). Beginning in the 1890s, Cather experienced the early philanthropic inklings of this movement toward civic clarity and order in Andrew Carnegie's concert hall, museum, and library in Pittsburgh's Oakland section, an important refuge for Cather on the ground as for her protagonist in "Paul's Case." "Paul's Case" is instructive for understanding Albert's case in "Double Birthday." Civic improvements notwithstanding, for neither Albert nor Paul does Pittsburgh pave an open road to liberation: the paths linking the Alberts' home to the larger city are as personal as the one Paul beats between Carnegie Hall and Cordelia Street. The city intensifies private experience, to a degree that is fatal for Paul, but salutary for Albert, whose realism and maturity are beyond Paul's adolescent reach. For Benjamin, too, the flâneur's private vision always outruns the intentions of the city planner. Although Benjamin perceives Haussmann's nineteenth-century boulevards in Paris as forms of social control, he nevertheless finds there new outlets for the urban allegorist's dialectical vision (*Arcades* 11–13). Likewise, Cather's Pittsburgh fosters dialectical convergences and afterimages beyond the comprehension of any formal civic plan.

The city's public passageways provide the settings for these personal illuminations. In contrast to the reclusive Judge, who travels by private car, the Alberts are continually ranging across the city in the public way. Albert first appears in the text as an uncanny face emerging from the crowd—"one of these men whom one does not readily place" (41). He commutes between South Side and his downtown clerkship on foot and on streetcar; and when he trudges up Squirrel Hill to accept the Judge's beneficent champagne, he finds it easier to dodge the Prohibition laws than the private automobiles that cut in his way. In his prime, Uncle Albert was a walker in Pittsburgh and New York. To this habit he owes the discovery of Marguerite Thiesinger, that "one

Voice" sounding from the open windows of Allegheny High School as he strolled by (48). When she died, he was sitting on a bench in Central Park. Even now Uncle Albert still ventures into the street, with Elsa, the housekeeper's granddaughter, "to join him and see him over the crossings" (53). Occasionally his nephew takes him by streetcar up Mt. Oliver to a German graveyard, presumably where Marguerite is buried. Elsa mimes the urban "crossings" of the Alberts in the "cross-stitch" she practices while chatting with Uncle Albert (54)—underscoring the relationship between urban space and domestic textiles suggested by Cather's opening remark about unusual urbanites typifying "a past more loosely woven" (41). For Benjamin, the flâneur domesticates urban space, immerses himself in its fleeting images and interstitial spaces, and glimpses its inner life. "[F]lanerie can transform Paris into one great interior," Benjamin suggests. "[O]n the other hand, the city can appear to someone walking through it to be without thresholds: a landscape in the round" (*Arcades* 422). Cather builds an ethics of crossing into her city, where the courage to step into its passageways is rewarded by discovery, and where assisting another there is an expression of charity. This is the meaning of the mysterious, slender gondolier in the stained glass at Allegheny, the image of those who bear the cross of others by bearing their crossings. Uncle Albert bore the cross of Marguerite's death. "That struggle took place in my body," he says. "Her dissolution occurred within me" (53).

Now Albert has assumed the role of gondolier for his aging uncle. But in another sense, Albert is his own passenger, negotiating interior crossings within a city whose dominant values are not his own. Two scenes illustrate his internal struggle in relation to bridges and public transit. In the first, Albert, en route to the Judge's, takes the streetcar across the Twenty-second Street Bridge past "the blazing steel mills" (54). There ensues a scene of confusion that exposes the economic realities over which Albert's life is suspended: "As he waited on Soho Hill to catch a Fifth Avenue car, the heavy frosty air suddenly began to descend in snow flakes. He wished he had worn his old overcoat; didn't like to get this one wet. He had to consider such things now. He was hesitating about a taxi when his car came, bound for the

East End" (54). Albert's vulnerability is exposed at the seams of the city—the bridge and transit exchange. In *The Image of the City*, Kevin Lynch invests such transitional sites with special significance in the urban landscape: "The junction, or place of a break in transportation, has compelling importance for the city observer. Because decisions must be made at junctions, people heighten their attention at such places and perceive nearby elements with more than normal clarity" (73). Albert's hesitation causes the reader, too, to pause and look around. One feature that stands out is those "blazing steel mills," which relate to Albert in a double sense. Earlier the Judge has commented that Albert would have done better to work in the steel mills than to fritter away his youth in Rome. In a larger sense the mills represent the city's great industrial engine, over which Albert has renounced his rightful control in favor of a middle age spent playing in its disapproving glare. In its confluence of economic anxiety and water crossing, this scene recalls an image of Uncle Albert crossing Jersey ferry to New York to oversee Marguerite's singing career: "He often shivered as he crossed the Jersey ferry; he was afraid of Fate. He would tell over her assets on his fingers to reassure himself" (51). Whitman—like, he is "a self-important man . . . standing by the rail of the ferry boat" (51). As Uncle Albert knows, it is such "disconcerting" folk who distinguish that "one Voice" calling through the city's open windows. For both Alberts, the city challenges but ultimately supports a life lived at crosscurrents with its economic norms.

Cather replays the same elements—water crossing, chill, anxiety, contemplation, resumption—in a final scene. It is the anticipated double birthday, and Albert, fighting off the "shiver" of another year, is walking home across the Smithfield Bridge:

> A thick brown fog made everything dark, and there was a feeling of snow in the air. The lights along the sheer cliffs of Mount Washington, high above the river, were already lighted. When Albert was a boy, those cliffs, with the row of lights far up against the sky, always made him think of some far-away, cloud-set city in Asia; the forbidden city, he used to call it. Well, that was a long time ago; a lot of water had run under this bridge since then, and kingdoms and empires had

> fallen. Meanwhile, Uncle Doctor was hanging on, and things were not so bad with them as they might be. Better not reflect too much. He hopped on board a street car, and old women with market baskets shifted to make room for him. (57)

Albert's passage over the waters of the Monongahela River typifies the dialectical structure of the story. Suspended between downtown and déclassé South Side, Albert sees in a single image the dream city of his privileged childhood and the actual city of his reduced middle age. He absorbs this contrast in the context of larger historical upheavals ("kingdoms and empires had fallen") and seems to recognize that his privileged witness to these changes is more precious than any illusion of control over history or of insulation from it. "Better not reflect too much": dropping the subject, Cather's narrative voice merges with the consciousness of her character, achieving a casual, "loosely woven" prose that suspends resolution in step with Albert's own suspense. Like Benjamin's Angel of History, Albert is propelled reluctantly into the future, unable to "make whole what has been smashed." He resumes his journey by mounting a streetcar and casting his lot with a feminine populace who "shifted to make room for him." The flâneur, writes Benjamin, "demanded elbow room" (*Illuminations* 172). So too, Albert glimpses and passes on, descending into the crowd but maintaining his uniqueness. Albert does not need to reflect, because, through his dialectical vision, the city reflects him, as it has supported his individuality and his freedom to be "out of tune with the times" (41).

"Double Birthday" has been considered a companion story to "Neighbour Rosicky," which Cather wrote immediately before and published just after (Slote xxx; Arnold 126–27), and it is worth asking why Rosicky seeks his fortunes beyond the city while Albert seeks his within it. It comes down to a matter of seeing. On a fateful Fourth of July, Rosicky experiences the sudden emptiness of lower Manhattan, "like the stillness in a great factory when the machinery stops and the belts and bands cease running." The change is "too great," and the city appears "blank" to him (29). Like Rosicky, Albert experiences the ruptures of urban life—that emptiness after the machinery stops—but whereas Rosicky removes to rural Nebraska, Albert bridges the gap and rejoins the urban crowd. Albert sees more deeply. He sees through the city's historical upheavals to the unorthodox social and geographical patterns to which his city life, and this story, bear witness, sketching what Cather calls "a future yet unforeseen." This vision lacks the clarity with which Alexandra Bergson's eyes survey the prairie and foresee its development in *O Pioneers!* Albert's vision, like Benjamin's, follows the oblique and shifting contours of a modern city where no overarching perspective, of time or space, is possible. Rather, he finds meaning and identity in the chance encounters and fragments of memory that give "Double Birthday" its form.

Cather called Pittsburgh her "birthplace" as a writer ("And Death Comes")—that second artistic birthday, which, as Thea Kronborg discovers, is longer and more personally demanding than the first (*Song of the Lark* 175–76). Pittsburgh was the first big city where Cather learned to embed personal expression into architecture and social geography, and to grapple with industrial capitalist America from the standpoint of art. Its strategic location, connecting the eastern seaboard to the continental interior; its rivers and dramatic, urbanized heights; its bridges and transit lines; its ethnic diversity and domestic retreats—all of this appealed to her imagination. In "Double Birthday," her final Pittsburgh-set story, Cather portrays a city that reflects as much the geography of her mature fiction as it does the city she experienced as an emerging author. Like her character Albert, fifty-five when the story appeared in 1929, with a December birthday, she perceived a city unified not by progress but by spaces and relationships struck across the currents of change, receding into the future. This imagined Pittsburgh is in a sense the space from which Cather was passing beyond modernity, from which she crossed to those ideal cities at Santa Fe and Quebec that she likewise constructed from the ruins of the past.

NOTES

1. Useful discussions of Benjamin's philosophy of the city include Buck-Morss; Gilloch; Caygill 118–48; and Cutler 100–107.

2. Although Cather based her depiction of Pittsburgh on her experi-

ences there a quarter century earlier, there were, to a thoughtful observer of the broader American scene in the later 1920s, forebodings of ill. Mechanization was rising, speculation was manic; at the same time, unemployment was increasing, wages were low, and workers were hard pressed to buy the goods they produced (Lorant 336, 340).

3. Demarest notes the commingling of classes in this depiction of Allegheny City, which was annexed to Pittsburgh in 1907 and is now called the North Side: "Cather presents the older city as a community in which people of different classes mingled in friendly intimacy, in which the round of daily errands performed on foot created a neighborhood familiarity" (144). For Benjamin, according to Caygill, "the experience of the city replaces substance and subject with *transitivity*" (120). Cather's likely prototype for the Engelhardt house was the residence of onetime Lincoln drama critic George Gerwig at 66 (now 906) Cedar Avenue in Allegheny (Sullivan 20–21).

4. Uncle Albert's throat bears "a long, jagged scar," which, according to his brother, resulted from an accidental fall into frames of glass (46–47).

5. On Richardson's Romanesque style, see Handlin 115–21. A guide to Richardson's courthouse evokes the experience of moving through it: "The design of the great three-story staircase is a celebration of the arch as an architectural form. . . . The many arches seem to move and interact as we move past them" (*H.H. Richardson's Allegheny County Courthouse*). On Cather's interest in Romanesque architecture, see Moseley 68–71.

WORKS CITED

"And Death Comes for Willa Cather, Famous Author." *Pittsburgh Sun-Telegraph* 25 Apr. 1947. Bridging the Urban Landscape site. Carnegie Library of Pittsburgh. 22 May 2003. http://www.clpgh.org/exhibit/neighborhoods/northside/nor_n111.html.

Arnold, Marilyn. *Willa Cather's Short Fiction*. Athens: U of Ohio P, 1984.

Benjamin, Walter. *The Arcades Project*. Trans. Howard Eiland and Kevin McLaughlin. Cambridge: Harvard UP, 1999.

———. *Illuminations*. Ed. Hannah Arendt. Trans. Harry Zohn. New York: Schocken, 1968.

———. *Reflections*. Ed. Peter Demetz. Trans. Edmund Jephcott. New York: Schocken, 1978.

Bennett, Mildred R. "Willa Cather in Pittsburgh." *Prairie Schooner* 33 (Spring 1959): 64–76.

Buck-Morss, Susan. *The Dialectics of Seeing: Walter Benjamin and the Arcades Project*. Cambridge: MIT P, 1989.

Byrne, Kathleen D., and Richard C. Snyder. *Chrysalis: Willa Cather in Pittsburgh*. Pittsburgh: Historical Society of Western Pennsylvania, 1980.

Cather, Willa. "Double Birthday." 1929. *Uncle Valentine and Other Stories: Willa Cather's Uncollected Short Fiction, 1915–1929*. Ed. Bernice Slote. Lincoln: U of Nebraska P, 1973. 41–63.

———. *Lucy Gayheart*. 1935. New York: Vintage, 1976.

———. "Neighbour Rosicky." 1930. *Obscure Destinies*. 1932. Willa Cather Scholarly Edition. Ed. Frederick M. Link with Kari A. Ronning and Mark Kamrath. Historical essay and explanatory notes Kari A. Ronning. Lincoln: U of Nebraska P, 1998. 7–61.

———. *O Pioneers!* 1913. Willa Cather Scholarly Edition. Ed. Susan J. Rosowski and Charles W. Mignon with Kathleen Danker. Historical essay and explanatory notes David Stouck. Lincoln: U of Nebraska P, 1992.

———. *The Song of the Lark*. 1915. Lincoln: U of Nebraska P, 1978.

———. "Uncle Valentine." 1925. *Uncle Valentine and Other Stories: Willa Cather's Uncollected Short Fiction, 1915–1929*. Ed. Bernice Slote. Lincoln: U of Nebraska P, 1973. 3–38.

———. *The World and the Parish: Willa Cather's Articles and Reviews, 1893–1902*. Ed. William M. Curtin. 2 vols. Lincoln: U of Nebraska P, 1970.

Caygill, Howard. *Walter Benjamin: The Colour of Experience*. London: Routledge, 1998.

Cutler, Edward S. *Recovering the New: Transatlantic Roots of Modernism*. Hanover: U of New Hampshire P, 2003.

Demarest, David P., Jr., ed. *From These Hills, from These Valleys: Selected Fiction about Western Pennsylvania*. Pittsburgh: U of Pittsburgh P, 1976.

Gilloch, Graeme. *Myth and Metropolis: Walter Benjamin and the City*. Cambridge, England: Polity P, 1996.

Gray, Thomas. "Elegy Written in a Country Churchyard." *Norton Anthology of English Literature*. 4th ed. New York: Norton, 1979. 1: 2444–47.

Handlin, David P. *American Architecture*. London: Thames and Hudson, 1985.

H.H. Richardson's Allegheny County Courthouse and Jail: Self-Guided Walking Tour. Pittsburgh: Living Architecture . . . Alive in Pittsburgh, 1999.

Lorant, Stefan. *Pittsburgh: The Story of an American City*. Pittsburgh: Esselmont Books, 1999.

Lynch, Kevin. *The Image of the City*. Cambridge: MIT P, 1960.

Moseley, Ann. "The Religious Architecture of *The Professor's House* and *Death Comes for the Archbishop*. *Willa Cather and the Culture of Belief*. Ed. John J. Murphy. Provo UT: Brigham Young UP, 2002. 63–80.

O'Brien, Sharon. *Willa Cather: The Emerging Voice*. New York: Oxford UP, 1987.

Rosowski, Susan J. "Willa Cather as a City Novelist." *Writing the City: Eden, Babylon, and the New Jerusalem*. Ed. Peter Preston and Paul Simpson-Housley. London: Routledge, 1994. 149–70.

Rybczynski, Witold. *City Life: Urban Expectations in a New World*. New York: Scribner, 1995.

Slote, Bernice. Introduction. *Uncle Valentine and Other Stories: Willa Cather's Uncollected Short Fiction, 1915–1929*. Ed. Bernice Slote. Lincoln: U of Nebraska P, 1973. ix–xxx.

Sullivan, Peter. "Willa Cather's Pittsburgh German Friends and Literary Connections." *Nassau Review* 7.2 (1996): 19–33.

Updike, John. Introduction. *The Best American Short Stories of the Century*. Ed. John Updike and Katrina Kenison. Boston: Houghton Mifflin, 1999. xv–xxiv.

Wilson, William H. *The City Beautiful Movement*. Baltimore: Johns Hopkins UP, 1989.

Antithetical Icons?
Willa Cather, Ernest Hemingway, and the First World War

STEVEN TROUT

In books and articles devoted to Willa Cather's fiction, Ernest Hemingway's name typically appears in connection with just one work—Cather's Pulitzer Prize–winning novel *One of Ours*, published in 1922. As Cather scholars rarely fail to mention, Hemingway hated this controversial and widely misunderstood text, a reaction he bitingly expressed to Edmund Wilson in a letter dated 25 November 1923. After stating his disappointment over the commercial failure of E. E. Cummings's *The Enormous Room*, Hemingway lashed out at *One of Ours*, one of the more successful titles from the previous year, and contemptuously described its "big sale[s]" and hopelessly inflated reputation. Then, in perhaps his most notorious critical witticism (at least among Cather aficionados), Hemingway sarcastically belittled the portrayal of war in *One of Ours*, especially the battle scene in the penultimate chapter: "Wasn't that last scene in the lines wonderful? Do you know where it came from? The battle scene in *Birth of a Nation*. I identified episode after episode, Catherized. Poor woman, she had to get her war experience somewhere" (*Selected Letters* 105).

Cather scholars have never forgiven Hemingway for this blatantly chauvinistic attack, and, as if to keep their readers ever mindful of Hemingway's ignominy, they have included his embarrassing diatribe in most of the book chapters and articles devoted to *One of Ours*. For example, in *Willa Cather: A Literary Life*,

James Woodress highlights Hemingway's attack within his discussion of male critics who "did not read carefully to see that Cather had no illusions about the war" (326). Book-length studies of Cather by Susan J. Rosowski, Hermione Lee, Joseph Urgo, Guy Reynolds, and Janis Stout also cite Hemingway's remarks.[1] And in articles specifically focused on *One of Ours*, Hemingway's contemptuous assessment remains a popular source of indignation: it appears, sometimes quoted in full, in nine of the fourteen critical essays published on *One of Ours* since 1980 (including, I should point out, my own essay devoted to that novel).[2] In short, among admirers of Willa Cather, that "poor woman [who] had to get her war experience somewhere," Hemingway has much to answer for.

Unfortunately, the attention lavished upon Hemingway's attack on *One of Ours* has only rarely led to deeper, more sustained comparisons of these two major American authors, both of whom arguably produced their best work in the 1920s, and both of whom were profoundly affected by the First World War.[3] Glen A. Love's masterful 1990 essay, "*The Professor's House*: Cather, Hemingway, and the Chastening of American Prose Style," remains virtually alone in its side-by-side treatment of the two writers; few scholars of American literature have followed its lead. At first sight, the reasons for this scholarly indifference seem obvious. Separated by age and gender, markedly dissimilar life experiences, and (at least on the surface) sharply contrasting artistic sensibilities, Hemingway and Cather never met, never corresponded, and never acknowledged even the slightest technical or thematic kinship. Indeed, neither artist apparently found the other particularly interesting. Michael Reynolds's *Hemingway's Reading* places only two Cather volumes, along with *One of Ours*, in Hemingway's library, and there is no evidence that Hemingway read them. As indicated on the publisher's bill, Pauline Pfieffer, Hemingway's second wife, ordered the copy of *A Lost Lady* that became part the Hemingway family's book collection in the late 1930s, and she may also have been responsible for the copy of *Shadows on the Rock* that remained in the couple's Key West home after Hemingway packed for Cuba in 1940. Moreover, Hemingway's correspondence contains only one other noteworthy reference to a Cather novel. In November 1923, just a few days after blasting *One of Ours*, Hemingway did some Catherizing of his own when, in a letter to Gertrude Stein, he facetiously referred to the transatlantic liner *Antonia*, on which he and his family had just booked their passage to Europe, as *My Ántonia* (Baker 119). Whether Hemingway had read *My Ántonia* is unclear. And so is the meaning of his joke. Is the title intended as a compliment? An expression of contempt? Or neither—simply an innocent play on words?

The record of Cather's responses to Hemingway is similarly inconclusive. In 1932 she praised *Death in the Afternoon*, the only Hemingway title she is known to have read, when recommending the book in a letter to Mabel Dodge Luhan (Stout, *Calendar* 169). Yet Cather's perceptions of Hemingway's work, and the currents in American culture with which it had become identified, were not always so transparent. A more ambiguous response to Hemingway appears in one of her letters to Ferris Greenslet, her former editor at Houghton Mifflin. Approached in 1936 by the English artist Stephen Tennant to help place a volume of erotic drawings with a reputable American publisher, a task she knew to be hopeless, Cather turned to Greenslet for assistance in explaining to Tennant the mysteries of American morality. As Woodress paraphrases, "She found it hard to explain why Americans were indecent in some things and drew the line at others. She thought Americans wanted Hemingway and the four-letter words but without any perfume" (467). Hardly an advocate of verisimilitude carried to the point of crudity, Cather perhaps intended this passing reference to Hemingway as something of a jab. Or perhaps not. Although "four-letter words" never appear in her own work (much to the detriment of *One of Ours*, where a good dose of profanity might have improved the novel's implausible rendering of soldier's speech), Cather was not a prude. Nor did she advocate the kind of reactionary censorship to which Hemingway fell victim in 1929, when authorities in Boston intercepted and impounded the serialized version of *A Farewell to Arms* contained in *Scribner's*. Like Hemingway's scattered references to Cather, Cather's remarks on the younger writer simply do not add up to a consistent attitude or judgment.

Thus, for critics interested primarily in literary influences or the interplay of artistic personalities, the Hemingway-Cather connection—or rather disconnection—has little to recommend it and seems to lead nowhere. However, for scholars seeking to understand the impact of World War I on American literature of the 1920s, there is, I contend, a great deal to gain by considering these two writers together. Although Hemingway may have loathed *One of Ours*, by 1925 Cather's vision of the war to end all wars had essentially come to resemble his own: by suggesting that four years of unprecedented carnage and destruction had hopelessly fractured modern history and crippled the means by which traditional narratives interpreted the past, Cather's novel *The Professor's House* uncannily dealt with many of the same themes as Hemingway's short-story collection *In Our Time*, published the same year. Moreover, as Love has demonstrated, by the mid-1920s Hemingway and Cather were in general agreement (though perhaps without knowing so)[4] regarding the aesthetics of serious fiction: both produced narratives rich in suggestive nuances and implied meanings (while maintaining an appearance of directness and transparency that separated their work from that of high modernists such as Joyce or Woolf); both experimented with the intentional removal of important information from the text—what Susan Beegel has called, in regard to Hemingway, a "craft of omission." Indeed, Hemingway's famous description of his writing as an iceberg with nine-tenths of the meaning concealed below the surface, invisible to all but the most astute reader, sounds curiously like Cather's emphasis, established in her 1923 essay "The Novel Démeublé," on the crucial importance of "the thing not named." Thus, if we set aside Hemingway's infamous critique of *One of Ours* and look beyond the profound experiential and temperamental differences that separate these writers, the two emerge as fellow modernists who reached many of the same conclusions about World War I and whose methods of storytelling proceeded from similar assumptions about the nature of their craft. As I will demonstrate through a comparison of two of their finest works of the

1920s, these two literary icons are hardly antithetical in either their choice of subject or their technique.

Hemingway's *In Our Time* and Cather's *The Professor's House* stand out from other literary responses to World War I through, among other things, the subtlety with which they evoke the conflict as a central subject. Shared aesthetic values—articulated first by Cather, then by Hemingway—account for this subtlety.[5] In "The Novel Démeublé" (composed, ironically enough, while she worked on *One of Ours*, a book that many readers regard as unnecessarily lengthy or "over-furnished"), Cather expressed impatience with the "mere verisimilitude" (40) achieved by authors, such as Sinclair Lewis, who cluttered their texts with lengthy descriptions of physical settings and cultural milieus. "High quality" in fiction, she insisted, stems less from what an author states than from what is left unsaid—from "the inexplicable presence of the thing not named" (41). In other words, the fictional world that mattered most to Cather was not the one that a writer builds, block by block, through the actual content of the narrative, but the one that a reader creates by *engaging* with the text, by responding to the work's "mood" or "emotional aura," as opposed to the mere *things* it describes, and then actively filling in what an author has omitted or only obliquely suggested (41).

Hemingway offered no such manifesto; even his oft-cited description of his work as an iceberg is fairly brief and lacks the theoretical complexity of Cather's arguments. However, when Hemingway looked back on his early career decades later in *A Moveable Feast*, his posthumously published memoir of Paris in the 1920s, he recounted the development of his craft along lines strikingly similar to Cather's. Consider, for example, the process of unfurnishing that Hemingway describes in his account of writing "Out of Season," one of the stories in *In Our Time*. In paradoxical language reminiscent of "The Novel Démeublé," Hemingway explained that he had removed the "real end" of the story—in which Peduzzi, the drunken fishing guide, commits suicide—based on the "new theory that you could omit anything if you knew that you omitted [it] and the omitted part would strengthen the story and make people feel something more than they understood" (75). *Make people feel something more than they understood*—here Hemingway sounds very much like Cather by describing, in his own way, the elevation of an "emotional aura" above "mere verisimilitude." At the same time, his remarkable reference to the absent suicide as the "real ending" places the artistic truth of his story beyond the actual words on the page. What is "real" and important in "Out of Season," or any other Hemingway work for that matter, exists only as a kind of phantom signature or shadowy trace—in other words, as "the thing not named."[6]

Hemingway's and Cather's aesthetics of absence and indirection play out on a grand scale in *In Our Time* and *The Professor's House*, where each writer establishes the overwhelming and terrifying significance of the Great War by, paradoxically, refusing to address that significance head-on. In both texts, the horror of a global conflagration that claimed eight million lives (and prepared the way for a global pandemic that claimed twenty-one million more) is simply a given. By moving the war out of direct sight—into the lower mass of the iceberg, if you will, or into the shadowy subtext implied by Cather's phrase "the thing not named"—these works imply that the defining event of early-twentieth-century history is too monstrous, too nihilistic in its implications, to be faced directly.

In *In Our Time*, Hemingway locates the experience of war at the very center of his age, an age characterized by discord and inhumanity. Yet with the exception of a few brief, vivid glimpses of the front line—these include the snapshot images of German soldiers "potted" while climbing over a barricade at Mons, drunken French soldiers on their way to another bloodbath, and Nick Adams lying critically wounded somewhere on the Italian front—the war enters the text primarily through its effects. We do not see the battles that blasted the protagonist of "Soldier's Home" out of "God's kingdom," out of the cultural frame where he once contentedly posed among a phalanx of fraternity brothers. By the same token, the traumatic events that prompt Nick Adams to seek refuge in the rituals of fishing and backpacking remain, apart from that quick glimpse of the Italian front, submerged within the text. In short, although the neomasculine "Papa" might not appreciate a description of his work drawn from an essay by a "poor woman" who lacked direct war experience, Cather's musings on "the thing not named" in "The Novel Démeublé" fit the dynamics of Hemingway's text with surprising accuracy: for much of *In Our Time*, World War I is indeed "felt upon the page without being named there"; it is "an overtone divined by the ear but not heard by it" (41). Only upon a second or third reading does the war's often nearly invisible ubiquity begin to stand out. Throughout the volume, scattered details foreshadow or echo the cataclysm—the "old ruin" that Nick and Majorie row past in "The End of Something"; the threadbare "military coat" that Peduzzi, apparently a down-and-out veteran of the Italian theater, wears in "Out of Season"; the ominous "war monument" that faces the couple's hotel room in "Cat in the Rain"; the Argonne Forest–like stretch of burnt timber that Nick crosses in "Big Two-Hearted River." Even the titles of stories set in prewar Michigan seem ominously, if indirectly, anticipatory of Nick Adams's war experience: "Indian *Camp*" (emphasis mine), "The End of Something," "The Three-Day Blow," "The Battler." Camps, endings, blows, and battles—World War I reaches into virtually every corner of Hemingway's text, albeit in an often ghostly and half-perceptible fashion.

The conflict Hemingway obliquely signifies throughout his collection of stories and vignettes plays a similarly central—and similarly phantomlike—role in *The Professor's House*, especially in the novel's complex treatment of historical epistemology. In his influential essay "*The Professor's House* and the Issues of History," David Stouck confines the significance of the Great War in Cather's narrative primarily to Outland's tragic metamorphosis from a romantic archaeologist who interprets humanity as part of nature to an industrial researcher who seeks domination, via technological "progress," over his environment. For Stouck, Outland's death on the western front, a gaseous inferno created through the very science that Outland venerates, is a fitting end for a young man who forsakes the mesa, with its fusion of people and place, for a vacuous modernity bent on separating the two: "When Tom takes his place in the modern world he becomes a scientist; he develops a theory of space that leads to the invention of the Outland engine. Then he is killed in a war that is the product of modern technology and dubious morality" (209).

Yet the conflict that destroys St. Peter's star student figures in a great deal more of the novel than Stouck's reading suggests. For example, the paucity of references to St. Peter's post-1915 scholarship—to *anything*, in fact, beyond his hobbylike editing of the Outland archaeological journal, a book that no one seems likely to read (or even publish)—implies that St. Peter's commitment to historical research has died, along with his protégé, in the trenches of Flanders. In this way, Cather registers, albeit indirectly, the sense of disenchantment and lassitude felt by many European and North American historians in the wake of a conflict whose immense scale, pervasive irrationality, and sheer monstrousness appeared to defy an orderly reconstruction. Moreover, through the mutual hostility that she establishes between St. Peter and his archrival, Horace Langtry, Cather addresses an intellectual fissure, one widened by four years of unthinkable slaughter, whose destabilizing effects reached into many American history departments in the early twentieth century—namely, the growing division between historians who aspired, as St. Peter does, to recover *the* truth about the past and those, such as Langtry, who viewed history as an infinite set of arbitrary constructs. Although Langtry's willingness to accept a report on *Tom Sawyer* as historical research on the Missouri Compromise is consistent with his shameless pandering to students, his academic shenanigans also point to a theoretical posture at odds with St. Peter's more traditional sense of his calling. By flippantly equating the version of truth offered by works of fiction with that provided through a historian's painstaking, albeit subjective, examination of verifiable sources, Langtry is essentially deconstructing his own discipline. As Peter Novick observes in his study of the "objectivity question" and American history departments, antifoundational notions of history appeared on American campuses well before 1914; however, the vast cultural and epistemological upheaval connected with World War I was critical to their proliferation. In short, then, the war does far more in Cather's text than kill off St. Peter's protégé. A historical conundrum, seemingly defying explanation or reconstruction, the war haunts St. Peter both personally and professionally, undermining his passion for research while reinforcing the postmodern trends within his discipline.[7]

The one passage in *The Professor's House* where St. Peter's thoughts turn directly to the war signals the conflict's importance on several additional levels. While musing over his lost opportunity to visit Paris in Outland's company, a scheme interrupted by the German invasion of Belgium, the professor visualizes the Delacroix monument in the Luxembourg Gardens and offers a terse but shattering assessment of how the war to end all wars has, in actuality, all but ended Western civilization: "He had wanted . . . to stand with [Outland] before the monument to Delacroix and watch the sun gleam on the bronze figures—Time, bearing away the youth who was struggling to snatch his palm—or was it to lay a palm? Not that it mattered. It might have mattered to Tom, had not chance, in one great catastrophe, swept away all youth and all palms, and almost Time itself" (261). In just a few brief phrases, Cather's world-weary protagonist consigns to oblivion an entire generation ("all youth"), Western notions of honor and courage (suggested by "palms"), and any sense of stability or authority within the discipline of history ("Time itself"). Moreover, he attributes the origins of this "catastrophe" not to historical forces that can be understood in terms of cause and effect, but to random "chance." As this chilling passage intimates, the Great War has left the professor's cultured view of the past, and of the civilization to which he contributes through his scholarly writings, as shattered and barren as the shell-churned battlefields of the western front.

At the same time, Cather's reference to the war nearly sweeping away "Time itself" seems closely tied to the growing sense of temporal dislocation that we see in St. Peter. How Cather's historian lives within time is a central concern in the novel. For most of his fifty-two years, St. Peter has moved through life in a predominantly linear and straightforwardly sequential fashion. The "Kansas boy" becomes a sophisticated and cosmopolitan adult. From an apparently contented bachelorhood, St. Peter slips into an equally contented marriage, then fatherhood. His career follows an orderly progression as well. Although a professional student of the past, he has existed largely in the present and the future, absorbed in his writing and research, in production as opposed to retrospection. One volume of his magnum opus follows upon another—almost, one might say, like clockwork.

By the opening of *The Professor's House*, however, St. Peter's internal clock has, if you will, begun to run backwards—a psychological phenomenon intimately tied up with the death of Tom Outland and, by extension, the "great catastrophe" in which he is destroyed. This backward thrust in St. Peter's consciousness begins, innocently enough, with his unwillingness to relinquish his uncomfortable and, it turns out, all-but-lethally-unventilated study. By the end of the novel, however, the implications of the professor's retreat into the past have become more sinister: disengaged from his wife and daughters, who live voraciously in the present, he slips backwards into his preadolescent, "primitive" self, then drifts toward the extinction of all consciousness, coming dangerously close to joining his lost student in the outland of the dead. Fittingly, St. Peter's near suicide at the end of the novel, the culmination of his psychological and temporal retreat from the postwar age, evokes World War I in a manner similar to Hemingway's oblique methods in *In Our Time*. Stupefied by "gas," a word whose connotations in the context of World War I require little comment, St. Peter becomes half conscious of the storm that rages outside his attic room—of the "the wind increasing in *violence*" and "things *banging* and *slamming* about" (276, emphasis mine). At the moment in the narrative when St. Peter comes closest to death, Cather uses imagery redolent of combat and bombardment to establish further World War I as "the thing not named."

The notoriously broken-backed design of *The Professor's House*, with its disconcertingly expansive account of "Tom Outland's Story" and staccato-like conclusion, works hand in hand with half-obscured textual details in conveying the violent impact of the war on St. Peter's psyche, an impact analogous to that of the "black" thunderhead that slams into his Victorian foursquare in the scene mentioned above (276). Indeed, it seems hardly coincidental that Cather reserves her most radical departure from conventional novelistic form for a book that focuses on a professional historian, a character who is—or at least *was*—a craftsman of linear plot lines. Mirroring the protagonist's paralyzing indifference to the present, to the postwar, to life without his star student, the narrative plunges us backwards into "Tom Outland's Story"—into the comparatively romantic and promise-filled setting of the American Southwest years before Father Duchene whisks Outland off to Flanders Fields. In other words, the novel's disjointed form, its jarring shift from Hamilton in the early 1920s to New Mexico in the early 1910s and then back again, reflects the way that the Great War has, like a bayonet blade, sliced time into two irrevocably sundered phases—the pre- and the postwar. As much a victim of the conflict as his protégé, whose death St. Peter sometimes regards with envy, Cather's historian lives in a temporal universe that has indeed broken in two. And, to add to the professor's personal and professional disorientation, the event located at the point of breakage between the prewar and the postwar defies historical understanding or recovery; a black hole into which "Time itself" has collapsed, along with "all youth" and "all plumes," the horrors of 1914 to 1918 stand as the ultimate vacuum in a text filled with wastes and nullities.

In much the same way as Cather's novel, Hemingway's *In Our Time* moves through space and time with alarming abruptness and relegates the Great War (at least explicitly) to a series of terse and cryptic vignettes that, much like St. Peter's equally terse and cryptic reference to the "great catastrophe," underscore the conflict's terrifying resistance to nineteenth-century rationalist conceptions of historical logic or causality. If *The Professor's House* is about a historian traumatized by the Great War, then Hemingway's book reads like the kind of demented antinarrative that such a historian might write. Indeed, the text seems metaphorically shell shocked. Here the epistemological center of St. Peter's prewar world, within which the professor confidently produced one linear and rational work of historical exegesis after another, truly no longer holds. Perceptual anarchy has been unleashed within the text, a point that quickly becomes clear when we contrast Hemingway's title, with its calm assurance of a definable subject, with the cubist jumble that follows. The volume is called *In Our Time*, but what exactly, we might ask, is *our time*? At every turn, the text problematizes its self-declared subject. For example, among the first five Nick Adams stories, which seem to follow a linear chronological order, Hemingway intersperses vignettes inexplicably narrated by Europeans and set amid the battles of the western and Italian fronts, events still distant from Nick's early adventures in Upper Michigan. *Whose* time, we wonder, is the focus here? And which time—the prewar or the wartime—is the narrative's chief concern?

In the second half of the book, from "Soldier's Home" onward, this scrambling of chronology seems largely absent. Violent shifts in voice and place still occur, but the vignettes, which deal mostly with bullfighting, now *appear* to be contemporaneous with the short stories they introduce (almost as if Hemingway wished to be inconsistent even in his use of inconsistency). Nevertheless, while generations of Hemingway scholars have posited one formalist interpretation of *In Our Time* after another, each attempting to tie the book's disparate elements into a cohesive artistic whole, the volume remains defiantly *un*interpretable, a seeming mishmash of fragmentary micro-texts that never quite form into a coherent mosaic. This is, it seems to me, precisely the point that Hemingway ultimately makes about *our* time: a universe that accommodates the horrors of a world war simply no longer makes sense; thus, its representation in a conventional narrative form is, at least according to the most avant-garde and openly modernist of Hemingway's works, an impossibility. Far from offering a lucid artistic vision of early-twentieth-century history, Hemingway's text demonstrates that in the aftermath of "the great catastrophe," events are no longer recoverable as part of a coherent, linear progression. World War I, brief glimpses of which rip through Hemingway's text like shrapnel, has blown "Time itself" to pieces.

My main argument has been quite simply that *The Professor's House* and *In Our Time*, both of which appeared in 1925, share a number of salient features. In both books, direct discussion of the Great War is relegated to mere snippets of text—that is, St. Peter's sentence-long rumination on "the great catastrophe," a passage that many first-time readers of *The Professor's House* may miss entirely, and the five snapshot-like sketches of combat, each containing approximately one hundred words, that Hemingway scatters parenthetically amid Nick Adams's prewar experiences in Michigan. At the same time, however, the world-shattering significance of the war seeps outward from these terse passages and, in a fashion at once palpable and vaporous, extends its phantomlike reach to the violent imagery, fragmentary structure, and overall sense of temporal dislocation that characterize both works. What larger conclusions, then, can we draw from this admittedly unorthodox pairing of writers? What do the similarities between *The Professor's House* and *In Our Time* offer us in terms of a new interpretive platform from which to explore one of Cather's most intensely analyzed works? And how much further does the artistic kinship between "Papa" and the "poor woman" extend?

Thorough and detailed answers to these questions fall beyond the scope of this essay. Nevertheless, I will offer, by way of conclusion, a tentative road map for the rich interpretive territory—or, if you prefer, "the last good country"—that a more extended comparison of these two writers could open for us. To begin with, the notion that Cather, who was forty-five years old in 1918, shared little in common with members of the so-called lost generation, a notion reinforced by the abundance of scholarship focused on Cather and Edith Wharton (as opposed to, say, Cather and Djuna Barnes or John Dos Passos), requires revision in the light of the thematic and structural similarities that link *The Professor's House* and *In Our Time*. Like her professor, Cather did feel increasingly distant from Americans who came of age in the 1910s or 1920s. Indeed, her attitude in this regard hardened. In 1936 she famously claimed to welcome only readers who were "not under forty." However, if I am correct in interpreting *The Professor's House* as a modernist response to war that enacts the same epistemological breakdown dramatized in Hemingway's short-story collection, then a host of opportunities for additional comparative analysis come into view. When approached as a work of World War I literature, *The Professor's House* suddenly resembles not only Hemingway's *In Our Time* but also Virginia Woolf's *To the Lighthouse*, with its similarly parenthetical treatment of "the great catastrophe," and John Dos Passos's *1919*, whose medley of first- and third-person narratives, combined with capsule biographies of American leaders and snippets of newspaper headlines and popular song lyrics, carries to a high-modernist extreme Cather's own experiment with the juxtaposition of disparate blocks of text. Cather sought out relatively few members of the lost generation, and despite her occasional forays into public lecturing (at Bread Loaf and elsewhere) and numerous acts of kindness to younger writers, she did not relish the role of mentor. For the most part, she left the cultivation of new talent to others—to Sherwood Anderson, who helped launch Hemingway's career (as well as Faulkner's), and to Gertrude Stein. Yet as demonstrated in *The Professor's House*, Cather's artistic vision of World War I was as dark and bitter, and as defiantly modernist, as anything recorded in the works of writers twenty to thirty years her junior. The work of situating her 1925 novel among the canonical texts of the Great War, a task likely to yield further insights into the nature of Cather's modernism, still awaits us.

So too does a more thorough exploration of the thematic affinities shared by Cather and Hemingway—affinities that extend, I believe, well beyond the two works we have considered. As a creator of memorably unconventional male characters, many of whom are tormented (or simply destroyed) by their culture's definition of manliness, Cather would have had little sympathy for the neomasculine Hemingway code hero, whose toughness, superhuman alcoholic capacity, and laconic speech all stand in direct antithesis to the sensitivity, sensual restraint, and verbal yearning of Jim Burden, Claude Wheeler, and Tom Outland. Yet the existential void—or vacuum—that Jake Barnes and Frederic Henry face, while wearing their protective masculine armor, is not so far removed from the dark reality that often breaks through the surface of Cather's deceptively sunlit fiction—a reality of death and inevitable decline, of chaos and oblivion.

Indeed, Cather's work is filled with moments when a fathomless abyss of Hemingway-esque nada suddenly opens up within the narrative. One such moment, for example, occurs in *Death Comes for the Archbishop* when Latour presses his ear to the floor of Jacinto's mysterious cavern and, in a rare instance of fear, senses an unnameable horror that exists beyond the understanding of his Christian faith. "It is terrible," he tells his guide (218).[8] By the same token, in *Shadows on the Rock*, Cécile's disastrous visit to the island reveals, as Susan J. Rosowski observes, a degree of darkness and disorder in her world that she has never before suspected (Rosowski 218). The experience sends Cécile running back to her clean, well-lighted place on the rock. And then there is the moment in *Sapphira and the Slave Girl* when Sapphira's orderly universe, with its seemingly indestructible foundation of racial prestige and power, is suddenly knocked out of kilter: momentarily filled with paranoid anxieties, Sapphira sees her dwelling as a "shattered, treacherous house," as part of "a dream of disaster" (106–7).

Of course, Cather's characters respond to this ever-threatening nada in a quite different fashion from Hemingway's. While Jake Barnes, a lapsed Catholic, braces himself against cosmic meaninglessness by wearing a stiff upper lip and ordering another drink, Latour vows never to enter a cavern again. Through an assertion of will—part courage, part denial—he chooses to remain within the structures of his faith. Similarly, Cécile finds refuge from the outer horror of the Canadian wilderness not in alcohol or sex (the primary sanctuaries offered Hemingway's young women) but in the meticulous rituals of fine French housekeeping. And Sapphira, whose imperious nature is both admirable and frightening, staves off her "dream of disaster" by seizing a tangible symbol of her aggressively asserted identity—the "clapper bell" with which she summons slaves. Nevertheless, although Cather's characters make different choices than Hemingway's, within texts that often accommodate spirituality and affirmation, both writers periodically acknowledge the same existential dilemma: how to live in a world without absolute meaning, a world broken in two. Further comparison of these two literary icons promises to open new pathways into Cather's textual universe, a place perhaps not so distant from Upper Michigan, wartime Italy, or the Caribbean waters plied by the fisherman Santiago.

NOTES

1. See Rosowski; Lee; Urgo; Reynolds; and Stout, *Willa Cather: The Writer and Her World*.

2. References to Hemingway's indictment of *One of Ours* appear in Boxwell; Gelfant; Griffiths; McComas; O'Brien; Ryan; Schwind; Trout, "Cather's *One of Ours*"; and Yongue.

3. To date only two articles have considered *One of Ours* alongside the work of Hemingway and other male writers of World War I: Miller and Rohrkemper.

4. Throughout this article I have steered clear of the problematic question of influence. Love contends that Hemingway might have actually borrowed Cather's conception of "the thing not named" as the basis for his own theory of artistic omission (307). However, since there is no direct evidence that Hemingway ever read "The Novel Démeublé" or that he ever discussed "the thing not named" with F. Scott Fitzgerald (although this seems likely enough), I have approached Hemingway and Cather as modernists who developed along parallel lines, without any influence *necessarily* operating between them.

5. Throughout this paragraph I am indebted to Love's "*The Professor's House*: Cather, Hemingway, and the Chastening of American Prose Style." Love is, to my knowledge, the first critic to recognize the remarkable similarities between Cather's conception of "the thing not named" and Hemingway's iceberg theory.

6. Julian Smith offers a succinct and groundbreaking analysis of Hemingway's editorial omissions in "Hemingway and the Thing Left Out." Note how the title perhaps unintentionally echoes Cather's "the thing not named." For additional discussion of Hemingway's Cather-like emphasis on the unstated, see Beegel and Stewart.

7. For a more detailed discussion of St. Peter and postwar trends in American historiography, see my *Memorial Fictions* 155–63.

8. This scene recalls Nick Adams's similarly fearful reaction to the "swamp" in "Big Two-Hearted River." Both settings—the cavern and the swamp—threaten the protagonist's confidence and faith.

WORKS CITED

Baker, Carlos. *Ernest Hemingway: A Life Story*. New York: Scribner, 1969.

Beegel, Susan. *Hemingway's Craft of Omission: Four Manuscript Examples*. Ann Arbor: UMI Research P, 1988.

Boxwell, D. A. "In Formation; Male Homosexual Desire in Willa Cather's *One of Ours*." *Eroticism and Containment: Notes from the Flood Plain.* Ed. Carol Siegel and Ann Kibbey. New York: New York UP, 1994. 285–310.

Cather, Willa. *Death Comes for the Archbishop.* 1927. Willa Cather Scholarly Edition. Ed. Charles W. Mignon with Frederick M. Link and Kari A. Ronning. Historical essay and explanatory notes John J. Murphy. Lincoln: U of Nebraska P, 1999.

———. *Not Under Forty.* New York: Knopf, 1936.

———. "The Novel Démeublé." 1936. *Willa Cather on Writing: Critical Studies on Writing as an Art.* Lincoln: U of Nebraska P, 1988. 35–43.

———. *One of Ours.* New York: Knopf, 1922.

———. *The Professor's House.* 1925. Willa Cather Scholarly Edition. Ed. Frederick M. Link. Historical essay James Woodress. Explanatory notes James Woodress with Kari A. Ronning. Lincoln: U of Nebraska P, 2002.

———. *Sapphira and the Slave Girl.* New York: Knopf, 1940.

———. *Shadows on the Rock.* New York: Knopf, 1931.

Cummings, E. E. *The Enormous Room.* 1922. New York: Liveright, 1978.

Dos Passos, John. *1919.* New York: Harcourt, 1932.

Gelfant, Blanche H. "'What Was It . . . ?' The Secret of Family Accord in *One of Ours*." *Willa Cather: Family, Community, and History.* Ed. John J. Murphy, Linda Hunter Adams, and Paul Rawlins. Provo: Brigham Young U Humanities, 1990. 85–102.

Griffiths, Frederick T. "The Woman Warrior: Willa Cather and *One of Ours*." *Women's Studies* 2 (1984): 261–85.

Hemingway, Ernest. *Death in the Afternoon.* New York: Scribners, 1932.

———. *Ernest Hemingway: Selected Letters, 1917–1961.* Ed. Carlos Baker. New York: Scribner, 1981.

———. *In Our Time.* 1925. New York: Simon, 1996.

———. *A Moveable Feast.* 1964. New York: Simon, 1996.

———. *The Sun Also Rises.* New York: Scribner's, 1926.

Lee, Hermione. *Willa Cather: Double Lives.* New York: Vintage, 1989.

Love, Glen A. "*The Professor's House*: Cather, Hemingway, and the Chastening of American Prose Style." *Western American Literature* 24.4 (1990): 295–311.

McComas, Dix. "Willa Cather's *One of Ours*: In Distant Effigy." *Legacy* 14.2 (1997): 93–109.

Miller, Paul W. "Anti-Heroic Theme and Structure in Midwestern World War I Novels from Cather to Hemingway." *Midamerica* 23 (1996): 99–108.

Novick, Peter. *That Noble Dream: The "Objectivity Question" and the American Historical Profession*. Cambridge: Cambridge UP, 1988.

O'Brien, Sharon. "Combat Envy and Survivor Guilt: Willa Cather's 'Manly Battle Yarn.'" *Arms and the Woman: War, Gender, and Literary Representation*. Ed. Helen M. Cooper, Adrienne Auslander Munich, and Susan Merrill Squier. Chapel Hill: U of North Carolina P, 1989. 184–204.

Reynolds, Guy. *Willa Cather in Context: Progress, Race, Empire*. New York: St. Martin's, 1996.

Reynolds, Michael. *Hemingway's Reading, 1910–1940*. Princeton: Princeton UP, 1981.

Rohrkemper, John. "The Great War, the Midwest, and Modernism: Cather, Dos Passos, and Hemingway." *Midwestern Miscellany* 16 (1988): 19–29.

Rosowski, Susan J. *The Voyage Perilous: Willa Cather's Romanticism*. Lincoln: U of Nebraska P, 1986.

Ryan, Maureen. "No Woman's Land: Gender in Willa Cather's *One of Ours*." *Studies in American Fiction* 18.1 (1990): 65–76.

Schwind, Jean. "The 'Beautiful' War in *One of Ours*." *Modern Fiction Studies* 30.1 (1984): 53–71.

Smith, Julian. "Hemingway and the Thing Left Out." *Ernest Hemingway: Five Decades of Criticism*. Ed. Linda Welshimer Wagner. Ann Arbor: Michigan State UP, 1974. 188–200.

Stewart, Matthew. *Modernism and Tradition in Ernest Hemingway's "In Our Time."* New York: Camden, 2001.

Stouck, David. "*The Professor's House* and the Issues of History." *Willa Cather: Family, Community, and History*. Ed. John J. Murphy, Linda Hunter Adams, and Paul Rawlins. Provo UT: Brigham Young U Humanities, 1990. 201–11.

Stout, Janis P., ed. *A Calendar of the Letters of Willa Cather*. Lincoln: U of Nebraska P, 2002.

———. *Willa Cather: The Writer and Her World*. Charlottesville: UP of Virginia, 2000.

Trout, Steven. *Memorial Fictions: Willa Cather and the First World War*. Lincoln: U of Nebraska P, 2002.

———. "Willa Cather's *One of Ours* and the Iconography of Remembrance." *Cather Studies 4: Willa Cather's Canadian and Old World Connections*. Ed. Robert Thacker and Michael A. Peterman. Lincoln: U of Nebraska P, 1999. 187–204.

Urgo, Joseph. *Willa Cather and the Myth of American Migration.* Urbana: U of Illinois P, 1995.

Woodress, James. *Willa Cather: A Literary Life.* Lincoln: U of Nebraska P, 1987.

Woolf, Virginia. *To the Lighthouse.* San Diego: Harcourt, 1927.

Yongue, Patricia Lee. "For Better and for Worse: At Home and War in *One of Ours.*" *Willa Cather: Family, Community, and History.* Ed. John J. Murphy, Linda Hunter Adams, and Paul Rawlins. Provo UT: Brigham Young U Humanities, 1990. 141–53.

Icons and Willa Cather

MERRILL MAGUIRE SKAGGS

I remain skeptical about the political tactic of calling any deeply admired or complex figure an icon. Icons, by definition, are easily recognized by simple people, are quickly replaced by fresher icons, and are magnetic to iconoclasts. Further, Cather's now-well-known habit of reversing elements in her work from one book or scene to the next seems her way of keeping herself a moving target. She herself bragged anonymously, as David H. Porter has shown, "One thing is certain—she will not repeat herself. There will never be a stereotyped Cather heroine or hero" (Porter 58). Normally, Cather will not sit still in any sense, as a stable icon should, but moves fast through juxtaposed works, with attendant surprises and innovations.

Nevertheless, I believe that at the end of her life Cather *did* begin to feel like an icon—visible, venerated, and vulnerable. At that point she was willing to behave like a good cultural icon, too. She thus prepared her final volume of fiction to sound as the work of a proper icon should: it would make clear statements and render usable summaries. She planned for it to appear as her last book, and she had it ready for the faithful A. A. Knopf to publish posthumously when she died, as he did. That a plan unfolds here is evident, I think, when Knopf, so careful to follow Cather's wishes to the letter, swiftly followed *The Old Beauty* (1948) with *Willa Cather on Writing* (1949); they are meant to be connected.

The best circumstantial evidence for this connection can be viewed in any collection preserving first editions with their book jackets on.[1] The book jackets of both of Cather's collections of essays—*Not Under Forty* (1936) and *Willa Cather on Writing*—exactly duplicate the jacket for *The Old Beauty* except for color or shade. Thus the book jackets make a visual point: the nonfiction statements and the fictional statements are closely related. Specifically, the story "The Old Beauty" is related to "A Chance Meeting," Cather's sketch about getting to know Flaubert's iconic niece Caro, in the lady's old age. The Faulkner references in "Before Breakfast"[2] are related to Faulkner's name inserted, after all Cather's resolutions not to comment on living writers—and after a stressed date for emphasis—in the addendum to her essay "148 Charles Street" (Skaggs, "Cather's War" 50). That essay, too, is collected in *Not Under Forty*. "The Best Years," the last story Cather wrote, relates to her essay on Katherine Mansfield. In the tribute to Mansfield, Cather refers to a writer's choice to use a nom de plume or a name not quite her birth name, to use the writer's family, Mansfield's alert delight in things around her, her definitions of home, and her waning vitality. Significantly, "Katherine Mansfield" reminds us that "The qualities of a second-rate writer can easily be defined, but a first-rate writer can only be experienced" (*Stories* 877). "Katherine Mansfield" is included in both essay collections, for emphasis, not only on writers generally, but on such autobiographical stories relating to writers as "The Best Years."

In the first story of her final collection, "The Old Beauty," Cather subtly and negatively comments on three of her contemporary American female fiction-writing competitors: Kate Chopin, Edith Wharton, and Ellen Glasgow. She shares with them, she concedes, the wry recognition that even world-recognized, iconic faces fade and die in the end, just like everybody else. But there, her comtpanion piece "A Chance Meeting" establishes, the comparison between herself and those three women writers ends. The contrast reveals Cather approaching a commanding old lady from different points of view, from different gender perspectives, from different degrees of connection and of displacement from home, and in different moods or attitudes. Cather shows her attentive readers that she can tell a tale from any angle, to make any point.

Cather focuses on her own work in the story she places second, though she wrote it last of the three. "The Best Years" serves as a bridge between her negative allusions in the first tale and her basically positive ones in the last. She is perhaps most positive, however, about herself. She carefully weaves into "The Best Years" a phrase, image, or keepsake from each of her twelve novels and from the three great short stories of *Obscure Destinies*. Thus she embraces her own great work but concludes that we find out, too late, that "our best years are when we're working hardest and going right ahead when we can hardly see our way out" (*Stories* 756). Then, with the regal composure of an icon doing justice, Cather ends her last volume by saluting the young ones with grit: especially she acknowledges William Faulkner, who she shrewdly guesses will dominate the future's next phase.

We turn now to look more closely at these three final stories. Since we know that Cather wrote "The Best Years" for her brother Roscoe in the last two years of her life (Woodress 500), although his death preceded her giving it to him, we can pinpoint the planning period for this last volume and see Cather deliberately wrapping up her life. The first thing that strikes us about the whole book is its summarizing tone. After the stunning technical experiments and massive destabilizations of *Sapphira and the Slave Girl*, this volume sits still. Even when looking forward, it looks backward as if with Henry Grenfell's dry eyes. Yet the moving pen here is still held by Willa Cather, and the stories repay with their density all the attention an alert reader can bring.

"The Old Beauty," for example, suggests that some feminist and queer studies critics have stopped reading too quickly. They have inaccurately surmised that Cather never dealt openly with lesbianism. She *did* eventually decide to save the subject for her last volume, perhaps to save herself the stress of facing the flack. But Woodress tell us that she initially wrote the story to be published immediately, withdrawing it only after the editor of *Woman's Home Companion* disliked it. Cather, conversely, continued to be especially fond of it and regarded it with pleasure. According to Lewis's account, "She put it aside for inclusion in a book of short stories, if she should publish one later. She herself thought highly of 'The Old Beauty.' She had found it interesting to write, and she felt that she had carried through her idea successfully" (Woodress 475). After writing the story at about the same time in 1936, she prepared the manuscript for her essay collection *Not Under Forty*, including for easy comparisons "A Chance Meeting."

In any case, "The Old Beauty" includes two lesbian couples. Gabrielle Longstreet and Cherry Beamish are the admirable focal characters. The two women who actually cause the accident that precipitates Gabrielle's death, named Jim and Marge, are briefly glimpsed negative caricatures. Initially, Cather had planned to publish the story in *Woman's Home Companion* so that her two versions of the tale would come out at about the same time, forcing this comparison.

"The Old Beauty" and "A Chance Meeting" tell differently the same essential story. The autobiographical sketch featuring Cather, speaking as herself, seems cheerful, wryly amused, and fondly deferent. The story is at best sardonic. The tale's sniffy tone, reminiscent of Myra Henshawe's "sniffy little nose" (*Stories* 561), fits the way Cather stretches out the sexual spectrum to teach a lesson to her rivals: more varieties of erotic energy can be imagined *and depicted* than are dreamt of in your published philosophies; your eros is too humdrum and small. The central lesbian couple here consists of two widows, both once-famous objects of admiration, though one liked boy toys, the other, husbands or suitors; their almost parodically gay male adorer is never a prospective lover of either. The combined story and sketch dramatize Cather's *deliberate choices* as she writes to achieve a main idea. Those choices involve tone, mood, characterizing details, driving purpose, and assumed fiction or ostensible fact.

In recognizing the women writers Cather brings to judgment in "The Old Beauty," we turn first to Ellen Glasgow. Gabrielle Longstreet's name itself invokes Virginia's other southern woman writer, whose career so closely paralleled Cather's. In 1912 Glasgow had published a novel entitled *Virginia*, which irritated Cather profoundly because it claimed the home state and the representative female character for that other writer, who would also eventually acknowledge she had written a "social history of Virginia," Cather's home territory (Skaggs, "Interlocking Works" 162). Those two literary offenses of Ellen Glasgow—that she claimed the name and the region—are intimated by the *Gabrielle* and the *Longstreet*. Glasgow's next novel, after *Virginia*, was published in 1916 and entitled *Life and Gabriella. Longstreet*, however, is the most representative southern regional name one could find, for it belonged to Civil War general and university president Augustus Baldwin Longstreet, who wrote *Georgia Scenes. Georgia Scenes* (1835) was the first fictional southern social history; Cather may be alluding to it in order to denigrate Glasgow's. Conveniently, Longstreet was buried in Oxford, Mississippi.

Gabrielle also has another name worth noticing, because her second husband was named De Coucy. The axiomatic motto of Enguerrand De Coucy, whose family is mentioned in *Brewer's British Royalty* (Williamson 16), is "*Roi je ne suis / Ni Prince, ni compte aussi. / Je suis le Sire de Coucy*" ("King I am not / Nor Prince, nor count. / I am the Sire de Coucy").[3] The allusion suggests the same arrogance Glasgow displayed for James Branch Cabell's amusement: "'Her shrewishness' wrote Cabell, in discussing her successful contemporaries was 'a never-failing well-spring of diverting malice; her remarks about Willa Cather were as unforgettable as they were unrepeatable'" (Skaggs, "Interlocking Works" 160). Cather, of course, strikes back here. She identifies her protagonist with a Glasgow-fingering name as a lady who "makes comments that are indecent, really" (*Stories* 714). Those comments are as arrogant as one would expect from a De Coucy.

Gabrielle Longstreet makes her abrasive remarks because she is now on the wrong half of a divide. Her world once broke in two as she was awakened to sexual facts she had not hitherto known. Also like Kate Chopin's Edna Pontellier in *The Awakening*, Cather's Gabrielle Longstreet has awakened from "a delicious, grotesque, impossible dream" (Chopin 32). Gabrielle's awakening occurs after Cather has referred to her *twice* as "unawakened" (*Stories* 702, 714). What awakens her, however, is a ghastly assault inside her own New York parlor, which is interrupted just in time by Henry Seabury, the character who provides our focal point of view (and who functions as the same kind of peephole Niel Herbert does in *A Lost Lady*). Having clipped Ellen Glasgow with Gabrielle's name, Cather seems also to remind Kate Chopin's readers here that horror can awaken a sleeping beauty as well as ecstasy can. It can change a beauty's style from "fresh" to arrogant, obscene, and judgmental. Cather seems to accuse Chopin of romantic naïveté.

It is the plot of Edith Wharton's "The Muse's Tragedy" (1900), however, that Cather reshapes in "The Old Beauty." While Wharton may be using her story to correct Henry James's *The Tragic Muse* (1890), Cather herself addresses the subject of world-recognized muses who are famous merely because "Great Protectors" have loved them.[4] In Wharton's offending story, a dead poet's muse-figure, now without male protectors, tests her waning powers on a younger male by provoking him to fall in love with her. Cather commented about such literary formulas and fashions as existed at the time she wrote her first novel: "The drawing-room was considered the proper setting for a novel, and the only characters worth reading about were smart people or clever people. . . . But Henry James and Mrs. Wharton were our most interesting novelists, and most of the younger writers followed their manner, without having their qualifications" (*Stories* 963–64). By 1916 Cather was expressing concern to Ferris Greenslet because an article had said she wrote like Mrs. Wharton (Stout no. 369), and she did not want to. In "The Old Beauty" Cather reminds Wharton that even great beauties or muses can attract younger male admirers by their "grand style" (*Stories* 714), without needing to prompt any male's predictable (if not formulaic) dreams of love, and the same point goes for "A Chance Meeting." Cather seems to think the other three ladies have expressed limited imaginations when it comes to the bonding emotions. In neither Cather's short story nor her sketch about meeting Flaubert's niece is the younger admirer a prospective lover. Thus, like the simpleton in a fairy tale, Cather finishes off three in one blow.

The collection's second story, "The Best Years," begins by featuring Miss Evangeline Knightly, Supervisor of Schools, wearing gauntlets. Here Cather throws down the gauntlet to all her critics by reviewing her own accomplishments. For example, Lesley Ferguesson, teaching in a one-room country school, keeps her head in a disaster she cannot stave off, saves others but perishes herself, and still remains the one everybody loves best, as Bartley does in *Alexander's Bridge*. The experimental farming with new ideas of *O Pioneers!* turns into a joke here, as is the name "Wide Awake Farm." Lesley's room at home duplicates Thea's private retreat in *The Song of the Lark*, but the standpipe Lesley spots so eagerly on her way into town shines up the one in which Thea's tramp drowns himself in Cather's third novel.

In *My Ántonia*, Cuzak children have natural good manners, as do Ferguesson pupils and brothers in "The Best Years." In both works, a town hotel importantly facilitates plot. While *One of Ours*, Cather's fifth novel, features as terrible a blizzard as "The Best Years," Wheelers justify the poor education they offer Claude, just as Miss Knightly rationalizes hiring a fourteen-year-old child to teach school in the story. *A Lost Lady* shares with this tale its panting trains, tributes of roses, and types of prints on parlor walls. In *The Professor's House* Roddy Blake objects to Tom's turning "Fourth of July speech" patterns on him; but Fourth of July speeches become the chief raison d'être of Lesley's useless father. In *My Mortal Enemy*, neighbors in Parthia, Illinois, love talking about Myra Driscoll's elopement, just as MacAlpin neighbors love talking about "Old Ferg," Lesley's father, and for the same reason: both legends produce glimpses of novelty and audacity. In fact, Mr. Ferguesson "talked a trifle as if from a rostrum, perhaps" (*Stories* 742), as ponderously as Captain Forrester, who saw no reason to vary his speech patterns.

In *Death Comes for the Archbishop* the keys to building a functioning southwestern church are Latour's authority and organizational ability; in "The Best Years" those talents belong to the Ferguesson mother, who runs her family effectively. In *Shadows on the Rock* Father Hector is the flower of the priestly flock, as *Hector* Ferguesson is "flower of the family" (*Stories* 738); and the children in both these works are distinguished by "the deepest, the most solemn loyalty" to their mothers and homes (741), a trait Cather usually approves.

"Old Mrs. Harris" and "The Best Years" both depict the same family of siblings—one adored sister and four adoring brothers; Cather inclined to erase her sisters in her so-called autobiographical fiction. The opening trope of "The Best Years" describes in loving language the act of driving through the beautiful land that "Neighbour Rosicky" also drives through so winningly, and admires so well; yet part of the beloved landscape in both stories is a comforting country cemetery. *Obscure Destinies* culminates in "Two Friends," and William Jennings Bryan wreaks havoc in "The Best Years" as he has done in the previous story. In fact, as Woodress reminds us, "Bryan is the only political figure she ever profiled" (102).

The self-described station master with no ambition in "The Best Years" duplicates Mr. Gayheart, the watch-repair man of *Lucy Gayheart*. And in *Sapphira and the Slave Girl*, as in "The Best Years," the big house feels more empty at the end because the girl its owners love is dead. What one realizes in so lengthy a set of parallels, of course, is that such a list of parallel details can go on for a long time. The point of the list, however, is that Cather left none of her works out: she embraced them all in her final summing up of her writing career. Those telling details, she knew always, were what good stories were made of.[5]

Thus Cather deftly acknowledges and salutes all her own fine work. Then she further acknowledges that a time comes when one feels diminished—a *Less-ley*. This pronunciation is even used by Lesley's mother to hiss her name (*Stories* 732). The stressed punctuation leads to guesses about creating fictions, as any *Fer-guess-on* might. When her spent time arrives, Lesley thinks of being home as of being replanted in the earth, as a kindly gardener might replace a washed-out plant. "The feeling of being at home was complete, absolute; it made her sleepy" (745). We can even notice with a catch of breath that in this, her final story, Cather uses the phrase her mentor William James said conveys the finished and dead: "complete, absolute" (Skaggs, "Cather's Radical Empiricism" 15).

Cather made a point of arranging this volume so that a determined note of affirmation ends it. Along with Faulkner, Cather, if somewhat grimly, hails the future here, toward which we are all still hopping as best we can. Yet at the end as at the beginning, we can see that "plucky youth is more bracing than enduring age" (*Stories* 769). Plucky youth shows every sign here that it has the gumption to stick to its chosen tasks, cold and hard as they may be. Cather does not allow herself this kind of final pronouncement, appropriate to a cultural icon, until her last page in her posthumous volume of stories. By then, however, she was clearly ready to stop.

Cather, however, must have had gauntlets on the mind as she arranged her last volume. The gauntlet she throws at Faulkner takes the form of her throwaway allusion to *Henry IV, Part I*. It lands before him—perhaps her best reader—as if she were playing Bolingbroke at the beginning of *Richard II*. In this, her last thunderously resonating literary reference, we can expect reverberations as well as flourishes. For one example, she gets in three Shakespearean plays for the space it takes to name one and leave one up to the reader: *Henry IV, Part I* can pair plausibly with either *Richard II*, whose plot leads up to it, or *Henry IV, Part II*, which follows it up. Grenfell has packed two little volumes bound alike (*Stories* 763).

Henry Grenfell's name suggests Shakespeare's troubled King Henry IV, formerly Harry Bolingbroke, whose grin fell away when, as a young man, he was crowned King of England in *Richard II*. Cather's Grenfell was equally young when he collided with his destiny. Since Cather's allusion initially concerns the personalities of the analogous Henrys, Grenfell and the King, she initially draws more from *Richard II*: here Bolingbroke plays foil to King Richard. Thus she underscores a doubleness that starts with Shakespeare: there will be two kings at the beginning and end of the sequence playing out here, plus two Harry juniors, Hal and Hotspur. Cather may be saluting an equal here, but she is also giving notice that she is not throwing in the towel; instead, she is throwing a *gaunt*let (thus alluding to a saga that begins with old John of Gaunt, time-honored Lancaster).

At the beginning of "Before Breakfast" Cather's now-elderly Grenfell ponders a recent moment when he sparred with his eldest son as he was packing to go away. He was preparing to enjoy "glorious loneliness" (*Stories* 766) when *Harrison* (Henry's or Harry's son) picks out of his open traveling bag an edition of *Henry IV, Part I* and the two converse tensely, ostensibly about the play. Even in Shakespeare's play the father-son relationship is labeled *punishing* (3.2.11). But Harrison does not err grossly enough to pick up the matching volume, so we are permitted to imagine it as either prelude or finale to King Henry's story. This setup may be crooked, but when the stakes are survival, the story points out, a frog-toad hops.

At the beginning of this carefully arranged swan song, then, Cather's Henry Grenfell and Shakespeare's Henry IV face two similar problems: first, how to imagine the undisturbed possession of a beloved island that is foundationally divided; and second, how to love a first son and heir whose values, interests, and manners seem utterly alien. Cather allows her churlish Henry, after dyspeptic fuming, to rediscover some fire in the belly, as well as his damaged appetite for food—or perhaps one should say, a good digestion.[6] What transforms Grenfell's outlook is seeing a plucky young person perform an elected task under difficult circumstances, without dodging. He returns to his cabin to find approvingly that his cook "William hadn't waited; he was wisely breakfasting" (*Stories* 769). The question that now dawns on readers as the story ends is, which William is Cather referencing here, Shakespeare or Faulkner? This question we might call a clear ambiguity.

If William Faulkner blinked to spot his name associated with a "man Friday" who was "'boarded out' in a fisherman's family" (*Stories* 766), he must have grasped the flattering bow to William's heartier appetite. William, at least, is not like Grenfell or Henry IV, to whom Fortune has given a feast and then taken away the stomach to enjoy it (*Part II*, 4.4.103–7). Grenfell, like Bolingbroke, has paid dearly for his achievements. And this Shakespearean sequence also references another Cather work. As Marvin Friedman has pointed out (61), "Before Breakfast" itself references *My Mortal Enemy*, in which Myra murmurs "Old John of Gaunt, time honored Lancaster," from *Richard II*, in her dying days; in those hard times she ponders being left alone with her mortal enemy and concedes that lovers can be enemies too. Grenfell, sounding like Myra, acknowledges: "The bitter truth was that his worst enemy was closer even than the wife of his bosom—was his bosom itself!" (*Stories* 765). We ourselves are invited to recall that admirers and rivals can blend as two in one body—and that Shakespeare's Harry and Hotspur embodied that kind of doubling first.

We may now consider "Before Breakfast" Cather's summarizing story of the relation between the two greatest twentieth-century American fiction writers, Faulkner and herself. While Cather always hid at least one Shakespearean allusion within every fiction she published, the lifting up of *Henry IV, Part I* is uncommonly obvious in this piece. It underscores the stakes she is playing for as she acknowledges the problems of having two kings in one kingdom. The Shakespearean play also highlights other themes: How does a power figure tolerate an uncivil successor? Do sins really require atonement (Shakespeare says *no*)? What finally is worth celebrating? For that matter, how far should good manners be expected to go? As *Richard II*–quoting Myra Henshawe says, "It's all very well to tell us to forgive our enemies; our enemies can never hurt us very much. But oh, what about forgiving our friends? . . . that's where the rub comes!" (*Stories* 554).

Leaving as wide open as possible that question about who one's mortal enemy might be, and whether there is any significant difference between what one loves most and what one fears most (questions robustly active in Shakespeare's trilogy about Henry IV), we turn back to Shakespearean resonances in "Before Breakfast." Cather seems to ask here, is this Henry a king, a rascal, or a clown? Like King Henry IV, Henry Grenfell has reached the pinnacle of his power at Grenfell and Saunders, Bonds, by accident (though it is surely no accident that Cecily *Saunders* and Jim *Bond* are Faulkner names). The "firm truth," however, can be interpreted two ways: as a businesslike way to identify Faulkner as the prototype for Grenfell, or as the *bond* between two equal partners. Grenfell, like Bolingbroke, once collided with another, rose to rescue something important, gained the favor of the powerful thereby, and thus found glory. In the process he has paid the bills of his children but come to look suspiciously on relatives and former friends. Yet from the first he has also displayed an occasional and quixotic willingness to forgive his enemies. He is now himself a loner, envious of his opponents' preferable children, and anxious about what his own sons "just reach out and *take*" (*Stories* 763) with no struggle (as Hal reaches to take the crown at the end of *Henry IV, Part II* when he thinks his father is dead). Grenfell's self-congratulatory regard for the way he worked hard to gain his kingdom seems defensively smug and potentially self-deceptive. We know him to be smart, ambitious, inconsistent, and energetic, but not necessarily trustworthy. It is therefore gratifying to see him regain some faith in the younger generation and their future, as Henry IV does also at the end of both parts of *Henry IV*.

Yet Henry Grenfell owns a cabin like Cather's on an island in the North Atlantic, which is very like her beloved Grand Manan. Here he, as she, loves to isolate himself and take long walks. The obvious walking path leads by waterfalls, as two busloads of Cather scholars discovered for themselves by visiting the island in 1995. Grenfell thus also begins to seem a lot like one of those autobiographical males in Cather's work: Jim Burden, Niel Herbert, Godfrey St. Peter, possibly even Bartley Alexander. We are therefore eventually forced to ask, is Grenfell really supposed to suggest only Faulkner, or is he also a surrogate for Cather herself? Or does he represent both? And is this glorious loneliness what both have come to? Who or what *is* this new Henry? Is this crown worth fighting over?

Once we look closely at Shakespeare's *Henry IV*, we find transferable images from the play that reappear in Cather's text. In the first lines of Shakespeare's play we glimpse King Henry IV looking for "frighted peace" with "opposed eyes . . . like the meteors of a troubled heaven," while he feels "shaken" and "wan with care." His hope is to "March all one way and be no more oppos'd / Against acquaintance, kindred, and allies." In our first glimpse of Grenfell after his sleepless night, his head and eyes are tipped upside down to receive eyedrops, from which odd posture he soon wonders whether he has treated his family exactly right. Yet he resents them because his wife and eldest son seem "a close corporation" (*Stories* 764), much as the Duke of York's wife and son comically incorporate their efforts at the end of *Richard II* to extract a pardon from Bolingbroke for the treason of which York accuses his son (5.3). Grenfell feels his sons do not chase the ball but reach out and take it with fine hands, as *both* Bolingbroke does in *Richard II* and Hal does in *IV, Part II*. Grenfell's bitterness toward professors and physicists in "Before Breakfast" alludes to Henry IV's bitterness before his death at the public failure to recognize the terrible effects on one's health of being a self-made king and of wearing a crown. The "intestine shock" Henry registers in the opening scene of *Part I* reflects Grenfell's "hair-trigger stomach" (*Stories* 765). At the least, Professor Fairweather's name is as transparent as Shakespeare's Shallow, Pistol, Silence, or Wart from *Part II*. And Grenfell's recognition that his "worst enemy" is "his bosom itself" corresponds to Henry IV's similar recognition at the end of *Part II* (4.5.182–220).

With his head awry, before breakfast, Grenfell spots the planet Venus. This glimpse of the morning star, however, follows his sight of the "big snowshoe hare" he remembers fondly from previous visits. The hare reminds us of "hare-brained Hotspur" (*Part I*, 5.2.19), whom the King admires, as well as the reluctance to "start a hare" (*Part I*, 1.3.197–98). Hotspur's remark that it is easier to "pluck honor from the pale-faced moon, / Or dive into the bottom of the deep" (*Part I*, 1.3.202–3), conversely, frames the sky-to-sea survey Grenfell accomplishes here, but reminds us that his tale begins after a troubled night of sleepless agitation because a geologist has told him the two ends of his preferred world don't match. Grenfell soon doffs his "easy robes of peace" (*Part I*, 5.1.13), in this case his "eiderdown bathrobe" (*Stories* 765), to dress for action that commences with dawn, as does the battle between Henry IV and Hotspur. But after all the parallels are noted, the main point is that Grenfell is an "unthankful king" of the island (*Part I*, 1.3.136) and a "forgetful man" (1.3.161), whose former allies cannot trust him. Yet Cather seems willing to make the charge, or allow us to make it, against either Faulkner or herself. They are the two disparate halves of a literary kingdom, two icons, who now have no choice but to stick to each other for "the eternities" (*Stories* 761; a Faulkner word), or at least for a long time (a Cather correction). Cather may then be suggesting in her last public pronouncement that she thinks they are bonded double permanently, two iconic sides of an American coin, and that's the end of it.

NOTES

This is a slightly shorter version of an address presented at Breadloaf in 2003.

1. One such is the Caspersen Cather Collection at Drew University, available to all scholars.

2. See my "Thefts and Conversations" for a thorough review of these references. I extend this argument further in "Cather's War and Faulkner's Peace." My book *Axes: Willa Cather and William Faulkner* is now in press at University of Nebraska Press and scheduled for publication in fall 2007.

3. A slightly different version of the famous motto can be found at the website advertising the De Coucy chateau: "*Roy ne suis, ne Prince, ne Duc, ne Comte aussi, suis le Sire de Coucy.*" http://photo.lrx.free.fr/Coucy-/htm.

4. The situation uncannily prefigures that of another cultural icon, Britain's Princess Diana, who was said to charm merely because she was fresh and beautiful.

5. Bintrim's recently completed dissertation (2004), covering Cather's early editing days in Pittsburgh, emphasizes Cather's advising the boys and girls from whom she is soliciting stories to try to find the details that make stories live: "try to tell the important details only, the ones which give life and color to your story," she advised her young readers (Bintrim 94).

6. I am fascinated that those two avid miners of Mark Twain, Cather and Faulkner, will share Twain's backhanded tribute to Shakespeare's *Henry IV*, which Twain drops into "1601." That frisky romp on Shakespeare's England, which some consider pornographic, is built around the implicit metaphor of constipation and digestion, that is, of farts and old farts. There is an analogy here to Grenfell's stomach.

WORKS CITED

Bintrim, Timothy K. "Recovering the Extra-Literary: The Pittsburgh Writings of Willa Cather." Diss. Duquesne University, 2004.

Cather, Willa. *Stories, Poems, and Other Writings*. Ed. Sharon O'Brien. New York: Library of America, 1992.

Chopin, Kate. *The Awakening*. New York: Norton, 1976.
Friedman, Marvin. "Lifting the Death Chill: 'Before Breakfast' as Sequel to *My Mortal Enemy*." *Willa Cather Pioneer Memorial Newsletter and Review* 45.3 (2002): 61–67.
Kittredge, George Lyman, ed. *The Complete Works of William Shakespeare*. Boston: Ginn and Co., 1936.
Porter, David H. "Cather on Cather." *Willa Cather Pioneer Memorial Newsletter and Review* 45.3 (2002): 55–60.
Skaggs, Merrill M. "Cather's Radical Empiricism." *Willa Cather Pioneer Memorial Newsletter and Review* 47.1 (2003): 15–19.
———. "Cather's War and Faulkner's Peace: A Comparison of Two Novels, and More." *Faulkner and His Contemporaries*. Ed. Ann Abadie and Joseph R. Urgo. Oxford: U of Mississippi P, 2004. 40–53.
——— "The Interlocking Works of Willa Cather and Ellen Glasgow." *Willa Cather's Southern Connections: New Essays on Cather and the South*. Ed. Ann Romines Charlottesville: UP of Virginia, 2000. 158–69.
———. "Thefts and Conversations: Cather and Faulkner." *Cather Studies* 3 (1996): 115–36.
Stout, Janis P., ed. *A Calendar of the Letters of Willa Cather*. Lincoln: U of Nebraska P, 2002.
Williamson, David. *Brewer's British Royalty*. London: Cassell, 1996.
Woodress, James. *Willa Cather: A Literary Life*. Lincoln: U of Nebraska P, 1987.

"A Critic Who Was Worthy of Her"

The Writing of *Willa Cather: A Critical Biography*

ROBERT THACKER

Writing to E. K. Brown in October 1946, Canadian poet Duncan Campbell Scott commented favorably on Brown's essay "Homage to Willa Cather," which had just appeared in the *Yale Review*. After naming the Cather titles he is familiar with—*My Ántonia*, *Death Comes for the Archbishop*, and *Shadows on the Rock*—Scott says, "I agree with your opinion as to their chance of permanence. I am sure she must have been pleased with your Homage and was conscious that here she had a critic who was worthy of her" (McDougall 177). Brown's essay, which followed after his earlier assessment, "Willa Cather and the West" (1936), defines Cather's trajectory as an artist, the writing history that produced the body of texts that concerns critics still. In "Homage to Willa Cather," Brown was able to construct that body as largely complete and to offer a judicious and sensitive overview. As he had written to Scott earlier in 1946, and with a factual assurance that would later evaporate, Cather "will be 70 this December" (McDougall 172).

For her part, Cather was taken with Brown. She had replied in a friendly way to the copy of "Willa Cather and the West" he had sent her years before, but her reaction to "Homage to Willa Cather" was out of step with her usual response to probing professors. As James Woodress writes, "Cather was charmed with the article and responded with a remarkable five-page letter in which she said it was hard for her tell Brown in temperate language how deeply she appreciated his careful and sympathetic reading of her books." "The tone of these letters," Woodress continues, "is friendly and unreserved, as though Cather were writing to a nephew of whom she greatly approved" (vii). While it is impossible to say just what might have happened had Cather and Brown met, Cather ends her late-January 1947 letter to Brown looking "forward to discussing their personal values when he comes to New York" (Stout 277).

Given Cather's response to Brown's essay, it is reasonable to think that a meeting between the two would have eventuated in a biography commissioned by the subject herself. But Cather died before the meeting could take place, and the decision about a biography and biographer fell to Edith Lewis, Cather's friend and literary executor, and to Alfred A. Knopf, her publisher since 1920.

I will return to these people and to the gestation of the Brown biography, but to set the stage for the story I am constructing here I want to highlight three phrases I have offered thus far: "Here she had a critic who was worthy of her"; "Homage to Willa Cather"; and "personal values." Equally, I want to add two more quotations: the first Cather's, the second Brown's. In "My First Novels (There Were Two)," Cather writes: "When I got back to Pittsburgh I began to write a book entirely for myself; a story about some Scandinavians and Bohemians who had been neighbours of ours when I lived on a ranch in Nebraska" (92). In his personal copy of *The Professor's House*, Brown wrote only a few notes. One, however, is especially striking: "I always think Willa Cather's books [are] too good for this (America[n]) continent."

Together, these quotations define the contexts of what I take to be a foundational act of Cather's establishment as a cultural icon: the making of E. K. Brown's *Willa Cather: A Critical Biography* (completed by Leon Edel). It emerged one of three books published on Cather in 1953—the others were Edith Lewis's *Willa Cather Living: A Personal Record* and Elizabeth Shepley Sergeant's *Willa Cather: A Memoir*. The Brown-Edel biography, beyond being the first scholarly life of Cather, is a book fraught by the complications of its own gestation. And that gestation, though generally well known among critics, has never been examined in detail through the prism of its archival sources: the E. K. Brown Papers at Yale University and the National Archives of Canada, the Dorothy Canfield Fisher Papers at the University of Vermont, and the Leon Edel Papers at McGill University.

These archives reveal a story of some intrigue surrounding the making of *Willa Cather: A Critical Biography*, one in which the major players are familiar: Cather herself, of course, but newly gone and grieved; Edith Lewis, Alfred Knopf, and E. K. Brown; and then Margaret Brown, Dorothy Canfield Fisher, A. S. P. Woodhouse, Ernest Sirluck, and Leon Edel. Throughout, who Cather was, what she wrote, and what she said about what she wrote are ever in play—that is, Willa Cather as emerging cultural icon. Or, putting the crux of this story another way, what is the definable critical value of Cather and her art? How, as Auden put it regarding Yeats, did Cather "become her admirers"?

CATHER, BROWN, AND THE QUESTION OF "PERSONAL VALUES"

In November 1950, when Brown was well embarked on his book, he received a letter from Elizabeth Shepley Sergeant; he had been in touch with her as one of Cather's friends, and she was keeping him abreast of her own book's progress. Sergeant writes: "I do agree with you about the lesser attraction of the mature Cather. It is as if she were greatly lured by the world in some obscure way, yet would never admit it. She had lost some of her early modesty about her own work." Just after this, Sergeant adds: "This is a dictated letter and I seem to have been indiscreet—but I am sure you will not reveal my indiscretions" (Sergeant to Brown, 26 November 1950). Brown did not reveal Sergeant's "indiscretions," but her comment catches some of the tone of the times in which Brown wrote. He was at work with Alfred A. Knopf's and Edith Lewis's approval and help; Sergeant, meanwhile, was shaping her own memoir of Cather, well aware of Cather's views on such writing and with what might be called

Lewis's acquiescent disapproval; a woman from Red Cloud, Nebraska, Mildred Bennett, who had never known Cather, was working, to Lewis's apparent horror, on what would prove to be the first biographical book to reach print, *The World of Willa Cather* (1951). Others worked on similar projects as well. As these people researched and wrote, an iconic Cather was beginning to emerge.

Throughout, Lewis and Knopf sought to manage such work. For example, when Cather died in 1947, George Seibel, a friend of Cather's from her time in Pittsburgh, approached Knopf with the idea of writing a biography. Dorothy Canfield Fisher, a mutual friend, had suggested it to him. Knopf rebuffed the idea, saying "there would not be a life."[1] Later, once Brown was working on the biography that Lewis and Knopf had authorized, Seibel wrote to Fisher that he did not "see what we can do but follow the line of least resistance with regard to Willa. After all you can't copyright your name or other people's memories. . . . Three or four people besides Prof. Brown have recently come to see me or have written. Mr. Knopf and Miss Lewis should be glad of such new and widening interest, which their reticence or reluctance may have helped to kindle" (Seibel to Fisher, 9 July 1949).

Seibel's phrase "reticence or reluctance" captures one dimension of Cather's own handling of her literary reputation during her lifetime: she acted in ways that would further that reputation. In this, Lewis and Knopf were only following Cather's lead in rejecting Seibel and recruiting Brown, a distinguished critic in the midst of a brilliant career. Writing to Brown in, presumably, the same vein that she had written Siebel, Fisher argued that Lewis's and Knopf's "wish to keep her [Cather's] girlhood days unchronicled was beginning to give rise to rather disagreeable surmises as to the cause of this wish of hers. Several people in the literary world have asked me quite horrid questions about this point—based on the idea that so great a desire to keep something hidden must mean that 'something' had a sinister color, or would be a disgrace to know" (Fisher to Brown, 27 March 1950).

Equally, Sergeant's comment to Brown that Cather had "lost some of her early modesty" is revelatory of another way of seeing Cather's handling of her reputation: Sergeant's comment rings true and extends the version of her apprenticeship Cather offered in 1931 in "My First Novels (There Were Two)." Writing that essay after a twelve-year span during which she produced seven novels (including one awarded the Pulitzer), a book of stories, and various occasional pieces, Cather made her apprenticeship and subsequent success sound serene, almost inevitable. The facts, both biographical and contextual, that form the basis for any such assessment need not be repeated here, but Cather's career between 1895 (when she graduated from college) and 1918 (when *My Ántonia* appeared) has still been insufficiently scrutinized. By and large, Cather's critics have followed her version.

But I do not accept that version of things, and it was probably for good reason that Brown left only one period in Cather's life for Edel to write *in toto*: the Pittsburgh years (it became two chapters in the finished book). Not at all serene, Cather worked doggedly during those years to discover ways to shape her fictions that both rejected the methods of the conventional novel and created on the page a sense of being that she called "life itself" (*Song of the Lark* 254). The notion that she wrote *O Pioneers!* "for herself" is a retrospective rationalization of the first order, and one made emblematic by the changed birth date that was to so vex Brown during his research, itself a lie perpetuated by Lewis on Cather's gravestone: after all, Cather had been sanitizing her own history for some time before Brown appeared to construct his Willa Cather.[2]

Brown was self-selected for the task. Born in Toronto in 1905, he was educated at the University of Toronto and at the Sorbonne, where he took a *doctorate-és-lettres*, a degree seldom earned by non-Francophones owing to the stringent French required, and one requiring two theses, a major (on Wharton) and a minor (on Matthew Arnold). (Another student in Paris, embarked on the same program and also with Canadian roots, was Leon Edel. He and Brown became good friends then.) Well before he finished his theses, Brown had returned to the University of Toronto to teach. And even before he had defended his theses, he left to head the English department at Manitoba. Brown later returned again to Toronto before going to Cornell and, finally, to the University of Chicago. Throughout, he published—from 1930 to 1950 he averaged fifteen to twenty publications a year: books, articles, and reviews reflecting broad interests (British, American, and Canadian literature), deep erudition, and a sharp critical sensitivity. An early champion of Wharton and E. M. Forster, Brown continued his work on Arnold and other Victorians and also published the first major critical book on Canadian writing, *On Canadian Poetry* (1943) (see Groening).

Brown's startling response in his copy of *The Professor's House*—that Cather's work is "too good for this (America[n]) continent"—owes to his British and Continental bias in literary preferences, a very usual one in a University of Toronto–trained critic of his generation. Yet however startling it is to us now, Brown's comment reveals just what his critical work on Cather was effecting: he was consciously moving her work into the realm of the first-rate writers.[3] And the beginning of "Homage to Willa Cather" makes it clear that he was doing so as an attack on Trilling and his cohort, whose writing Brown refers to in his first paragraph (though not by name) as "among the gross abuses of much recent American criticism" (77). What he offers, instead, in his homage to Cather is a sensitive, nuanced reading of her work that holds up very well today because it hinges on values apprehended from the stories she writes; that is, as a critic Brown got what Cather was trying to do. He writes, as two examples, that Cather "had always understood that a person's relation to a place might be valuable to him, and as decisive in his growth or retardation, as any relation he might have with other persons. What happens in one place could not happen in same way in any other" (85). Having offered this precise—and utterly compelling—formulation, Brown demonstrates it through *Death Comes for the Archbishop*, asserting that its "language" "makes the impression of the New Mexico landscape superior to any presentation of setting in the earlier books" (86).

Thus what Cather likely apprehended in Brown's essay were shared "personal values" about literature generally and, most particularly, about ways of understanding her books. By background, education, and inclination, Brown proved himself to be a critic who had a point of view similar to Cather's own: rooted in the European literary tradition, he was able through his critical writings to "bring the Muse" into his North American "country." That is, by his own work Brown demonstrated that he was, in Scott's phrasing, "a critic worthy of" Cather. He did, and he was. And through the warmth of the letters Cather wrote to him after she had read Brown's homage, there is every reason to think that she saw Brown's worth. Edith Lewis and Alfred Knopf certainly did.

BROWN'S WRITING OF *WILLA CATHER: A CRITICAL BIOGRAPHY*

For his part, Brown seems to have mounted a campaign to position himself as Cather's first biographer. With the connivance of Helen McAfee, managing editor of the *Yale Review*, Cather was sent (with Brown's compliments) three extra copies of the issue containing his article. McAfee, who knew and had dealings with Cather herself, seems keen to help further Brown's case (McAfee to Brown, 30 October 1946, Yale).[4] After Cather died—in fact, the day after she was buried—Brown probably wrote Knopf to propose a critical biography. Knopf replied: "I am much interested in your suggestion, but do not feel able to attempt to act on it at this time. I must wait until Miss Cather's literary executor can size up the whole situation created by her death, when we will be able to decide how best to deal with the many suggestions that, quite naturally, are now coming in one way and another" (Knopf to Brown, 8 May 1947).

It took Lewis and Knopf time to sort things out, but in April 1948 Lewis wrote to Brown to ask "if there is a likelihood of your being in New York" soon, since "I should like very much to consult you about a biography of Miss Cather." In her initial letter, Lewis describes her longtime relationship with Cather (including her work on Cather's books), her position as literary executor, and her having talked to Mr. Knopf about the matter. Of Brown's "Homage," Lewis writes, "It pleased Miss Cather, I think, more than anything that has been written about her books." Lewis writes that she has "just finished" Brown's book on Matthew Arnold, and it "has impressed me very deeply." Closing, she reiterates her need to talk to Brown, saying, "I shall be grateful if you can help me to make it possible" (Lewis to Brown, 20 April [1948]). Brown doubtless responded at once, for on 4 May Lewis is writing to give him her unlisted telephone number (Yale), and on 11 June Helen McAfee asks Brown, "How did you come out on the Cather proposal—or is that a secret?" (McAfee to Brown, 11 June 1948).

In late July, Lewis writes that "Mr. Knopf and I both consider it a piece of great good fortune that you will write the biography of Miss Cather. When I asked you to do it, it was with the knowledge that Miss Cather herself felt you had a very true understanding and appreciation of her work." She and Knopf hope to give Brown "every help that we can, and to put all the available material at your disposal." He should feel free to approach any of "Miss Cather's friends . . . please do so with my fullest consent and encouragement" (Lewis to Brown, 29 July 1948).[5]

Brown set to work at once, and, surveying the papers, one cannot but be impressed by his enterprise: he crisscrossed the country, corresponded with and interviewed people, and generally ferreted out all the materials he could find. Looking over his shoulder, writing people on Brown's behalf, and passing things on, Lewis was as good as her word. And while Brown was engaged in this work, he kept at numerous other projects: 1948 and 1949 saw more than thirty publications each, and 1950 saw twenty-seven, among them *Rhythm in the Novel*, a published set of lectures Brown gave at Toronto which includes a discussion of *The Professor's House* that bears reading today (Groening 218–20). Brown began writing "in earnest" on 1 August 1950, and by early 1951 he had drafted all of the biography save the chapter on the Pittsburgh years and most of the epilogue (Brown to Fisher, 29 November 1950).

By then Brown was a very sick man—sicker, in fact, than he was himself aware, since his wife and doctor worked together to keep the seriousness of his condition from him (Margaret Brown to Fisher, 28 April [1951]).[6] He was dying of brain cancer. Once he had completed his work on Brown's book, Leon Edel deposited the manuscript and many of Brown's notes in the Beineke

Library at Yale; the manuscript shows that Brown began the epilogue—its published first sentence is his—but broke it off to go back to draft the introduction. Given his own circumstances, this was an understandable and poignant decision. On 23 April 1951, at the age of forty-five and in the midst of a brilliant career, E. K. Brown died.

"MR. KNOPF'S SAGACITY": MARGARET BROWN, DOROTHY CANFIELD FISHER, LEON EDEL, AND THE COMPLETION OF *WILLA CATHER: A CRITICAL BIOGRAPHY*

In late 1935, Brown had married Margaret Deaver, described by Sandra Djwa as "a vivacious young Minneapolis society woman" (158) and by Brown's biographer as "no academic . . . but she was widely if eccentrically read, perpetually amused by professorial mannerisms and gossip (as was Brown himself) and striking in appearance and dress" (Groening 48).[7] At the time of his death the couple had two young sons, who were Margaret's preoccupation and her greatest concern, especially in view of their father's sudden passing. Even so, it fell to Margaret to decide just what would become of Brown's biography of Cather, and she is at the center of the rest of this story.

The Dorothy Canfield Fisher Papers at the University of Vermont contain correspondence between E. K. Brown and Fisher in connection with the biography—Fisher wrote up reminiscences for his use, and in the late summer of 1949 Brown visited the Fishers at Arlington, Vermont.[8] Brown and Fisher clearly developed a rapport. So when Margaret Brown begins to settle her husband's literary affairs, she writes on the same day, less than a week after her husband's death, to Lewis and Fisher. A month later she also wrote to Lorne Pierce—head of the Ryerson Press, Toronto—and offered some useful context:

> I think you would be interested to know that after Edward discovered his condition, he put the Scott ahead of the Cather, for personal reasons, mainly that he was devoted

> to Mr Scott. I think if he had let the Scott go entirely he would have finished the Cather. As it is, the Cather is being estimated at the moment, and although it is done in part the balance will largely depend on Mr Knopf's sagacity. I am hoping for the best. (28 May 1951)

Margaret is referring here to Brown's memoir—forty typed pages—included in *Selected Poems of Duncan Campbell Scott* (1951). To another Ryerson correspondent, she writes that her husband "was engaged with this extremely complicated Cather biography at the time of his death, and I have had to put that ahead of all the other literary matters he was pursuing" (Brown to Joan Trebell, 26 May 1951).

"This extremely complicated Cather biography," indeed. In her 28 April 1951 letter to Fisher, in which she tells Fisher of her husband's death, Brown writes: "I have just had my first breathing spell, and am not thinking very clearly, but I think it important that I do not do anything to jeopardize the book on Miss Cather. Edward has long told me of Miss Lewis's personality. I wrote her a note in an attempt to calm her (no doubt) assorted fears. Edward had the greatest admiration for you, so I thought I should write you and ask, in fact, urge any useful suggestions." Toward the end of this letter, too, Margaret writes, "Poor Miss Lewis, she must be terribly upset." This may well be an understatement. In her 28 April 1951 letter to Lewis, Brown tells her that her husband "did not know how little time he had left. He knew of its seriousness, and had been working very hard on the biography." She also tells Lewis that the manuscript is being looked at by "a very competent friend" of her husband's, that Lewis should not worry about the materials she had given Brown, and that Margaret "will do all I can to facilitate matters for Mr. Knopf—and I really *do* think the biography can still be finished without losing too much." In her letter to Fisher written the same day, Margaret says, "But my worry is that Miss Lewis doesn't 'fall apart' over this and cause any trouble."

Although there is ample evidence that once Lewis and Knopf had decided on Brown for the biography Lewis worked to help Brown (the text of *Willa Cather Living* is, after all, is based on the "notes" Lewis wrote for Brown), there is also evidence that Lewis wavered in her support. During the summer of 1949, for example, Knopf wrote to E. K. Brown, "I don't honestly feel that I can shed much light on Miss Lewis and her present attitude" (Knopf to Brown, 16 August 1949). And when writing to Fisher as matters surrounding the biography were coming to a head in August 1951, Margaret Brown wrote that Edward "more than once said that when he was with Miss Lewis he often had the uncomfortable feeling that Miss Lewis expected Miss Cather to pop up around the door and possibly rebuke Miss Lewis for something she had said." In the same letter, Margaret expresses no residual anger toward Lewis and Knopf—"I think they are both doing what they think is the right thing, Miss Lewis is trying to protect her Idol"—and says that Knopf is being firm with a person—Mrs. Brown—he sees as a "Small Fry" (Brown to Fisher, 11 August 1951).

Writing retrospectively of the circumstances of the Brown biography after its author's death, in his own "Homage to Willa Cather" at the first International Cather Seminar, Leon Edel says that Brown wrote "in relative independence" from Lewis and, had Brown "lived to finish it," "His book would have been even more independent" (188). But Brown did not live to finish it, so his wife had to decide what to do with the manuscript, one she described as "4/5s finished" (Brown to Fisher, 28 April [1951]; Edel said "three-quarters done" ["Homage" 189]). In doing so she had to confront Lewis and Knopf. And though in the same essay, written just after Lewis's death in 1972, Edel is at pains to treat Lewis in a balanced way, he nevertheless offers a characterization of her that warrants quotation: "I am not suggesting that Edith Lewis was a sort of dragon guarding a sacred shrine" (189). Perhaps not, but she was certainly a formidable person from Margaret Brown's point of view.

The first person to read the manuscript after Brown's death, the "very competent friend" whom Margaret mentions to Lewis, was Ernest Sirluck, one of Brown's former students and then a junior colleague at the University of Chicago. At the same time, she consulted A. S. P. Woodhouse, head of English at University College, Toronto, and a man whom she described to Fisher as

"Edward's closest and oldest friend"; Woodhouse suggested that someone read the manuscript—thus Sirluck, whose doctoral thesis Woodhouse had supervised at Toronto. This was being done in "protecting Edward's interests," whereupon Margaret would "then send all the material, etc. to Mr. Knopf" (Brown to Fisher, 8 May [1951]). Neither of these men—both Miltonists—knew much about Cather, but each certainly knew something about scholarship, and that Margaret Brown looked to their advice over the next months augured much to benefit her husband's biography. In due course Sirluck reported, as he recalls in his autobiography, that Brown's manuscript needed "considerable work" (193).[9]

"What is worrying Miss Lewis," Margaret Brown continues to Fisher in early May, "is that she has sent Edward these famous notes she has made and copies that (I think) Miss Bloom has taken of letters Miss Cather wrote. Nothing less than a guard posted on each door of my house, and a (loaded) sub-machine gun in the front hall would apparently satisfy Miss Lewis that her material is safe." Brown called Knopf and offered to bring the materials to New York and leave them with him. He "seemed very sensible," she wrote to Fisher, "but I wondered if he understood the point that I was trying to make which was that I not only want to quiet Miss Lewis now, but to somehow keep her in a frame of mind so that she won't start over again being difficult with the person who has to finish the book" (Brown to Fisher, 8 May [1951]).[10] Given what she knows of Lewis, she doubts that this is possible, but she needs to make the attempt.

On 16 May, less than a month after her husband's death, Margaret Brown traveled to New York and turned over the manuscript and other materials to Knopf. During the interview Knopf was "pleasant and direct" (Brown to Fisher, 16 May 1951), but he also remarked that in completing Brown's book Miss Lewis "hopes for literary fame . . ." (Brown to Fisher, 22 May 1951). In this last letter, Margaret also enclosed a letter from E. K. Brown to Woodhouse addressing her husband's deteriorating health as well as a copy of Sirluck's "revised (and final) report of the Cather mss."

Thus, within a month of Brown's death those concerned with

the fate of his uncompleted Cather manuscript are divided: Lewis and Knopf, on the one hand, and Margaret Brown and her advisers on the other. Having authorized E. K. Brown to produce the biography they envisioned—one of taste and circumspection focused on Cather's works more than on her private life; that is, one Cather herself would have endorsed—Lewis, Cather's literary executor, and Knopf, her publisher, wanted to ensure the outcome of their project in the ways they had envisioned. Margaret Brown, self-admittedly not a literary person, but as her husband's heir and executor the person who owned his nearly completed manuscript biography, wanted to ensure its completion in a way that confirmed E. K. Brown's reputation. In contention throughout this standoff is Cather's iconic status: What will she become? How will she be constructed? Who will have the job of completing E. K. Brown's critical biography of Cather?

Of particular significance in this standoff is Edith Lewis. Easy to caricature as some sort of "dragon guarding a sacred shrine," Lewis has often been seen as a kook in Cather criticism, especially just after Cather's death, yet very little is known about her.[11] What is known—for example, Lewis's editorial role in the shaping of Cather's manuscripts appears to be significant—suggests that learning more about her will lead to significant revision of our understanding of the Cather-Lewis relationship.[12]

Yet there is considerable reason to question Lewis's actions regarding this biography after Brown's death. Even before Brown was authorized to begin his work on the biography, Lewis and Knopf had created an atmosphere of, as Seibel characterized it to Fisher, "reticence or reluctance" surrounding any biographical work on Cather. There is evidence that Lewis sought to stymie Mildred Bennett's research. More than this, the archival records make it clear that in helping Brown and Edel, Lewis not only corrected facts but also sought to shape particular interpretations of Cather's life, friends, and works. And on least one occasion she wrote Edel to discourage him from assisting Sergeant's memoir in any material way (Lewis to Edel, 6 February 1952). Without question, too, Lewis took such actions in the same spirit in which she wrote to Carrie Miner Sherwood when Lewis and Knopf were considering candidates to write the biography. Then

Lewis wrote that she and Knopf "both feel that it [the biography] must be done by a writer of the highest standing, someone with a deep and true understanding of Willa's work and a high order of critical ability—above all, one who can be trusted to write it in a way she herself would have approved" (15 November [1947]). Given all of this, most of it known to Margaret Brown, Knopf's remark to her in May 1951 that in finishing Brown's biography Lewis "hopes for literary fame" had a chilling effect. Based on Lewis's actions since Cather's death, it should have.

One of the solutions contemplated was to publish the manuscript as it was—that is, without anyone completing it, just copy-editing and mechanics. Thus in late June, Brown wrote to Fisher:

> Your remark about finishing the book as is, is very well taken, but as the book lacks a satisfactory introduction and a satisfactory conclusion, I don't know. Mr. Knopf if [is] now acting like a member of the British Foreign Office, very chary with his remarks. His only questions have been in the direction of the person to finish the Pittsburgh chapter (which does have to be finished, but could remain fairly pedestrian, if necessary). Also, he reassures me that he has had two carbons made of the mss. It is possible that he thinks as you do, but is waiting to talk it over with Miss Lewis. (24 June 1951)

Just after this, Knopf wrote to Brown and endorsed Lewis as the person to finish the book: "I would like very much indeed to be able to arrange with Miss Lewis to prepare Mr. Brown's manuscript for publication. I know that the resulting job will be competent, in good taste, and will respect at every point the work which Mr. Brown himself completed. I won't say any more in this letter because Miss Lewis is writing you" (26 June 1951).

Margaret Brown rejected this possibility, writing to Fisher after receiving Lewis's letter of proposal: "I read from her letter that she intends to fill in the gaps in the mss as though they have been written by Edward, and then write the final part as her own. If I understand that properly, it seems impossible to let her finish it." She also mentions that Sirluck noted that Brown had rewritten

Lewis's notes, making them come "alive and [have] style, whereas in the original form they were flat and dull" (Brown to Fisher, n.d. [return address "until July 14, 1951"]). Brown sent copies of Lewis's letter to both Sirluck and Woodhouse; Woodhouse ultimately drafted Brown's reply to Lewis and to Knopf.

Fisher's reply to Brown deserves to be quoted at length:

> This proposition that Miss Lewis finish your husband's book about Willa Cather is very much more of a drama than you realize, probably, young as you are. I have known Edith Lewis, as I think I told you, since we were both little girls. So I know very well, from a little distance that is, the circumstances of Miss Lewis going to live with Miss Cather. She was a singularly attractive, sensitive, and everybody thought gifted girl who went to New York to see what she could do in the literary world. She was getting on very well and had had some recognition, and had indeed won a prize for a short story in a contest of considerable importance. And then because she and Miss Cather had both lived in Lincoln, Nebraska, they came together. Miss Lewis fell at once completely under Miss Cather's influence and as far as her family and friends could see disappeared from view thereafter, until she is quite an old lady as I am. She has made every imaginable sacrifice, much more than a wife would make for her husband, because a wife has at least some legal position and definite recognition as a helper. This she has never had. So I can see that the opportunity to have a part in what will certainly be the very best book ever written about Willa Cather, means an enormous amount to her.
>
> But I agree with you that to have her go on with the book in the way which she seems to wish to do it, that is finishing it up, and touching up the parts which your husband has already written would be the worst possible way to treat that. You wouldn't want anybody to do over or fill in any gaps in what he has already written. (Fisher to Brown, 8 July 1951)

Fisher's portrait of Lewis here ought to be read with the knowledge that, for her part, Lewis also has doubts about Fisher (see

Lewis to Edel, 20 June 1952; in *Willa Cather Living* there is only one reference to "the Canfield Family" as Cather's friends in Lincoln), yet it captures a view of Lewis confirmed by others and by her own actions when confronted with Margaret's firmness on Edel as the person to finish her husband's book. This standoff, moreover, was very much about what Cather was to become as an icon—an "Idol," as Margaret had Lewis's Cather, or the person supported by the biographical facts sought by E. K. Brown, Margaret Brown's "Board of Experts" (as she once called them), and ultimately Leon Edel (Brown to Fisher, 17 August 1951).[13]

Margaret Brown's preference for Edel merits some comment. As indicated, E. K. Brown had met Edel when the two were graduate students at the Sorbonne in the 1920s. There, for his part, Edel embarked on his lifelong career as a Jamesian and as a literary biographer. During the early 1930s, he sought out and interviewed the subject of one of Brown's theses, Edith Wharton, for his research (a file of letters addressed to Brown by Edel during the 1930s at McGill University recounts this meeting). Edel's papers also confirm that the two men remained friends and were in regular contact during the subsequent years. Margaret Brown and Edel address each other by first name throughout their correspondence regarding the biography, indicating that they were longtime friends. And when Brown died, probably before he was approached to finish the Cather book, Edel wrote to A. S. P. Woodhouse—whom he did not know at the time—volunteering to participate in a memorial volume in Brown's honor (Edel to Woodhouse, 29 May 1951). At the time, too, Edel was deep in the first volume of his five-volume biography of James, but he was willing to take on his friend's book in order to see it published. Objectively, then, Edel was a far more appropriate choice to complete the book than Lewis.[14]

Replying to Fisher's advice about Lewis, Margaret shows herself feeling the force of Fisher's retrospective assessment of Lewis: "My only objection to Miss Lewis was that she would make an objective book subjective. From what you wrote, I see the lady would emerge finally as an Author of Distinction." Not wishing to accept Lewis under such terms, although still wishing to see the book into print through Knopf, Margaret proposed Edel—in very firm and clear terms, as drafted by Woodhouse—as the person to complete her husband's book. Her letter to Knopf is firm and businesslike; the letter to Lewis is apologetic and understanding (Brown to Knopf, Brown to Lewis, 11 August 1951). In early August she wrote to Fisher that "My suggestion was received with anger and resentment" (Brown to Fisher, 7 August 1951).

Even though she was no academic, Margaret saw what Lewis and Knopf were doing to her and, thereby, to her husband and his work. Indeed, through all this she came to something of the same realization Henry Colbert has that morning at his breakfast table in *Sapphira*: "*I see through all this, see to the bottom*" (7). Thus she continues, writing to Fisher from Chicago, caustically appraising the situation confronting her back east:

> Mr. Knopf has made up his mind. Very practical one, too. If accepted by me, Miss Lewis, or I should say, Miss Cather's literary executor, would be forever Mr. Knopf's friend, and forever agreeable to his suggestions and even beyond the horizon it would be bright for Miss Lewis must die one day and so must Mr. Knopf, *but* there is the Firm, and what better heritage than being Miss Cather's 2nd literary executor? The dollars lost over the kind of book Miss Lewis would finish would be nothing compared to the long term gains. So from his point of view he is quite right in rejecting Mr. Edel. However, now enter into the more torturous recesses of the mind—which I think exist in most people that have managed to make millions in one lifetime: Mr. Knopf is thinking "let's play both ends against the middle"—so instead of rejecting Mr. Edel as a person to do the job—for there is no telling what that wretched woman in Chicago will dream up—let us hand her the problem, with the stipulation that before anything more is done there is a *contract*. And a well-written contract can seal a fate subtly but as certainly as a judge donning the black cap[e]. Then *let* Mr. Edel see Miss Lewis, discover she has been adequately impressed to reject him, and the book can only be written by Miss Lewis. The only gamble is that the woman in Chicago is lying and is

> *anxious* that the book be published. Mr. Knopf and Miss Lewis then feel the greatest emotional delight of all—self righteousness, etc., etc. (Brown to Fisher, 7 August [1951])

Sensing Margaret's frustration at all this, one is tempted to quote Roddy Blake: "it would come to money in the end. 'Everything does'" (*The Professor's House* 243). But the real currency here was not money but reputation—Cather's versus Brown's. Writing to Fisher in August, just before Lewis announced herself "not [willing] to take any further part in Mr. Brown's biography" (Lewis to Brown, 16 August 1951), Margaret recalled that when her husband "told me the stories about Miss Lewis he did not try to dissuade me from my conviction that she was being silly. Mr. Knopf he once mentioned as 'a very shrewd man.' . . . Edward felt this *kind* of book was needed, which is not Miss Lewis's kind" (Brown to Fisher, 11 August 1951).

On 11 August, Brown also told Fisher about the letter in which she informed Lewis of her preference for Edel: "I must say, I hated to send that letter to Miss Lewis. After all the work she has done, and considering her great attachment to Miss Cather, and the fact she isn't young any more, and is so sensitive and suspicious. Neither of those people seem to realize that Edward *died*, except inasmuch as he did it very inconveniently for them." Brown ultimately reversed herself regarding Knopf, but not Lewis. And when Lewis announced her decision to withdraw from consideration, Margaret commented to Fisher, "It seems that Miss Lewis has picked up her dolls and gone home" (17 August 1951).

After receiving his copy of Lewis's withdrawal letter, Edel wrote to Brown that "Mr. Knopf has clearly done the ungentlemanly thing of showing his private correspondence [to Lewis]—a breach of discretion in such an instance which can only, I suspect, be a calculated act. We can only guess what his motives are, but her reaction, so prompt and angry, strikes me as confirming precisely that she has hardly an objective view of the matter." He concludes: "I think what's happening confirms all your suspicions and justifies entirely what you've done" (Edel to Brown, 20 August 1951).

In his "Homage to Willa Cather," Edel asserts that "Miss Lewis could only write a worshipful life, and it would no longer be the life of Brown's researches" (190). Once the dust from Brown's decision to have him complete the book settled, Edel was able to complete the biography as Margaret Brown had hoped and to see it to print as a Knopf book. Edel had the advantages of being in New York at the time and having a well-established reputation as a scholar to which Knopf deferred. First he met with Knopf, whom he did not know, on 11 October 1951, and between then and 23 October he met with Lewis. When they met, as Edel writes, "I said to her that we were each mourning a friend: that we were each trying to be loyal to that friend" (191). Clearly, Lewis accepted that argument. Once the difficulties of August had passed, and once a contract had been arranged—between Knopf on the one hand and Brown ("the owner") and Edel ("the editor") on the other—Lewis resumed her position as helpful adviser to the project.

The numerous letters in the Edel Papers at McGill show that Lewis and Edel established a good rapport, just as Edel later remembered in his homage. He kept her informed of the book's progress and, once the manuscript was completed in spring 1952, asked her to read it and comment. This she did, writing Edel a twenty-one-page letter commenting page by page on matters of fact, interpretation, and syntax (Lewis to Edel, 21 May 1952). In addition to this, they met to go over the manuscript.[15] This done, the book appeared in early 1953 to positive reviews. It remains among the best Cather biographies.

E. K. Brown's *Willa Cather: A Critical Biography*, completed by Leon Edel (and no more than that, completed), embodies in its provenance the issues that confront Cather critics still as scholars, and which confront especially any attempt to gauge Cather as a "cultural icon." Like her character Eden Bower in "Coming, Aphrodite!," who "knew that she was to be Eden Bower," Cather worked doggedly during her early career to become Willa Cather, well-known author (28). During the 1910s, once her star began to ascend—again like Eden Bower—she carefully shaped the persona she became, most especially through such essays as "My First Novels (There Were Two)." And while not all would agree with Sergeant when she wrote to E. K. Brown that the older Cather "lost some of her early modesty about her own work," that assessment seems inescapable. In responding to Brown's "Homage" as she did, Cather effectively directed Lewis toward him as her first scholarly biographer. Brown, for his part, also knew that he was going to be E. K. Brown, a leading, sensitive, and admired critic who espoused real literary values, and so was "a critic worthy of" Willa Cather. So too was Leon Edel. We do not know, nor can we ever know, just how Brown would have finished *Willa Cather: A Critical Biography*, but one thing is certain: the standoff between Margaret Brown and her "Board of Experts," on the one hand, and Edith Lewis and Alfred A. Knopf, on the other, offers an initial and critical instance of "Willa Cather as cultural icon" as she ceased to be Willa Cather and became her admirers.

NOTES

1. Among the Brown Papers at the Beinecke Library at Yale University there is an alphabetized accordion file in which Brown organized his and other relevant materials connected to the biography. The note in which Knopf told Seibel that "there would not be a life" is in slot D.

2. See Edel's "Homage to Willa Cather," the published version of the address he gave at the first International Cather Seminar in 1973, for a detailed account of Brown's—and Edel's—difficulties with Cather's changed birth year. Edel's account of his negotiations with Lewis over the publication of the date in the Brown biography is both revealing and contextually important here. In a letter to Edel, Lewis concedes that 1873 is the correct birth year (Lewis to Edel, 6 May 1952). See Murphy for a thorough and balanced survey of the Cather-Lewis relationship.

David H. Porter has probed and traced Cather's construction of her own history, looking especially at two biographical sketches—one written in 1903 and other in 1915—and at a manuscript "interview" with herself that Cather wrote in 1926. My examination of Cather's numerous personal approaches to key reviewers who would subsequently do her reputation good—H. L. Mencken and H. W. Boynton the most prominent among them—complements Porter's (see Thacker). The conclusion that Cather was enormously ambitious and intent on literary success, and willing to do what she need to do to ensure that success, is both inescapable and little scrutinized. By 1931, when she wrote "My First Novels (There Were Two)," her very real success allowed her to forget the grasping details of her struggle before she switched to Alfred A. Knopf in 1920. Knopf, for his part, made that success real.

3. Brown's work is characterized throughout by his assertion that contemporary authors demand close critical scrutiny. This can be seen in his early thesis on Wharton's work, his stated enthusiasm for the work of E. M. Forster and Virginia Woolf, and especially in his work on Canadian writers. Brown's publication list is filled with newspaper reviews in which he treats a wide range of authors and books, primary and secondary, British, American, and Canadian. His "Causeries" were a frequent feature in the *Winnipeg Free Press*.

4. In late 1921, Wilbur Cross, editor of the *Yale Review*, approached Cather to see if she would send them her lecture "Obstacles to American Art." Cather indicated willingness initially, but ultimately she did not do so. Part of this correspondence was with Ms. McAfee, whom Cather invited to their "at homes" on Bank Street (Cather to McAfee, 7 February 1924).

5. An example of Lewis's work to help Brown is the following letter to Carrie Miner Sherwood:

> I do not know if Willa sent you the very fine review of her work by Mr. Brown which was published in the 1946 autumn number of the YALE REVIEW. Willa herself liked it better than anything that had been written about her books—thought it written with the greatest sympathy and understanding. She wrote Mr. Brown several long letters that last winter and spring—the kind of letters she would not have written to anyone in whom she not had great confidence.
>
> It was chiefly because of Willa's own feeling about Mr. Brown that Mr. Knopf, her publisher, and I, after many talks in which we tried to canvas the various possibilities, decided to ask Mr. Brown to do Willa's biography.
>
> A new book of his which appeared this spring—a critical study of Matthew Arnold—seemed to us added evidence of his fine ability as a writer.
>
> Mr. Brown came to New York in May at Mr. Knopf's and my request and we went over the thing thoroughly with him. Both Mr. Knopf and I feel that he is a person of the highest standards, fitted by his scholarship and his gifts as a writer and his long-felt interest and sympathy with Willa's work, to write the kind of biography she would have approved.
>
> I have told Mr. Brown that through your life-long friendship

with Willa, and your close companionship with her as a child and a young girl, you can give him better material than anyone else about her life in Red Cloud. I hope so much, Mrs. Sherwood, that you will help him all you can when he comes there. I feel sure that Willa would have wished it. I think when you see him you will feel the same confidences in him that Mr. Knopf and I feel. (Lewis to Sherwood, 27 July 1948)

6. Just after E. K. Brown died, his wife, Margaret, wrote to Fisher: "If Edward had known the true and hopeless nature of his illness (melano sarcoma) he would, I think, have finished the book. But of course I valued his peace of mind more than anything else and didn't tell him" (28 April 1951). Ernest Sirluck, who shared an office with Brown during his illness, writes that Brown turned to a "quack" in Toronto "when his doctors had told him there was no hope" (183). While Margaret did confide her husband's condition to Sirluck and to his wife, Lesley, she did so without her husband's knowledge. Margaret said they could discuss the matter with Edward only if he brought it up. He never did; nor did he tell any of his close Toronto friends that he had cancer. Sirluck concludes: "I have never understood why he was so insistent about keeping his illness secret" (184).

7. Professor Gordon Roper, who knew the Browns when he was at the University of Chicago with them, described Margaret as "a dish"—an impressive woman striking in appearance and dress, unlike most faculty wives (pers. comm., 6 August 2003). Ernest Sirluck, who met Margaret while he was an undergraduate at Manitoba, describes her as "an attractive young woman who was cutting her own considerable swath in Winnipeg society (she was an American with money and knowledge of how to use it)" (40).

8. In her 11 August 1951 letter to Fisher, Margaret is a bit perplexed that her husband did not anticipate a course of action should he die before the Cather biography was finished. Not an academic and his sole literary executor, she concludes that he knew she was good at seeking and taking expert advice. Some of that material—most significantly, a ten-page letter dated 10 December 1950 describing Pittsburgh during Cather's time there—is in the Leon Edel Papers at McGill University.

9. In his 12 May 1951 memorandum to Margaret Brown, Sirluck notes that "two-thirds of the introduction has been written" and that the chapter on the Pittsburgh years "would require both research and criticism"; in addition, a chapter on Cather's last years (1941–47) is needed, as is a conclusion that provides an estimate of her career. While Brown had done most of the introduction, "the quality of the work" on it "is not as high as the quality of the rest of the book." Regarding the

Pittsburgh chapter, Brown had written his analysis of *The Troll Garden*, the "major critical portion of the chapter." In addition to this assessment of the manuscript, Sirluck made suggestions regarding the person to finish the job, the nature of the contract, and the function of the preface. He thought Knopf should select the person, who would be paid for the work without any claim to royalties. The book's preface should make clear just what material was added to Brown's and, if required, any difference of viewpoint in the concluding critical assessment of Cather's career should be specified.

10. Throughout these exchanges, Margaret sees Knopf's position as one of expediency; in view of his ongoing relationship with Lewis over the Cather copyrights, having Lewis finish Brown's book is the easiest thing to do.

11. Indicative of this attitude toward Lewis is a commonly held belief that she is buried, in Jaffrey, New Hampshire, at Cather's feet. She is not: she is beside Cather to the right, her stone flush with the ground beside Cather's large stone replete with *My Ántonia* quotation and incorrect birth date.

12. Manuscript materials that have recently come to light suggest that Lewis was deeply involved in shaping Cather's fiction. A manuscript of *The Professor's House* at the University of Nebraska, for example, reveals that Lewis made numerous, and substantive, revisions to the text. Many of these were retained in the published book. See Philip L. and Helen Southwick Collection, Love Library, University of Nebraska–Lincoln. Melissa Homestead and Anne Kaufman are now at work on an extended biographical analysis of Lewis that has already radically changed the accepted view of the Lewis-Cather partnership. They promise to change that view much further.

13. Brown notes, and it is confirmed by Lewis's subsequent correspondence with Leon Edel, that Lewis consistently referred to the Brown-Edel book as "*the Biography*"—that is, always a proper noun. See, for example, Lewis to Edel, 23 October 1951.

14. Ernest Sirluck offered me his recollection of these "difficult days":

> The only thing I might add is that Leon Edel was fully aware of the difficulty posed by the difference between his approach to biography, which emphasized psychological analysis, and Brown's, which emphasized the explication of texts. He came to Chicago at Peggy Brown's invitation, and after going through Edward's materials met with me for an entire morning. I knew the quality of his work and wanted him to do the job, while he wanted to be sure that I understood the difference between his approach and Edward's. We talked at length about the difference between completing another

man's work and writing an autonomous portion of a book, and he finally said he was willing to subordinate his role to Edward's for his old friend's sake. I thought then and still think it was rather a noble act. (Sirluck to author, e-mail, 16 January 2004)

15. Margaret Brown also read—and warmly approved of—the manuscript, marveling at Edel's ability to add material while retaining her husband's tone and pace (Brown to Edel, 1 October [1952]). Edel also had Fisher sent a set of page proofs (Edel to Fisher, 18 October 1952). Only Lewis, apparently, offered line-by-line commentary.

WORKS CITED

Brown, E. K. Correspondence and notes for *Willa Cather: A Critical Biography*. Yale Collection of American Literature. Beinecke Rare Book and Manuscript Library, Yale U, New Haven CT.

———. "Homage to Willa Cather." *Yale Review* 36 (1946): 77–92.

———. Letter to Dorothy Canfield Fisher. 29 Nov. 1950. Leon Edel Papers. Rare Books and Special Collections Division, McGill U Libraries, Montreal, Quebec.

———. "Memoir." *Selected Poems of Duncan Campbell Scott*. Toronto: Ryerson, 1951. xi–xlii.

———. Personal copy of *The Professor's House* by Willa Cather. Yale Collection of American Literature. Beinecke Rare Book and Manuscript Library. Yale U, New Haven CT.

———. *Rhythm in the Novel*. Toronto: U of Toronto P, 1950.

———. *Willa Cather: A Critical Biography*. Completed by Leon Edel. 1953. Foreword by James Woodress. Lincoln: U of Nebraska P, 1987.

———. "Willa Cather and the West." *University of Toronto Quarterly* 5 (1935–36): 544–66.

Brown, Margaret. Letters to Dorothy Canfield Fisher. Dorothy Canfield Fisher Papers. Special Collections, U of Vermont Library, Burlington.

———. Letters to Edith Lewis. Leon Edel Papers. Rare Books and Special Collections Division, McGill U Libraries, Montreal, Quebec.

———. Letter to Alfred A. Knopf. 11 August 1951. Leon Edel Papers. Rare Books and Special Collections Division, McGill U Libraries, Montreal, Quebec.

———. Letter to Joan Trebell, Editorial Secretary, Ryerson. 26 May 1951. E. K. Brown Papers. National Archives of Canada, Ottawa, Ontario.

———. Letter to Leon Edel. 1 Oct. [1952]. Leon Edel Papers. Rare

Books and Special Collections Division, McGill U Libraries, Montreal, Quebec.
———. Letter to Lorne Pierce. 28 May 1951. E. K. Brown Papers. National Archives of Canada, Ottawa, Ontario.
Cather, Willa. "Coming, Aphrodite!" *Youth and Bright Medusa*. 1920. New York: Vintage, 1975. 3–63.
———. Letter to Helen McAfee. 7 Feb. 1924. Yale Collection of American Literature. Beinecke Rare Book and Manuscript Library, Yale U, New Haven CT.
———. "My First Novels (There Were Two)." *On Writing: Critical Studies as Writing as an Art*. Foreword by Stephen Tennant. 1949. Lincoln: U of Nebraska P, 1988. 89–97.
———. *The Professor's House*. 1925. Willa Cather Scholarly Edition. Ed. Frederick M. Link. Historical essay James Woodress. Lincoln: U of Nebraska P, 2002.
———. *Sapphira and the Slave Girl*. New York: Knopf, 1940.
———. *The Song of the Lark*. 1915. Intro. Sherrill Harbison. New York: Penguin, 1999.
Djwa, Sandra. *Professing English: A Life of Roy Daniells*. Toronto: U of Toronto P, 2002.
Edel, Leon. "Homage to Willa Cather." *The Art of Willa Cather*. Ed. Bernice Slote and Virginia Faulkner. Lincoln: U of Nebraska P, 1974. 185–204.
———. Letter to A. S. P. Woodhouse. 29 May 1951. Leon Edel Papers. Rare Books and Special Collections Division, McGill U Libraries, Montreal, Quebec.
———. Letter to Dorothy Canfield Fisher. 18 Oct. 1952. Dorothy Canfield Fisher Papers. Special Collections, U of Vermont Library, Burlington.
———. Letter to Margaret Brown. 20 Aug. 1951. Leon Edel Papers. Rare Books and Special Collections Division, McGill U Libraries, Montreal, Quebec.
Fisher, Dorothy Canfield. Letter to E. K. Brown. 27 Mar. 1950. Leon Edel Papers. Rare Books and Special Collections Division, McGill U Libraries, Montreal, Quebec.
———. Letter to Margaret Brown. 8 July 1951. Dorothy Canfield Fisher Papers. Special Collections, U of Vermont Library, Burlington.
Groening, Laura Smyth. *E. K. Brown: A Study in Conflict*. Toronto: U of Toronto P, 1993.
Knopf, Alfred A. Letters to E. K. Brown. Yale Collection of American Literature. Beinecke Rare Book and Manuscript Library, Yale U, New Haven CT.

———. Letter to Margaret Brown. 26 June 1951. Dorothy Canfield Fisher Papers. Special Collections, U of Vermont Library, Burlington.

Lewis, Edith. Letters to Carrie Miner Sherwood. Willa Cather Pioneer Memorial, Red Cloud.

———. Letters to E. K. Brown. Yale Collection of American Literature. Beinecke Rare Book and Manuscript Library, Yale U, New Haven CT.

———. Letters to Leon Edel. Leon Edel Papers. Rare Books and Special Collections Division, McGill U Libraries, Montreal, Quebec.

McAfee, Helen. Letter to E. K. Brown. 30 Oct. 1946. Yale Collection of American Literature. Beinecke Rare Book and Manuscript Library, Yale U, New Haven CT.

———. Letter to E. K. Brown. 11 June 1948. E. K. Brown Papers. National Archives of Canada, Ottawa, Ontario.

McDougall, Robert L., ed. *The Poet and the Critic: A Literary Correspondence between D. C. Scott and E. K. Brown*. Ottawa: Carleton UP, 1983.

Murphy, John J. Introduction. *Willa Cather Living*. By Edith Lewis. 1953. Lincoln: U of Nebraska P, 2000. v–xix.

Porter, David H. "Cather on Cather: Two Early Self-Sketches." *Willa Cather Newsletter and Review* 45.3 (2002): 55–60.

———. "Cather on Cather II." *Willa Cather Newsletter and Review* 46.3 (2003): 1, 49, 53–58.

Seibel, George. Letter to Dorothy Canfield Fisher. 9 July 1949. Dorothy Canfield Fisher Papers. Special Collections, U of Vermont Library, Burlington.

Sergeant, Elizabeth Shepley. Letter to E. K. Brown. 26 Nov. 1950. Yale Collection of American Literature. Beinecke Rare Book and Manuscript Library, Yale U, New Haven CT.

Sirluck, Ernest. *First Generation: An Autobiography*. Toronto: U of Toronto P, 1996.

———. Letter to Mrs. E. K. Brown. 12 May 1951. Yale Collection of American Literature. Beinecke Rare Book and Manuscript Library, Yale U, New Haven CT.

Stout, Janis, ed. *A Calendar of the Letters of Willa Cather*. Lincoln: U of Nebraska P, 2002.

Thacker, Robert. "She's Not a Puzzle So Arbitrarily Solved: Willa Cather's Violent Self-Construction." *Violence, the Arts, and Willa Cather*. Ed. Merrill Skaggs and Joseph R. Urgo. Forthcoming. Madison NJ: Fairleigh Dickinson UP, 2007.

Woodress, James. Foreword. *Willa Cather: A Critical Biography*. By E. K. Brown. Completed by Leon Edel. Lincoln: U of Nebraska P, 1987. v–xii.

CONTRIBUTORS

Timothy C. Blackburn is English Chair at Forsyth Country Day School, near Winston-Salem, North Carolina. He has taught at several colleges in Minnesota and independent schools in Minnesota and New Jersey. His previous publications include papers on Defoe's *Captain Singleton* and *Robinson Crusoe.*

Joshua Dolezal is an erstwhile wilderness ranger and visiting Assistant Professor of English at Central College, in Iowa. His creative and scholarly work has also appeared in *Medical Humanities*, *Hudson Review*, *Gettysburg Review*, and elsewhere.

Jonathan D. Gross is Professor of English at DePaul University and Interim Director of the DePaul Humanities Center. He is the author of *Byron: The Erotic Liberal* and editor of *Byron's "Corbeau Blanc": The Life and Letters of Lady Melbourne*; *Emma, or the Unfortunate Attachment*; and *Thomas Jefferson's Scrapbooks.* He taught a course for DePaul University in 2002, featuring the One Book/One Chicago choice, which was Cather's *My Ántonia.* His essay in this volume grew out of that experience.

Erika Hamilton is a graduate student and researcher at the University of Nebraska–Lincoln, where she recently received an MA in English and creative writing. She is currently working on her PhD in literature with an emphasis on Willa Cather and Renaissance Studies. Hamilton is a Program Officer with the Nebraska Humanities Council.

Richard C. Harris, Professor and Director of Humanities at Webb Institute, Long Island, New York, has previously published on Cather in a number of journals, including volumes 1 and 4 of *Cather Studies*. He is volume editor of the Scholarly Edition of Cather's *One of Ours* and is currently working with Dr. Mary Weddle on a book on Willa Cather's aunt France "Franc" Cather, the prototype for Mrs. Wheeler in *One of Ours*.

Mark J. Madigan, an Associate Professor of English at Nazareth College of Rochester, has published widely on Cather, Dorothy Canfield Fisher, and other American writers. He is the editor of *Keeping Fires Night and Day: Selected Letters of Dorothy Canfield Fisher* as well as Fisher's *The Bedquilt and Other Stories* and *Seasoned Timber*. He is the volume editor of *Youth and the Bright Medusa*, forthcoming in the Willa Cather Scholarly Edition. He taught American literature at the University Ljubljana, Slovenia, as a Fulbright Scholar in 2004.

Richard H. Millington is Professor of English at Smith College. He is author of *Practicing Romance: Narrative Form and Cultural Engagement in Hawthorne's Fiction* and of essays on Hawthorne and Cather. He is the editor of *The Cambridge Companion to Nathaniel Hawthorne* and the coeditor of *Hitchcock's America*, which includes his essay on *North by Northwest*.

John J. Murphy, Professor of English at BYU, is the author of *"My Ántonia": The Road Home* and over sixty essays and chapters on Cather and other American writers. He has edited *Critical Essays on Willa Cather* and *Willa Cather: Family Community, and History*, and is volume editor of the Cather Scholarly Editions of *Death Comes for the Archbishop* and *Shadows on the Rock*.

Joseph C. Murphy is Assistant Professor of English at Fu Jen University, Taiwan, where he serves on the editorial board of *Fu Jen Studies*. His publications and conference papers have focused on Whitman, Howells, Henry Adams, and Flannery O'Connor, as well as on Cather, and on the areas of American architecture, painting, and religion. He is completing a book entitled *Exposing the Modern: Worlds' Fairs and American Literary Culture, 1853–1907*.

Elsa Nettels is Professor of English Emeritus at the College of William and Mary. Her publications include *James and Conrad*; *Language, Race, and Social Class in Howells's America*; and *Language and Gender in American Fiction: Howells, James, Wharton, and Cather*. For six years, from 1997 to 2002, she wrote the chapter on Wharton and Cather for *American Literary Scholarship*.

Robert Pinsky, Poet Laureate of the United States (1997–2000), is poetry editor of the online journal *Slate* and a contributor to *The NewsHour with Jim Lehrer* on PBS. He teaches in the graduate writing program at Boston University. His book-length poem *An Explanation of America*, awarded the Saxifrage Prize when published in 1980, has been reissued by Princeton University Press in a new edition.

Jessica G. Rabin is author of *Surviving the Crossing: (Im)migration, Ethnicity and Gender in Willa Cather, Gertrude Stein, and Nella Larsen*, along with several articles on Cather. She is Assistant Professor of English at Anne Arundel Community College and teaches American Literature, Women's Studies, and Bible and Literature. She also serves as Associate Editor of *Philip Roth Studies* and Secretary/Treasurer of the Philip Roth Society.

Guy Reynolds is a Professor in the Department of English at the University of Nebraska–Lincoln, where he also directs the Cather Project and serves as General Editor of the Cather Scholarly Edition. He is the author of *Willa Cather in Context: Progress, Race, Empire* and *Twentieth-Century American Women's Fiction*.

Michael Schueth earned a PhD from the University of Nebraska–Lincoln in 2005. His dissertation was entitled "Willa Cather and Celebrity: The Writer's Self-Image and the Literary Marketplace." He has presented several papers on Cather and currently teaches at Creighton University.

Merrill Maguire Skaggs is author of *After the World Broke in Two: The Later Novels of Willa Cather* and of numerous essays on Cather and other subjects. She edited *Willa Cather's*

New York: New Essays on Cather in the City and now does research within, as well as helps other scholars to use, the Caspersen Cather Collection at Drew University, where she serves as Baldwin Professor of the Humanities.

Janis P. Stout is Professor Emerita of English at Texas A&M University. Her most recent books are *Through the Window, Out the Door: Women's Narratives of Departure, from Austin and Cather to Tyler, Morrison, and Didion*; *Willa Cather: The Writer and Her World*; and *Coming Out of War: Poetry, Grieving, and the Culture of the World Wars*. She is the editor of *Willa Cather and Material Culture: Real-World Writing, Writing the Real World* and *A Calendar of the Letters of Willa Cather*.

John N. Swift is Professor of English and Comparative Literary Studies at Occidental College in Los Angeles, where he teaches British and American modernism and psychoanalytic approaches to literature. A past president of the Willa Cather Pioneer Memorial and Educational Foundation, he has published many essays on Cather and her work and is coeditor of *Willa Cather and the American Southwest*.

Robert Thacker is Professor of Canadian Studies and English at St. Lawrence University, and has been Molson Research Fellow there. He codirected the Sixth International Seminar in Quebec City and coedited its volume of essays, *Cather Studies, Volume 4: Willa Cather's Canadian and Old World Connections*. His recent work on Cather has appeared in *American Literary Realism*, the *Canadian Review of American Studies*, and *A Companion to the Regional Literature of America*. His *Alice Munro, Writing Her Lives: A Biography* was published in 2005.

Steven Trout is an Associate Professor of English at Fort Hays State University. He is the author of *Memorial Fictions: Willa Cather and the First World War* and a coeditor of *The Literature of the Great War Reconsidered: Beyond Modern Memory*. His articles on twentieth–century fiction have appeared in numerous journals, including *Hemingway Review*, *Studies in Short Fiction*, and *Twentieth Century Literature*. Most recently he edited *Cather Studies, Volume 6: Willa Cather and the Great War*.

Joseph R. Urgo is Professor and Chair of the Department of English at the University of Mississippi. His works include *Novel Frames: Literature as a Guide to Race, Sex, and History in American Culture* and *Willa Cather and the Myth of American Migration*, as well as journal articles, book reviews, and encyclopedia entries on Cather and Faulkner. He was coeditor of *Willa Cather and the American Southwest* and appears in the PBS production *The Road Is All: Willa Cather*.

INDEX

Page numbers in italics refer to illustrations.